Voices of Shakespeare's England

Voices of Shakespeare's England

Contemporary Accounts of Elizabethan Daily Life

John A. Wagner, Editor

VOICES OF AN ERA

 GREENWOOD

AN IMPRINT OF ABC-CLIO, LLC
Santa Barbara, California • Denver, Colorado • Oxford, England

Library of Congress Cataloging-in-Publication Date
Voices of Shakespeare's England : contemporary accounts of Elizabethan daily life / edited by John A. Wagner.
    p. cm.
  Includes bibliographical references and index.
  ISBN 978-0-313-35740-4 (hard cover : acid-free paper) — ISBN 978-0-313-35741-1 (ebook)
  1. Great Britain—History—Elizabeth, 1558-1603—Sources. 2. Great Britain—Social life and customs—16th century—Sources. 3. Great Britain—Politics and government—1558-1603—Sources. 4. English literature—16th century—History and criticism. 5. Shakespeare, William, 1564-1616—Appreciation. I. Wagner, J. A. (John A.)
  DA350.V65 2010
  942.05'5—dc22   2009053677

14 13 12 11 10   1 2 3 4 5

This book is also available on the World Wide Web as an eBook.
Visit www.abc-clio.com for details.

ABC-CLIO, LLC
130 Cremona Drive, P.O. Box 1911
Santa Barbara, California 93116-1911

This book is printed on acid-free paper ∞
Manufactured in the United States of America

For John, Olivia, Dolores, Charles, and Matthew, who now all wait to
tell me the truth about Shakespeare

Some say Shakespeare could not be
sprung from such simplicity,
from letterless rusticity,
from merchant stock, ungowned, ungloved,
where useless learning went unloved,
where words of warriors, ways of courts
were unknown ways of unknown sorts,
a place, it seems, where none could grow
knowing all one had to know
to come to truth so sure and near
as did whoever wrote Shakespeare.

—Anonymous

Therefore reader . . . I beseech thee to take it patiently to peruse this
work, which is but little, and taste nothing but the fruit of it . . . .
—From the Introduction to
Princess Elizabeth's translation (1544)
of Marguerite de Navarre's poem,
"Miroir de l'ame pecheresse"
(Mirror of the Sinful Soul)

And if then you do not like him, surely you are in some manifest danger, not to understand him. And so we leave you to other of his Friends,
whom if you need, can be your guides: if you need them not, you can
lead yourselves, and others. And such Readers we wish him.
—From "To the Great Variety of Readers,"
the Preface written by John Heminges
and Henry Condell for the First Folio
edition (1623) of William Shakespeare's plays

CONTENTS

Contents

PREFACE

Voices of Shakespeare's England: Contemporary Accounts of Elizabethan Daily Life contains excerpts from 51 documents from the time of the revered English dramatist William Shakespeare, whose life extended from 1564 to 1616. These years cover most of the reigns of Elizabeth I (1558–1603) and her Scottish successor James I (1603–1625). If she were alive today, Queen Elizabeth would no doubt be both perplexed and not a little unhappy to know that the years of her reign are now often considered "Shakespeare's England," a period defined not by the monarch, who in her own time was a symbol of pride and patriotism to her people, but by a low-born playwright, a member of a profession that, however popular, was still considered rather disreputable. Nonetheless, the popular interest that Elizabeth's reign now draws in the United States, as witnessed by a host of Web sites and recent films (e.g., *Shakespeare in Love*), cable television programs (e.g., *Elizabeth I* with Helen Mirren), and both fiction and nonfiction books (e.g., novels by Patricia Finney, Judith Cook, or Fiona Buckley and biographies of the queen by David Starkey and Alison Weir), is far in excess of the interest generated by any other period of English history. Certainly not the Wars of the Roses, the seventeenth-century civil war, nor even the matrimonial trials of Elizabeth's father, Henry VIII, attract the attention, either in society or in the classroom, that Shakespeare bestows on the reign of Elizabeth.

PRIMARY DOCUMENTS

Primary documents offer a unique method of learning about the peoples of the past, allowing us to listen to those people speak in their own voices. The document excerpts reproduced in this volume provide all manner of readers with engaging and informational insights into the way life was lived when Shakespeare wrote and Elizabeth ruled. For example, John Hooker, who sat in the legislatures of both England and Ireland, tells us how a sixteenth-century Parliament functioned. Robert Greene, who frequented the London underworld, uses the language of that world to tell us about the lives of thieves, whores, and con artists. Richard Wigmore, an eyewitness to the execution of Mary, Queen of Scots, describes in detail the queen's death.

From these documents, one can begin to understand Elizabethan views and attitudes, even flatly contradictory ones. For instance, one can see how seriously Protestant Elizabethans viewed Catholic threats to queen and country, as well as how committed some English Catholics were to preserving or restoring their faith in England. Or one can understand why moralists such as Stephen Gossen attacked the frivolity of poetry and what he saw as the inde-cency of the public theater, while court poets such as Sir Philip Sidney praised poetry's power for good and London citizens such as Simon Forman thrilled at witnessing performances of Shakespeare's plays. For these reasons, high school students, college undergraduates, public library patrons, and anyone with an interest in Elizabeth/Jacobean history or literature will find these documents highly useful in pursuing classroom or personal study of the period and its people.

ORGANIZATION OF SECTIONS

The 51 document excerpts are divided into 40 numbered sections, with some sections offering two or three related documents. These sections are divided into four topical cate-gories, with ten sections relating to some aspect of the Elizabethan/Jacobean economy or social structure; ten to the Elizabethan/Jacobean Church and State, particularly Parliament and the fear of Catholicism; ten to the literature of the period, particularly the writing of poetry and history and the writing and performance of stage plays; and ten to the monar-chy, particularly the life of Queen Elizabeth, into whose reign most of Shakespeare's liter-ary career fell, but also, to some extent, the lives of King James and his mother, Mary, Queen of Scots.

The document selections include a wide variety of types—letters, plays, poems, speech-es, polemics, novels, official reports, promotional works, and descriptive narratives of peo-ple and events. Some of these documents are well known and often excerpted, such as selec-tions from the plays and sonnets of Shakespeare himself, from the queen's "Golden Speech," and from the *Chronicles* of Raphael Holinshed or the *History* of William Camden. Others are more obscure but often just as rewarding to modern readers, such as the *Autobiography* of the hunted Jesuit John Gerard, the queen's letters to King James explaining the execu-tion of his mother, and Robert Laneham's enthusiastically detailed account of the Earl of Leicester's lavish entertainment of the queen at Kenilworth in 1575. The spelling in each of the documents in this volume has been modernized for easier understanding by modern readers. However, see the document reproductions in the "Evaluating and Interpreting Primary Documents" section for a discussion of Elizabethan spelling and handwritings styles. Elizabeth remarked famously in regard to religion that she would not make "win-dows into men's souls," but each of these documents, using the words of contemporaries, offers the reader a window into the soul of the age of Shakespeare, providing an under-standing that cannot be had even from the best modern textbooks or monographs.

In addition to the excerpts themselves, each numbered section offers various tools to help the reader more fully understand the meaning, purpose, and importance of each doc-ument. These tools include an "Introduction" providing relevant historical background for the selection; a "Keep in Mind As You Read" listing of context points to help evaluate the document; an "Aftermath" section describing the results and consequences that flowed from the document; an "Ask Yourself" section listing questions about the document and life during the period, often relating both to present times; a "Topics and Activities to Consider" section suggesting several themes or ideas to explore in a paper, essay, online project, or class presentation, often making use of other documents, books, films, and Web sites; and a "Further Information" section listing important print and electronic informa-tion resources as well as any relevant films or television programs. All documents are also accompanied by a brief sidebar that further illuminates some topic or concept related to the document, such as "Elizabethan London," "Priest Holes," the "Shakespearean Sonnet," or "Royal Progresses."

OTHER FEATURES

Other important features of *Voices of Shakespeare's England* include a general introduction that defines and explains the importance and scope of the Elizabethan/Jacobean period for users, an appendix of brief biographical entries on the most important individuals mentioned in the document sections, and a glossary of unfamiliar terms encountered in the sections. All names and terms included in the appendix or glossary are highlighted as cross-references upon their first mention in any section. Any unfamiliar terms appearing in the documents themselves are also highlighted, and brief definitions will appear after the document text so that they may be quickly referred to while reading the selection.

An "Evaluating and Interpreting Primary Documents" section provides users with a series of questions—Who wrote it? When and where was it written? Who was it written for? Why was it written?—to assess the historical context of the document. It also advises users on how to identify and define keywords and passages, the main thesis of the document, and the assumptions the author brought to the document from his or her class, religious background, or economic circumstances. Users will also be urged to understand how the document was produced and circulated and to compare it to other similar documents of the period. Photos of Elizabethan documents accompany the text, briefly explaining for students and modern users familiar only with modern electronic document production, how documents were produced during the period and by whom, and, where appropriate, the various writing styles used.

Finally, the volume includes a chronology of English history from the birth of Elizabeth I (1533) to the death of Shakespeare (1616), listing important events both in the life of the nation and in the life of the playwright; a detailed and current bibliography of print materials and Web sites, divided by broad topic, to provide readers with other useful information resources; and a detailed subject index to allow readers to easily and quickly access information in the document sections.

ACKNOWLEDGMENTS

I wish to thank the staffs at Arizona State University's Hayden Library and at the Scottsdale (Arizona) Public Library for assisting me in finding important document collections, research materials, and possible illustrations. Although much is now available on the Internet, there are still some materials that can only be obtained with the assistance of a librarian.

At ABC-CLIO, I want to thank Gary Kuris and Vince Burns for encouraging me to undertake this project and Kevin Ohe for helping me understand how such documentary materials may best be used by students and researchers. My thanks also to Mariah Gumpert at ABC-CLIO for helping me with the design of the volume and the series and to both her and Lisa Connery at Publication Services for so effectively seeing this volume through production to publication. Also, I must remember to mention the little Shih Tzu, Snuffle, and the King Charles spaniel, Schultzy, who kept me quiet (and sometimes not-so-quiet) company through long hours of reading, research, and writing. Finally, as usual with anything I try to do, nothing of any value would have been possible without the love and support of my wife, Donna.

Introduction: Shakespeare's England

WILLIAM SHAKESPEARE

William Shakespeare was born on April 23, 1564, in the Warwickshire market town of Stratford-on-Avon. His father, John Shakespeare (c. 1530–1601), was a Stratford glove maker and grain dealer, who married Mary Arden (c. 1540–1608) in about 1557. The couple had eight children, of whom five survived into adulthood: William, the eldest; his three brothers, Gilbert (1566–1612), Richard (1574–1613), and Edmund (1580–1607), and his sister, Joan (1569–1646). In the 1560s, the Shakespeare family prospered. John was a town alderman and owned several houses in Stratford. In the 1570s, John's fortunes declined. He mortgaged and lost much of his property, including his wife's inheritance, and was dropped from the town council in 1586. He thereafter appears in the record mainly in relation to lawsuits for debt.

William Shakespeare married Anne Hathaway (c. 1556–1623) in 1582, only a few months before the birth of their daughter Susanna (1583–1649), a not uncommon occurrence in Elizabethan England. In 1585, Anne gave birth to twins, a son named Hamnet, who died at age 11 in 1596, and a daughter Judith, who lived until 1662. Sometime in the late 1580s, Shakespeare left Stratford and his family and moved to London, where he began a successful career as an actor and playwright, coming eventually to be a shareholder in an acting company, the Chamberlain's Men, later known as the King's Men. In 1596, William helped his father obtain a coat of arms, allowing John to die a gentleman in 1601 when William inherited his remaining properties in Stratford.

William produced the bulk of his plays and poems between 1590 and 1613 when he retired again to Stratford. In his will, made on March 25, 1616, about a month before his death, Shakespeare leaves his long abandoned wife "my second best bed with the furniture" (Lambert, p. 87). No mention is made in the will of any manuscripts or other literary property. At his death, Shakespeare had only one grandchild, Elizabeth Hall (1608–1670), the daughter of Susanna and her husband John Hall, a Puritan physician. Shakespeare's other daughter, Judith, married Thomas Quiney in 1616 and gave birth to two sons, Richard in 1618 and Thomas in 1620. However, both of these grandsons died childless in 1639, as did Elizabeth Hall in 1670, leaving William Shakespeare with no further direct descendants.

Beyond this, little is known of the life and career of William Shakespeare, the man who is considered by many to be the greatest writer in the English language. Because we know so little about large parts of Shakespeare's life, many questions and much speculation have arisen about his education, his appearance, his religion, his sexuality, and, most importantly, his authorship of the works ascribed to him. Arguing that Shakespeare's education was brief and his early life provincial, opponents of Shakespeare's authorship believe that he could not have obtained the learning and experience to write brilliant plays that spoke clearly of the playwright's familiarity with the royal court, the military camp, the legal world, and other specific realms of experience. As a result, many other Elizabethan writers have been proposed as the true author of the works of Shakespeare, including, most notably, Sir Francis Bacon, Christopher Marlowe, and Edward de Vere, Earl of Oxford. Other writers argue that the works of Shakespeare were the result of a collaboration of writers that may have included the man from Stratford, as well as Oxford, Marlowe, and other London dramatists.

Fueling these arguments is a severe lack of documentary evidence for Shakespeare's life and career. No manuscripts exist for any of Shakespeare's plays, and only six signatures can positively be attributed to him. Eighteen of Shakespeare's plays appeared in print for the first time only in 1623 with the publication of the First Folio, the first published collection of Shakespeare's dramatic works. However, most modern Shakespeare scholars reject these arguments for alternative authorship as unconvincing and maintain that the outlines of Shakespeare's life are well known and that he was well established in the London theater community as a talented playwright by the late 1590s. Certainly, the genius of Shakespeare was already recognized within a few years of his death. In the preface to the First Folio, which was edited by Shakespeare's acting colleagues, John Heminges and Henry Condell, the playwright Ben Jonson declared that Shakespeare was "not of an age, but for all time."

QUEEN ELIZABETH I

Princess Elizabeth was born on September 7, 1533, the daughter of Henry VIII and his second wife, Anne Boleyn. Proclaimed heir to the throne at her birth, Elizabeth was removed from the succession and declared illegitimate upon the execution of her mother for treason and adultery in May 1536. As an adult, Elizabeth is said never to have spoken of her mother. The succession was settled in 1537 with the birth of Elizabeth's half-brother, who became king as Edward VI upon Henry's death in January 1547. Under the terms of the late king's will, Elizabeth was restored to the succession, standing next in line after Edward and her elder half-sister Mary.

When Edward died childless in 1553, Elizabeth supported her sister against an unsuccessful coup attempt endorsed by the late king, who, as a Protestant, feared that his devoutly Catholic sister Mary would return England to Rome. He was right, and Elizabeth's reluctance to accept Catholicism and her position as a Protestant alternative to Mary cost Elizabeth the queen's favor. Imprisoned in the Tower of London in 1554 on suspicion of involvement in Wyatt's Rebellion, an uprising that sought to dethrone Mary, Elizabeth admitted nothing and was eventually released for lack of evidence.

Upon Elizabeth's accession to the throne in November 1558, the two most pressing problems facing her were the question of her marriage and the succession. Because Elizabeth's heir was her Catholic cousin, Mary, Queen of Scots, and because the age expected a woman ruler to take a husband to help her govern, Elizabeth's ministers and Parliaments urged her to marry and produce a Protestant heir. Although for a time she seemed likely to marry Robert Dudley, her favorite and the love of her life, and though many other suitors were proposed, Elizabeth confounded expectations by remaining unmarried and refusing to formally name a successor.

Elizabeth also steadfastly maintained the moderate Anglican Church that Parliament had mandated largely according to her wishes in 1559. This policy frustrated Puritans, English Protestants who thought the Church was still too close to Catholicism in ritual and practice, but also spared England the religious wars that decimated sixteenth-century France. Catholic conspiracies to place Mary on the English throne and the threat of invasion from a Spanish, Catholic Netherlands forced Elizabeth to intervene militarily in the Netherlands Revolt against Spain in 1585, a decision that drew England into war with Spain. In 1588, one year after Elizabeth reluctantly consented to the execution of Mary, who had been a prisoner in England for 19 years, Philip II of Spain launched the Spanish Armada against England. The defeat of the Armada destroyed the myth of Spanish invincibility, cemented Elizabeth's hold on the affection of her people, and heartened Protestants across Europe.

Although the years after the defeat of the Armada witnessed military failure and economic decline, they also saw the flowering of the greatest cultural renaissance in English history. Remarkable developments in music, architecture, art, and, especially, drama and poetry, as well as brilliant achievements in commerce and exploration, made England's Elizabethan Age a period of confidence and progress. Almost 70, Elizabeth died on March 24, 1603, still loved and respected by most of her people.

Little contemporary evidence survives as to the queen's physical appearance. She was described as slightly above average height for an upper-class woman of her time, with fair skin, dark eyes, a long slightly hooked nose, and reddish-gold hair that curled naturally. She had a slim figure and beautiful hands with long fingers of which she was quite proud. She apparently resembled her father more than her mother and her paternal grandfather, Henry VII, most of all. She also shared certain personality traits with her grandfather, both monarchs being accused of frugality to the point of meanness. Neither displayed the bluff openhandedness of Henry VIII when it came to distributing rewards for royal service, and both strove to remain solvent by limiting expenditure, particularly for war. Elizabeth and her grandfather also shared a strong sense of national responsibility, carefully weighing the benefits and risks of each action for the nation as a whole. In Elizabeth, this caution often exasperated her ministers, who saw it merely as procrastination and indecision and confirmation of their own notions about the unfitness of women to rule. However, over time, her ministers and most of her subjects came to appreciate her sound judgment and common sense, and, after her death, many English people came to look upon Elizabeth's reign as a lost golden age.

Elizabeth always considered the love of her people to be her strongest asset in governing, and she strove all her life to win and retain that love. Even such political and religious enemies as Philip II, who approved and financed plans for her overthrow and murder, gave her a grudging respect as an intelligent and worthy opponent. Historians today consider Elizabeth one of the greatest monarchs in English history and one of the greatest women rulers of all time. By refusing to be pressured into marrying, Elizabeth allowed England to survive as an independent power. By crafting and maintaining a broadly based religious settlement, by pursuing peace and financial prudence, and by inspiring achievement in others through competition for her favor, Elizabeth gave England a new national unity and a new national confidence.

KING JAMES I

On Elizabeth's death, her throne passed quietly to her kinsman, King James VI of Scotland, the son of Mary, Queen of Scots. Born on June 19, 1566, James became king a year later upon the forced abdication of his mother. Because Mary fled to England in 1568 and was held prisoner there for the rest of her life, James never knew her and was brought up as a Protestant, a fact that eventually cleared his way to the English throne. James' early years as king were characterized by political disorder and civil war. In 1583, the king, now 16, initiated his personal rule, striving throughout the 1590s to secure his control over the kingdom, the nobility, and the Scottish Church, a more Calvinistic institution enjoying greater independence from the Crown than its counterpart in England.

In 1589, James married Anne of Denmark. The queen bore him three children who lived to adulthood—Henry, who died in 1612; Charles, later king as Charles I; and Elizabeth, from whom later monarchs of England, including Queen Elizabeth II, descend. In two books published in the 1590s, *The True Law of Free Monarchies and Basilikon Doron*, James set forth his theory of divine right kingship, arguing that an anointed monarch was answerable only to God and thus could be removed from his throne only by God, not by the will or action of the people.

James tried to persuade Elizabeth to formally name him her heir, but this she steadfastly refused to do, remembering her sister's reign when she had been the popular alternative to an unpopular queen. Elizabeth, however, granted James a pension in 1586 and promised not to oppose his claims to the Crown so long as his policies in Scotland, particularly as to religion and foreign affairs, met her approval. These favors limited James' reaction to his mother's execution in 1587 to formal protests and ensured his neutrality when the Spanish Armada entered the English Channel in 1588. James had no intention of jeopardizing his chance to rule England for a mother he could not remember. Although James frequently annoyed Elizabeth by ignoring the stream of advice she sent northward in her letters, he never provoked her unduly. By 1601, many English courtiers, including the queen's chief minister, Sir Robert Cecil, were secretly corresponding with James, thereby tacitly acknowledging him as the next ruler of England. He therefore succeeded to the English throne without incident upon Elizabeth's death in March 1603.

Following his accession, James took Shakespeare's acting company, the Chamberlain's Men, under his direct patronage, making them the King's Men. The company performed frequently at court, especially for Queen Anne and her daughter, Princess Elizabeth. The accounts of the treasurer of the king's chamber record court performances of numerous of Shakespeare's plays, including *Much Ado About Nothing, The Tempest, The Winter's Tale, Julius Caesar, The Merchant of Venice,* and both parts of *Henry IV.* Because James was less parsimonious than his predecessor, court entertainments became more frequent and more lavish, with Ben Jonson producing many masques and pageants. James died on March 27, 1625, and was succeeded by his surviving son, Charles I.

ECONOMIC LIFE

Agriculture formed the heart of the Elizabethan economy, employing far more English people than any other industry or occupation. Elizabethan England grew or produced most of the food and raw materials its people required, including hides for leather, wool for cloth, hemp for naval supplies, tallow for candles and soap, and horses for transport. Over the course of the reign, Elizabethan agricultural production transformed from being mainly for the subsistence of the farmer or local community to production for sale to wider markets. This change was the result of a rapidly growing population, which caused a steep rise in both the demand and price of food. Small peasant farmers gave way to gentleman and yeoman farmers, whose larger acreages allowed them to produce grain surpluses that could be sold in London and anywhere in the kingdom where demand outstripped supply.

The growth of the English cloth industry, which thrived on the increased production of English wool growers, enhanced this demand. As more rural workers engaged in the manufacture of cloth, they joined the growing populations of London and other towns, which relied on others to grow food. As a result of this demand, new farming methods were devised to improve yields, and marginal lands, out of production since the Black Death of the fourteenth century, went back into production. Many gentleman and yeoman farmers practiced enclosure, whereby land that had been pasture for the common use of a village was enclosed with a hedge or fence and given over by the landlord to the production of grain for the commercial market. Enclosure sometimes led to economic hardship for husbandmen and cottagers, who often lost the land they rented when their gentry landlords realized they could increase profits by working the land themselves with hired laborers. Nonetheless, except for the 1590s, when bad harvests necessitated grain imports, Elizabethan agriculture supplied the ordinary needs of the English people.

SOCIAL LIFE

Elizabethan society was characterized by a high degree of stratification, with people divided into various clearly delineated classes and ranks. As a consequence of the medieval feudal system, whereby the king granted land to a lord in return for military service, Elizabethan social distinctions were based primarily on the holding of land. Although feudal institutions had largely broken down, Elizabethan society was still heavily rural, with almost 90 percent of the population living on isolated farmsteads or in villages or towns under 2,000 people. Political and economic power was concentrated in the 3 to 4 percent of the population that constituted the landholding elite—the royal family, the titled nobility, and the gentry. Under Elizabeth, who had no spouse, children, or living siblings, the royal family consisted largely of the queen herself, although she had many distant cousins among the nobility and gentry. Under James, the royal family expanded to include a spouse and three children. Possessing titles of nobility and the right to be summoned to the House of Lords, the peerage numbered about 60 during Elizabeth's reign, but rapidly expanded under James, who was far more willing than his predecessor to grant noble titles. The number of Elizabethans who possessed the land, lifestyle, and local influence to claim the status of gentleman numbered about 16,000 at James' accession and grew during his reign. Both the nobility and gentry were further subdivided by title and degree of wealth.

Over 80 percent of the population consisted of rural residents lacking the land and lifestyle to qualify as gentry. These rural commons were divided into yeomen, husbandmen, cottagers, and landless laborers. A yeoman farmed at least 50 acres of freehold, which was land not rented or leased from a nobleman or gentleman and capable of being inherited by the yeoman's heirs. A yeoman also had an annual income of at least 40 shillings, the income required for a man to vote in county elections for Parliament. Husbandmen rented between 5 and 50 acres of land from larger landholders. Cottagers worked a few acres of land attached to their cottages and supplemented their income by working for others. Landless laborers had no land at all and depended entirely on wage work. Husbandmen, cottagers, and landless laborers comprised the great majority of the English rural population.

The remaining 10 to 15 percent of the Elizabethan and Jacobean population comprised a growing body of town dwellers—professionals (e.g., lawyers or physicians), merchants, craftsmen, and civil and military officers of the Crown. With the wealthier yeoman, these groups were called the "middling sort." They constituted the most upwardly mobile portion of society. As they grew more prosperous, these groups gradually acquired the land and adopted the lifestyle that would qualify them as gentlemen, a status often unofficially conferred by local society, if not officially by the College of Arms. The clergy represented English society in miniature with the archbishops and bishops recognized as an ecclesiastical nobility. Some of the vicars and chaplains of the poorer villages shared the low social status of the cottagers and laborers in their parishes. Despite its rigid formal distinctions of class, Elizabethan and Jacobean society was becoming increasingly fluid as wealthy merchants and lawyers rose into the gentry and poorer gentlemen sank to yeoman status.

RELIGIOUS LIFE

From her sister, Mary I, Elizabeth inherited an English Catholic Church that recognized the authority of the pope. Elizabeth's own theological views and liturgical preferences remain unclear even today, but she had been educated by anti-papal reformers, and she recognized the great unpopularity that Mary's burning of Protestant heretics had brought to the Crown and to Catholicism. As regards religion, the queen and her ministers wanted to satisfy as many people as possible by making as few changes as possible. While disliking papal authority, most English people in 1558 were not strong Protestants and probably would have been content with a church freed from papal control, but essentially Catholic in doctrine and practice. Thus, the two main issues for Elizabeth's government and Parliament were defining the relationship between Church and Crown and determining a form of worship. However, Catholic nobles and Mary's bishops opposed even the most moderate changes while returning Marian exiles, English Protestants who had fled to the continent during Mary's reign, demanded a radically Protestant church.

In light of this opposition, the government gave up on placating Catholics and proposed more Protestant religious legislation that gave England a church largely based on the doctrines of Calvinism. The Act of Supremacy abolished papal authority, but heeded complaints about a laywoman heading the Church and gave Parliament a larger role in directing religious affairs. The Act of Uniformity abolished the Catholic Mass and restored an altered version of the 1552 *Book of Common Prayer* to appease Catholics and conservatives. By giving the Church a form of worship that was too radical for Catholics and too conservative for Protestants, the queen and Parliament established a religious settlement that became known as the *via media*, the "middle way," an attempt to accommodate as many viewpoints as possible within the new Church.

Nonetheless, Elizabeth was determined that the English Church would serve the needs of the English state as she herself defined those needs. Thus, the Anglican Church was Calvinist in doctrine, episcopal in structure, and governed by the Crown through Parliament. Although bishops had disappeared from the Calvinistic churches of Europe, Elizabeth retained them because they served as useful instruments of royal control. Although she insisted on conformity to the manner of worship laid down by Parliament in the Act of Uniformity and the *Book of Common Prayer*, Elizabeth allowed a wide variety of beliefs and practices to exist within this mandated framework. Anglicans could largely believe as they wished, so long as they outwardly conformed and kept their unapproved opinions to themselves. The Anglican Church was thus based on the idea that matters of worship and church government not specifically outlined in the Bible and authorized by the state could be left to local practice and national custom as things indifferent to salvation and true belief.

Puritans, however, maintained that almost all religious practices were strictly prescribed in Scripture and could not be left to local or national tradition. At the Church's creation in 1559, Anglican doctrine and liturgy were vaguely defined because the government sought to include as many people as possible, whether conservatives or advanced reformers, within the new church. But the parameters of Anglicanism became sharper during the course of the reign as Roman Catholics fell away and Puritans began to distinguish themselves from the national church through disputes over vestments, governance, and liturgy. By Elizabeth's death in 1603, her Anglican Church had won the allegiance and devotion of most of her subjects.

Puritans looked forward to the accession of James I, whom they considered a convinced Calvinist willing to undertake the reforms Elizabeth had refused. But the king disappointed his Puritan subjects, being unwilling to abolish bishops or make any other changes that he believed weakened his control over the Church. The king did, however, agree to the Puritan request for better lay access to the Word of God, ordering the creation of a new English translation of the Bible to be used by all Anglicans. This Authorized or "King James" version of the Bible is still in use today.

POLITICAL LIFE

The highest expression of English national government in the reigns of Elizabeth and James was the King (Queen) in Parliament, the monarch acting with and through the consent of the national legislature. Parliamentary statute, passed by the two houses of Parliament, the Lords and Commons, and approved by the monarch, was the highest law of the realm, controlling and modifying even the common law. However, Parliament was not a permanent part of government, being summoned and dismissed by the Crown. Elizabeth called 10 Parliaments during her 44-year reign. James summoned four during a 22-year reign. Because Parliament was usually summoned to approve new taxation, its irregularity was not necessarily unpopular. Elizabeth summoned fewer parliaments in the early years of her reign, when she sought to avoid war, promote trade, and keep taxes low. After 1585, the continuance of war with Spain saw more frequent parliaments, longer sessions, and increased Crown demands for taxation. Under James, Parliament slowly developed into a focus for discontent with Crown policies, leading James to summon only two Parliaments during the first 18 years of his reign. The Parliament of 1614 was so quarrelsome and ineffective that it became known as the "Addled Parliament."

The Elizabethan House of Lords consisted of 70 to 80 members—two archbishops, 26 bishops, and the rest titled noblemen summoned by special writ. Under James, the House of Lords expanded as the king created many new peers. By 1603, the House of Commons numbered 462—90 representatives from the counties of England and Wales and 372 from 191 parliamentary towns, with London sending four representatives. In the counties, only male residents holding lands worth at least 40 shillings per year could vote, a qualification that essentially restricted the franchise to the gentry. In the towns, voting qualifications depended upon how the town's charter defined a voter. In many boroughs, the vote was narrowly restricted.

Parliament provided legislative remedies for public matters brought before it by the Privy Council, which handled day-to-day administration. Privy councilors were often elected to Parliament, where they were expected to further the Crown's interests. The Commons, which met in St. Stephen's Chapel at Westminster, had the right to initiate all tax bills. Debate in the Commons was directed by the speaker, a Crown nominee elected by the House at the start of each session. To become statute, bills passed through three readings. The first reading informed members of the bill's content, the second initiated debate, and the third, after revision, refined the wording of the measure. Upon receiving the royal assent, a bill passed after a third reading became statute. The debates and decisions of the Lords and Commons were recorded by the clerk of each House, who kept journals of all parliamentary activities.

The main units of local government in Shakespeare's England were the 53 shires (or counties) into which England and Wales were divided. Because the Crown had no professional and salaried bureaucracy, it relied on the gentry, the social and political elite of the counties, to administer the shires in the royal interest. Through a series of largely unpaid local offices, the gentry implemented government policy in the shires by enforcing royal proclamations and parliamentary statutes. The most important local officials were the justices of the peace (JPs), who had both administrative and judicial functions. Each year, the Crown appointed a commission of the peace for each county that included between 30 and 60 men selected on the basis of their social, political, and economic position within the shire. Most of the work of the commission was undertaken by the quorum, a specially nominated inner circle of JPs that often included members with legal experience. Another important county official was the sheriff, who supervised local prisons, impaneled juries, and implemented criminal sentences imposed by the JPs.

Other shire officials included the coroner, who investigated suspicious deaths; the escheator, who enforced the Crown's feudal rights; the customer, who collected certain taxes; and the constable, who kept peace within the hundred, an administrative subdivision of the shire. A more recent local office was that of lord lieutenant, a military official responsible for supervising the county militia, storing and maintaining stocks of arms and ammunition, and organizing local defenses. Local noblemen were often named lord lieutenant for a group of counties, with deputy lieutenants under them responsible for one county each. Until the start of the Spanish war in 1585, lord lieutenants were appointed on an ad hoc basis, but wartime demanded more regular arrangements for local defense, and lord lieutenants were thereafter appointed for life. Working under the JPs were also such parish officers as the constables, who kept the peace within a parish; watchmen, who assisted the constables; and surveyors of the highways and overseers of the poor, who maintained roads and supervised poor relief within each parish.

LITERARY LIFE

The last two decades of the reign of Elizabeth and the first two of James witnessed the writing and production of some of the finest plays in the English language. In 1500, English drama consisted of medieval morality plays and cycles of mystery plays, religious drama performed by amateur actors in town streets during fairs and holidays. Over the next century, a professional theater developed from these beginnings. The Reformation freed English drama from religious themes and provided playwrights with secular plots while English nationalism generated by the break with Rome caused writers to mine English history for stories and characters. English humanism put Elizabethan and Jacobean writers in touch with classical Greek and Roman styles and imbued them with a love of drama and literature. Wary of the political and religious purposes for which drama could be used, Elizabeth banned the performance of unlicensed plays in 1559 and suppressed religious play cycles in the 1570s.

In 1572, the Queen forbade anyone but noblemen to sponsor professional troupes of players, and, in 1574, she authorized her master of revels to license all plays and acting companies. These actions placed the English theater under royal control and accelerated the secularization of Elizabethan drama. Beginning with Leicester's Men, an acting troupe sponsored by Robert Dudley, Earl of Leicester, who used the stage to promote his political program and his hopes for a royal marriage, numerous professional companies arose under the patronage of important courtiers. Along with the development of groups of professional players came the building of permanent theaters, the first being James Burbage's London playhouse, The Theatre, constructed in 1576.

Other theaters soon appeared in and around London, including Burbage's Blackfriars (1576), the Rose (1587), and the Swan (1595). Many company actors became shareholders in particular theaters. For example, William Shakespeare and the other principals of the Chamberlain's Men were part owners of the Globe Theater. The development of a professional theater meant that playwrights no longer had to attach themselves to noble patrons or limit themselves to the themes and forms their patrons favored, but could, within government guidelines, write plays on themes that interested themselves and their audiences. These developments opened the playwriting profession to many who otherwise might not have been able to develop their talents, such playwrights as John Lyly, Robert Greene, Christopher Marlowe, Ben Jonson, and Shakespeare.

Stretching across the reigns of Elizabeth and James, the period from 1575 to 1610 was one of the most creative and prolific in the history of English poetry. This poetic flowering began in the previous quarter century when humanist scholars and Protestant reformers used English, long considered inferior to Latin and Greek as a literary language, to teach and preach. Prose works of scholarship like Roger Ascham's *The Schoolmaster* (1570) and religious works like John Foxe's *Book of Martyrs* and Thomas Cranmer's *Book of Common Prayer* (1549, 1552), illustrated the strength and flexibility of Elizabethan English. Poetry, the pastime of courtiers in earlier decades, reached a wider audience in the 1560s with the publication of Richard Tottel's anthology *Songs and Sonnets* (1557), a work generally known as "Tottel's Miscellany." By popularizing the court poetry of Henry VIII's time and the work of unknown contemporary poets, Tottel inspired a host of similar poetry collections that built demand for English verse.

This growing interest in poetry was illustrated by the popularity of *A Mirror for Magistrates*, a collection of poetic laments supposedly spoken by participants in the Wars of the Roses. Compiled by various editors and containing the efforts of such contemporary poets as Thomas Sackville and Thomas Churchyard, the *Mirror* went through four editions between 1559 and 1587. The plainer, simpler poetry published by Tottel and the *Mirror* in the 1560s was superseded in the next two decades by the more ornate and innovative lyric poetry written by Edmund Spenser and Sir Philip Sidney. Spenser was the first English poet to use print to deliberately disseminate his work to a wider public. His *The Faerie Queen* (1590–1609) was a lyric epic of Protestant nationalism, casting Elizabeth as the Faerie Queen herself. Sidney's work was also infused with Protestant fervor and tied to the cult of Elizabeth, the Virgin Queen. Where Spenser inspired every English poet of the 1590s to try lyric poetry, Sidney, through his *Astrophel and Stella* (1591) cycle, initiated a great flood of sonnet sequences, including one published by William Shakespeare in 1609. In the 1590s and the 1600s, English poetry was being enriched by many talented poets innovating new forms and exploring new themes and topics.

Bibliography

Doran, Susan. *Queen Elizabeth I.* New York: New York University Press, 2003.

Dunn, Jane. *Elizabeth and Mary: Cousins, Rivals, Queens.* New York: Alfred A. Knopf, 2004.

Erickson, Carolly. *The First Elizabeth.* New York: Summit Books, 1983.

Greenblatt, Stephen. *Will in the World: How Shakespeare Became Shakespeare.* London: W.W. Norton & Company, 2004.

Guy, John. *Queen of Scots: The True Life of Mary Stuart.* Boston: Houghton Mifflin, 2004.

Haigh, Christopher, ed. *The Reign of Elizabeth I.* Athens: University of Georgia Press, 1987.

Hibbert, Christopher. *The Virgin Queen: Elizabeth I, Genius of the Golden Age.* Reading, MA: Addison-Wesley, 1991.

Hurstfield, Joel. *Elizabeth I and the Unity of England.* London: The English Universities Press, 1960.

Johnson, Paul. *Elizabeth I: A Biography.* New York: Holt, Rinehart and Winston, 1974.

Lambert, D.H., ed. *Cartae Shakespeareanae: Shakespeare Documents; A Chronological Catalogue of Extant Evidence Relating to the Life and Works of William Shakespeare.* London: George Bell and Sons, 1904.

Loades, David. *Elizabeth I.* New York: Hambledon Continuum, 2006.

MacCaffrey, Wallace. *Elizabeth I.* London: Edward Arnold, 1993.

———. *Elizabeth I: War and Politics 1588–1603.* Princeton, NJ: Princeton University Press, 1992.

———. *Queen Elizabeth and the Making of Policy, 1572–1588.* Princeton, NJ: Princeton University Press, 1981.

———. *The Shaping of the Elizabethan Regime: Elizabethan Politics 1558–1572.* Princeton, NJ: Princeton University Press, 1968.

Neale, J.E. *Queen Elizabeth I: A Biography.* Chicago: Academy Chicago Publishers, 1992.

Olsen, Kirstin. *All Things Shakespeare: An Encyclopedia of Shakespeare's World.* 2 vols. Westport, CT: Greenwood Press, 2002.

Palliser, D.M. *The Age of Elizabeth: England Under the Later Tudors, 1547–1603.* 2nd ed. London: Longman, 1992.

Palmer, Alan, and Veronica Palmer. *Who's Who in Shakespeare's England.* New York: St. Martin's Press, 1981.

Rex, Richard. *Elizabeth I: Fortune's Bastard.* Stroud, Gloucestershire, Tempus, 2003.

Ridley, Jasper. *Elizabeth I: The Shrewdness of Virtue.* New York: Viking, 1988.

Smith, Lacey Baldwin. *Elizabeth Tudor: Portrait of a Queen.* Boston: Little, Brown and Company, 1975.

———. *The Elizabethan World.* Boston: Houghton Mifflin, 1991.

Starkey, David. *Elizabeth: The Struggle for the Throne.* New York: HarperCollins, 2001.

Stewart, Alan. *The Cradle King: The Life of James VI and I, the First Monarch of a United Great Britain.* New York: St. Martin's Press, 2003.

Wagner, John A. *Historical Dictionary of the Elizabethan World.* Phoenix: Oryx Press, 1999.

Warnicke, Retha M. *Mary Queen of Scots.* London: Routledge, 2006.

Weir, Alison. *The Life of Elizabeth I.* New York: Ballantine Books, 1998.

Willson, D. Harris. *King James VI and I.* New York: Henry Holt and Company, 1956.

EVALUATING AND INTERPRETING PRIMARY DOCUMENTS

In historiography, which is the study of the writing of history and the employment of historical methods, a primary source is a document, recording, artifact, work of art or literature, or other information resource that was created at or near the time being studied, usually by someone with direct, personal knowledge of the particular past events, persons, or topics being described. Primary sources are original sources of information about the past, unlike secondary sources, which are works historians later create from a study, citation, and evaluation of primary sources. A modern textbook of British history; a modern biography like David Loades' *Elizabeth I*; a modern monograph like Wallace MacCaffrey's three-volume study of the reign of Elizabeth I; or a modern film like *Shakespeare in Love* may be helpful in explaining the Elizabethan period and its people to twenty-first century readers and viewers, but they are all secondary descriptions and depictions based upon the firsthand experiences and recollections recorded and preserved in the primary documents of the period.

Primary documents—as illustrated by the document selections included in *Voices of Shakespeare's England*—come in many forms and types, including letters, diaries, polemics, notes of speeches, literary works, and public records and documents. All these types of sources were written by a particular person at a particular time in a particular place for a particular reason. Some were written with no expectation that they would ever be read by anyone other than the original recipient; others were written for publication or at least with an eye to wider distribution. Some were meant to inform, some to persuade, some to entertain, and some to obfuscate. Each exhibits the political, religious, class, ethnic, or personal biases of their creators, whether those attitudes were consciously or unconsciously expressed. Some are the product of poor memories, bad information, or outright deception, but all are authentic voices of someone alive at the time, and all can add at least a little to the information we have of an otherwise irrecoverable past age or person. Nonetheless, historians must carefully evaluate and test all primary sources to determine how much weight and credibility each should be given.

HOW TO READ PRIMARY DOCUMENTS

When evaluating a primary source, historians ask the following questions:

1. Who wrote or produced it? What is known about this person's life or career?
2. When was the source written or produced? What date? How close or far was that date from the date of the events described?

3. Where was it produced? What country? What region? What locality?
4. How was the source written or produced? What form did it originally take? Was it based upon any preexisting material? Does the source survive in its original form?
5. Why was the source written or produced? What was its creator trying to do? And for whom?
6. Who was the source written or produced for? Who was its audience? Why? What do we know about the audience?
7. What is the evidential value of its contents? How credible is it?

Readers of the document selections contained in this volume should apply these same questions to the selections they read or study.

When analyzing a primary document, scholars also seek to identify the keywords and phrases used by the author and try to understand what the author meant by those terms. They will also try to summarize the main thesis of the source to understand what point the author was trying to make. Once the author's thesis is understood, historians evaluate the evidence the author provided to support that argument and try to identify any assumptions the author made in crafting those arguments. Historians also examine the source within the context of its time period by asking if the document is similar to others from the same period, how widely it was circulated, or what tone, problems, or ideas it shares with other documents of the period. Scholars will also seek to determine if the author agrees or disagrees with other contemporary authors on the same subject and whether or not the source supports what they already know or have learned about the subject from other sources.

Primary sources offer modern readers and researchers the actual words of people who lived through a particular event. Secondary sources, like textbooks, offer an interpretation of a historical person or event by someone who did not know the person or witness the period. Reading primary sources allows us to evaluate the interpretations of historians for ourselves and to draw our own conclusions about a past personage or events. Asking the questions listed above will help users of this volume better understand and interpret the documents provided here. Because of unfamiliar and archaic language or terminology or very different modes of expression or styles of writing, some primary sources can be difficult to read and hard to understand.

However, an important part of the process of reading and using historical sources is determining what the documents can tell about the past and deciding whether one agrees with the interpretation offered, both by the author of the original source and by later creators of secondary works based on the original document. By using primary sources, modern readers become aware that all history is based on sources that are themselves interpretations of events rooted in the interpreter's own opinions and biases. This awareness allows modern students to recognize the subjective nature of history. Thus, reading primary sources provides modern readers with the tools and evidence needed to make informed statements about the world of the past and of the present.

ELIZABETHAN AND JACOBEAN PRIMARY DOCUMENTS

The actual source documents of Shakespeare's England can sometimes be difficult for modern nonspecialist users to read and understand. Elizabethan writing styles were often very different in construction and cadence from modern styles. In literature, for instance, the euphuic style popularized in the 1580s by John Lyly was very elaborate and artificial, much given to the use of alliteration and packed with historical, philosophical, and mythological allusions. Much of Lyly's work could be confusing and meaningless to a reader who does not understand the allusions. Also, students who have struggled through their first exposure to the plays or poems of William Shakespeare or other Elizabethan literary figures know that Elizabethan English can be difficult to follow. Indeed, modern books and Web sites have appeared that place the original text of Shakespeare next to a "translation" in modern English to help readers better understand the meaning.

In medieval England, French was the language of the law and the royal court while Latin was the language of literature, scholarship, and diplomacy. English came into fashion at court and among the nobility in the late fourteenth century when the Hundred Years War with France encouraged a more self-conscious English nationalism. By Elizabeth's accession in 1558, English was the language of government and was rapidly becoming the language of literature and scholarship. Unlike the fourteenth-century English of Geoffrey Chaucer, which is largely unintelligible to a twenty-first-century ear, the English of Shakespeare, Marlowe, and other Elizabethan writers is close enough to modern English to be generally comprehensible.

Although some Elizabethan words had different meanings from the ones they bear today and other words have today fallen out of use (e.g., "thee" and "thou" as familiar forms of address), the main difference between Elizabethan and modern English consists of variations in the pronunciation of certain vowels (e.g., the Elizabethan pronunciation of "weak" rhymed with "break"). Elizabethan pronunciation varied widely from region to region, and no standard pronunciation existed, although the London dialect was beginning to achieve a certain dominance by the end of the reign. Elizabethan English had no official form, and widely varying dialects could even be heard spoken at court by nobles and gentlemen from different parts of the realm. Of more importance to modern readers of Elizabethan documents is the fact that spelling also lacked consistency, and people tended to spell words as they pronounced them, with wide variations in pronunciation producing equally wide variations in spelling. This variety even affected proper names. Sir Peter Carew's name, for instance, appears in surviving documents in numerous spellings, including "Caroo," "Carowe," and "Care." However, despite this variety, Elizabethan English was a vigorous and flexible language. During Shakespeare's lifetime, English, through exploration and political and commercial expansion, extended itself into Wales, Lowland Scotland, Ireland, and America.

Another difficulty for readers of Elizabethan/Jacobean documents is handwriting. Figure 1, below, is a reproduction of a letter, dated 26 August 1588, from William Cecil, Lord Burghley, to Charles Howard, Lord Howard of Effingham, admiral of the English fleet. The letter is actually a brief covering note to another letter from the Earl of Sussex, which Burghley is sending on to the admiral.

This letter is written in two distinct hands. The first twelve lines are written in what is called a "Secretary hand" by one of Burghley's clerks. The Secretary writing style originated in Italy, but came into wide use in England in the late fifteenth and early sixteenth centuries. As the volume of government, business, and personal correspondence grew in the early modern period, so did development of the Secretary hand. The Secretary hand was characterized by the use of certain letter forms and abbreviations. For instance, the first two lines of Burghley's note (with original spelling) read as follow:

> After my most hartie Commendacions to yo[u]r good l[ordship]
> Having this verie morning receiued the inclosed l[ett]re to
> yo[u]r L[ordship]

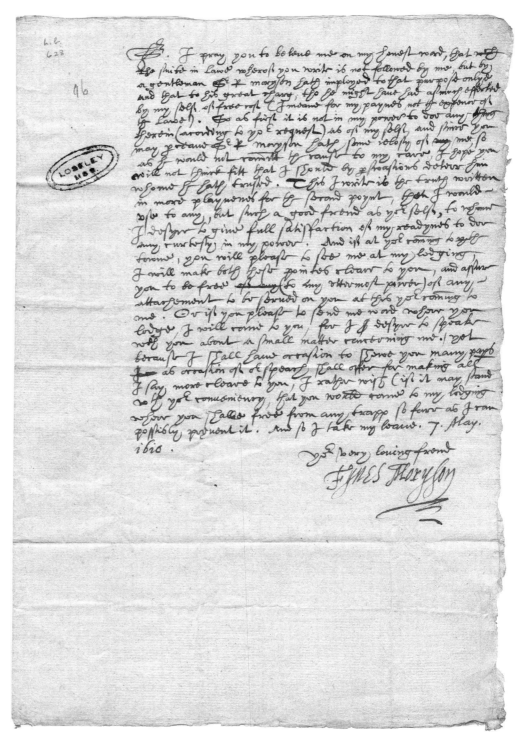

Letter from Lord Burghley to Lord Howard of Effingham, dated 26 August 1588. *By Permission of the Folger Shakespeare Library.*

Note that the frequent mention of 'lord' or 'Lordship' is abbreviated rather indifferently, with an "l" or an "L," a common Secretary hand abbreviation. Note also the long umbrella-like "s" in "most," the third word in the first line, a distinctive letter form of the Secretary hand. Note that the date in the last line of the Secretary hand uses Roman numerals ("xxvjth of August. 1588"), another characteristic of Elizabethan correspondence.

The second part of this letter is done in Burghley's own handwriting, an Italic hand that is difficult to read largely because Burghley uses a large number of technical abbreviations, such as "Culv." for Culverin, a type of gun. The Italic hand rose to prominence in England in the sixteenth century and was often used by women. Its letter forms are closer to modern handwriting, so it is usually easier for modern readers to follow. It was less used in Elizabethan government correspondence because it was considered easier to forge.

This letter was carried by dispatch riders from London to Canterbury. We know this because the arrival times (not shown in Figure 1) at each postal station along the route were noted by the postal officers. Thus, the letter left London about 9:00 AM, reached Dartford at 1:00 PM, Rochester at 5:00 PM, Sittingbourne at 6:00 PM, and Canterbury after 8:00 PM. Sussex's letter, which is now lost, was apparently urgent, for Burghley wrote on the back of his note, "post hast for life."

Figure 2 reproduces a portion of an autograph letter from Queen Elizabeth to King James VI of Scotland. The letter is dated March 16, 1592, which is, in fact, 1593 by the Gregorian calendar, which was not then in use in England or Scotland.

Elizabeth usually wrote in an Italic hand, and she has done so here, though it is rather difficult to read because it appears the queen was writing very quickly. (She herself describes the letter as "suche skribled Lines.") She has mixed in many Secretary letter forms and abbreviations, making the handwriting a sort of hybrid. The first two lines of the letter read as follows:

> Me thinks I frame this Lettar Like
> to a Lamentatio[n] wiche you wyl pardo[n]

Note the similarity between the queen's Italic hand in this letter and Burghley's Italic hand in the second portion of the letter in Figure 1. Note also the queen's distinctive signature in the bottom right corner of Figure 2.

Figure 3 reproduces a letter, dated May 7, 1610, from Fynes Moryson to a Mr. Gresham. The letter is in regard to a lawsuit being conducted by the writer's brother, Sir Richard Moryson.

The first three lines of the letter read as follows:

> Sir, I pray you to beleue me on my honest word, that [which]
> the suite in Lawe whereof you write is not followed by me, but by
> a gentleman Sir R Moryson hath imployed to that purpose onlye

The letter is written in a most traditional Secretary hand, with few errors or corrections. The wavy lines at the ends of lines 12 and 18 are simply line filler, not letters. Notice the use of "u" where we would use "v," as in "beleue" in the first line. That is traditional sixteenth-century spelling. Note also the ending "e" on many words, such as "Lawe" and "onlye," again a commonplace of Tudor spellings. See how much easier this exact Secretary hand is to read than the queen's hurried Italic hand in Figure 2. Finally, notice that the date, using an Arabic "7" rather than the roman "vij," and the signature are written in an Italic hand rather than in Secretary.

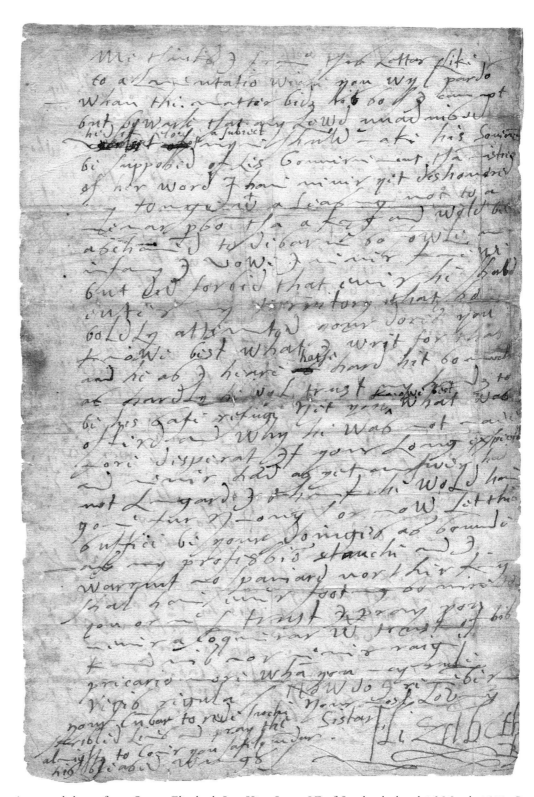

Autograph letter from Queen Elizabeth I to King James VI of Scotland, dated 16 March 1593. *By Permission of the Folger Shakespeare Library.*

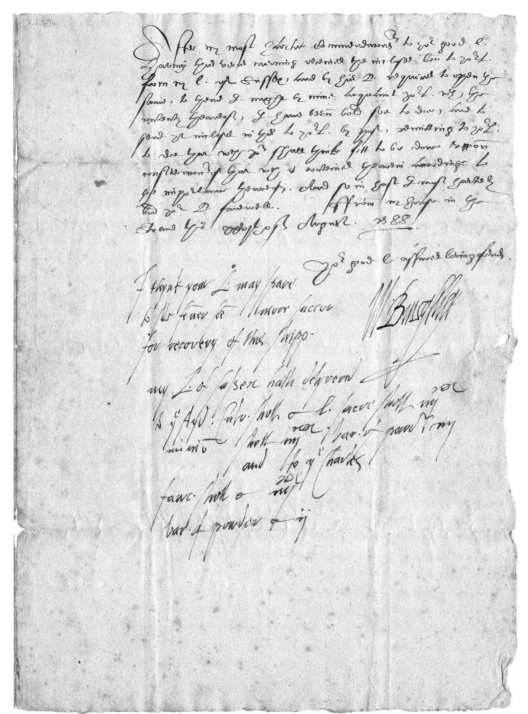

Letter from Fynes Moryson to Mr. Gresham, dated 7 May 1610. *By Permission of the Folger Shakespeare Library.*

Bibliography

Burgess, Peter H. *Shakespeare in Modern English*. Lutterworth, England: Tynron Press, 1992.

Preston, Jean F., and Laetitia Yeandle. *English Handwriting 1400–1650: An Introductory Manual*. Binghamton, NY: Medieval and Renaissance Texts and Studies, 1992.

Web Sites

No Fear Shakespeare: http://nfs.sparknotes.com/asyoulikeit/page_2.html

Shakespeare in Modern English: http://www.enotes.com/william-shakespeare/shakespeare-modern-english

Chronology of English History from the Birth of Elizabeth I to the Death of William Shakespeare, 1533–1616

1533	January 25	Henry VIII secretly marries Anne Boleyn
	September 7	Birth of Princess Elizabeth later Elizabeth I
1536	May 19	Execution of Anne Boleyn for treason
1537	October 12	Birth of Prince Edward later Edward VI, son of Henry VIII and Jane Seymour and half-brother of Elizabeth I
1542	December 8	Birth of Princess Mary of Scotland, daughter of James V and Marie de Guise and cousin of Elizabeth I
	December 14	Six-day-old Princess Mary becomes queen of Scotland on the sudden death of her father
1547	January 28	Death of Henry VIII; Accession of Edward VI
1550	April 12	Birth of Edward de Vere, future seventeenth Earl of Oxford
1553	July 6	Death of Edward VI
	July 10	Lady Jane Grey, a cousin of Elizabeth I and her half-siblings, is proclaimed queen
	July 19	Queen Jane is deposed; Accession of Mary I; Princess Elizabeth becomes heir presumptive to the English Crown
1554	January/February	Sir Thomas Wyatt leads an unsuccessful rebellion against Queen Mary's proposed marriage to Prince Philip later Philip II of Spain. Replacing Mary with her sister Elizabeth is an avowed aim of some of the rebels
	March 18	Princess Elizabeth, suspected of supporting Wyatt's Rebellion, is imprisoned in the Tower of London
	May 19	Princess Elizabeth is removed from the Tower and confined at the royal manor of Woodstock
	July 25	Queen Mary marries Prince Philip of Spain
1555	April	Princess Elizabeth is allowed to return to Court, but remains confined to her apartments
	October	Princess Elizabeth is allowed to withdraw from Court to her house at Hatfield
1558	April 24	Mary of Scotland marries the Dauphin Francis, son of Henri II and heir to the French throne

	November 17	Death of Mary I; Accession of Elizabeth I
	November 20	Elizabeth appoints Sir William Cecil secretary of state and principal secretary
1559	January 10	Philip II of Spain, husband of the late Queen Mary, proposes marriage to Elizabeth, who refuses him
	January 15	Coronation of Elizabeth I
	January 23	First parliamentary session of the reign opens; Parliament passes [April 29] the Act of Supremacy, severing England from Rome, and the Act of Uniformity, giving England a Protestant Church
	June 5	Elizabeth rejects marriage proposal of Charles, the Catholic archduke of Austria
	July 7	Scottish Protestants occupy Edinburgh, beginning civil war between Protestant lords of Scotland and French-backed Catholic regency government of Marie de Guise, mother of Mary of Scotland
	July 10	Death of Henri II of France; Accession of Francis II and his wife, Mary of Scotland, to the French throne
	July 17	Shane O'Neill succeeds to earldom of Tyrone in northern Ireland
	September 24	Scottish Protestants appeal to Elizabeth for help in Scottish civil war
	December 17	Matthew Parker becomes Elizabeth's first Archbishop of Canterbury
1560	January 12	Irish Parliament passes Act of Uniformity, giving Ireland a Protestant Church
	February 22	Elizabeth signs Treaty of Berwick with Scottish Protestants
	July 6	Conclusion of Treaty of Edinburgh, whereby English and French troops withdraw from Scotland, Mary is pledged to recognize Elizabeth as rightful queen of England, and a Protestant provisional government rules Scotland in Mary's absence
	August 24	Scottish Parliament establishes a Protestant Church
	September 8	Amy Robsart Dudley, wife of Robert Dudley, favorite of Elizabeth, dies under mysterious circumstances, and rumors spread that Dudley murdered his wife to marry the Queen
	December 5	Death of Francis II of France widows Mary of Scotland; Accession of Charles IX to French throne
1561	July 13	Elizabeth refuses Mary safe passage to Scotland because Mary refuses to ratify the Treaty of Edinburgh
	August 19	Queen Mary returns to Scotland from France and continues Protestant government under her half-brother, James, Earl of Moray
1562	August 24	Recoinage of debased English currency restores European confidence in English money
	September 20	Elizabeth concludes treaty with French Protestants, providing military assistance in exchange for English possession of Le Harve
	October	Elizabeth falls seriously ill with smallpox, raising fears of civil war should she die without a clear successor; Elizabeth names Dudley protector in event of her death
	October	John Hawkins launches first slaving expedition to Africa and first trading expedition to Spanish America
	November/ December	Shane O'Neill rises in rebellion in Ulster in northern Ireland

1563		Publication of John Foxe's *Acts and Monuments*, known popularly as *The Book of Martyrs*
	January 11	Second parliamentary session of the reign opens; Parliament unsuccessfully petitions Elizabeth to marry and settle the succession and passes an Act of Artificers, which regulates wages and conditions of employment, and an Act for Relief of the Poor
	April	Parliament orders a Welsh translation of the *Book of Common Prayer*
	September 11	Shane O'Neill, the Earl of Tyrone, submits to the Queen's deputy in Ireland and ends his rebellion
1564	March	Elizabeth proposes Robert Dudley as husband for Mary of Scotland
	April 11	Calais, lost to France by Queen Mary in 1558, is officially recognized as a French possession in the Anglo-French Treaty of Troyes
	April 23	Birth of William Shakespeare
	April 26	Baptism of William Shakespeare, son of John Shakespeare, is entered in the Stratford Parish register
	September 28	Elizabeth raises Robert Dudley to peerage as Earl of Leicester
	October	Riots occur in Ireland against the plantation of English colonists in the Irish counties of Offaly and Leix renamed by the English Queen's and King's Counties
	October 18	John Hawkins launches his second voyage to Africa and America
1565	July 25	Mary of Scotland marries Henry Stuart, Lord Darnley, a great-grandson of Henry VII
	Summer	Queen visits Coventry on her summer progress
	October 6	Mary of Scotland defeats pro-English, pro-Protestant forces under her half-brother, James, Earl of Moray
1566	March	Various London clergy are suspended for refusing to wear vestments
	March 9	A group of Protestant lords, with the support of Lord Darnley, seize and murder David Rizzio, Queen Mary's French secretary, in the Scottish queen's presence; Mary is placed under arrest
	March 20	Mary of Scotland resumes control of the Scottish government with the support of Lord Darnley
	June 19	Birth of Prince James of Scotland later James I of England, son of Queen Mary and Lord Darnley
	August/September	Elizabeth's summer progress takes her to Stamford, Woodstock, and Oxford
	September 30	Third parliamentary session of the reign opens; Parliament unsuccessfully petitions Elizabeth to marry and settle the succession and seeks unsuccessfully to make Protestant alterations in the Anglican settlement of 1559
1567	February 10	Lord Darnley, ill with syphilis, is murdered at Kirk o'Field outside Edinburgh
	April 24	James Hepburn, Earl of Bothwell, abducts and imprisons Queen Mary at Dunbar Castle
	May 15	Mary of Scotland marries Bothwell
	June 2	Death of the Irish rebel Shane O'Neill, Earl of Tyrone
	June 15	Scottish nobles defeat Queen Mary at Carberry Hill; Bothwell flees Scotland

	July 24	Queen Mary, imprisoned at Lochleven, abdicates the Scottish Crown in favor of her son
	August 22	James, Earl of Moray, proclaimed regent for young King James VI of Scotland
	October 2	John Hawkins launches his third voyage to Africa and America
1568	May 2	Queen Mary escapes from Lochleven
	May 13	Mary defeated at Langside
	May 16	Mary of Scotland flees into England and is imprisoned by Elizabeth
	September 21	John Hawkins is routed by Spanish at San Juan de Ulloa
	December	Elizabeth orders seizure of Spanish bullion onboard ships driven by privateers into Plymouth and Southampton
1569	June	James Fitzmaurice Fitzgerald leads a rebellion against English rule in southern Ireland
	November 1	Thomas Howard, Duke of Norfolk, is arrested for conspiring with Mary of Scotland
	November 14	Rebels led by Thomas Percy, Earl of Northumberland, and Charles Neville, Earl of Westmoreland, enter Durham and restore Catholic worship in the cathedral; the Northern Rebellion, attracting no support elsewhere in the kingdom, fades away by the end of the year
1570	January 23	James, Earl of Moray, the regent for James VI, is assassinated
	February	Pope Pius V issues the bull *Regnans in Excelsis*, which declares Elizabeth excommunicated and deposed
	August	The Duke of Norfolk is released from the Tower but remains under house arrest
	September	Elizabeth considers marriage proposals from Archduke Charles of Austria and Henri, Duke of Anjou later Henri III of France
1571	February 25	Elizabeth raises Sir William Cecil to the peerage as Lord Burghley
	April	The Ridolfi Plot, involving Mary of Scotland, the Duke of Norfolk, and the Spanish ambassador in a scheme to overthrow Elizabeth, is uncovered
	April 2	Fourth parliamentary session of the reign opens; Parliament, reacting to the Northern Rebellion and the Queen's excommunication, makes publishing a papal bull or calling theQueen a heretic treason, but is frustrated by the Queen in attempts to compel Catholics to attend Anglican services or to pay ruinous fines for not attending
	September 3	The Duke of Norfolk is imprisoned in the Town for his involvement in the Ridolfi Plot
	December	Sir John Perrot begins an Anglicization program in southern Ireland, the scene of recent rebellions against English rule
1572	March 1	Elizabeth closes English ports to the Dutch Sea Beggars
	April 1, 22	Sea Beggars capture the Dutch ports of Brill and Flushing, thus igniting a Dutch revolt against Spanish rule
	April 21	Treaty of Blois with France provides for mutual assistance in case of attack and an Anglo-French effort to settle the ongoing conflict between pro- and anti-Mary factions in Scotland
	May 8	Fifth parliamentary session of the reign opens; Parliament works unsuccessfully for the execution of Mary of Scotland and successful-

		ly for the execution of the Duke of Norfolk, and Puritan members seek unsuccessfully to alter the 1559 settlement and establish a Presbyterian Church structure
	June 2	Execution of Thomas Howard, Duke of Norfolk, for involvement in the Ridolfi Plot
	Summer	Queen visits Warwick on her summer progress
	August 24	Saint Bartholomew's Day Massacre of Protestants occurs in France; many Huguenots subsequently seek asylum in England
	August 29	Francis Drake seizes Spanish treasure ships in the West Indies
1573	July 9	Elizabeth grants Walter Devereux, Earl of Essex, right to colonize Ulster in Northern Ireland
	August 9	Drake returns from America with enormous treasure taken from Spanish
	December	Sir Francis Walsingham, a strong Puritan, is made secretary of state
1574		Arrival of first seminary priests in England
	May 30	Death of Charles IX of France; Accession of Henri III formerly a suitor of Elizabeth as Duke of Anjou
	Summer	Queen visits Bristol and the West on her summer progress
1575	May 17	Death of Archbishop Matthew Parker
	May 22	Elizabeth withdraws her support for Essex's plans to colonize Ulster in Ireland
	Summer	Elizabeth visits Reading, Windsor, Woodstock, and other towns north and west of London on her summer progress
	July 26	Essex's army in Ireland massacres the inhabitants of Rathlin Island
	December 24	Edmund Grindal becomes Elizabeth's second Archbishop of Canterbury
1576		James Burbage opens the Theater, which is considered the first playhouse in London
	February 8	Sixth parliamentary session of the reign opens; Parliament again petitions the Queen to marry, and Puritan members again seek unsuccessfully to alter the 1559 settlement of religion
	March 15	Peter Wentworth, a Puritan member of Parliament, is imprisoned in the Tower for criticizing the Queen and demanding Parliament's right to freedom of speech without interference from the Crown
	June 7	Martin Frobisher launches his first voyage of exploration to America
	September 22	Death of the Earl of Essex in Ireland
	December 20	Archbishop Grindal refuses to suppress prophesyings as ordered by Elizabeth
1577		James Burbage opens The Theatre, the first permanent, professional theater in England, on the south bank of the Thames opposite London
	May 25	Martin Frobisher launches his second voyage of exploration to America
	June	Archbishop Grindal is placed under house arrest and suspended from his office for his refusal to suppress prophesyings
	December 13	Francis Drake launches his voyage of circumnavigation
1578	April 4	Mary of Scotland's last husband, the Earl of Bothwell, dies in a dungeon in Denmark

	May 31	Martin Frobisher launches his third voyage of exploration to America
	June	Elizabeth entertains marriage proposal from Francis, Duke of Alençon, brother of Henri III of France
	Summer	Elizabeth visits Norwich and eastern England on summer progress
	September 21	Robert Dudley, Earl of Leicester, marries Lettice Knollys Devereux, Countess of Essex and cousin of theQueen, without Elizabeth's knowledge or consent
	September 26	Sir Humphrey Gilbert launches his first voyage of exploration to America
1579	July	James Fitzmaurice Fitzgerald and a papal force land in southern Ireland at Smerwick
	August	The Duke of Alençon arrives in England to woo Elizabeth
	August 18	Death in battle of the Irish rebel James Fitzmaurice Fitzgerald
1580	June	Jesuit missionaries Edmund Campion and Robert Parsons arrive in England
	September 26	Drake enters Plymouth harbor, completing his three-year circumnavigation of the globe
	November 10	English forces capture the rebel fortress at Smerwick and crush latest Irish rebellion
1581	January 16	Seventh parliamentary session of the reign opens; Parliament imposes ruinous fines on Catholic recusants i.e., Catholics who refuse to attend Anglican services and make converting or being converted to Catholicism treason
	April 4	Elizabeth knights Drake on the deck of the *Golden Hind*
	November 2	Duke of Alençon arrives in London to finalize marriage agreement with Elizabeth
	December 1	Execution of the Jesuit priest Edmund Campion
1582	February	Alençon leaves England after Elizabeth backs out of marriage
	November 28	Marriage bond between William Shakespeare and Anne Hathaway entered in the Registry of the Diocese of Worcester
1583	c. May 23	Birth of Shakespeare's daughter, Susanna
	May 26	Baptism of Susanna, daughter of William Shakespeare
	June 11	Sir Humphrey Gilbert launches his second voyage of exploration to America
	July 6	Death of Archbishop Grindal while still under house arrest
	July/August	Sir Humphrey Gilbert discovers and explores Newfoundland
	September 9	Sir Humphrey Gilbert is lost at sea
	September 23	John Whitgift becomes Elizabeth's third Archbishop of Canterbury
	November	Discovery of the Throckmorton Plot to replace Elizabeth with Mary of Scotland
1584	March 25	Sir Walter Raleigh, half-brother of Sir Humphrey Gilbert, obtains a patent from the Queen to plant English colonies in America
	April 27	Sir Walter Raleigh sends out an exploratory mission to America under Philip Amadas and Arthur Barlowe; the expedition explores a portion of the North American coast that is subsequently named Virginia by Raleigh in honor of Elizabeth, the "Virgin Queen"
	June 10	Death of the Duke of Alençon; Assassination of the Dutch Protestant leader, William of Orange

	November 23	Eighth parliamentary session of the reign opens; Parliament banishes all Catholic priests, recalls all Englishmen in Catholic seminaries in Europe, and prescribes death for anyone conspiring to overthrow or assassinate the Queen
	October	Formation of the Bond of Association, pledging members to protect Elizabeth from her enemies
1585	February	Baptism of Hamnet and Judith, twins, son and daughter of William Shakespeare
	April 9	Sir Walter Raleigh sends out a colonizing expedition to Virginia under his cousin Richard Grenville; the expedition establishes the first English colony at Roanoke
	May	Anglo-Spanish relations deteriorate to war; Philip II orders seizure of all English vessels in the Atlantic ports of Spain
	June 7	John Davis launches his first voyage of exploration to America
	August 10	Elizabeth concludes a treaty of alliance with the Dutch, promising the Dutch military assistance against Spain
	September 7	Drake sets sail on a raid of Spanish America
	December	The Earl of Leicester sails to the Netherlands with an army of 7,000
1586	May 7	John Davis launches his second voyage of exploration to America
	June	Sir Francis Drake evacuates the English colonists from Roanoke; Philip II begins massing an armada for an attack on England
	September 20	Execution of Anthony Babington and six others for their involvement in the Babington Plot to replace Elizabeth with Mary of Scotland
	October 14	Mary found guilty of treason for her involvement in the Babington Plot
	October 15	Ninth parliamentary session of the reign opens; Parliament, reacting to the Babington Plot and the trial and condemnation of Mary of Scotland, petitions the hesitant queen to go forward with Mary's execution
1587	February 8	Execution of Mary of Scotland at Fotheringay Castle
	April 21	Drake attacks Cadiz, destroying most of the fleet being gathered there for Philip's invasion of England
	May 8	Sir Walter Raleigh sends out a second colonizing expedition to Virginia under John White; the colonists establish second colony on Roanoke Island
	May 19	John Davis launches his third voyage of exploration to America
	August 18	Birth at Roanoke Colony of Virginia Dare, first English child born in America
	December 24	Lord Willoughby replaces Leicester as commander of the English forces in the Netherlands
1588	May 20	Spanish Armada leaves Lisbon for England
	June	Preparations begin in England and around London to repel Spanish Armada; Earl of Leicester is put in command of English army of defense
	July 19	Spanish Armada is sighted
	July 28/August 8	English fleet meets Armada in a series of naval battles in the English Channel, culminating in the Battle of Gravelines; after which, the Armada is driven north by storms
	September 4	Death of the Earl of Leicester

	September 11	Storms off Ireland destroy many of the remaining Armada vessels
	October	Marprelate Tracts attacking the bishops of the Church of England begin to circulate in London
	November 24	Royal thanksgiving service held at Saint Paul's Cathedral for England's delivery from the Armada
1589	February 4	Tenth parliamentary session of the reign opens; Parliament seeks again to alter the religious settlement of 1559 and is again unsuccessful
	April 8	Drake and Sir John Norris launch the ultimately unsuccessful Portugal Expedition against Spain
	July 22	Murder of Henri III of France; Henri of Navarre, a Protestant, is proclaimed King as Henry IV
1590		Edmund Spenser publishes the first three books of *The Faerie Queen* William Shakespeare begins the writing of the three parts of his *Henry VI*
	April 6	Death of Sir Francis Walsingham; Robert Cecil, Burghley's son, succeeds Walsingham as secretary of state
	August 17	John White's relief expedition lands at Roanoke, but finds no trace of the colonists or their whereabouts
1591	May 13	Puritans associated with the Marprelate Tracts are charged with sedition
	August 3	Robert Devereux, Earl of Essex, stepson of the late Earl of Leicester and new favorite of the Queen, leads an English military expedition to France to assist Henri IV
	September 3	Death of Sir Richard Grenville and loss of the *Revenge* in a naval battle between English and Spanish squadrons in the Azores
1592		Robert Greene criticizes Shakespeare in his *A Groatsworth of Wit*, which is the first print reference to Shakespeare as a playwright
	January	The Earl of Essex is recalled from command of English forces in France
	February 25	The lord mayor of London petitions Archbishop Whitgift to do something about the corrupting influence plays and playhouses are having on the apprentices and servants of the city
	August 7	Sir Walter Raleigh imprisoned for seducing one of the Queen's ladies-in-waiting
	September	Fears of a new Spanish invasion, which prove to be unfounded, sweep the southern coast of England; William Shakespeare is working as an actor and playwright in London, where he will write some of his most famous plays in the 1590s
1593		First likely performance of *Richard III*
	February 19	Eleventh parliamentary session of the reign opens; Parliament passes a measure punishing Puritans and other Protestants who refuse to conform to the Church of England with imprisonment and then exile for continued refusal
	April 6	Radical Protestants Henry Barrow and John Greenwood are hanged for sedition
	April 18	William Shakespeare's poem "Venus and Adonis" entered in the register at Stationers' Hall

	May 30	Death of playwright Christopher Marlowe in a mysterious tavern brawl
	May 31	John Penry hanged for his role in publishing the Marprelate Tracts
	June/July	Severe visitation of the plague
	July	Henri IV of France converts to Catholicism
1594		Probable first performance of *The Taming of the Shrew*
	February 6	William Shakespeare's play *Titus Adronicus* entered in the Stationers' Register
	February 19	Birth of Prince Henry, son of James VI of Scotland
	March 12	William Shakespeare's play *Henry VI, Part 1* entered in the Stationers' Register
	Summer	Three-year period of rainy summer weather and bad harvests begins
1595		Probable first performances of *Richard II*, *Romeo and Juliet*, and *A Midsummer Night's Dream*
	January 25	Beginning of Irish rebellion led by Hugh O'Neill, Earl of Tyrone
	February 6	Sir Walter Raleigh launches a voyage of American exploration to search for El Dorado
	March 15	Payment made by the treasurer of the royal chamber to William Kempe, William Shakespeare, and Richard Burbage for two comedies performed before the Queen at Christmas 1594
	February 22	Execution of Robert Southwell, a Jesuit priest
	August 28	Drake and Hawkins launch a raiding expedition against the Spanish West Indies
1596	January 29	Drake dies at sea off Panama
	March 17	Spanish raid English coast near Plymouth
	July 6	Earl of Tyrone raises a new rebellion in southern Ireland
	June 20	Earl of Essex captures Cadiz and holds it until 4 July
	July 5	Sir Robert Cecil is made principal secretary
	July/August	One of the worst harvests of the century leads to food riots in Kent and elsewhere
	August 11	Burial of Hamnet, son of William Shakespeare
	October	Second Spanish Armada is wrecked by storms
	October 20	Grant of arms is made to John Shakespeare, father of William Shakespeare
1597	July	Raleigh and the Earl of Essex launch the ultimately unsuccessful Islands Voyage against Spain
	August 29	William Shakespeare's play *Richard II* entered in the Stationers' Register
	October	Third Spanish Armada is wrecked by storms
	October 20	William Shakespeare's play *Richard III* entered in the Stationers' Register
	October 24	Twelfth parliamentary session of the reign opens; Parliament petitions the Queen for redress of monopolies and passes a new Act for Relief of the Poor
1598	July 22	William Shakespeare's play *The Merchant of Venice* entered in the Stationers' Register
	August 4	Death of William Cecil, Lord Burghley

	August 14	Irish rebels under the Earl of Tyrone defeat the English at the Battle of Yellow Ford in northern Ireland
	September 13	Death of Philip II of Spain
	November	Tyrone and other Irish rebels raid Dublin
1599		Probable first performances of *Henry V* and *Julius Caesar*
		Richard Burbage builds the Globe Theatre; Shakespeare is a shareholder in the Globe, as well as an actor and principal playwright
	March 12	Earl of Essex is made lord lieutenant of Ireland
	April 15	Essex arrives in Dublin with an English army
	September 8	Essex arranges a truce with Tyrone in Ireland
	September 24	Essex returns to England without the Queen's permission
1600		Likely first performance of Hamlet
	May	Charles Blount, Lord Mountjoy, the new lord deputy of Ireland, arrives in Dublin
	June 5	Elizabeth pardons Essex, but deprives him of most of his offices and places him under house arrest
	August 14	William Shakespeare's play *Henry V* entered in the Stationers' Register
	August 26	Essex is released from confinement, but barred from the Court
	October 8	William Shakespeare's play *A Midsummer Night's Dream* entered in the Stationers' Register
1601	February 7	Supporters of Essex request a special performance of Shakespeare's Richard II, with its scene depicting the deposition of the monarch, at the Globe Theatre
	February 8	The Earl of Essex raises a rebellion in London
	February 25	Execution of the Earl of Essex at the Tower of London
	April	Sir Robert Cecil opens a secret correspondence with James VI of Scotland, the Queen's likely heir
	September	Spanish fleet lands at Kinsale in Ireland to aid Tyrone and the Irish rebels against the English government
	September 8	Burial of John Shakespeare, father of William Shakespeare
	October 27	Thirteenth and last parliamentary session of the reign opens; Parliament again petitions the Queen to reform her use of monopolies
	November 30	Elizabeth delivers Golden Speech on monopolies to a deputation from Parliament
	December 24	Mountjoy wins a resounding victory over Tyrone and the Irish rebels at Kinsale
1602	January 2	Spanish commander at Kinsale in Ireland surrenders to Mountjoy
	January 18	William Shakespeare's play *The Merry Wives of Windsor* entered in the Stationers' Register
	July 26	William Shakespeare's play *Hamlet* entered in the Stationers' Register
1603	March 24	Death of Elizabeth I; Accession of James VI of Scotland, the son of the late Queen Mary, to the English throne as James I
	April	English Puritan ministers present the Millenary Petition to the new King; the Millenary petition, so named because it was supposedly signed by a thousand ministers, asked James to remove or modify various Church rituals and ceremonies in accordance with Puritan views

	April 10	James VI of Scotland is officially proclaimed James I, King of England, Scotland, France, and Ireland
	May 17	Issuance of a royal warrant for a patent authorizing the theatrical company to which William Shakespeare belongs to put on theatrical performances at the Globe Theater
	June 23	James I issues a proclamation ending England's war with Spain
	Summer	Two plots against James I the Catholic Bye Plot and the Protestant Main Plot are uncovered and suppressed; Sir Walter Raleigh is implicated in the Main Plot and imprisoned in the Tower of London
1604		Likely first performance of *Othello*
	January 14–18	Hampton Court Conference, a debate between Anglican and Puritan divines chaired by James I, is held at Hampton Court Palace
	March 19	First Parliament of James I is convened
	June 24	Death of Edward de Vere, Earl of Oxford
	July 22	King appoints 54 scholars to serve as translators on a project to produce a new and government authorized version of the English Bible
	August 19	Treaty of London officially ends the war with Spain
	September	Canons of 1604 are officially announced to the Church of England
1605		Probable first performance of *King Lear*
	November 5	Gunpowder Plot, a Catholic scheme to blow up the King and Parliament, is uncovered and foiled
1606		Probable first performance of *Macbeth*
	Spring	Parliament debates and passes new Penal Laws against Roman Catholics, including one ordering recusants suspected of disloyalty to take an oath to the King
	November	In Bate's Case, the Court of Exchequer establishes the Crown's right to levy impositions, taxes on imports, and sometimes exports imposed by royal decree rather than by consent of Parliament
	December 26	William Shakespeare's company gives a performance of his play *King Lear* before the King at Whitehall Palace
1607	May 14	Jamestown Colony is established in Virginia
	November 29	William Shakespeare's play *Romeo and Juliet* entered in the Stationers' Register
	December 31	Burial of Edmund Shakespeare, brother of William Shakespeare
1608	February 18	Birth of Elizabeth Hall, Shakespeare's only granddaughter
	June 26	Treaty is concluded with the Netherlands
	September 9	Burial of Mary Shakespeare, mother of William Shakespeare
1609	April 9	Start of the Twelve Years' Truce between Spain and the Netherlands
	June 17	Establishment of an English alliance with the Netherlands and France to guarantee the Twelve Years' Truce
	May 20	William Shakespeare's *Sonnets* entered in the Stationers' Register
1610	February	Robert Cecil, Earl of Salisbury, the lord treasurer, proposes that Parliament grant the King an annual revenue of £200,000; Parliament turns the proposal into the so-called Great Contract by demanding abolition of wardship and other reforms
	April 20	Dr. Simon Forman attends a performance of William Shakespeare's play *Macbeth* at the Globe Theater

	July 23	Parliament is prorogued with the Great Contract unpassed
	October	Parliament reconvenes and rejects the Great Contract
1611		Completion of the Authorized Version of the Bible, known as the King James Bible
	February 9	James I dissolves his first Parliament
	May 22	King James creates a new rank in the English peerage, the baronet
1612	May 24	Death of Robert Cecil, Earl of Salisbury, lord treasurer of England
	November 5	Death of Henry, Prince of Wales, eldest son of James I and heir to the throne
1613	February 14	Elizabeth, daughter of James I, marries Frederick V, elector of the Palatinate of the Rhine; Elizabeth's great-grandson will become King of England as George I in 1714
	March 10	William Shakespeare buys a house in Blackfriars in London
	June 29	Globe Theater burns to the ground during a performance of Shakespeare's *Henry VIII*
1614	April 5–June 7	Short life of James I's second Parliament, known as the Addled Parliament
1616	February 10	Marriage of Judith Shakespeare to Thomas Quiney
	March 25	William Shakespeare makes his will, leaving his wife "my second best bed with the furniture"
	April 23	Death of William Shakespeare in Stratford
	April 25	Burial of William Shakespeare
1623		Publication of the First Folio, the first collected edition of Shakespeare's plays

SOCIETY AND ECONOMY

1. An Englishman Claims Land in Elizabethan Ireland: *The Life and Times of Sir Peter Carew* (1568)

INTRODUCTION

This selection comes from the "Life of Sir Peter Carew," a manuscript written in the 1580s by John HOOKER, the chamberlain of the city of Exeter, and first published in 1857 as *The Life and Times of Sir Peter Carew*. Sir Peter CAREW was an English gentleman who, in the late 1560s, laid claim to numerous lands in Ireland that had in previous centuries belonged to several of his ancestors. In the following excerpt, Hooker describes how he met Carew and, through his ability to decipher old documents in the Carew family archive, how he became Carew's advance agent in Ireland for pursuit of his land claims.

KEEP IN MIND AS YOU READ

1. Carew, a Protestant, had rebelled against ELIZABETH's Catholic half-sister and predecessor, MARY I, who had spent much of her reign in exile or prison. His properties in England were seized and granted or leased to others in Queen Mary's favor. While most of these lands were formally restored to Carew after Elizabeth became Queen in 1558, Carew suffered severe financial consequences because of his rebellion, something that helps explain his willingness to undertake long and difficult legal action to recover long-lost properties in Ireland.

2. In the 1560s, English rule in Ireland, while theoretically covering the entire island, was, in fact, effective only in a small area known as the Pale, which comprised the city of Dublin and four surrounding counties. The rest of Ireland was divided into independent ANGLO-IRISH lordships, where English law and custom were generally followed, and independent native Irish lordships ruled according to Irish law and custom (see "Elizabethan Ireland" below). The lands Carew claimed as his own were mainly outside the Pale, where the authority of the English Crown and the influence of English law were weak. In most cases, these lands had belonged to the families of their current holders for almost two centuries.

3. As chamberlain of the city of Exeter in the western county of Devonshire, John Hooker's most important work was the organization and archiving of the city's records. He was also a historian and antiquary (see "Elizabethan Antiquarianism," Document 30), who wrote or edited several important Elizabethan works, including *The Order and Usage of the Keeping of a Parliament in England* (see Document 13), which described the organization and functioning of Elizabethan Parliaments,

and the 1586–1587 edition of Holinshed's *Chronicles* (see Document 24), a popular Elizabethan history of Britain that was used by William SHAKESPEARE as a source for his history plays.

4. When Hooker writes that Carew could not understand his documents because he was "unlearned," he means that Carew could not read Latin, the language of most of the documents.

Document: The "Life Sir Peter Carew"

It was not long after but [Sir Peter Carew] returned him into his own country of **Devon**, and there rested himself, attending such affairs of the commonwealth as the time required. And being now at some leisure, he bethought himself of such lands as he was persuaded he should have by inheritance, within the realm of Ireland. And, although he had **sundry** writings of evidences for the same, yet they being old, and he unlearned, he could neither read them himself, nor was acquainted with any who could and would sufficiently instruct him. And having continual speeches thereof unto his friends and acquaintance, bemoaning, as it were, the want of some expert and skillful man to instruct him, it was, at length, advertised unto him, that the writer hereof [John Hooker], being to him then unacquainted, was a man greatly given to seek and search old records and ancient writings, and was very skillful in reading of them, and that he was best able of any in the city of Exeter to do him pleasure in this behalf.

Sir Peter being very earnest and desirous to have his humor to be satisfied, sought means of acquaintance with him, and having attained the same, he did forthwith show and impart unto him, two or three old writings of evidence, concerning the said his lands, and of which one was very old, and had been trodden under foot, and by that means the letters were almost worn out. Nevertheless, this man did read them, and declare the effect of them unto him, which he did like so well, that then he committed unto him the view and search of all his evidences, of which he served only those out of so many as he thought did appertain to this matter. And all these he wrote out into a fair book, and thereof, as also only of his other evidences, he drew out his pedigree and descent. And then, Sir Peter Carew, being satisfied of his title, and instructed of his right, did, by the advice of this writer, make his repair to her highness, and to the council, laying before them, and giving them to understand, what title and right he had to sundry pieces of lands in the realm of Ireland, most humbly requesting that he might have the liberty to travel over into that realm for the recovery thereof.

Her majesty and council seemed to be glad thereof, and did not only grant his request, but also sent several letters to the **lord-deputy** of that realm, and to all her officers for his furtherance and help therein. When he had obtained all these things according to his own mind, he came down into the country [Devon], sent for this writer, and imparted unto him the whole success of his journey; and conferred with him what were best to be done. At length, upon good advice and conference between them, it was concluded that someone should be first sent over to learn and

attainder: legislative act imposing forfeiture of property or death for commission of treason or other serious crimes

Devon (Devonshire): county of southwestern England

Ilfracombe: English port town in Devon on Bristol Channel

loath: unwilling

lord-deputy: Queen's representative who headed English administration in Ireland

sundry: miscellaneous; various

Waterford: seaport of southern Ireland

understand here the same, and in what case the right of the matter was there, and whether any **attainder**, statute, or alienation, were made by any of the ancestors of this gentleman, by which his right were extinct; and there being none who would, or who was meet to, take this matter upon him, then he entreated this writer to do it; who, notwithstanding that he was very **loath**, yet at length he yielded thereunto: and forthwith he took shipping at **Ilfracombe**, being then the beginning of May [1568], and arrived at **Waterford**, and from thence taking his journey towards Dublin, he passed through the country of Odrone, which was a barony, and parcel of the inheritance of the said Sir Peter, and sundry of whose ancestors had been barons of the same.

Source: Hooker, John. "Life of Sir Peter Carew." In John Maclean, ed. *The Life and Times of Sir Peter Carew, Kt.*. London: Bell and Daldy, 1857, pp. 71–73.

AFTERMATH

Hooker spent several years in Ireland helping Carew, who came to the island himself in August 1568 to institute legal proceedings to recover his lands. However, Carew's suits caused much unrest among the current holders of those lands and, in one instance, triggered an uprising known as the BUTLER WARS. Angered by the difficulty and expense of quelling this uprising, the Queen ordered Carew to cease legal action and, when he came to England to plead his case, refused him permission to return to Ireland. Carew eventually did return to the neighboring island, dying in Ireland in November 1575, but his land claims were never effectively secured because the English government feared the disaffection his efforts spread among Irish and Anglo-Irish landholders.

ELIZABETHAN IRELAND

In the sixteenth century, the English lordship of Ireland (the monarch was titled Lord of Ireland) was divided into the Englishry and the Irishry. The Englishry consisted of independent Anglo-Irish lordships held by descendants of Norman and English invaders who had conquered and settled parts of Ireland in the Middle Ages, and districts under direct English control, comprising the city of Dublin and its surrounding counties, an area known as the Pale. The Anglo-Irish held their lands from the English Crown and generally followed English law and custom. The Irishry consisted of independent native Irish lordships following Irish law and custom. Until the 1530s, when the Irish Parliament extended the English Reformation to Ireland, the Crown ruled Ireland through an Anglo-Irish governor (see "English Reformation," Document 14). In 1541, the Irish Parliament declared HENRY VIII King of Ireland, a change that signaled the Crown's desire to rule a unified Irish state recognizing only English law and custom. Ireland now experienced English lord deputies commanding English troops, English colonists settled on Irish lands, and English Protestantism imposed on the Irish Church, all efforts that Peter Carew, when he came to Ireland, strongly supported.

However, Elizabeth refused to spend the money or commit the military resources required to effectively and permanently extend English rule into the Irish lordships. Late in her reign, Ireland witnessed a series of native Irish revolts that culminated in 1593 with the NINE YEARS WAR, an insurrection that eventually led to Spanish intervention in Ireland. The defeat in 1603 of Hugh O'NEILL, Earl of Tyrone, leader of the Irish rebels, left JAMES I, Elizabeth's successor, an Irish kingdom that was economically ravaged, but politically subordinated. The war also left the Irish and Anglo-Irish firmly committed to a Catholic Church closely identified with resistance to Protestant English rule.

ASK YOURSELF

1. By the 1560s, Carew's ancestors had not held lands in Ireland for almost 200 years, so many of the properties Carew sought to recover had belonged to the families of their current holders for generations. How would you feel if someone suddenly appeared with the backing of the government to claim ownership of your family's long-held house or property?

2. Carew was a strong Protestant while most of the holders of the lands he claimed were Roman Catholics. How might this difference in religion have affected Carew's decision to seek possession of these properties? How might it have affected the decision of most of the landholders to resist Carew's efforts, either by legal means or otherwise?

3. Notice in the above selection how Carew's first step was to seek permission from the Queen and PRIVY COUNCIL to travel to Ireland and begin legal proceedings to recover his lands. Travel to and from Elizabethan England by English subjects was tightly controlled. How does this compare to the ability of modern American citizens to travel abroad? Why might the Elizabethan government have been so careful to control foreign travel? Why and how do modern governments regulate travel and secure their borders?

TOPICS AND ACTIVITIES TO CONSIDER

- The English Crown governed Ireland, with varying degrees of success, for almost 800 years. Carew's experiences in Ireland convinced him of the need for more vigorous action to strengthen English rule in the neighboring island. Accordingly, he advocated more English settlement, a strengthened English military presence, and more repressive government for Ireland, all measures that gained increasing support in government circles after 1580. Consider how Elizabethan action in Ireland may have contributed to the Anglo-Irish conflicts of the last two centuries and to the disorder that still afflicts Northern Ireland today.

- On a map, study the proximity of the islands of Britain and Ireland to each other. Why do you think the Elizabethans were so concerned about unrest in Ireland or about the possibility of foreign intervention in the island? How did the question of religion heighten or lessen this concern?

- When the modern state of Israel was founded in 1948 it created a situation in which two peoples—Palestinians and Jews—had ancient and conflicting claims to some of the same territory. Consider how the modern Palestinian question is similar to and different from the conflicting land claims of English and Irish in sixteenth-century Ireland.

- Consider the effect of the interaction of economic self-interest and religious belief on the territorial conflicts in Elizabethan Ireland, as well as on those in modern Ireland, the modern Middle East and India, and elsewhere.

Further Information

Canny, Nicholas. *The Elizabethan Conquest of Ireland: A Pattern Established, 1565–1576.* New York: Barnes and Noble, 1976.

Colm, Lennon. *Sixteenth-Century Ireland: The Incomplete Conquest.* Dublin: Gill and Macmillan, 1994.

Ellis, Steven G. *Ireland in the Age of the Tudors, 1447–1603: English Expansion and the End of Gaelic Rule.* 2nd ed. London: Longman, 1998.

Morgan, Hiram. *Tyrone's Rebellion: The Outbreak of the Nine Years War in Tudor Ireland.* Rochester, NY: Boydell Press, 1993.

Wagner, J.A. *The Devon Gentleman: The Life of Sir Peter Carew.* Hull, England: University of Hull Press, 1998.

2. THE SWORD OF ELIZABETHAN EDUCATION: ROGER ASCHAM'S *THE SCHOOLMASTER* (1570)

INTRODUCTION

Roger ASCHAM was tutor to Princess ELIZABETH from 1548 to 1550; Latin secretary to Elizabeth's two siblings and predecessors on the throne, EDWARD VI and MARY I; and then Latin secretary to Elizabeth herself after her accession in 1558. The following excerpt from Ascham's most famous work, *The Schoolmaster* (1570), describes a discussion that occurred at Windsor Castle in 1563 between Secretary of State William CECIL (later Lord Burghley) and a number of other ministers and courtiers, including Ascham. The discussion centers around the proper way to maintain discipline in schools, with Ascham agreeing with Cecil that children "were sooner allured [to learning] by love, than driven by beating."

KEEP IN MIND AS YOU READ

1. Although Elizabethan England had no national educational system, education was gradually becoming more available to the children of the middle classes, the sons of urban merchants and craftsmen, and those of rural landholding GENTRY (see "Elizabethan Education" below).
2. Formal education, whether through private tutors or local schools, was limited almost exclusively to boys.
3. Grammar schools, private educational foundations that sought to give boys a basic grounding in Latin grammar and vocabulary, were established in many towns in the Elizabethan period, becoming the chief engine for extending educational opportunity to middle-class boys and to a few lower-class students who showed promise. As a boy, William SHAKESPEARE is believed to have attended the grammar school in his hometown of Stratford-upon-Avon.
4. Most learning in Elizabethan schools was by rote, with students reciting what they had memorized.
5. Discipline in Elizabethan schools was commonly harsh, with most teachers using a birch rod to beat students who did not properly apply themselves to their studies or who broke school rules.

6. Although the English Reformation had largely freed schools from Church control, Elizabethan schools still had a strong religious component, with prayers and the catechism used to teach reading. Also, much Latin translation was done out of the Bible, as well as out of the works of classical authors (see "Elizabethan Education," Document 14).

Document: Roger Ascham's The Schoolmaster

Not long after our sitting down "I have strange news brought me," said Master Secretary [William Cecil], "this morning, that diverse **Scholars** of Eaton, be run away from the School, for fear of beating." Whereupon, Master Secretary took occasion to wish that some more discretion were in many Schoolmasters, in using correction, than commonly there is. Who many times, punish rather, the weaknesses of nature, than the fault of the Scholar. Whereby, many Scholars, that might else prove well, be driven to hate learning, before they know, what learning means: and so, are made willing to forsake their book, and be glad to be put to any other kind of living.

Master Peter, as one somewhat severe of nature, said plainly, that the Rod only, was the sword, that must keep, the School in obedience, and the Scholar in good order. Master Wotton, a man mild of nature, with soft voice, and few words, inclined to Master Secretary's judgment, and said, "in mine opinion, the Schoolhouse should be indeed, as it is called by name, the house of play and pleasure, and not of fear and bondage. And as I do remember, so says Socrates in one place of Plato. And therefore, if a Rod carry the fear of a Sword, it is no marvel, if those that be fearful of nature, chose rather to forsake the Play, than to stand always within the fear of a Sword in a **fond** man's

handling." Master Mason, after his manner, was very merry with both parties, pleasantly playing, both, with the shrewd touches of many curst boys, and with the small discretion of many lewd Schoolmasters. Master Haddon was fully of Master Peter's opinion, and said, that the best Schoolmaster of our time, was the greatest beater, and named the Person. "Though," quoth I, "it was his good fortune, to send from his School, unto the University one of the best Scholars indeed of all our time, yet wise men do think, that that came so to pass, rather, by the great **towardness** of the Scholar, than by the great beating of the Master: and whether this be true or no, you yourself are best-witness." I said somewhat farther in the matter, how, and why, young children, were sooner allured by love, than driven by beating, to attain good learning: wherein I was the bolder to say my mind, because Master Secretary courteously provoked me thereunto: or else, in such a company, and namely in his presence, my wont is, to be more willing, to use mine ears, than to occupy my tongue.

Eaton: public school for boys established in 1440 by Henry VI and located in Eaton, across the River Thames from Windsor
fond: foolish; silly
scholars: students
towardness: promise; potential

Source: Ascham, Roger. *The Scholemaster*. Edited by Edward Arber. Birmingham, 1870, pp. 17–19.

ELIZABETHAN EDUCATION

Elizabethan England had no national system of education, and only a small fraction of Elizabethan children, mostly boys, received formal schooling. The sons of the nobility and wealthier gentry might be privately tutored or receive training in manners, religion, and statecraft while serving in another noble or gentle household. Cecil House, the home of William CECIL, Lord Burghley, became well known as an educational establishment, with as many as 20 young men in residence at one time. Sons of urban merchants and craftsmen and of lesser gentlemen often were educated in petty schools, private local establishments run by a town, guild, or parish. Some petty schools were attached to a local grammar school, private educational foundations designed to give boys a basic grounding in Latin grammar and literature. Petty schools taught the fundamentals of reading and writing in English and perhaps basic arithmetic. Although the Reformation had freed much education from Church control, the petty school had a strong religious component, with prayers and the catechism used to teach reading.

Discipline in petty schools was often harsh, with the birch rod used freely to correct misbehavior or poor performance, a practice that Roger Ascham severely criticized. Bright or upper-class students might proceed around age 10 to grammar school and from there to one of the universities or the INNS OF COURT for legal training (see "English Universities," Document 22). Perhaps 30 percent of men and 10 percent of women were literate by the end of Elizabeth's reign in 1603. Literacy was higher in the towns, especially London, and in the more PURITAN areas, where emphasis was placed on being able to read the Bible (see "Elizabethan London," Document 7).

AFTERMATH

After the discussion described above, one of the participants, Sir Richard SACKVILLE, the Queen's treasurer, approached Ascham about recommending an educational program for Sackville's young grandson. The treasurer, who had vivid memories of hating school because of the harshness of his teacher, agreed wholeheartedly with Ascham regarding the need for gentle encouragement rather than the rod in promoting learning. Urged by Sackville to put his ideas into writing, Ascham wrote *The Schoolmaster*, which outlined an educational program that was grounded in the classics, focused on the development of character, and employed patience and persuasion rather than corporal discipline to stimulate learning.

ASK YOURSELF

1. Study of Latin and of Latin classics was the main (and sometimes only) focus of Elizabethan grammar schools. Why do you think training in Latin was considered so important in the sixteenth century? What benefits do you think Elizabethan students derived from the study of Latin? How did the Reformation affect the use and study of Latin? How would you compare the emphasis on training in other languages in the United States with that of Elizabethan England and with that of other nations in the twenty-first century?

2. Prior to the sixteenth century, education in Europe was controlled mainly by the Church, with most schools run by priests and monks and located in monasteries, convents, and local churches. How did Elizabethan schools differ? What role did religion play in Elizabethan schools? What affect did the Protestant Reformation, with its emphasis on the reading of Scripture, have on Elizabethan education? What influence, if any, did the religious turmoil of the Reformation have on the

development of American and European education as it exists in the twenty-first century?

TOPICS AND ACTIVITIES TO CONSIDER

- ❧ Elizabethan education was reserved mainly for boys of certain social and economic classes. Consider how this differs from public education in the United States and elsewhere in the twenty-first century. Consider also what this says about the assumptions Elizabethan society made about the purpose and aims of formal education and how those compare with the basic assumptions that underlie the purpose and goals of modern education.
- ❧ Humanism was an educational program based on the moral and intellectual value of studying the literature of ancient Greece and Rome. Humanist training also sought to imbue students with the classical civic virtues—active involvement in public affairs and the rendering of service to the state. Use the Internet to research what is meant today by the term "secular humanism" and compare it to the humanism of the sixteenth century. Consider how the current debate between advocates of a religious-based education and those of a secular humanist education compares and contrasts to the sixteenth-century notions of humanism and the role of religion in education.
- ❧ How does the debate over the use of corporal punishment that still rages in child-rearing and educational circles today compare and contrast to the same debate, if indeed you think it existed, in the sixteenth century?

Further Information

Ascham, Roger. *The Scholemaster*. Edited by R.J. Schoeck. Don Mills, Ontario: Dent, 1966.
Cressy, David. *Education in Tudor and Stuart England*. New York: St. Martin's Press, 1976.
Ryan, Lawrence V. *Roger Ascham*. Stanford, CA: Stanford University Press, 1963.
Simon, Joan. *Education and Society in Tudor England*. Cambridge: Cambridge University Press, 1979.

Web Sites

Educating Shakespeare: http://www.likesnail.org.uk/welcome-es.htm
Elizabethan Education: http://www.elizabethan-era.org.uk/elizabethan-education.htm
What Every Schoolboy Knows: http://www.elizabethan.org/compendium/54.html

3. ENGLISH WOMEN: ACCOUNTS OF MALE ENGLISH OBSERVERS (1550, 1577)

INTRODUCTION

In the following excerpts, two sixteenth-century Englishmen express their opinions on contemporary women's fashions (see Document 4 for foreign perceptions of Englishwomen). The first selection, a poem by ardent Protestant preacher and reformer Robert CROWLEY, leaves no doubt as to the poet's opinion of the fashions he sees worn by women on the streets of London. Crowley does not confine his criticism to the high fashion of court ladies, but denounces primarily the wives of London citizens. Note particularly Crowley's blatant anti-Semitism, a common and unremarkable feature of sixteenth-century clerical writing and preaching. Crowley can think of no worse insult than to compare London women to "Jewish whores."

The second selection comprises two excerpts drawn from "The Description of England," a detailed account of life in Elizabethan times by the historian and antiquary William HARRISON (see "English Antiquarianism," Document 30). Writing 27 years after Crowley, Harrison, who was also a cleric, expresses a similar opinion regarding the extravagance of women's (and men's) fashions, only in somewhat more temperate language. Harrison is particularly critical of the dress of bishops' widows, whom, he believes, should know better. Concluding with remarks that today would be considered sexist, but that would have occasioned little contemporary comment, Harrison declares that women will be women regardless of their class or station.

KEEP IN MIND AS YOU READ

1. In sixteenth-century England, married women were considered to be under the guardianship of their husbands, and their legal rights were largely subsumed in their spouse's (see "Elizabethan Women," Document 4). Even the Queen, who could inherit the Crown, was expected to marry so that her husband could help her govern, if not rule for her.

2. Although social mobility was increasing, Elizabethan society was highly class conscious, and modes of dress were important in delineating one class from another. Attempts to ape one's social superiors by affecting types of dress considered inappropriate to one's class were scorned and even subject to punishment under the law (see "Sumptuary Laws" below).

3. By the 1580s, the PURITANS—Protestants who desired more extensive reform of the English Church than the Queen would allow—were demanding stronger measures to root out immorality from English society. Specifically, they called for the closure of theaters and the end of traditional holiday festivities, especially at Christmas. The demand for modesty in dress, especially as expressed in Crowley's poem, but also to some extent in Harrison's prose, is religiously based, reflecting a Puritan sensibility.

Document 1: Robert Crowley's View of Women's Fashion (1550)

What should we think of the women
  that in London we see?
For more wanton looks
  I dare boldly say,
Were never in Jewish whores
  than in London wives this day.
And if gait and garments
  do show anything,
Our wives do pass their hours
  in whorelike decking.
I think the abominable
  whores of the **Stews**,
Did never more whorelike
  attirements use.
The cap on her head
  is like a sow's maw:
Such another fashion
  I think never Jew saw.
Then fine gear on the forehead
  settle after the new trick,
Though it cast a crown or two,
  What then? they may not stick.
If their hair will not take color,
  then must they be new;
And lay it out in **tussocks**:
  this thing is too true.
At each side a tussock
  as big as a ball.
A very fair sight
  for a fornicator bestial.
Her face fair painted
  to make it shine bright,
And her bosom all bare
  and most whorelike **dight.**
Her middle braced in,

as small as a wand;
  And some by waists of wire
    at the paste wife's hand.
A bum like a barrel,
    with hoops at the skirt,
Her shoes of such stuff
    that may touch no dirt.
Upon her white fingers
    many rings of gold
With such manner stones
    as are most dearly sold.
. . .

I have told them but truth,
    let them say what they will;
I have said they be whorelike,
    and so I say still.

> **dight:** dressed; adorned
> **Stews:** a district of whorehouses
> **tussocks:** compact tufts of grass or other vegetation

Source: Crowley, Robert. "Of Nice Rogues." *One and Thyrtye Epigrammes* (1550), reprinted in Furnivall, Frederick, ed. *Harrison's Description of England in Shakspere's Youth*. London: Published for the New Shakspere Society by N. Trübner and Co., 1877, pp. 170–71.

_____

Document 2: Excerpts on Fashion from William Harrison's Description of England (1577)

In women also it is most to be lamented, that they do now far exceed the **lightness** of our men (who nevertheless are transformed from the cap even to the very shoe) and such staring attire as in time past was supposed meet for none but light housewives only is now become an habit for chaste and sober matrons. What should I say of their **doublets** with pendant **codpieces** on the breast, full of jags and cuts, and sleeves of sundry colors? their **galligaskins** to bear out their **bums** and make their attire to fit plum-round (as they term it) about them? their **farthingales** and diversely colored **netherstocks** of silk, jersey, and suchlike, whereby their bodies are rather deformed than commended? I have met some of these **trulls** in London so disguised that it has passed my skill to discern whether they were men or women.

  . . . .

    If you say that their [the bishops'] wives be **fond**, after the decease of their husbands, and bestow themselves not so advisedly as their calling requires . . . I beseech you then to look into all states of the laity and tell me whether some duchesses, countesses, barons' or knights' wives do not fully so often offend in the like as they? For Eve will be Eve, though Adam would say nay.

> **bum:** vulgar term for butt or buttocks
> **codpiece:** flap or bag concealing an opening in the front of men's breeches
> **doublet:** close fitting jacket worn by men
> **farthingale:** hoop support worn under a woman's skirt to extend it at the hipline
> **fond:** foolish, silly
> **galligaskins:** loose wide hose or trousers
> **lightness:** shallowness; lack of seriousness or gravity
> **netherstocks:** tights
> **trulls:** prostitutes; strumpets

SUMPTUARY LAWS

English sumptuary laws restricted the wearing of certain types, qualities, and colors of apparel to certain social classes. The laws attempted to maintain class distinctions in an increasingly fluid social environment. Sumptuary laws arose out of religious concerns that extravagance in dress (and diet) led to a degeneration of public morals and out of economic concerns that the enthusiasm for and overconsumption of foreign fashions could harm the domestic cloth industry. Based upon earlier enactments, the 1559 Elizabethan sumptuary statute restricted cloth of gold to earls and above, woolen cloth of foreign manufacture to noblemen and their families, and fur trim to men whose annual income exceeded £100. Servants could wear no fur at all unless they served noblemen or gentlemen (i.e., no merchant could dress his servants in fur), and husbandmen and common laborers could wear no hose worth more than 10 pence a yard. The color purple was confined to the royal family, and scarlet was reserved for the monarch and the highest nobility.

Punishment for violations of the statute ranged from confiscation of the offending article to fines running from a few shillings to a ruinously high £10. The fact that sumptuary statutes had to be regularly reenacted meant that the laws, as the above two excerpts attest, were little enforced and often ignored. Because Elizabethans so little heeded sumptuary laws, the Queen, in 1597, issued a PROCLAMATION calling for stricter adherence to the statute and expanding and elaborating existing restrictions.

Source: Furnivall, Frederick, ed. *Harrison's Description of England in Shakspere's Youth.* Part 1. London: Published for the New Shakspere Society by N. Trübner and Co., 1877, pp. 34, 170–71.

AFTERMATH

Later in his life, Robert Crowley became a strong Puritan. He resigned his clerical position in 1567 because he refused to wear the vestments mandated for Anglican ministers by the Queen through Parliament (see "Elizabethan Parliaments," Document 11). Crowley considered them too gaudy and too similar to the vestments worn by the Catholic clergy, whom he despised. William Harrison had no trouble with the English Church as maintained by the Queen and Parliament. He served the Essex parish of Radwinter from 1559 until his death in 1593. Nonetheless, as his writings show, Harrison was strongly anti-Catholic and a staunch adherent of the Protestant Anglican Church (see "Anglican Church," Document 20).

ASK YOURSELF

1. Beyond the sixteenth-century racial and religious biases they reveal, how do Crowley's criticisms of the fashions of his time compare and contrast to criticisms of current fashions made by both religious and secular commentators? Do you think that today, when it comes to clothing and fashion, differences in taste between generations matter more than religious objections? How might your friends' criticisms of clothing differ from the criticisms of your parents or your children? What else does Crowley's poem say about his views of women and of Elizabethan society in general?
2. Consult the "Further Information" section below or the Internet for an accessible print or electronic version of *The Description of England* and read several selections. How hard or easy was it to read and understand Harrison's writing? Why do you

think his work was hard or easy to read? Did you enjoy reading from the *Description*? Why or why not?

3. What do you think of Harrison's final comment about Eve and Adam? Does it seem like something that Crowley would say or agree with? What is Harrison saying in this excerpt about men's fashions and about Elizabethan society in general?

TOPICS AND ACTIVITIES TO CONSIDER

☙ Crowley and Harrison both grounded their criticism of women's fashions in their religious beliefs, yet the former was frequently at odds with the English Church establishment while the latter was not. Consider the tone of the two excerpts and see if you can discern any differences in the nature and basis of their criticisms. If you find a difference, research more fully the lives of the two men and try to determine the reason for it.

☙ Using the Internet or books on Elizabethan fashion, find pictures of the various articles of clothing mentioned by Harrison (see the "Further Information" section below for some useful resources). Once you have an idea of what they looked like, consider whether or not you agree with Harrison regarding the frivolousness of such attire. Consider also what current or recent fashions might excite similar distaste in a modern commentator and why.

☙ With John HOOKER (see Documents 1 and 13) and others, Harrison was part of the editorial team that produced the Elizabethan editions of Holinshed's *Chronicles* (see Document 24), for which Harrison's *Description of England* served as the introduction. Consult the "Further Information" section below or the Internet for an accessible print or electronic version of *The Description of England* and read several selections on various topics, such as food, education, pets, or architecture. Consider how Elizabethan society compares to modern society in each of these areas.

Further Information

Cioni, Maria L. *Women and Law in Elizabethan England*. New York: Garland, 1985.

Crowley, Robert. *The Select Works of Robert Crowley*. Edited by J.M. Cowper. English Text Society, extra series, vol. 15. London: Trubner, 1872, reprint ed. 1987.

Emerson, Kathy Lynn. *Wives and Daughters: The Women of Sixteenth Century England*. Troy, NY: Whitston Publishing Company, 1984.

Harrison, William. *The Description of England*. Edited by Georges Edelen. New York: Dover Publications, 1994.

Hogrefe, Pearl. *Tudor Women*. Ames: Iowa State University, 1975.

Jardine, Lisa. *Still Harping on Daughters: Women and Drama in the Age of Shakespeare*. Totowa, NJ: Barnes and Noble, 1983.

Mendelson, Sara, and Crawford, Patricia. *Women in Early Modern England 1550–1720*. Oxford: Oxford University Press, 2000.

Parry, G.J.R. *A Protestant Vision: William Harrison and the Reformation of Elizabethan England*. Cambridge: Cambridge University Press, 1987.

Prior, Mary, ed. *Women in English Society, 1500–1800*. New York: Methuen, 1985.

Warnicke, Retha M. *Women of the English Renaissance and Reformation*. Westport, CT: Greenwood Press, 1983.

Web Sites

Elizabethan Clothing: http://www.elizabethan-era.org.uk/elizabethan-clothing.htm
Elizabethan Costume: http://www.elizabethancostume.net/
Harrison's *Description of England*: http://www.fordham.edu/halsall/mod/1577harrison-england.html

4. English Women: Accounts of Male Foreign Observers (1575, 1585)

INTRODUCTION

The descriptions of Elizabethan women reproduced here are by foreign men. The first is from the writings of the Flemish historian Emanuel VAN METEREN, who was much more complimentary of the appearance and dress of Englishwomen than were either of the Englishmen quoted in Document 3 above. The second selection is from the travel diary of Samuel KIECHEL, a German merchant who visited London in the 1580s. Kiechel also found English women to be attractive and was particularly taken with the English custom of greeting guests with a kiss.

KEEP IN MIND AS YOU READ

1. Both Van Meteren and Kiechel came mainly into contact with the wives and daughters of wealthy gentlemen, who had homes in London, and the women of urban merchant and professional class families, who were able to afford servants. Thus, the wives of these classes, while their rights were limited in the legal sense (see "Elizabethan Women" below), attained a certain independence and authority in overseeing the proper functioning of their husband's households.

2. One of the most important roles of the mistress of a great noble, gentle, or merchant household was to exhibit to any guests, especially foreign ones such as Van Meteren and Kiechel, her family's prosperity, influence, and position, thus dressing properly and demonstrating her command of the accepted social graces and conventions was of great importance and certainly colored the observations of such observers.

3. The vast majority of women in England were not members of landed or urban merchant families, but rural women whose husbands were small independent farmers, tenant farmers who rented landed from the nobility or GENTRY, or landless laborers. Their workday and mode of dress would have been far different from that described below by Van Meteren and Kiechel.

Document 1: Account of English Wives by Emanuel van Meteren (1575)

Wives in England are entirely in the power of their husbands, their lives only excepted. Therefore, when they marry, they give up the surname of their father and of the family from which they are descended, and take the surname of their husbands, except in the case of duchesses, countesses and baronesses, who, when they marry gentlemen of inferior degree, retain their first name and title, which, for the ambition of the said ladies, is rather allowed than commended. But although the women there are entirely in the power of their husbands, except for their lives, yet they are not kept so strictly as they are in Spain or elsewhere. Nor are they shut up; but they have the free management of the house or housekeeping, after the fashion of those of the Netherlands, and others their neighbors. They go to market to buy what they like best to eat. They are well dressed, fond of taking it easy, and commonly leave the care of household matters and drudgery to their servants. They sit before their doors, decked out in fine clothes, in order to see and be seen by the passers-by. In all banquets and feasts they are shown the greatest honor; they are placed at the upper end of the table, where they are the first served; at the lower end they help the men. All the rest of their time they employ in walking and riding, in playing at cards or otherwise, in visiting their friends and keeping company, conversing with their equals (whom they term gossips) and their neighbors, and making merry with them at child-births, christenings, **churchings**, and funerals; and all this with the permission and knowledge of their husbands, as such is the custom. Although the husbands often recommend to them the pains, industry, and care of the German or Dutch women, who do what the men ought to do both in the house and in the shops, for which services in England men are employed, nevertheless the women usually persist in retaining their customs. This is why England is called the Paradise of married women. The girls who are not yet married are kept much more rigorously and strictly than in the Low Countries.

The women are beautiful, fair, well-dressed, and modest, which is seen there more than elsewhere, as they go about the streets without any covering . . . of . . . mantle, hood, veil, or the like. Married women only wear a hat both in the street and in the house; those unmarried go without a hat, although ladies of distinction have lately learnt to cover their faces with silken masks or vizards, and feathers,—for indeed they change very easily, and that every year, to the astonishment of many.

> **churching:** Christian ceremony wherein a woman who has recently given birth is blessed and gives thanks for a safe delivery

Source: Furnivall, Frederick, ed. *Harrison's Description of England in Shakspere's Youth.* London: Published for the New Shakspere Society by N. Trübner and Co., 1877, pp. lxii–lxiii.

Document 2: Account of English Women by Samuel Kiechel (1585)

Item, the women there [England] are charming, and by nature so mighty pretty, as I have scarcely ever beheld, for they do not falsify paint or bedaub themselves as in Italy or other places; but they are somewhat awkward in their style of dress; for they dress in splendid stuffs, and many a one wears three cloth gowns or petticoats, one over the other. Item, when a foreigner or an inhabitant goes to a citizen's house on business, or is invited as a guest, and having entered therein, he is received by the master of the house, the lady, or the daughter, and by them welcomed—as it is termed in their language;—he has even a right to take them by the arm and to kiss them, which is the custom of the country; and if any one does not do so, it is regarded and imputed as ignorance and ill-breeding on his part: the same custom is also observed in the Netherlands.

Source: Furnivall, Frederick, ed. *Harrison's Description of England in Shakspere's Youth.* London: Published for the New Shakspere Society by N. Trübner and Co., 1877, p. lxii.

ELIZABETHAN WOMEN

As Emanuel van Meteren observed above, English wives were "entirely in the power of their husbands." Under English COMMON LAW, married women could not inherit or administer land, make wills, sign contracts, sue or be sued, or make trusts or bonds. The legal term for the status of married women, *coverture*, literally meant that a woman's legal identity was "hidden" or "covered" by her husband's. A minor girl was under the guardianship of her father who arranged her marriage. A wife passed to the guardianship of her husband, who controlled any land she brought to the marriage. The husband could not sell or lease his wife's land, and one-third of his estate (the widow's dower) passed to her upon his death. The rest of the estate could be disposed of in any manner the husband saw fit. This common law tradition even affected princesses. When ELIZABETH I inherited the greatest property right in law, the Crown, she was expected to marry and have her right to rule limited or completely taken up by her husband.

Elizabethan women did have certain rights under other types of law. Even under the common law, widows and unmarried adult women could inherit land, make wills, sign contracts, and exercise other legal and property rights. Under EQUITY law, married women had a legal identity and could sue or be sued, and premarital agreements giving the wife her own income or the right to administer her own property were recognized. Canon (or Church) law also allowed married women to make bonds to protect their rights to property or the rights of children by a former marriage. Church courts also handled the probate of wills and dealt frequently with widows as executors of their husband's wills or estates.

AFTERMATH

After serving as trade consul in London for the Dutch merchant community in the early 1580s, Emanuel van Meteren in 1599 wrote a history describing the first part of the long war between Spain and the Netherlands (see "Spanish Netherlands," Document 38). Because he had for a time been secretary to the Dutch Protestant leader William the Silent, Van Meteren was himself eyewitness to some of the events he wrote about, making his history a valuable source for the war, just as his earlier accounts of life in London are important sources for various aspects of Elizabethan social life.

In the years following his sojourn in London in the mid-1580s, Samuel Kiechel, a trader from the German city of Ulm, traveled widely in eastern Europe and the Middle East, visiting the cities of Istanbul, Damascus, and Jerusalem. His accounts of these journeys were published in 1866 as *Die Reisen des Samuel Kiechel* (The Travels of Samuel Kiechel).

ASK YOURSELF

1. Note that little mention is made in the two accounts below of childrearing, but much is said of leisure activities, such as riding, card-playing, and conversing with neighbors. How might the descriptions of Van Meteren and Kiechel differ in this regard if they had gone into the countryside to observe the daily activities of the wives of yeoman and tenant farmers or those of landless laborers (see "Social Class and Land Holding," Document 5)?

2. Read the accounts reproduced in Document 3, above, which were written by English observers. How do they differ from the accounts of foreign observers offered here? How do they compare? Where they differ? Why do you think this is so?

3. What impact, if any, does religious belief and attitude seen to have on the observations of Van Meteren, who was a Dutch CALVINIST, and Kiechel, who was a German LUTHERAN?

TOPICS AND ACTIVITIES TO CONSIDER

- ❧ Using books and the Internet, find illustrations of sixteenth-century women's fashions in various European countries, particularly Germany, the Netherlands, and France, and compare the clothing styles of upper class women across the period. See the "Further Information" section below for some information resources to get you started. Was there a sixteenth-century center of fashion trends from which changes in clothing styles originated, as they do from Paris or New York in the twenty-first century? Design your own fashions based on basic sixteenth-century styles for a queen, a noblewoman of the royal court, a prosperous merchant's wife, and a yeoman farmer's wife. Or write an essay about how the royal court was a center of fashion in the sixteenth century.

- ❧ How do differences in religious belief affect fashion? Research how the wife of a PURITAN minister or gentleman might have dressed in the sixteenth century. Research how devout women of a particular faith dress today, such as Amish women or Muslim women or women of other faiths who wear distinctive attire. Choose one of these sixteenth- or twenty-first-century religious groups, and write an essay analyzing how differences in dress styles affect perceptions of that group within the mainstream society.

Further Information

Cioni, Maria L. *Women and Law in Elizabethan England*. New York: Garland, 1985.

Emerson, Kathy Lynn. *Wives and Daughters: The Women of Sixteenth Century England*. Troy, NY: Whitston Publishing Company, 1984.

Harrison, William. *The Description of England*. Edited by Georges Edelen. New York: Dover Publications, 1994.

Hogrefe, Pearl. *Tudor Women*. Ames: Iowa State University, 1975.

Jardine, Lisa. *Still Harping on Daughters: Women and Drama in the Age of Shakespeare*. Totowa, NJ: Barnes and Noble, 1983.

Mendelson, Sara, and Crawford, Patricia. *Women in Early Modern England 1550–1720*. Oxford: Oxford University Press, 2000.

Prior, Mary, ed. *Women in English Society, 1500–1800*. New York: Methuen, 1985.

Warnicke, Retha M. *Women of the English Renaissance and Reformation*. Westport, CT: Greenwood Press, 1983.

Web Sites

Elizabethan Clothing: http://www.elizabethan-era.org.uk/elizabethan-clothing.htm

Elizabethan Costume: http://www.elizabethancostume.net/

Harrison's *Description of England*: http://www.fordham.edu/halsall/mod/1577harrison-england.html

5. HIGH RENTS AND HARD TIMES FOR LAND TENANTS: WILLIAM HARRISON'S *DESCRIPTION OF ENGLAND* (1577)

INTRODUCTION

In these selections from William HARRISON's *Description of England* (see also Document 3), the author, an Elizabethan antiquary and clergyman, describes the terrible plight of the landless rural poor and the severe economic effect of rising rents on small tenant farmers, who rented the land that provided them and their families with a livelihood. Copyholders were descendants of medieval villeins, who had been bound through service to the land of their lord. By the sixteenth century, work service had been commuted to rent paid in either cash or kind. Copyhold tenants paid fines upon taking possession of the tenement on the death of the previous holder. If the amount of the fine was not fixed, the landlord could raise it beyond the tenant's means, thus causing him to lose the lease and his standard of living. (See Document 8 for a very different view of the landlord-tenant relationship.)

The landless poor, described in the second paragraph, suffered real poverty. Many had a small cottage and plot of ground for a garden, but could not keep even these if they could not find work in their area or if the plot given them was swallowed up in ENCLOSURE, a process whereby land held in common by the local village or parish community was reserved for the use of the lord or of one individual or family. Although the outcry against enclosures was exaggerated, they did cause real hardship in certain areas of Tudor England. (See "Social Class and Land Holding" below and "Elizabethan Antiquarianism," Document 30.)

KEEP IN MIND AS YOU READ

1. Tenant farmers and landless laborers in the countryside comprised perhaps 70 to 75 percent of the total population of Elizabethan England.
2. The sixteenth century was a period of European-wide inflation, with prices for food, housing, and basic commodities rising sharply throughout the Tudor period, and especially in the middle decades of the century.
3. Although Elizabethan society was highly class conscious, it was also increasingly fluid. Despite Harrison's generalizations about the hardships suffered by tenant farmers, many innovative and enterprising yeoman and tenant farmers expanded their holdings and prospered while less forward-thinking or less lucky gentlemen and even noblemen lost wealth and status.

Document: Excerpts from William Harrison's
Description of England

> copyholder: one who held tenure to land by right of being recorded in the court of the manor of which the land was a part; the copyholder paid rent to the manor lord
>
> God wot!: God knows!

[T]here things . . . are grown to be very grevious unto them [copyholders], to wit: the enhancing of rents . . . ; the daily oppression of **copyholders**, whose lords seek to bring their poor tenants almost to plain servitude and misery, daily devising new means and seeking up all the old how to cut them shorter and shorter, doubling, trebling and now and then seven times increasing their fines, driving them also for every trifle to lose and forfeit their tenures (by whom the greatest part of the realm does stand and is maintained) to the end they may fleece them yet more, which is a lamentable hearing. The third thing they talk of is usury, a trade brought in by the Jews, now perfectly practiced almost by every Christian and so commonly that he is accounted but for a fool that does lend his money for nothing. . . .

[T]he inhabitants of many places of our country are devoured and eaten up and their houses either altogether pulled down or suffered to decay little by little, although sometimes a poor man peradventure does dwell in one of them, who, not being able to repair it, suffers it to fall down and thereto thinks himself very friendly dealt withal, if he may have an acre of ground assigned unto him whereon to keep a cow or wherein to set cabbages, radishes, parsnips, carrots, melons, pumpkins, or suchlike stuff, by which he and his poor household live as by their principal food, since they can do no better. And as for wheat bread, they eat it when they can reach unto the price of it, contenting themselves in the meantime with bread made of oats or barley: a poor estate, **God wot**!

Source: Furnivall, Frederick, ed. *Harrison's Description of England in Shakspere's Youth*. Part 1. London: Published for the New Shakspere Society by N. Trübner and Co., 1877, pp. 241–42, 258–59.

AFTERMATH

The significant rise in prices experienced by the Elizabethans continued into the middle of the seventeenth century when the rise in the cost of living began to slow. The Elizabethans ascribed this price rise to many different causes, with Harrison's greedy and oppressive landlords being but one theory. Some lords certainly did raise entry fines exorbitantly and profited thereby, but many other landholders faced their own economic hardships, finding the rents and fines they collected insufficient to meet their own rising costs. Like other broad generalizations by other Elizabethan economic commentators, Harrison's observations described only one small part of a complex economic reality.

Today, most historians explain the sixteenth-century rise in prices as a consequence of demographic growth. As the rate of population growth increased after 1450, prices, especially for food, rose as demand grew. Because adherence to tradition inhibited new agricultural practices and technologies, production of food could not rise fast enough to match the growing demand for food and other goods stimulated by a growing population.

SOCIAL CLASS AND LANDHOLDING

Arising out of the medieval system of feudalism, whereby the king granted land and the peasants who worked the land to a lord in return for military service, Elizabethan social distinctions were based primarily on the holding of land. Although feudal institutions no longer accurately reflected Elizabethan society, political and economic power was still concentrated in the hands of the titled peerage and gentry, the 3 to 4 percent of the population that constituted the landholding elite. The peers, who possessed titles of nobility and the right to be summoned to the House of Lords in Parliament, numbered about 60 individuals during ELIZABETH I's reign, but grew significantly under JAMES I, who was far more generous than his predecessor with the granting of titles. The number of Elizabethans entitled through landed wealth, lifestyle, and degree of local influence to claim the status of gentleman numbered about 16,000 in 1603.

Over 80 percent of the English population consisted of yeomen, husbandmen, cottagers, and landless laborers—rural residents lacking the land and lifestyle to qualify as gentry. Yeomen farmed at least 50 acres of freehold, land not rented or leased, usually from a nobleman or gentleman, and capable of being inherited by the yeoman's heirs. Yeomen also had annual incomes of at least 40 shillings, the income required for a man to vote in county elections for Parliament. Husbandmen rented between 5 and 50 acres of land from larger landholders. Cottagers worked a few acres of land attached to their cottages and supplemented their income by working for others. Landless laborers had no land and depended entirely on wage work. Yeomen and husbandmen who held land by copyhold rented it from the nobleman or gentleman who owned the manor to which the land belonged. These are the tenants who concerned William Harrison. Husbandmen, cottagers, and landless laborers comprised the great majority of the English rural population.

ASK YOURSELF

1. As mentioned in Document 3 above, William Harrison was an Anglican clergyman and a strong Protestant. How does Harrison make his religious beliefs apparent in these observations on rural economics? How do you think religious belief might have affected Elizabethan economic relationships? What different perspectives might an Anglican, a PURITAN, and an English Roman Catholic bring to economic decisions? Why would these differences exist?

2. What do you think happened to landless laborers and their families who lost their houses and garden plots? What sorts of options do you think they had? What sorts of options would be available to a modern family that lost its house that were not available to an Elizabethan family? How do you think Elizabethan society perceived such unfortunates? How might modern perceptions of a family in a similar situation compare or differ?

TOPICS AND ACTIVITIES TO CONSIDER

> Research the topic of medieval feudalism, a system whereby all land belonged to the monarch, who granted it out, along with the villeins to work the land, to support a knight who was thereby freed to specialize in the arts of warfare and provide military service to the Crown. Trace how, over the centuries, feudalism evolved from its original form to the type of copyhold tenure prevalent in Elizabethan England. Devise a simple genealogical chart of your family with yourself as an Elizabethan

copyholder, yeoman farmer, or gentleman or nobleman, and describe what type of land ownership your father, grandfather, or great-grandfather might have had.

☙ Research the concept of usury mentioned by Harrison, and explain why he said it was "brought in by the Jews" and seemed to be a bad practice. Explain how what Harrison called usury works in the modern American economic system and how it became untangled from the religious connotations with which Harrison surrounded it.

☙ Access the online edition of Patricia Skinner's *Jews in Medieval Britain: Historical, Literary and Archaeological Perspectives* at http://books.google.com/books, and read one of the essays offered in this collection, paying particular attention to the connection between Jews and medieval English finance.

Further Information

Bowden, Peter J., ed. *Chapters from the Agrarian History of England and Wales. Volume 1: Economic Change: Prices, Wages, Profits and Rents, 1500–1750.* Cambridge: Cambridge University Press, 1990.

Braudel, F., and F. Spooner. "Prices in Europe from 1450–1750." In E.E. Rich and C.H. Wilson, eds. *The Cambridge Economic History of Europe*, vol. 4: *The Economy of Expanding Europe in the Sixteenth and Seventeenth Centuries.* Cambridge: Cambridge University Press, 1967.

Brown, Henry Phelps, and Shiela V. Hopkins. *A Perspective of Wages and Prices.* London: Methuen, 1981.

Harrison, William. *The Description of England.* Edited by Georges Edelen. New York: Dover Publications, 1994.

Kerridge, Eric. *Agrarian Problems in the Sixteenth Century and After.* Reprint ed. London: Routledge, 2006.

Kinney, Arthur F., ed. *Elizabethan Backgrounds: Historical Documents of the Age of Elizabeth I.* North Haven, CT: Shoe String Press, 1990.

Outhwaite, R.B. *Inflation in Tudor and Early Stuart England.* 2nd ed. London: Palgrave Macmillan, 1982.

Tawney, R.H. *The Agrarian Problem in the Sixteenth Century.* New York: Harper and Row, 1967.

Web Site

Harrison's *Description of England*: http://www.fordham.edu/halsall/mod/1577harrison-england.html

6. The Cost of Defending the Realm: The Forced Loan of 1588

INTRODUCTION

Although ELIZABETH I, like her grandfather, HENRY VII, was known for her parsimony, the start of war with Spain in the 1580s burdened the Queen's government with charges that far exceeded her normal revenues. To meet this need, the Queen was dependent on Parliament for grants of taxation, and, after 1585, she summoned that body more frequently than she had during the years of peace (see "Elizabethan Parliaments," Document 11). However, when even parliamentary grants proved unable to meet the financial demands of war, Elizabeth resorted to more questionable means of raising revenue, such as the highly unpopular practice of extorting forced loans from her wealthier subjects, especially among the citizens of London (see "Elizabethan London," Document 7). Reproduced below is a letter, issued under the Queen's seal, which was sent to Roger Columbell, a Derbyshire gentleman, in 1588 as part of the government's increasingly desperate effort to raise the large sums of money required to defend the realm against threatened invasion from Spain. Asked for the sizable sum of £25, Columbell paid the required amount three months later (see "Forced Loans and Benevolences" below).

KEEP IN MIND AS YOU READ

1. In times of peace, the Queen was expected to support herself and conduct the business of government entirely from her own ordinary revenues. These regular annual revenues came largely from two sources—income derived from the royal estates and the custom taxes, which were collected on imports and exports.

2. The Crown was expected to ask Parliament for grants of taxation only in times of emergency or extraordinary expense. War, which was enormously expensive, was the most frequent reason for heavy taxation. Elizabeth hated the waste and expense of war, hence her strenuous efforts to avoid entering into it in the first decades of her reign.

3. On average, the Queen received between £50,000 and £100,000 per year from the royal lands and another £75,000 from the customs, making her normal annual revenue, exclusive of parliamentary grants, less than £200,000.

4. In 1588 alone, the cost of defending the realm against the Spanish Armada exceeded £160,000.

5. The Queen's many other military expenses after 1585 included maintaining the fleet and the naval war against Spain, maintaining an English army in the Netherlands, maintaining coastal defenses, and supporting the Protestant party in the French civil wars.

Document: Letter under the Queen's Privy Seal to Roger Columbell of Derbyshire (January 1588)

By the Queen

Trusty and well-beloved, we greet you well, whereas for the better withstanding of the intended invasion of this realm, upon the great preparation made by the King of Spain, both by sea and land the last year, the same having been such as the like was never prepared at any time against this realm, we are now forced for the defense of the same, and of our good loving subjects, to be at infinite charges both by sea and land, especially for that the same intended invasion tends directly to the conquest of this realm, and finding also by such intelligences as we daily receive that the like preparations are now making for the like intent the next year, by the said King, for the withstanding whereof it shall be necessary for us to prepare both by sea and land, which cannot be performed without great charges, we have therefore thought it expedient, having always good and loving subjects most ready upon such like occasion to furnish us by way of loan some convenient portions of money, agreeable to their **estate**, (which we have and mind always to repay,) to have recourse unto them in like manner at this present.

And therefore, having made choice in the several parts of our realm of a number able to do us this kind of service, which is not refused between neighbor and neighbor, amongst the number we have also particularly named you, Roger Columbell, for your ability and good-will you bear to us and our realm, to be one; wherefore we require you to pay to our use the sum of five-and-twenty pounds to such person as by our lieutenant of that county shall be named to you by his handwriting. And these our letters of **privy seal**, subscribed by the party so named, by our **lieutenant** that shall receive the same, confessing the time of the receipt thereof, shall be sufficient to bind us, our heirs, and successors, duly to repay the said sum to you or your assigns, at the end of one year, from the 26th day of January, in the thirty-first year of our reign.

Thos. Kery.

Received of Mr. Roger Columbell, the 12th day of April, for her Majesty's use, the above said sum, twenty and five pounds, at Haddon, by me.

John Maners
Clerk in Engham

estate: class or degree

lieutenant: a local official, usually a nobleman, who was given charge of training militia, collecting military supplies, and organizing local defenses for one or a group of English counties

privy seal: seal used by the monarch and held by an official called the lord privy seal to authenticate documents, such as royal commands, answers to petitions, and special money transactions, such as these letters which, in effect, command their recipient to contribute to a loan

Source: Wright, Thomas, ed. *Queen Elizabeth and Her Times: A Series of Original Letters.* Vol. 2. London: Henry Colburn, Publisher, 1838, pp. 361–62.

FORCED LOANS AND BENEVOLENCES

Forced loans were demands for money made by the English Crown without parliamentary consent on the kingdom's wealthier subjects. The loans were usually levied to meet financial emergencies, particularly those arising during times of war or rebellion. Although the Crown promised to repay the money raised in this manner, such repayment was often irregular and incomplete. Making prompt repayment, Henry VII, Elizabeth's grandfather, levied small forced loans in the 1480s. Elizabeth's father, HENRY VIII, and her siblings, EDWARD VI and MARY I, were less scrupulous in repayment and encountered growing resistance to their demands. Elizabeth, who turned to forced loans in the 1580s and 1590s to meet the rising cost of the Spanish war, found herself increasingly unable to repay her loans. When Charles I tried to extend payment of forced loans throughout the kingdom in the 1620s, resistance became intense, and their use was condemned by the Petition of Right in 1628 and outlawed by the Bill of Rights in 1689.

Unpaid loans to the Crown became, in effect, benevolences, a type of financial levy initiated by EDWARD IV in the 1470s. A benevolence was a voluntary contribution made to the Crown by wealthier subjects at the Crown's request. The money was looked upon as a gift made through the donor's "good will and benevolence" without any promise or expectation of repayment. Benevolences were outlawed by RICHARD III's Parliament in 1484, but revived by the Tudors, who considered all Ricardian statutes invalid. The Petition of Right also condemned benevolences, and no attempt was made to raise one after 1633.

AFTERMATH

Although the crisis of 1588 passed with the defeat of the Spanish Armada (see "Spanish Armada," Document 18), the Crown's war expenditure continued to climb, especially in the early 1590s when Elizabeth intervened in the French civil wars by monetarily supporting the Protestant king, HENRI IV, against the Spanish-backed CATHOLIC LEAGUE. Fear and loyalty made payment of the 1588 loan fairly full and prompt, but, when the Queen demanded new loans in 1590, 1591, and 1596, resistance grew with each new levy as those called upon sought new ways to evade payment. By 1592, the Crown had fallen into arrears on its loan payments, and the failure to promptly reimburse previous loans, combined with new requests for parliamentary taxation, only increased the anger and resentment aroused by new demands. In 1598, when rumors swept London that a new loan was being contemplated, many wealthy citizens fled the city for the countryside, hoping thereby to avoid payment.

ASK YOURSELF

1. Understanding that no one can directly refuse the Queen but anyone can try various indirect evasions, what steps might you, as an Elizabethan country gentleman or a London merchant, take to avoid paying a forced loan?
2. If you were the Queen or one of her ministers, what steps might you take to enforce or encourage payment? Why might you be unwilling to be too harsh in your actions? What would be the best way to convince people to pay, however reluctantly?
3. As one of Elizabeth's ministers, can you suggest any way to change how government is financed so that the Queen, even in time of war, will not have to resort to such unpopular measures as forced loans?

TOPICS AND ACTIVITIES TO CONSIDER

- ❧ After reading the Queen's letter to Roger Columbell carefully, analyze its language to determine how the government made a demand for money sound like a request. Suppose you are the monarch and you need money to conduct a foreign war, such as Elizabeth's wars in the Netherlands and France. Write your own letter "requesting" a loan in such a way as to encourage the most positive response.

- ❧ As the Queen's chief minister in charge of raising a new forced loan, devise a plan explaining who (what types or groups of people) would be sent letters and how you might modify the wording of the letters to tailor them to most effectively appeal to each group.

- ❧ Consider how the use of forced loans and benevolences by the English government in the sixteenth and seventeenth centuries may have affected the financing of government in the United States in the twenty-first century.

Further Information

Dietz, F.C. *English Public Finance 1485–1641*. 2nd ed. London: F. Cass, 1964.

Guy, John. *The Tudor Monarchy*. Oxford: Oxford University Press, 1997.

Outhwaite, R.B. *Inflation in Tudor and Early Stuart England*. 2nd ed. London: Palgrave Macmillan, 1982.

Somerset, Anne. *Elizabeth I*. New York: Alfred A. Knopf, 1991.

7. The Elizabethan Underworld: Robert Greene's Cony-Catching Pamphlets (1592)

INTRODUCTION

The Elizabethan playwright and pamphleteer, Robert GREENE, spent much of the 1580s living a dissolute life among the rogues, pickpockets, and prostitutes of the London underworld (see "Elizabethan London" below). Seeking to earn his living as a writer in an age when professional authors were almost unknown, Greene later used his experiences as the basis for his popular "cony-catching" pamphlets, vivid tales of London rakes and thieves who ingeniously and often humorously defrauded ordinary citizens of their money and property. "Cony-catching," in Elizabethan slang, meant a confidence game or a scam. In the following tale from one of Greene's pamphlets, a prosperous farmer, who, by calling his neighbor foolish for allowing his purse to be stolen, makes himself an irresistible target to the London thieves who overhear him and so becomes himself a victim.

KEEP IN MIND AS YOU READ

1. Greene is seen by Elizabethan literary scholars as the most talented of a group of sixteenth-century writers who produced what, thanks to Greene, has become known as "cony-catching literature," a genre of urban fiction that purports to instruct honest citizens in the ways of London criminals, but, in fact, constitutes a highly sensationalized form of popular entertainment based on the shocking and unseemly behavior of the unscrupulous urban poor.

2. The center of law, government, and commerce, London in the late Elizabethan period was a teeming metropolis without an organized police force that drew to it people of all classes and conditions.

3. Aside from court poets like Sir Philip SIDNEY, who would have viewed making money from their writings as demeaning, writers, playwrights, players, and others who did seek to earn a living from the pen were often considered disreputable figures in Elizabethan society, and some, such as Greene, Thomas KYD, and Christopher MARLOWE, fitted rather easily into and drew much inspiration out of London's seamy street life.

4. *A Disputation Between a He Cony-Catcher and a She-Cony Catcher*, the pamphlet from which the following excerpt is taken, is largely a dialogue between Laurence and Nan, two experienced London tricksters who debate the relative skills of men and women in the art of defrauding their fellow citizens.

Document: Tale of the Proud Farmer and the Cutpurse from A Disputation Between a He Cony-Catcher and a She-Cony Catcher

A pleasant tale of a country farmer that took it in scorn to have his purse cut or drawn from him, and how a foist served him.

It was told me for a truth that not long since here in London, there lay a country Farmer, with **divers** of his neighbors about Law matters, amongst whom, one of them going to Westminster-Hall, was by a **Foist** stripped of all the pence in his purse, and coming home, made great complaint of his misfortune, some lamented his loss, and others exclaimed against the **Cutpurses**, but this Farmer he laughed loudly at the matter, and said such fools as could not keep their purses no surer, were well served, and for my part quoth he, I so much scorn the Cutpurses, that I would thank him heartily that would take pains to foist mine, well says his neighbor, then you may thank me, since my harms learns you to beware, but if it be true, that many things fall out between the cup and the lip, you know not what hands Fortune may light in your own lap. Tush, quoth the Farmer, here's forty pounds in this purse in gold, the proudest Cutpurse in England win it and wear it; as thus he boasted, there stood a **subtle** Foist by and heard all, smiling to himself at the folly of the proud Farmer, and vowed to have his purse or venture his neck for it, and so went home and **bewrayed** it to a crew of his companions, who taking it in **dudgeon**, that they should be put down by a Peasant, met either at Laurence Pickering's, or at Lambeth . . . but wheresoever they met they held a convocation, and both consulted and concluded all by a general consent, to bend all their wits to be possessors of this Farmer's **Boung**, and for the execution of this their vow, they haunted about the Inn where he lay, and dogged him into divers places, both to Westminster Hall and other places, and yet could never light upon it, he was so watch-full . . . that all their travail was in vain, at last one of them fled to a more cunning policy, and went and learned the man's name and where he dwelt, and then **hied** him to the **Counter** and entered an Action against him of trespass, damages two hundred pounds, when he had thus done, he **feed** two **Sergeants**, and carried them down with him to the man's lodging, wishing them not to arrest him till he commanded them, well agreed they were, and down to the Farmer's lodging they came, where were a crew of Foists, whom he had made privy to the end of his practice, stood waiting, but he took no knowledge at all of them, but walked up and down, the Farmer came out and went to Paul's, the Cutpurse bad stay, and would not yet suffer the Officers to meddle with him, till he came into the West end of Paul's Churchyard, and there he willed them to do their Office, and they stepping to the Farmer arrested him, the Farmer amazed, being amongst his neighbors, asked the Sergeant at whose suit he was troubled, at whose suit soever it be, said one of the Cutpurses that stood by, you are wronged honest man, for he has arrested you here in a place of privilege, where the Sheriff's nor the Offices have nothing to do with you, and therefore you are unwise if you obey him, tush, says another Cutpurse, though the man were so simple of himself, yet shall he not offer the Church so much wrong, as by yielding to the **Mace**, to abolish **Paul's liberty**, and therefore I will take his part, and with that he drew his sword, another took the man and **haled** him away, the Officer he stuck hard to him, and said he was his true prisoner, and cried Clubs, the **Prentises** arose, and there was a great hurly burly, for they took the Officer's part, so that the poor Farmer was mightily turmoiled amongst them, and almost haled in pieces, whilst thus the strife was, one of the Foists had taken his purse away, and was gone, and the Officer carried the man away to a Tavern, for he swore he knew no such man, nor any man that he was indebted too, as then they sat drinking of a quart of wine, the Foist that had caused him to be arrested, sent a note by a Porter to the Officer that he should release the Farmer, for he had mistaken the man, which note the Officer showed him, and bad him pay his fees and go his ways: the poor Country-man was content with that, and put his hand in his pocket to feel for his purse, and **God wot** there was none, which made his heart far more cold then the arrest did, and with that fetching a great sigh he said, alas masters I am undone, my purse in this fray is taken out of my pocket and ten pounds in gold in it . . . . Indeed, said the Sergeant, commonly in such brawls the cutpurses be busy, and I pray God the quarrel was not made upon purpose by the pickpockets, well says his neighbor, who shall smile at you now, the other day when I lost my purse you laughed at me, the Farmer **brook** all, and sat malcontent, and borrowed money of his neighbors to pay the Sergeant, and had a learning I believe ever after to brave the cutpurse.

bewrayed: divulged; betrayed

boung: purse

brook: stand for; tolerate

Counter (or Compter): small prison built in London in 1555 and used mainly to confine debtors and those guilty or suspected of various misdemeanors

cutpurse: a pickpocket who worked by cutting open a pocket or purse

divers: various

dudgeon: indignation; taking offense

feed: paid a fee to

foist: a pickpocket who worked by reaching into a pocket or purse

God wot: God knows

haled: hauled; pulled; compelled to go

hied: quickly got (himself) to; hastened to

Mace: refers here to the authority or jurisdiction of the city of London

Paul's liberty: exclusion of the precincts of St. Paul's Cathedral from the jurisdiction, in certain matters, of the city of London

Prentises: apprentices; in Tudor England, and especially in London, these usually young men were common causes of riot and disorder

Sergeants: officers of the local courts

subtle: unnoticed or concealed

Source: Greene, Robert. *The thirde and last part of Cony-catching. With the newly devised knauish Art of Foole-taking. The like Cosenages and Villenies neuer before discouered. A Dispvtation Betweene a Hee Cony-catcher and a Shee Cony-catcher.* Edited by G.B. Harrison. New York: E. P. Dutton and Co., 1923, pp. 7–8.

AFTERMATH

In his later years, Greene repented of his dissolute former life, and his cony-catching pamphlets are written from the perspective of a now-reformed street rogue relating, as a former insider, colorful tales of life on the London streets. Indeed, the pamphlets incorporated much of Greene's own history, including tales of his drinking and gambling and a thinly veiled description of the abandonment of his wife for the sister of a notorious London thief. Witty and biting in the way they exposed the ill deeds of all sorts of London citizens, including prosperous merchants and craftsmen, Greene's pamphlets were popular and made him a well-known figure in London. Written just before his death in 1592, Greene's best-known pamphlet, *A Groatsworth of Wit Bought with a Million of Repentance*, criticized other London literary figures, including William SHAKESPEARE, who is famously characterized as "an upstart crow" (Palmer and Palmer 96).

ASK YOURSELF

1. What part does humor play in the anecdote related above? Why, if the pamphlets were for the moral instruction of readers, would Greene include so much humor?
2. How are the foists (i.e., pickpockets) and thieves characterized in the above tale? How would a reader react to their characterization? With revulsion? With sympathy? With anger? How are the farmer and other solid citizens characterized? How might a reader react to them? What do you think Greene is really saying about London society?
3. How does the jargon, the various names for thieves, such as foists and cutpurses, add to the appeal of the story? Does it really give you a sense that the writer has lived what he writes about?

TOPICS AND ACTIVITIES TO CONSIDER

- ❧ Compare this form of Elizabethan popular entertainment with modern forms of entertainment, such as popular novels or reality television shows. Draft a proposal for a novel or television program based on Elizabethan street life, as described by Greene.

ELIZABETHAN LONDON

Robert Greene's cony-catching pamphlets, which were popular reading in the 1590s, took for their theme the clever trickery of urban rogues, thieves, and vagabonds. Elizabethan London, the scene of these exploits, was the seat of English government and the largest and richest city in the British Isles. By 1603, London was one of the largest cities in Europe, with a population of about 200,000, and far more populous than Norwich, the second-largest city in England with about 15,000 people. Economic opportunity drew people from all over Britain to London. About one-eighth of the population of Elizabethan England lived in London at some time in their lives. Poor sanitary conditions gave London a high death rate, but the arrival of an estimated 3,000 new immigrants per year kept the city growing and gave the city's thieves many opportunities to ply their trade.

London was the political and economic capital of England. Parliament and the courts of COMMON LAW were situated a mile away at Westminster. Over half the Crown's tax revenue from towns came from London, as did more than two-thirds of it customs revenue and huge amounts of loan money from city merchants. Although geographically a small town confined within its medieval walls, London was divided into 26 wards, including Southwark across the Thames, an area notorious for the kinds of characters described by Greene. The wards were subdivided into 242 precincts. Each ward was administered by an alderman and each precinct by a common councilman. The courts of aldermen and councilmen performed important legislative and judicial functions within the city government. London was also divided into 111 parishes and contained 100 liveried companies, which regulated the city economy, collected taxes, and provided various social services. Only company members were citizens, or freemen, and only freemen could vote, establish a business, or enjoy other civic and economic rights.

∽ The lives and careers of outlaws, mobsters, and scam artists have long interested people, as illustrated by the medieval tales of Robin Hood, and still fascinate people today, as shown by films like *The Godfather*. Make a list of tales, short stories, novels, plays, television programs, and films that take some sort of criminal figure or group for their central character(s).

∽ Go to http://books.google.com and search for *Rogues, Vagabonds, and Sturdy Beggars*, edited by Arthur Kinney, or simply Google that book title to access this collection of Elizabethan rogue or cony-catching literature. Read a selection from one of the other Elizabethan writers included in the volume and compare it to Greene's work. How are they similar? How do they differ?

Further Information

Crupi, Charles W. *Robert Greene*. Boston: Twayne, 1986.

Jordan, John Clark. *Robert Greene*. New York: Octagon Books, 1965.

Kinney, Arthur F., ed. *Rogues, Vagabonds, and Sturdy Beggars: A New Gallery of Tudor and Early Stuart Literature*. Amherst, MA: University of Massachusetts Press, 1990.

Palmer, Alan, and Veronica Palmer. "Robert Greene." In *Who's Who in Shakespeare's England*. New York: St. Martin's Press, 1981, p. 96.

Salgado, Gamini. *The Elizabethan Underworld*. Charleston, SC: The History Press, 2006.

Web Sites

Robert Greene's Cony-Catching Pamphlets: http://darkwing.uoregon.edu/~rbear/greene4.html

Robert Greene's Groats-worth of Wit: http://darkwing.uoregon.edu/~rbear/greene1.html

8. THE DANGERS OF LENGTHY LEASES FOR LAND TENANTS: THOMAS WILSON'S *THE STATE OF ENGLAND, ANNO DOM. 1600* (1600)

INTRODUCTION

In Document 5 above, William HARRISON depicted rent-raising Elizabethan landlords as oppressors of their tenants. In the following selection, Thomas WILSON, a government official writing an assessment of the state of England in 1600, saw the landlord-tenant relationship the other way round. Meant as a document of guidance and advice for Sir Robert CECIL, the son and political heir of the late William CECIL, Lord Burghley, Wilson's *The State of England* portrays landlords as victims of their tenants, who took advantage of the mid-century coinage debasements to decrease the real value of their rent payments, thus impoverishing their landlords while at the same time making handsome profits for themselves from the rising demand for their agricultural products (see "Tudor Coinage Debasement" below). The crux of the problem, according to Wilson, was the landlords' unfortunate habit of renting land on long leases, in some cases up to 200 years, a practice that prevented them from raising rents and thus themselves taking advantage of the sixteenth-century inflation on the price of food grown on their land.

KEEP IN MIND AS YOU READ

1. Debasement of the coinage by the English government lowered the value of the coinage, meaning that the coin in which a landlord was paid had less purchasing power. If he could not raise the amount of the rent because that amount was set by a lease running for a long term of years, the landlord would soon have difficulty paying his own debts because debasement also causes inflation, that is, a rise in prices, and rising prices are most damaging to people with fixed incomes.

2. Governments debased coinage to realize a financial gain. Debasement reduced the silver or gold content of coins, thus allowing the government to mint more coins with the same amount of precious metal. This is what the English government did in the 1540s and 1550s to pay for war with France and Scotland.

3. Prices rose steadily throughout the sixteenth century, but the debasement was only an aggravating factor. The basic underlying cause of the Tudor inflation was a steady increase in population coupled with the inability of sixteenth-century agricultural techniques to produce sufficient food to meet rising demand.

Document: Excerpt from Thomas Wilson's The State of England, Anno Dom., 1600

The cause that has made the **yeomanry** in England so great [in times past] I cannot rightly call a policy, because it was no matter invented and set down by authority for the bettering of that state of people, but rather by the subtlety of them and simplicity of gentlemen; for the yeomanry and **mean** people being servants and vassals to the gents, who are the possessors and lord[s] of the lands and lordships and could not occupy all their lands themselves but placed farmers therein at a time when by reason of the great wars money was scarce and all things else cheap, and so lands let at a small rent, the yeoman and farmers told the gentlemen, their landlords, that they could not be at so great charges to manure and enclose and improve their grounds, and repair and re-edify their houses ruined by war unless they would let them the said land for some time. And if they would do so, and at a smaller rent, they would pay them some piece of money for a fine, and so much money yearly. The gentlemen, improvident of what should come after, and glad to have money in their hands, did let unto the said farmers all their lands and lordships (saving their dwelling) after the rate aforesaid, some for 30, some 40 and some 50, some 200 years. Soon after, the king, by reason of the want of money, altered the coin and caused that which was before but 6d. to go for 12d. and after that again lessened it as much more, so that he that was wont to pay but 3d. which though it were all one in value yet hereby it came to pass that he which paid before 1 pound weight in silver for his farm, paid now but a quarter, and the yeoman at that time having most money, carrying it to the Mint, had for every pound 4, paying for the minting, and the king besides got a great mass of money by his said mint. This device, and then the price of corn, cattle and all farmers' commodities increasing daily in price, and the gentleman who is generally inclined to great and vain expense had no more than would keep his house and some small rent, and therefore could not spend away prodigally much of the wealth of the land, because he had no superfluity. And the **baser sort**, which by this means had got the wealth, had never the inclination to spend much . . . . But since these long leases are grown to expire the gentlemen by this begin to beware how to be so overreached.

baser sort: people of common or humble birth

mean: common

yeomanry: small land holders below the nobility and gentry in social rank

Source: Wilson, Thomas. "The State of England, anno dom. 1600." *Camden Miscellany* xvi. London: Camden Society, 1936, pp. 38–39.

TUDOR COINAGE DEBASEMENT

Thomas Wilson's mention of how the king "altered the coin" refers to a series of debasements of English coinage carried out by the governments of HENRY VIII and EDWARD VI. Undertaken, according to Wilson, for "want of money," the debasements were attempts to increase the amount of money available to fund foreign wars. In Tudor England, money consisted mainly of silver coins, the value of which was closely tied to the amount of precious metal they contained. Debasement meant government manipulation of the coinage to reduce the weight and fineness (ratio of alloy to precious metal) of silver in the coin while maintaining its original face value. Although the government made an enormous short-term profit because it could issue more coinage with the same nominal purchasing power without increasing the available amount of bullion, the resulting lack of public confidence in the debased issues drove up prices, disordered markets and exchange rates, and caused people to hoard good coin and refuse bad.

Henry VIII authorized the first debasement in 1544 to conduct war in Scotland and France. By 1551, the silver content of English coins was one-sixth what it had been. Because people were accustomed to treating money as if it possessed the real value of the precious metal it contained, sellers of goods soon refused to accept debased coins as equal to the old issues, causing prices to rise quickly and sharply. As Wilson describes, the coinage debasement aggravated the problem of long leases because landowners found themselves paid rents in coin that no longer had the buying power of its nominal face value, if it were being accepted at all. The problem was not completely resolved until 1560 when the government of Elizabeth issued new coinage that allowed English money to regain both a proper silver content and public confidence.

AFTERMATH

Like Harrison's theories of rural economic hardship expressed in Document 5, Wilson's ideas were overly simplistic. Where Harrison, the cleric, identified with tenants, Wilson, the bureaucrat, identified with the political classes, the landlords. Some landlords did suffer because of long leases and fixed incomes, but many others adapted and prospered. In 1600, when Wilson was writing, the country was just shaking off the effects of a series of bad harvests in the 1590s and was still experiencing a period of high taxation (see Document 6) caused by the need to conduct the war with Spain on both land and sea. Scarcity caused prices to rise and hurt both landlord and tenant, while higher taxes further hurt landholders with fixed incomes. The end of the Spanish war in 1604, better weather and better harvests after 1600, and a gradual slowing of population growth eased inflationary pressure on all English subjects in the seventeenth century.

ASK YOURSELF

1. After reading William Harrison's arguments in Document 5 for landlords taking advantage of tenants and Thomas Wilson's arguments above for tenants taking advantage of landlords, who do you think makes the most convincing case? Why do you think that?

2. How has inflation affected the American economy in the last century? Why did the American economy experience inflation at various points in the twentieth century? How did that inflation affect various groups of Americans, such as homeowners and renters or those on fixed incomes? How does this modern inflation compare or contrast to the sixteenth-century inflation?

3. One of the most serious problems arising out of a government's debasement of the coinage is the public's loss of confidence in the coinage. What steps do you think a government could take to restore the people's confidence in and use of their money?

TOPICS AND ACTIVITIES TO CONSIDER

- ❧ In the *State of England*, Wilson analyzed and described the political and economic state of the kingdom as he perceived it to be in the year 1600. Write a brief account assessing the state of your neighborhood, city/town, state, or even country as you perceive it to be at the present time. You could focus your attention on the current state of society, the economy, politics, or anything else that you deem worthy of attention. Use examples to support your comments and observations.

- ❧ Using books and the Internet, research trends in the American economy since 1900 to identify periods of economic growth, periods of inflation, and periods of economic depression or recession. Use the data you gather to create an economic timeline for the United States since 1900, noting important economic events and their dates and durations.

Further Information

Bowden, Peter J., ed. *Chapters from the Agrarian History of England and Wales. Volume 1: Economic Change: Prices, Wages, Profits and Rents, 1500–1750.* Cambridge: Cambridge University Press, 1990.

Kerridge, Eric. *Agrarian Problems in the Sixteenth Century and After.* Reprint ed. London: Routledge, 2006.

McRae, Andrew. *God Speed the Plough: The Representation of Agrarian England, 1500–1660.* Cambridge: Cambridge University Press, 2002.

Medine, Peter E. *Thomas Wilson.* Boston: Twayne, 1986.

Outhwaite, R.B. *Inflation in Tudor and Early Stuart England.* 2nd ed. London: Palgrave Macmillan, 1982.

Spring, Eileen. *Law, Land, and Family: Aristocratic Inheritance in England, 1300 to 1800.* Chapel Hill: University of North Carolina Press, 1997.

Tawney, R.H. *The Agrarian Problem in the Sixteenth Century.* New York: Harper and Row, 1967.

Wilson, Sir Thomas. "The State of England Anno Dom. 1600, by Thomas Wilson." Edited by F.J. Fisher. *Camden Miscellany* 16. Camden, 3rd series, 52. London: Royal Historical Society, 1936.

9. A Piece of Elizabethan Self-Promotion: William Kempe's *Nine Days Wonder* (1600)

INTRODUCTION

William KEMPE, an Elizabethan comic actor, was famous for his humorous song-and-dance sketches called "jigs." These jigs were so popular that a London writer observed in 1598 that "whores, bedles [parish officers], bawds [pimps], and sergeants [city officers] filthily chant Kempe's jig" all about town (Gale 619). However, his best-known exploit was the 100-mile-long morris dance that he danced from London to Norwich in February and March 1600 (see "Morris Dancing" below). Although the venture took a month in total, only nine days were actually employed in dancing, with the rest of the time given over to resting and promotion. The following selection, describing part of the fifth and sixth days of dancing, comes from the book, *Kempe's Nine Daies Wonder*, which the actor published after the dance to further exploit his notoriety.

KEEP IN MIND AS YOUR READ

1. Kempe's dance was a publicity stunt, as we would call it today, and a money-making enterprise, with Kempe enjoying a good profit not only from sales of his book, but also from wagers laid before the dance and from gifts gathered along the way.

2. Kempe was apparently among the favorite actors of Queen ELIZABETH herself, who is known to have particularly enjoyed the outrageous Shakespearean character, Sir John Falstaff, who appeared in the two *Henry IV* plays and *The Merry Wives of Windsor* and who was likely written specifically for Kempe.

Document: Excerpt from Kempe's Nine Daies Wonder

The fifth day's journey, being Wednesday of the second week.

Taking advantage of my 3 miles that I had danced the day before, this Wednesday morning I tripped it to Sudbury; whither came to see a very kind

Gentleman, Master Foskew, that had before traveled on foot from London to Berwick, who giving me good counsel to observe temperate diet for my health, and other advise to be careful of my company, besides his liberal entertainment, departed, leaving me much indebted to his love.

In this town of Sudbury, there came a lusty tall fellow, a butcher by his profession, that would in a Morris keep me company to Bury: I being glad of his friendly offer, gave him thanks, and forward we did set: but ere we had measured half a mile of our way, he gave me over in the plain field, protesting, that if he might get a 100. pound, he would not hold out with me; for indeed my pace in dancing is not ordinary.

As he and I were parting, a lusty Country lass being among the people, called him faint hearted lout: saying, "if I had begun to dance, I would have held out one mile though it had cost my life." At which words many laughed. "Nay," said she, "if the Dancer will lend me a leash of his bells, I'll venture to tread one mile with him myself." I looked upon her, saw mirth in her eyes, heard boldness in her words, and beheld her ready to tuck up her russet petticoat, I fitted her with bells: which she merrily taking, garnished her thick short legs, and with a smooth brow bade the **Taberer** begin. The Drum struck, forward marched I with my merry Maid Marian: who shook her fat sides: and footed it merrily to Melford, being a long mile. There parting with her, I gave her (besides her skinfull of drink) an English crown to buy more drink, for good wench she was in a piteous heat: my kindness she requited with dropping some dozen of short curtsies, and bidding God bless the Dancer, I bad her adieu: and to give her her due, she had a good ear, danced truly, and we parted friendly. But ere I part with her, a good fellow my friend, having writ an odd Rime of her, I will make bold to set it down.

> *A Country Lasse browne as a berry,*
> *Blith of blee in heart as merry,*
> *Cheekes well fed and sides well larded,*
> *Euery bone with fat flesh guarded,*
> *Meeting merry Kemp by chaunce,*
> *Was Marrian in his Morrice daunce.*
> *Her stump legs with bels were garnisht,*
> *Her browne browes with sweating varnish[t];*
> *Her browne hips when she was lag,*
> *To win her ground, went swig a swag,*
> *Which to see all that came after,*
> *Were repleate with mirthfull laughter.*
> *Yet she thumped it on her way,*
> *With a sportly hey de gay,*
> *At a mile her daunce she ended,*
> *Kindly paide and well commended.*

At Melford, divers Gentlemen met me, who brought me to one Master Colts, a very kind and **worshipful** Gentleman, where I had unexpected entertainment till the Saturday. From whose house having hope somewhat to amend my way to Bury, I determined to go by Clare, but I found it to be both farther and fouler.

The sixth days journey, being Saturday of the second week.

From Wednesday night till Saturday having been very troublesome, but much more welcome to Master Colt's: in the morning I took my leave, and was accompanied with many Gentlemen a mile of my way. Which mile Master Colts his **fool** would needs dance with me, and had his desire, where leaving me, two fools parted fair in a foul way: I keeping on my course to Clare, where I a while rested, and then cheerfully set forward to Bury.

Passing from Clare towards Bury, I was invited to the house of a very bountiful widow, whose husband during his life was a Yeoman of that Country, dying rich no doubt, as might well appear, by the riches and plenty, that abounded in every corner of the house. She is called the Widow Everet.

At her house were met above thirty Gentlemen. Such, and so plentiful variety of good fare, I have very seldom seen in any Commoner's house. Her behavior being very modest and friendly, argued her bringing up not to be rude. She was a woman of good presence: and if a fool may judge, of no small discretion.

From this widow's I danced to Bury, coming in on the Saturday in the afternoon, at what time the right Honorable, the Lord Chief Justice [Sir John Popham] entered at another gate of the town, the wondering and regardless multitude making his honor clear way, left the streets where he past to gape at me: the throng of them being so great, that poor Will Kemp was seven times stayed ere he could recover his Inn. By reason of the great snow that then fell I stayed at Bury from Saturday in the second week of my setting forth, till Thursday night the week following.

Source: Kempe, William. *Kempe's Nine Daies Wonder: Performed in a Daunce from London to Norwich.* Edited by Alexander Dyce. London: Printed for the Camden Society by John Bowyer Nichols, 1840, pp. 9–11.

---

fool: a jester; a retainer kept at court or in noble or gentle households to provide entertainment, usually comedic

worshipful: notable; distinguished

taberer: drummer playing a small drum known as a taber (or tabor)

MORRIS DANCING

The morris dance was a ritual dance, usually performed by a group of (mostly) male dancers, especially as part of the celebrations and activities that accompanied May Day and Whitsunday (Pentecost) festivals in the late spring and early summer. Although there were regional variations, morris dancers usually dressed in outlandish costumes liberally adorned with bells, ribbons, and garlands. Larger dance troupes usually included certain stock figures, one of which was a "Maid Marian," the term used above by Kempe to describe the country girl who danced with him to Melford, although, in most morris dances, the Maid Marian was actually a man dressed as a woman. Other characters included a "hobby horse," which was a man surrounded by a horse costume so as to appear as if he were riding, and a "fool," which was a clownish figure dressed in jester's attire. Music was usually provided by a pipe (i.e., a flute) and tabor (i.e., a drum)—Kempe says above that he was accompanied by the latter—or by a fiddle. PURITANS denounced morris dancing, like plays and other pastimes they considered frivolous or immoral, and efforts were made in the seventeenth century to suppress it, but morris dancing survived all such efforts and is still popular throughout present-day Britain.

AFTERMATH

As the above excerpts indicate, Kempe, who was originally accompanied only by his musicians and an overseer charged with ensuring that he danced every mile, attracted crowds of followers and even fellow dancers. Upon entering Norwich, Kempe was met by a triumphal procession that escorted him to the town Guildhall, where he ceremoniously hung up his dancing shoes. The dance was timed to coincide with the installation of Norwich's new mayor, who awarded Kempe the handsome sum of £5 and an even more generous annual stipend of 40 shillings. Kempe's venture was widely celebrated, with references to it appearing in numerous letters and pamphlets written and published at the time. Interest was so great that Kempe wrote his subsequent book in part to forestall others from attempting to profit from their own descriptions of his exploit.

ASK YOURSELF

1. If Kempe were alive today, how do you think he would promote his dance? What new tools and media not available in 1600 could Kempe use today? How do you think he would employ them?
2. How do you think Puritans viewed Kempe and his humor? How do you think Kempe viewed Puritans?

TOPICS AND ACTIVITIES TO CONSIDER

- View the DVD for the 1998 Oscar-winning film *Shakespeare in Love*, in which the character of William Kempe appears played by Patrick Barlow. Compare the portrayal of Kempe in the film to the image of Kempe that emerges from *Kempe's Nine Daies Wonder*. Do you think Barlow's portrayal was accurate?
- Kempe was said to be able to improvise words to his jigs while dancing. Make a list of recent or current comedic actors who display this same innovative style of comedy, and give reasons why you believe each is like Kempe.
- Besides Falstaff, the Shakespearean roles Kempe is known or thought to have performed are Peter (*Romeo and Juliet*), Dogberry (*Much Ado About Nothing*), Bottom (*A Midsummer Night's Dream*), Costard (*Love's Labour's Lost*), Launce (*The Two Gentlemen of Verona*), and Launcelot Gobbo (*The Merchant of Venice*). Read one or two of these roles written by Shakespeare, and write a brief description of what you think might have been Kempe's style of acting.

Further Information

Harrison, G.B. *Elizabethan Plays and Players*. Ann Arbor: University of Michigan Press, 1956.
Rossiter, A.P. *English Drama from Early Times to the Elizabethans*. Folcroft, PA: Folcroft Library Editions, 1977.
Singman, Jeffrey L. *Daily Life in Elizabethan England*. Westport, CT: Greenwood Press, 1995.

Web Sites

Kempe's Nine Daies Wonder: http://darkwing.uoregon.edu/~rbear/arte/arte.htm
William Kempe: http://www.globe-theatre.org.uk/william-kempe-actor.htm

10. THE ELIZABETHAN POOR LAW OF 1601

INTRODUCTION

Tudor England witnessed a significant rise in the number of poor and rootless people with no trade or assured livelihood who moved about the country seeking work or better living conditions. Many factors contributed to this trend (see also Documents 5 and 8), including population growth, price inflation, coinage debasement, poor harvests, and the decline in private charity engendered by the breakdown of communal feudal society and the DISSOLUTION OF THE MONASTERIES (see "Tudor Coinage Debasement," Document 8). Tudor society considered these vagrants to be threats to national security and public order, "masterless men" who lived dangerously beyond the control of their social superiors. To cope with the situation, sixteenth-century Parliaments passed a series of Poor Laws to make some provision for the control and care of these individuals, thus making poor relief a matter of state concern for the first time (see "Elizabethan Parliaments," Document 11). Reproduced below are excerpts from the 1601 Act for the Relief of the Poor, which, with periodic amendment, served as the basis of the English system of poor relief until well into the nineteenth century (see "Elizabethan Poor Laws" below).

KEEP IN MIND AS YOU READ

1. In medieval times, poor relief in the countryside was a function of the village community, where the local parish priest was expected to set aside part of his income from TITHES to support the poor of the parish. As part of their duty as Christians, wealthy noble and gentry households also supplied alms for the local poor, as did the many monastic communities throughout the realm.

2. The Reformation, by discouraging begging, emphasizing personal responsibility, and overthrowing monasteries, further disrupted the already declining medieval system of poor relief and made some form of state action necessary.

3. The Poor Law of 1536 outlawed private almsgiving by most individuals, but did provide for a voluntary collection in all parishes to educate children, maintain the disabled, and employ the healthy. Although it gave some help to the truly needy, the act's main thrust was the punishment and control of able-bodied beggars and vagrants.

Document: Act for the Relief of the Poor, 1601

churchwarden: parish lay officer with responsibility for parish property and almsgiving

gaol: jail

meet: proper; fit; appropriate

quorum: a select body of county justices of the peace, at least one member of which must be present for the other justices to act

tithes: annual payments in cash and kind made by parishioners to support their parish clergyman

underwoods: underbrush; undergrowth

Be it enacted by the authority of this present parliament that the **churchwardens** of every parish, and four, three or two substantial householders there as shall be thought **meet**, having respect to the apportion and greatness of the same parish or parishes, to be nominated yearly in Easter week or within one month after Easter, under the hand and seal of two or more justices of the peace in the same county, whereof one to be of the **quorum**, dwelling in or near the same parish or division where the same parish doth lie, shall be called overseers of the poor of the same parish: and they or the greater part of them shall take order from time to time, by and with the consent of two or more such justices of peace as is aforesaid, for setting to work of the children of all such whose parents shall not by the said churchwardens and overseers or the greater part of them be thought able to keep and maintain their children; and also for setting to work all such persons married or unmarried having no means to maintain them, [or] use no ordinary and daily trade of life to get their living by; and also to raise weekly or otherwise, by taxation of every inhabitant parson, vicar and other, and of every occupier of lands, houses, **tithes** impropriate or propriations of tithes, coal mines or saleable **underwoods**, in the said parish, in such competent sum and sums of money as they shall think fit, a convenient stock of flax, hemp, wool, thread, iron and other necessary ware and stuff to set the poor on work, and also competent sums of money for and towards the necessary relief of the lame, impotent, old, blind and such other among them being poor and not able to work, and also for the putting out of such children to be apprentices, to be gathered out of the same parish according to the ability of the same parish; and to do and execute all other things as well for the disposing of the said stock as otherwise concerning the premises as to them shall seem convenient: which said churchwardens and overseers so to be nominated, or such of them as shall not be let by sickness or other just excuse to be allowed by two such justices of peace or more as aforesaid, shall meet together at the least once every month in the church of the said parish, upon the Sunday in the afternoon after Divine Service, there to consider of some good course to be taken and of some meet order to be set down in the premises, and shall within four days after the end of their year and after other overseers nominated as aforesaid, make and yield up to such two justices of peace as is aforesaid a true and perfect account of all sums of money by them received, or rated and assessed and not received, and also of such stock as shall be in their hands or in the hands of any of the poor to work, and of all other things concerning their said office; and such sum or sums of money as shall be in their hands shall pay and deliver over to the said churchwardens and overseers newly nominated and appointed as aforesaid; . . . .

And be it further enacted that it shall be lawful for the said churchwardens and overseers, or the greater part of them, by the assent of any two justices of the peace aforesaid, to bind any such children as aforesaid to be apprentices, where they shall see convenient, till such man-child shall come to the age of four and twenty years, and such woman-child to the age of one and twenty years, or the time of her marriage; the same to be as effectual to all purposes as if such child were of full age, and by indenture of covenant bound him or herself.

And the said justices of peace or any of them to send to the house of correction or common **gaol** such as shall not employ themselves to work, being appointed thereunto as aforesaid.

Source: Bland, A.E., P.A. Brown, and R.H. Tawney, eds. *English Economic History: Select Documents.* New York: Macmillan Company, 1919, pp. 380–81.

AFTERMATH

The statute of 1601 formalized many earlier practices by creating a national system of poor relief based on the compulsory payment of a poor rate, essentially an income tax, levied in the local parish. From this beginning developed in the seventeenth and eighteenth centuries the system of workhouses that was made infamous in the writings of such Victorian authors as Charles Dickens. Workhouses were not mentioned in the Elizabethan statute, although it did call for the provision of materials to put able-bodied poor to work and the erection of housing for the disabled poor.

Workhouses, as they developed in the seventeenth century, were usually ordinary houses rented by the local parish or town government for the housing and feeding of those who were unable to support themselves. Able-bodied poor were expected to work for no wages to compensate the community for their room and board. In 1723, Parliament gave parishes the option of halting so-called "outdoor relief" (direct payment of money, food, or clothing without any requirement to enter an institution) and offering those who applied for relief only the workhouse. By the nineteenth century, the notion that workhouse life should be deliberately harsh to deter the able-bodied poor from relying upon poorhouses made conditions in some institutions truly deplorable.

ELIZABETHAN POOR LAWS

During the reign of ELIZABETH I, Parliament enacted poor laws in 1563, 1572, and 1576, but the poor law of 1598, as revised in 1601, repealed all previous statutes and established a national system of poor relief that lasted into the nineteenth century. The impetus for Tudor legislation on poor relief arose from concern that growing numbers of poor and homeless people constituted a threat to the political and social order. Beginning in 1536, Parliament passed the first of a series of statutes designed to create a national, parish-based system for helping and controlling the poor. The 1536 act dealt with begging and vagabonds by forbidding the former and dividing the latter into two classes—the sturdy and the impotent. Sturdy beggars were put to work and charged with felony if they refused. Parishes were given responsibility for care of the impotent poor, who were to receive relief from a voluntary parish collection, which was to be distributed among the local needy.

The 1598 act made parish collections for the poor compulsory. Each parish had to appoint overseers of the poor who were empowered to confiscate the goods of any parishioner refusing to contribute to the poor rates. The law defined vagrants as "masterless men," that is, those not rooted in a community and under the authority of their social superiors, and men in so-called "dangerous" professions, such as minstrels and peddlers, or men refusing to work for the wages set by statute. Vagabonds could be whipped and returned to their home parishes. Disabled poor were to be given employment funded by the poor rates. Although the poor laws alleviated some poverty, their real accomplishment was to reinforce the social status quo by encouraging deference to authority and discouraging vagabondage and disorder.

ASK YOURSELF

1. How did the framers of the 1601 Poor Law view poverty? What were their main goals in enacting the statute?
2. What distinctions does the statute seem to make regarding the poor? Were all poor perceived in the same light, or were special provisions made for different groups, such as the disabled, the elderly, the able-bodied, or children?
3. Do you think religious groups such as Roman Catholics or PURITANS may have differed with the views on poverty and how to relieve it that are embodied in the 1601 statute? If so, how and why? If not, why not?

TOPICS AND ACTIVITIES TO CONSIDER

꙾ Read the section "Of Provision Made for the Poor" in Book II of William HARRISON's *Description of England* (see also Documents 3 and 5), which can be found in the printed edition edited by Georges Edelen (1994) or online at Harrison's *Description of England*, http://www.fordham.edu/halsall/mod/1577harrison-england.html. From your reading, determine whether Harrison, an Anglican cleric, reflected in his writing the principles embodied in the 1601 statute or whether his view of the subject differed from those of the framers of the law.

꙾ Access and read one of the following online descriptions of English workhouses in the Victorian era: George Eliot's "A Village Workhouse" (1830) http://www.victorianweb.org/authors/eliot/workhouse.html; Charles Dickens' "A Walk in a Workhouse" (1850) http://www.victorianweb.org/authors/dickens/poorlaw.html; or George R. Sims' poem, "Christmas Day in the Workhouse" (1903) http://lyricsplayground.com/alpha/songs/xmas/christmasdayintheworkhouse.shtml. Or read the workhouse descriptions in Dickens' novel *Oliver Twist* (1837–1839). Although these works describe conditions as they were over 200 years after the Elizabethan period, those conditions were a direct result of the foundations for poor relief laid down by the 1601 statute. Compare what you read in these Victorian writers with the kind of poor relief envisioned by the Elizabethan law, and list reasons why you think that law led to workhouses.

Further Information

Beier, A.L. *The Problem of the Poor in Tudor and Stuart England.* London: Routledge, 1983. [Available online at http://books.google.com.]

Pound, John. *Poverty and Vagrancy in Tudor England.* London: Longman, 1971.

Slack, Paul. *The English Poor Law, 1531–1782.* Cambridge: Cambridge University Press, 1995.

———. *Poverty and Policy in Tudor and Stuart England.* San Francisco: Addison-Wesley Publishers, 1988.

Webb, John, ed. *Poor Relief in Elizabethan Ipswich.* Suffolk Records Society, vol. 9. Ipswich: Suffolk Records Society, 1966.

Web Site

Poor Law of 1601: http://www.victorianweb.org/history/poorlaw/elizpl.htm

CHURCH AND STATE

11. THE POWERS OF PARLIAMENT: SIR THOMAS SMITH'S *DE REPUBLICA ANGLORUM* (1565)

INTRODUCTION

Sir Thomas SMITH was an Elizabethan scholar and civil servant, whose many government posts included serving Elizabeth as ambassador to France and secretary of state. The most famous of his many writings is *De Republica Anglorum* (1584), which is a detailed description of the functioning of Elizabethan government and therefore of great value to modern historians. Reproduced here is a well-known passage from *De Republica Anglorum* describing the nature and powers of Parliament (see "Elizabethan Parliaments below; for more on Parliament, see also Document 13).

KEEP IN MIND AS YOU READ

1. In the Elizabethan period, many functions of government were considered outside the jurisdiction of Parliament and reserved for the Crown, including ordering the succession, conducting foreign policy, and declaring war and peace.
2. ELIZABETH I also sought to limit Parliament's involvement in the governing of the English Church and the ordering of official doctrine and practice, although many, especially PURITANS, tried to increase Parliament's role in ecclesiastical affairs.
3. When speaking of the authority of Parliament, Smith always means the King/Queen in Parliament. For Elizabethans, the monarch functioning with the consent of the community of the realm as given through Parliament was the ultimate expression of national authority.

Document: Excerpt from Sir Thomas Smith's De Republica Anglorum

The most high and absolute power of the realm of England, consists in the Parliament. For as in war where the King himself in person, the nobility, the rest of the gentility, and the **yeomanry** are, is the force and power of England: so in peace and consultation where the Prince is to give life, and the last and highest commandment, the Barony for the nobility and higher, the knights, esquires, gentlemen and commons for the lower part of the commonwealth, the bishops

> **Centuriatis comitiis/tributis:** democratic assemblies of Roman soldiers (*comitia centuriata*) and citizens (*comitia tributa*) during the Roman Republic
>
> **procuration:** the naming or appointing of another to act as one's agent or attorney
>
> **sanctum:** holy; sanctioned
>
> **tailes (tailles):** land taxes
>
> **yeomanry:** small landholders below the nobility and gentry in social rank

for the clergy be present to advertise, consult and show what is good and necessary for the commonwealth, and to consult together, and upon mature deliberation every bill or law being thrice read and disputed upon in either house, the other two parts first each a part, and after the Prince himself in presence of both the parties does consent unto and allow. That is the Prince's and whole realm's deed: whereupon justly no man can complain, but must accommodate himself to find it good and obey it.

That which is done by this consent is called firm, stable, and **sanctum**, and is taken for law. The Parliament abrogates old laws, makes new, gives orders for things past, and for things hereafter to be followed, changes rights, and possessions of private men, legitimates bastards, establishes forms of religion, alters weights and measures, gives forms of succession to the crown, defines of doubtful rights, whereof is no law already made, appoints subsidies, **tailes**, taxes, and impositions, gives most free pardons and absolutions, restores in blood and name as the highest court, condemns or absolves them whom the Prince will put to that trial: And to be short, all that ever the people of Rome might do either in **Centuriatis comitiis** or **tributis**, the same may be done by the parliament of England, which represents and has the power of the whole realm both the head and the body. For every Englishman is intended to be there present, either in person or by **procuration** and attorneys, of what preeminence, state, dignity, or quality soever he be, from the Prince (be he King or Queen) to the lowest person of England. And the consent of the Parliament is taken to be every man's consent.

Source: Smith, Sir Thomas. *De Republica Anglorum: A Discourse on the Commonwealth of England*. Edited by L. Alston. Cambridge: Cambridge University Press, 1906, pp. 48–49.

ELIZABETHAN PARLIAMENTS

Parliament is the supreme legislature of England, comprising the monarch, the House of Lords, and the House of Commons. The Elizabethan House of Lords consisted of 70 to 80 members (2 archbishops, 26 bishops, and the rest titled lay peers summoned to each session by special writ). By 1603, the House of Commons numbered 462 (90 representatives from the counties of England and Wales and 372 from the 191 parliamentary towns, with London sending 4 representatives).

In the counties, only male residents holding lands worth at least 40 shillings per year could vote, a qualification that restricted the franchise to GENTRY. In the towns, voting qualifications varied according to how each town's charter defined a voter. In many towns, the vote was narrowly restricted. According to law, town representatives were to be residents, but, with the exception of London, most Elizabethan town representatives were county gentry. Summoned and dismissed by the monarch, the Elizabethan Parliament was an irregular, occasional, and brief part of government. Elizabeth called only 10 Parliaments in 44 years. Parliament provided legislative remedies for public matters brought before it by the PRIVY COUNCIL and for private matters brought before it by petition. Parliamentary statute, passed by the Lords and Commons and approved by the monarch, was the highest law of the realm.

The Commons had the right to initiate all tax bills. Debate in the Commons was directed by the speaker, a Crown nominee elected by the House at the start of each session. To become statute, bills passed through three readings. The first reading informed members of the bill's content, the second initiated debate, and the third refined the wording of the measure. Upon receiving the assent of the monarch, a bill passed after third reading became statute.

AFTERMATH

In the seventeenth century, Parliament, in response to what was perceived by many as the tyranny of the Crown, sought to acquire new powers, including the limitation of Crown rights, control of the military, oversight of foreign policy, and greater direction of ecclesiastical matters. In the eighteenth century, the Crown's right to veto legislation lapsed, and, by the nineteenth century, Parliament had established the principle that Crown ministers should serve only with the confidence and support of Parliament. By the twentieth century, the monarch, although still the official head of state, had become merely a figurehead, and the kingdom was governed by the House of Commons, the majority party in which, as determined by regular, popular elections, governed the country.

ASK YOURSELF

1. Although Smith declared that Parliament "represents and has the power of the whole realm," he said little in this passage about how members of Parliament are selected or by whom. How were Elizabethan elections for Parliament conducted? Who could vote, and who could not? Why, despite numerous restricting on voting, do you think Smith believed the Elizabethan Parliament was fairly representative of the realm?
2. What did Smith mean when he wrote that Parliament "restores in blood"?
3. How and in what instances did Parliament function as a court of law?

TOPICS AND ACTIVITIES TO CONSIDER

- ❧ Access the Web site of the British Parliament at http://www.parliament.uk and read particularly the History and How Parliament Works sections to get an idea of key dates in parliamentary history and how Parliament functions today. Select one of the topics mentioned in either of these sections, such as elections, the Houses of Lords or Commons, the Parliament building, or the process whereby laws are enacted, and write a brief description of the topic that could serve future readers as a useful description of the way things were at the start of the twenty-first century, just as Smith's writing helps present-day readers understand the character of Elizabethan Parliaments.
- ❧ Access the Web sites of the U.S. House of Representatives at http://www.house.gov or the U.S. Senate at http://www.senate.gov, and, as in the topic above, write a description of some aspect of either body that would serve as a useful snapshoot of the present-day U.S. Congress for future readers.

Further Information

Dewar, Mary. *Sir Thomas Smith*. London: Athlone Press, 1964.

Elton, G.R. *The Parliament of England 1559–1581*. Cambridge: Cambridge University Press, 1986.

Graves, Michael A.R. *Elizabethan Parliaments 1559–1601*. London: Longman, 1987.

Hartley, T.E. *Elizabeth's Parliaments: Queen, Lords and Commons 1559–1601*. New York: St. Martin's Press, 1992.

Neale, J.E. *Elizabeth I and Her Parliaments*. 2 vols. New York: St. Martin's Press, 1958.
Snow, Vernon F., ed. *Parliament in Elizabethan England: John Hooker's Order and Usage.* New Haven, CT: Yale University Press, 1977.
Wagner, John A. *Historical Dictionary of the Elizabethan World*. Phoenix: Oryx Press, 1999.

Web Site

De Republica Anglorum: http://www.constitution.org/eng/repang.htm

12. Government Control of the Printing Press: Star Chamber Censorship Ordinances (1566, 1586) and Philip Stubbs' Comments on Censorship (1593)

INTRODUCTION

The Elizabethan government, like most European governments of the time, sought to closely control the content of all books, plays, pamphlets, and other printed materials produced in the country. In 1559, ELIZABETH I confirmed the licensing system established in the reign of her sister MARY I. Under this system, most printed materials had to be registered with the Stationers' Company, an organization of professional printers and booksellers. Any publications not so registered were unlicensed and subject to confiscation by the government (see "Stationers' Register" below).

During the course of Elizabeth's reign, particularly as religious debates grew more heated and political and war with Spain became a reality, the government expanded and elaborated the rules governing registration and censorship of printed materials. Below are excerpts from two such censorship decrees issued in 1566 and 1586 by the STAR CHAMBER, the royal EQUITY court that, under Elizabeth, focused on criminal misdemeanors and matters of public order. Also reproduced here is a brief comment from the Elizabethan moralist Philip STUBBS, who, in his 1593 publication, *A Motive to Good Works*, decried the quick and easy licensing of works he found scurrilous and immoral, such as Robert GREENE's cony-catching pamphlets (see Document 7).

KEEP IN MIND AS YOU READ

1. By making possible for the first time the wide and rapid dissemination of dissenting opinion on matters both political and religious, the invention of the printing press in the fifteenth century confronted European governments with a new and perplexing problem. The need to address this problem led to the extensive use of censorship.
2. Despite these censorship regulations, unlicensed presses were common and hard to control, and enforcement of censorship rules, as modern research has shown, was neither regularly pursued nor consistently applied.
3. There was no concept of copyright, such as exists today, in Elizabethan England. Printers who were members of the Stationers' Company purchased works from authors and thus acquired a perpetual monopoly on the printing of those works. Authors could not become Company members, so they could not legally self-publish

their own works. Nor could they receive any royalties on a work of theirs that sold well because, once printed, that work was owned by the printer.

Document 1: Excerpts from the Star Chamber Censorship Ordinance of 1566

I. That no person should print . . . or bring . . . into the realm printed any book against the force and meaning of any ordinance . . . contained in any the statutes or laws of this realm or in any injunctions, letters patents or ordinances set forth by the Queen's authority.

II. That whosoever should offend against the said ordinances should forfeit all such books, and from thenceforth should never exercise . . . the feat of printing; and to sustain three months' imprisonment.

III. That no person should sell, bind or sew any such books, upon pain to forfeit all such books and for every book 20*s*.

IV. That all books so forfeited should be brought into Stationers' Hall, . . . and all the books so to be forfeited to be destroyed or made waste paper'

V. That it should be lawful for the wardens of the [Stationers'] Company . . . to make search in all workhouses, shops . . . and other places of printers, booksellers and such as bring books into the realm . . .; and all books to be found against the said ordinances to seize and carry to the Hall to the uses above said and to bring the persons offending before the Queen's Commissioners in causes ecclesiastical.

VI. Every stationer, printer, bookseller . . . should . . . enter into several **recognizances** of reasonable sums of money to her Majesty . . . that he should truly observe all the said ordinances . . . .

Upon the consideration before expressed and upon the motion of the Commissioners, we of the Privy Council have agreed this to be observed and kept . . . . At the Star-Chamber the 29th of June, 1566.

Source: Prothero, G.W., ed. *Select Statutes and Other Constitutional Documents Illustrative of the Reigns of Elizabeth and James I.* Oxford: Clarendon Press, 1894, pp. 168–69.

> **recognizance:** a legal obligation entered into before a court of record or public magistrate requiring the performance of a certain act (e.g., to observe the censorship ordinances) usually under penalty of forfeiture of a sum of money

Document 2: Star Chamber Censorship Ordinance of 1586

Whereas sundry decrees and ordinances have upon grave advice and deliberation been heretofore made and published for the repressing of such great enormities and abuses as of late more than in time past have been commonly used and practiced by **divers** contentious and disorderly persons professing the art or **mystery** of printing or selling of books, and yet notwithstanding the said abuses and enormities are nothing abated, but, as it is found by experience, do rather daily more and more increase to the willful and manifest breach and contempt of the said ordinances and decrees, to the great displeasure and offence of the Queen's most excellent Majesty, by reason whereof sundry intolerable offences, troubles and disturbances have happened as well in the church as in the civil government of the state and commonwealth of this realm, which seem to have grown because the pains and penalties contained and set down in the said ordinances and decrees have been too light and small for the correction and punishment of so grievous and heinous offences, and so the offenders and malefactors in that behalf have not been so severely punished as the quality of their offences have deserved. Her Majesty therefore, of her most godly and gracious disposition, being careful that speedy and due reformation be had of the abuses and disorders aforesaid, and that all persons using or professing the art, trade or mystery of printing or selling of books should from henceforth be ruled and directed therein by some certain and known rules and ordinances, which should be inviolably kept and observed and the breakers and offenders of the same to be severely and sharply punished and corrected, has straitly charged and required the most reverend [father] in God the Archbishop of Canterbury and the right honorable the lords and others of her Highness' Privy Council to see her Majesty's said most gracious and godly intention and purpose to be duly and effectually executed and accomplished.

Whereupon the said most reverend father and the whole presence sitting in this honorable court, this 23rd day of June in the 28th year of her Majesty's reign, upon grave and mature deliberation, have ordained and decreed that the ordinances, constitutions, rules and articles hereafter following from henceforth by all persons be duly and inviolably kept and observed, according to the tenor, purport and true intent and meaning of the same, as they tender her Majesty's high displeasure and as they will answer to the contrary at their uttermost peril: viz.

1. **Imprimis**, That every printer and other person . . . which at this time present hath erected or set up or hereafter shall erect . . . any printing-press, roll or other instrument for imprinting of books, charts, ballads, portraitures, paper called damask paper, or any such matter or things whatsoever, shall bring a true note or certificate of the said presses [&c.] already erected, within ten days next coming after the publication hereof, and of the said presses [&c.] hereafter to be erected . . . within ten days next after the erecting thereof, unto the Master and Wardens of the Company of Stationers of the City of London for the time being, upon pain that every person failing or offending herein shall have all the said presses [&c.] utterly defaced and made unserviceable for imprinting forever, and shall also suffer twelve months' imprisonment without bail or **mainprise**.

2. Item, That no printer of books nor any other person shall set up any press . . . but only in the city of London or in the suburbs thereof, and except one press in the University of Cambridge and one other press in the University of Oxford, and no more; and that no person shall hereafter erect in any secret or obscure corner or place any such press, but that the same shall be in such open place or places in his or their house or houses as the Wardens of the said Company of the Stationers may from time to time have ready access unto, to search for and view the same; and that no printer or other person shall at any time hereafter withstand or make resistance to any such view or search, nor deny or keep secret any such press: upon pain that every person offending in anything contrary to this article shall have all the said presses defaced and made unserviceable for

imprinting forever, and shall also suffer imprisonment one whole year, and be disabled forever to keep any printing-press or to be master of any printing-house or to have any benefit thereby other than only work as a **journeyman** for wages.

3. Item, That no printer nor other person that hath set up any press within six months last past shall hereafter use the same, nor any person shall hereafter erect any press till the excessive multitude of printers . . . be abated . . . or otherwise brought to so small a number of masters or owners of printing houses, being of ability and good behavior, as the Archbishop of Canterbury and Bishop of London for the time being shall thereupon think it requisite and convenient, for the good service of the realm, to have some more presses erected and set up. And that when and as often as the said archbishop and bishop shall so think it requisite and convenient and shall signify the same to the said Master and Wardens of the said Company of Stationers . . ., the said Master and Wardens shall . . . call the assistants of the said company before them and shall make choice of one or more . . . of such persons being free stationers as . . . shall be thought . . . meet to have the charge of a press, and . . . shall present [them] before the High Commissioners in causes ecclesiastical, or six or more of them, whereof the Archbishop of Canterbury and Bishop of London to be one, to admit every such person so chosen and presented to be master of a press . . . upon pain [as in previous §]. Provided that this article shall not extend to the office of the Queen's Majesty's printer for the service of the realm, but that the said office and officer shall be at the pleasure and disposition of her Majesty . . . .

4. Item, That no person shall imprint . . . any book . . . or thing whatsoever, except the same book . . . or any other thing . . . shall be allowed . . . according to the order appointed by the Queen's Majesty's injunctions', and be first seen and perused by the Archbishop of Canterbury and Bishop of London for the time being, or one of them (the Queen's Majesty's printer . . . and such as are privileged to print the books of the common law of this realm, for such of the same books as shall be allowed of by the two Chief Justices and Chief Baron for the time being or any two of them, only excepted), nor shall imprint any book against the form or meaning of any restraint or ordinance contained in any statute or laws of this realm . . . .

6. That it shall be lawful for the Wardens of the said company . . . to make search . . ., and all books contrary to the intent of these ordinances to stay and take to her Majesty's use, . . . and the parties offending . . . to bring before the said High Commissioners or some three or more of them, whereof the said Archbishop of Canterbury or Bishop of London for the time being to be one . . . .

8. Item, That for the avoiding of the excessive number of printers within this realm, it shall not be lawful for any person being free of the Company of Stationers, or using the trade or mystery of printing, bookselling or bookbinding, to have at one time any greater number of apprentices than shall be hereafter expressed . . . Provided always that this ordinance shall not extend to the Queen's Majesty's printer . . ., but that he have liberty to keep apprentices to the number of six at any one time.

---

divers: various

Imprimis: first

journeyman: someone who has learned a trade or craft but who continues to work for another rather than setting up his own shop

mainprise: a procedure at law whereby someone charged with a crime is allowed to go free if he finds persons, called mainpernors, who will stand surety for his appearance in court

mystery: an occupation or profession with specialized or secret practices and procedures

9. Item, That none of the printers in Cambridge or Oxford for the time being shall be suffered to have any more apprentices than one at one time at the most: but it shall be lawful for the said printers and their successors to use the help of any journeyman being freeman of the city of London without contradiction . . . .

Source: Prothero, G.W., ed. *Select Statutes and Other Constitutional Documents Illustrative of the Reigns of Elizabeth and James I.* Oxford: Clarendon Press, 1894, pp. 169–72.

Document 3: Excerpt from Philip Stubbs' A Motive to Good Works

I cannot but lament the corruption of our time for (alas) now-a-days it is grown to be a hard matter to get a good book licensed without **staying**, peradventure, a quarter of a year for it; yea, sometimes two or three years before he can have it allowed, and in the end happly rejected too. So that that which many a good man has . . . travailed long in . . . shall . . . never see the light, while . . . other books, full of all filthiness, scurrility, bawdry, dissoluteness, **cosinage, cony catching** and the like . . . are either quickly licensed or at least easily tolerated.

> **cony catching:** confidence games; scams
> **cosinage:** trickery; deceit
> **staying:** waiting

Source: Raleigh, Walter Alexander, Sidney Lee, C.T. Onions, eds. *Shakespeare's England: An Account of the Life and Manners of His Age.* vol. 2. Oxford: Clarendon Press, 1917, p. 222.

STATIONERS' REGISTER

Every book printed in Elizabethan England, except for those printed on the presses of the universities at Oxford and Cambridge, had to be registered with the Stationers' Company, a corporate body to which all professional printers and booksellers belonged. Mary I issued the Stationers' Company charter in 1557, and Elizabeth confirmed it in 1559. By entering books or plays in the Stationers' Register, printers established copyright to works they had purchased and forestalled the production of unauthorized editions. When used in conjunction with other kinds of internal and external evidence, the date of registration can today help set the chronology for the works of important Elizabethan poets and playwrights, especially William SHAKESPEARE.

Besides establishing copyright, the Stationers' Company and its register allowed the government to restrict publishing it found to be subversive or inflammatory in either politics or religion and to create lucrative publishing monopolies (see "Monopolies," Document 39). For instance, the Queen sold Richard Tottel a monopoly on the printing of law books and William Seres a patent on the printing of psalters and prayerbooks. Because these kinds of monopolies left many smaller printers virtually without work, the Company had to root out the inevitable proliferation of unauthorized editions that followed upon the granting of a publishing monopoly. In 1586, the PRIVY COUNCIL, seeking to suppress the activities of unlicensed Catholic and PURITAN presses, also empowered the Stationers' Company to inspect all printing sites and to confiscate all illegal publications and equipment. The fact that almost one-third of the surviving works for the Elizabethan period were never entered in the Stationers' Register suggests the difficulty of the Company's efforts in this regard.

AFTERMATH

Printing was a vibrant and growing trade in Elizabethan England, but it declined in the seventeenth century as increasing religious and political conflict led to harsher government restrictions. Also, the government granted more monopolies on certain types of printing to particular printers, thus choking off all competition in the printing trade. Finally, traditional English mistrust of foreigners prevented important technical innovations made by European printers from entering England, thus causing English printers to fall behind their continental counterparts in terms of skill and equipment.

With the advent of the English Civil War in the 1640s, Parliament rescinded the privileges of the Stationers' Company and abolished Star Chamber, acts that led in the next two decades to an explosion of new publications in all forms, particularly in London. Although some press censorship was restored by the parliamentary regimes of the 1640s and 1650s, rival political and religious factions produced numerous tracts offering their points of view, and so-called disorderly printing flourished. In 1662, after the restoration of the monarchy, press censorship became more effective, especially in terms of religious materials. However, after the Glorious Revolution of 1689, royal control of the press declined, and, in 1709, Parliament passed the groundbreaking Copyright Act, which ended the control of the Stationers' Company by vesting authors, rather than printers, with a monopoly on the reproduction of their works.

ASK YOURSELF

1. Access the U.S. Constitution at http://www.usconstitution.net/const.html#Am1, and read the very brief First Amendment to the Constitution regarding freedom of speech. What impact do you think the history and tradition of Crown censorship in England had on the United States and on the writing of this Amendment?
2. What topics, issues, and controversies have caused censorship debates in the United States in the last 50 years? What kinds of materials have people tried to ban from their libraries or communities, and why?

TOPICS AND ACTIVITIES TO CONSIDER

- Read the various definitions of censorship provided by PBS at http://www.pbs.org/wgbh/cultureshock/whodecides/definitions.html. Then draft your own definition of censorship.
- Access a copy of the 1709 Copyright Act at http://en.wikisource.org/wiki/Copyright_Act_1709. Write an essay analyzing this statute and how it changed perceptions of who controlled written material.

Further Information

Auchter, Dorothy. *Dictionary of Literary and Dramatic Censorship in Tudor and Stuart England*. Westport, CT: Greenwood Press, 2001.

Clegg, Cyndia Susan. *Press Censorship in Elizabethan England*. Cambridge: Cambridge University Press, 1997. [Available online at http://books.google.com.]

Rostenberg, Leona. The *Minority Press and the English Crown: A Study in Repression, 1558–1625*. Nieuwkoop, Netherlands: B. De Graaf, 1971.

13. WHO MAY SUMMON PARLIAMENT AND WHY: JOHN HOOKER'S *ORDER AND USAGE* (1571)

INTRODUCTION

John HOOKER (see also Document 1), chamberlain of the city of Exeter, sat in the Irish Parliament of 1569 and was member for Exeter in the English Parliament of 1571. As a result of these experiences, Hooker wrote *The Order and Usage of the Keeping of a Parliament in England* (1571) as a manual explaining how a Parliament was conducted in Elizabethan England. Reproduced here is an excerpt from *The Order and Usage* describing how and for what reasons a Parliament should be summoned into being. Accurate and detailed, Hooker's descriptive analysis of Elizabethan Parliaments is of immense value to modern historians (see "Elizabethan Parliaments," Document 11).

KEEP IN MIND AS YOU READ

1. Although Sir Thomas SMITH provided an extensive list of parliamentary powers in Document 11, that body's main functions involved the enactment of legislation and the approval of taxation. If the Crown required neither new laws nor new taxes, Parliament need not be summoned and often was not for long periods of time. As Hooker clearly indicated, the Crown alone decided when Parliament was to be called or dismissed.

2. Throughout *The Order and Usage*, Hooker focused more heavily on the House of Commons than on either the House of Lords or the Convocation of bishops and clerics, which usually met at the same time as Parliament. This emphasis reflected a growing belief among the GENTRY and the urban middle classes, the groups who sat in the Commons, that lawmaking was the business of all the politically aware classes of the realm, and not simply a prerogative of the Crown and nobility.

Document: Excerpt from John Hooker's The Order and Usage of the Keeping of a Parliament in England

By whom and for what cause a Parliament ought to be summoned and called

> **aid:** a grant of taxation by Parliament to the monarch for some extraordinary purpose
>
> **estates:** the great social and political classes of the realm, such as the nobility, clergy, and commons

The King who is God's anointed being the head and chief of the whole Realm and upon whom the government and estates thereof do wholly and only depend: has the power and authority to call and assemble his Parliament, and therein to seek & ask the advice, counsel and assistance of his whole Realm, and without this his authority: no parliament can properly be summoned or assembled. And the King having this authority, ought not to summon his Parliament: but for weighty & great causes, and in which he of necessity ought to have the advice and counsel of all the **estates** of his Realm, which be these and such like as follows.

First for Religion, for, for as much as by the Laws of God and this Realm, the King next and immediately under God is his deputy and Vicar on Earth, and the chiefest ruler within his Realms and dominions: his office, function and duty is, above all things to seek and see that God be honored in true Religion and Virtue, and that he and his people do both in profession and life live according to the same.

Also that all Idolatries, false Religions, heresies, schisms, errors, superstitions, and whatsoever is contrary to true Religion, all disorders and abuses, either among the Clergy or Laity, be reformed, ordered and redressed.

Also the assurance of the King and Queen's persons, and of their Children their advancement & preferment in marriages, the establishing of succession, the suppression of Traitors, the avoiding or eschewing of wars, the attempting or moving of wars, the subduing of Rebels, and pacifying of civil wars and commotions, the levying or having any **aid** or Subsidy for the preservation of the King and public estate.

Also the making and establishing of good and wholesome Laws, or the repealing or debarring of former Laws, as whose execution may be hurtful or prejudicial to the estates of the Prince or commonwealth. For these and such like causes being of great weight, charge and importance: the King (by the advice of his council) may call & summon his high Court of Parliament, and by the authority thereof establish and order such good Laws and orders as then shall be thought most expedient and necessary.

Source: Snow, Vernon F., ed. *Parliament in Elizabethan England: John Hooker's Order and Usage.* New Haven, CT: Yale University Press, 1977, pp. 145–47.

AFTERMATH

In the sixteenth century, thanks in part to its role in making the English Reformation (see "English Reformation," Document 14, and "Royal Supremacy" below), Parliament was firmly established as the supreme legislative body of the realm. All its enactments were held as binding. However, only in the seventeenth century, in response to what was perceived as the tyranny of the Stuart kings, did Parliament begin to demand to be a regular part of government that should meet by law at regular intervals, and not simply at the will of the monarch. Parliament had to fight and win a war with the King in the 1640s; govern the country, in various forms, without a monarch in the 1650s; and replace one monarch with another in 1688–1689 before the principle of regular Parliaments was firmly established. In 1694, the Triennial Act required a meeting of Parliament every three years and stipulated that no Parliament could legally run for more than three years. Thus, by the eighteenth century, Parliament became increasingly independent from royal control and a regular and indispensible part of government.

ROYAL SUPREMACY

As John Hooker observed, the monarch was God's "deputy and Vicar on Earth," an idea that formed the basis of the royal supremacy, the right of the English monarch to control the English Church. Prior to the 1530s, control over the English Church was shared between the Crown and the papacy, but HENRY VIII, during the struggle to annul his first marriage, forced the English Church to accept him as its supreme head. Because the king's headship over the Church was seen as coming from God, not Parliament, the 1534 Act of Supremacy only acknowledged the royal right to control the Church and gave the King authority to punish anyone who denied that right.

In 1559, when Elizabeth sought to reestablish the royal supremacy, which her sister MARY I had abolished, she faced difficulties imposed by her gender and by the growth of English Protestantism. That a woman should govern the state, let alone the Church, was a difficult proposition for most Englishmen. That any layperson, male or female, should hold absolute sway over ecclesiastical matters was a proposition increasingly questioned not only by Catholics, but also by radical Protestants. To meet these objections, Parliament gave the Queen the title of supreme governor rather than her father's more exalted title of supreme head. Also, by stating that the right to govern the Church was given to the Crown by Parliament, the act associated Parliament with the Queen in the leadership of the Church and gave Parliament greater authority over Church doctrine and administration.

ASK YOURSELF

1. How does what Hooker wrote about Parliament compare to what Sir Thomas Smith wrote about Parliament in *De Republica Anglorum* (see Document 11). If you wish to read more of Smith's work, you can access it at http://www.constitution .org/eng/repang.htm.

2. Considering the reasons for summoning a Parliament listed by Hooker, why might some people prefer to see fewer sessions of Parliament? Who might these people be? Why might other people prefer more frequent sessions of Parliament? Who might these people be?

TOPICS AND ACTIVITIES TO CONSIDER

- ➤ Leopold von Wedel wrote an account in his diary of ELIZABETH I's formal opening of the Fifth Parliament of her reign in 1584. Access and read this account at http://www.aasd.k12.wi.us/VOS/Textbook_Links/SS/7th/docs/ 091.pdf. Then search the Internet for stories, pictures, and videos of recent openings of Parliament conducted by the current monarch of England, Queen Elizabeth II. Write an essay describing how the opening of the British Parliament, as conducted at the start of the twenty-first century, compares and contrasts to the opening of a late sixteenth-century Parliament.

- ➤ Using the Internet and reference books such as the *Historical Dictionary of the Elizabeth World*, listed below, make a list of all the Elizabethan Parliaments and the dates of their sessions. From your list, determine the average length of sessions, the average amount of time between sessions, and whether there was any change in the length and frequency of parliamentary sessions between the first and second halves of Elizabeth's reign.

Further Information

Elton, G.R. *The Parliament of England 1559–1581*. Cambridge: Cambridge University Press, 1986.

Graves, Michael A.R. *Elizabethan Parliaments 1559–1601*. London: Longman, 1987.

Hartley, T.E. *Elizabeth's Parliaments: Queen, Lords and Commons 1559–1601*. New York: St. Martin's Press, 1992.

Neale, J.E. *Elizabeth I and Her Parliaments*. 2 vols. New York: St. Martin's Press, 1958.

Snow, Vernon F., ed. *Parliament in Elizabethan England: John Hooker's Order and Usage*. New Haven, CT: Yale University Press, 1977.

Wagner, John A. *The Devon Gentleman: The Life of Sir Peter Carew*. Hull: University of Hull Press, 1998.

———. *Historical Dictionary of the Elizabethan World*. Phoenix: Oryx Press, 1999.

14. Protecting Queen and Realm from Catholic Plots: Letter of the Bishop of London to Lord Burghley (1572)

INTRODUCTION

On August 24, 1572, the feast of St. Bartholomew, King CHARLES IX of France and his mother Queen CATHERINE DE MEDICI ordered the murder of leading HUGUENOTS (i.e., French Protestants) and then assembled in Paris for a royal wedding. As news of the murders spread, heavily Catholic Paris exploded in anti-Protestant violence that left thousands more dead and even threatened the life of ELIZABETH's ambassador to France, Sir Francis WALSINGHAM. It is to this horrific event, which became known as the ST. BARTHOLOMEW'S DAY MASSACRE, that Edwin SANDYS, bishop of London (see also Document 15), was reacting when he wrote the following letter.

Fearing that outraged young preachers might go too far in their denunciations of the French king, who was still technically Elizabeth's ally, the bishop was anxious for guidance from William CECIL, Lord Burghley, Elizabeth's chief minister. How, the bishop needed to know, did the Queen wish her clergy to respond to the massacre? The bishop, fearing that Catholic violence might soon threaten England, also added an unsolicited addendum—a list of nine recommended actions for securing the safety of both Queen and realm.

KEEP IN MIND AS YOU READ

1. As far as historians can determine, Bishop Sandys' list contains the first direct call for the execution of MARY, Queen of Scots, a proposal that was to become increasingly common over the next 15 years.
2. The Queen was away from the capital on summer progress (see "Royal Progresses," Document 31) when news of the massacre reached England, hence the bishop's concern that Elizabeth hurry back to the safety of London.
3. Because of the season and the Queen's absence from London, a series of young, zealous, but politically inexperienced clergymen had been appointed to preach at Paul's Cross, the public pulpit outside St. Paul's Cathedral in London. Because government policies and positions, especially on religion, were often unveiled in Paul's Cross sermons, Sandys was concerned that no preacher say anything that might be misconstrued as the Queen's official reaction to events in France.

4. In the last half of the sixteenth century, France suffered a devastating series of religious wars as a weakened monarchy, spurred on by a conservative Catholic party backed by Spain, sought to suppress the growing Huguenot minority. These internal upheavals left France unable to play a significant role in European affairs and made Elizabethan England the main counterbalance to the growing power of Catholic Spain.

Document: Letter of Edwin Sandys, Bishop of London, to William Cecil, Lord Burghley (5 September 1572)

These evil times trouble all good men's heads, and make their hearts ache, fearing that this barbarous treachery will not cease in France, but will reach over unto us. Neither fear we the mangling of our body, but we sore dread the hurt of our head, for therein consists our life and safety. We shall dutifully pray, give you good advice, and God, I trust, will deliver us out of the mouth of the roaring lion. The citizens of London in these dangerous days had need prudently to be dealt withal; the preachers appointed for the cross in this vacation are but young men, unskillful in matters political, yet so carried with zeal, that they will enter into them and pour forth their opinions. If the league stands firm between her Majesty and the French king, (as I suppose it does,) they may perhaps, being not directed, utter speech to the breech thereof; how that will be liked of I doubt. If I may receive from your Lordship some direction or advice herein, I will not fail to direct them so well as I can. The Dean of Paul's and I will first occupy the place, giving example how others may follow.

Sundry have required a public fast and prayer to be had, for the confounding of these and other cruel enemies of God's gospel, but this I will not consent unto, without warrant from her Majesty.

Thus am I bold to unfold a piece of my mind on the sudden, and to make you partaker of my simple cogitations, knowing that according to your old wont, you will take the same in good part. Hasten her Majesty homewards, her safe return to London will comfort many hearts oppressed with fear. God preserve you, and direct you with his spirit to counsel to his glory.

In haste, from my house at Fulham, this 5th of September, 1572.

Your Lordship's humble at commandment,

Ed. London.

[Enclosure]

The safety of our Queen and Realm, if God will.

1. Forthwith to cut off the Scottish Queen's head: *ipsa est nostril fundi calamitas.* [she herself is our utter calamity]

2. To remove from our Queen **papists**, and such as by private persuasion overthrow good counsel.

> **papists:** Roman Catholics
> **Popish:** Catholic

3. The Queen's Majesty to be guarded strongly with Protestants, and others to be removed.

4. Order must be taken for the safekeeping of the Tower, and for good order to be had in London; for strengthening of the city, and that they receive no Papists of strength to sojourn there this winter.

5. A firm league to be made with the young Scottish King, and the Protestants there.

6. A league to be made with the Princes Protestants of Germany, offensive and defensive.

7. The chief Papists of this realm are to be shut up in the Tower, and the **Popish** old Bishops to be returned thither.

8. The gospel earnestly to be promoted, and the church not burdened with unnecessary ceremonies.

9. The Protestants, which only are faithful subjects, are to be comforted, preferred, and placed in authority. The papists to be displaced.

These put in execution would turn to God's glory, the safety of the Queen's Majesty, and make the realm flourish and stand.

Source: Wright, Thomas, ed. *Queen Elizabeth and Her Times: A Series of Original Letters.* Vol. 1. London: Henry Colburn, Publisher, 1838, pp. 438–39.

ENGLISH REFORMATION

The English Reformation began in the 1530s as a political act of the Crown rather than as a popular movement of the people. Unable to obtain from the pope an annulment of his marriage, HENRY VIII used Parliament to end papal authority in England and make himself supreme head of the English Church (see "Royal Supremacy," Document 13). Besides permitting his annulment, the break with Rome allowed Henry to abolish the monasteries and seize their property for himself and his supporters. However, beyond altering the governance and economic position of the Church, Henry made few doctrinal changes. In the 1540s, English Protestants were few, but support for the pope was slight, anticlericalism was strong, and resistance to royal policies was negligible.

A truly Protestant Church appeared during the reign of EDWARD VI when Parliament abolished the mass, permitted the marriage of clergy, and seized chalices and other valuable religious paraphernalia, which was no longer needed for the new service. Worship services were conducted in English according to the BOOK OF COMMON PRAYER, the 1552 version of which was based squarely on the doctrines of Calvinism. However, upon Edward's death in 1553, his half-sister MARY I used Parliament to restore papal Catholicism and sought to eradicate heresy through the unpopular policy of burning Protestants.

At Elizabeth's accession in 1558, a majority of English people probably tended toward Catholicism, though few opposed the new Queen's decision to restore Protestantism. The Anglican Settlement of 1559 made Elizabeth supreme governor of the church, restored the prayer book, and based Anglican Church doctrine on CALVINIST principles. Despite increasing opposition from Puritans, those within the Church seeking more radical reform, and a minority that continued to adhere to papal Catholicism, Elizabeth stoutly maintained her church, and, by 1603, it claimed the allegiance of the majority of her people.

AFTERMATH

Although Bishop Sandys, like most Protestants in Europe, was horrified by the massacre, much of Catholic Europe reacted very differently to the event. Pope GREGORY XIII ordered the singing of a *Te Deum* (a hymn of praise to God) and commissioned the striking of a gold medal that showed an angel with a cross and sword standing over the bodies of slain Protestants. (View the medal at http://www.answers.com/topic/st-bartholomew-s-day-massacre.) King PHILIP II of Spain called the massacre "one of the greatest joys of my life," and the French Catholic poet Jean-Antoine de Baïf wrote a sonnet praising the murders.

More moderate Catholics, such as the Holy Roman Emperor Maximilian II, who described the massacre as "shameful," were shocked and began to work for accommodation with Protestants. In England, Elizabeth dressed her entire court in mourning and listened in stern silence to the French ambassador's attempt to explain the event. Huguenot refugees, who flooded into London and southeastern England after 1572, spread stories of the massacre throughout England. One such account later became the basis of playwright Christopher MARLOWE's anti-Catholic and anti-French play, *The Massacre at Paris*.

ASK YOURSELF

1. How do you think English Catholics reacted to news of the St. Bartholomew's Day Massacre? Why might they have reacted so?
2. Who do you think Sandys saw as the chief threat to the Queen and country—foreign Catholic rulers, such as the kings of Spain and France, or English Roman Catholics living within the realm? What steps does the bishop propose for dealing with both groups?
3. Why do you think the bishop is so hesitant to take action without direct instructions from either the Queen or Burghley?

TOPICS AND ACTIVITIES TO CONSIDER

- Access and read De Thau's eyewitness account of the events that initiated the St. Bartholomew's Day Massacre at http://www.fordham.edu/halsall/mod/1572stbarts.html. Then view the famous painting of the massacre by another reputed eyewitness, François Dubois, at http://www.folger.edu/imgdtl.cfm?imageid=1068&cid=1624massacre. By analyzing these, can you tell whether De Thau and Dubois were sympathetic to the Huguenot or the Catholic cause? List reasons to support your opinion.
- Put yourself in the place of an English minister of state in August 1572 when news of the massacre arrived. Like Bishop Sandys, draft a list of recommended actions for the Queen to take to secure herself and the realm from the threat of Catholic violence and to secure the Catholic minority in the country from the threat of English Protestant reprisals.

Further Information

Beckingsale, B.W. *Burghley, Tudor Statesman*. New York: St. Martin's Press, 1967.

Bossy, John. *The English Catholic Community 1570–1850*. New York: Oxford University Press, 1976.

Gerard, John. *The Autobiography of a Hunted Priest.* Translated from Latin by Philip Caraman. New York: Pellegrini and Cudahy, 1952.

Houliston, Victor. *Catholic Resistance in Elizabethan England: Robert Person's Jesuit Polemic, 1580–1610.* Farnham, Surrey: Ashgate, 2007.

Kingdon, Robert McCune. *Myths about the St. Bartholomew's Day Massacres, 1572–1576.* Cambridge, MA: Harvard University Press, 1988.

Lunn, David. *The Catholic Elizabethans.* Bath: Downside Abbey, 1998.

Morey, Adrian. *The Catholic Subjects of Elizabeth I.* Totowa, NJ: Rowman and Littlefield, 1978.

Nogueres, Henri. *The Massacre of Saint Bartholomew.* New York: Macmillan, 1962.

Pritchard, Arnold. *Catholic Loyalism in Elizabethan England.* Chapel Hill: University of North Carolina Press, 1979.

Read, Conyers. *Lord Burghley and Queen Elizabeth.* New York: Alfred A. Knopf, 1960.

———. *Mr. Secretary Cecil and Queen Elizabeth.* London: Jonathan Cape, 1965.

Sutherland, N.M. *The Massacre of St. Bartholomew and the European Conflict, 1559–1572.* London: Macmillan, 1973.

Web Site

Elizabethan Catholics by J.P. Sommerville: http://history.wisc.edu/sommerville/361/361-18.htm.

15. An Illegal Celebration of the Catholic Mass: Letters from the Bishop of London to Lord Burghley and the Earl of Leicester (1573)

INTRODUCTION

Celebration of the Catholic Mass had been outlawed in England since 1559, and Church authorities, such as Bishop Edwin SANDYS of London, sought to suppress illegal Catholic rites in their dioceses. This was particularly true following the SAINT BARTHOLOMEW'S DAY MASSACRE in France (see Document 14) in 1572 when fear of Catholic intrigues escalated in England. In the following two letters, one to William CECIL, Lord Burghley, the Queen's chief minister, and the other to Robert DUDLEY, Earl of Leicester, the Queen's favorite, Sandys described how his officers, apparently on Burghley's orders, invaded the London house of the Portuguese ambassador Signor Giraldi (anglicized as "Francis Gerald" in the letter) and broke up the secret Catholic services that had regularly occurred there.

KEEP IN MIND AS YOU READ

1. Sandys was appointed to the important bishopric of London on the strength of his credentials as a strong Protestant reformer. Perhaps by way of justifying his selection, he frequently ordered raids on London homes suspected of housing Catholic priests or services.

2. The number of English subjects arrested in Sandys' periodic raids (45 persons were arrested in one raid alone in April 1574) indicates how many Roman Catholics still lived in England. The fact that they were willing to risk arrest and imprisonment by attending secret Catholic services also indicates the strength of their commitment to their faith.

3. The residences of ambassadors from Catholic states had long been a favorite resort for English Catholics seeking to attend the services of their Church. Catholic ambassadors were reluctantly allowed to hold Mass privately in their homes, but they could not permit English subjects to attend those services, although, as is evident from Sandys' letters, many secretly did so. Indeed, the recorder of London complained in 1576 that as many as 200 English Catholics could be found at Mass in the Portuguese ambassador's house on major holy days. The government was thus always suspicious of the activities of resident Catholic ambassadors, but had

to proceed against them carefully so as not to offend the Catholic ruler who had sent them.

Document 1: Letter of Edwin Sandys, Bishop of London, to William Cecil, Lord Burghley (2 March 1573)

Your Lordship's letters found me at Fulham. The intolerable business wherewith I was burdened at London made me fly hither . . . that I may have leisure to pry into my book for four or five days. I leant that the Mayor of London has fully advertised your Lordship touching our dealings with this **Portingal**, who of too much boldness and without any color of authority, has suffered **massmongers** of long time in his house, to the great derogation of God's glory, the great offense of the godly and religious, and contrary to the laws of this realm. I, understanding of it, with my associate in commission, required the Sheriff of London, Mr. Pipe, to apprehend such as he should find there committing idolatry. Sundry he found there ready to worship the calf; only he apprehended four students at law, freshmen the most of them, I suppose. These I committed to the **Flete**, until your further pleasure be known. Francis Gerald, the Portingale, offered to shoot dogs, to smite with his dagger, and to kill, in his rage.

> **Flete:** Fleet Prison, a notorious London prison on the Fleet River that was used to incarcerate prisoners from the 1190s to the 1840s
>
> **massmongers:** a pejorative term for persons who conduct or support the holding of a Catholic Mass
>
> **Portingal (Portingale):** Portuguese
>
> **secundum virtutes:** according to your will or order

There was found the altar prepared, the chalice, and their bread god; and in the house, as I hear, a great number of Englishmen hid, as minded to hear mass. Because the Sheriff had neither apprehended the Portingale, neither the mass priest, I gave commission to the Queen's messenger Noriss, to apprehend them both, but the messenger returned to me, signifying that the Portingale is at the court to complain; which to be true I understand by your Lordship's letters. Truly, my Lord, such an example is not to be suffered, God will be mightily angry with it, it is too offensive; if her Majesty should grant it or tolerate it, she can never answer God for it. God's cause must be carefully considered of . . . .

God will that his ministers purge the church of idolatry and superstitions; to wink at it is to be partaker of it. You that well serve God, to see that idolater and godless man sincerely punished, if you will let him over to me, and give me authority, I will had him *secundum virtutes*. Your order I look for, and that I will see executed so far as my power will reach, upon the receipt of the Queen's letter. This much I thought my duty to write. God preserve your Lordship, and direct all your doings to his glory.

Scribbled at Fulham in haste, this March 2, 1572.

Your servant at commandment,

Ed. London.

Source: Wright, Thomas, ed. *Queen Elizabeth and Her Times: A Series of Original Letters.* vol. 1. London: Henry Colburn, Publisher, 1838, pp. 466–68.

Document 2: Letter of Edwin Sandys, Bishop of London to Robert Dudley, Earl of Leicester (4 March 1573)

. . . The **Portingale** has complained at the court as if he should have been evil used; no, My Lord, he has been evil suffered . . . . This idolatrous proud Portingale has daily, Sundays and holydays, had Mass in his house this twelvemonth, as I am credibly informed, whereunto has resorted from time to time twenty at the least of her Majesty's subjects . . . . This wicked blasphemy, this vile idolatry, her Majesty in conscience may not suffer: to suffer it were to be partaker of it . . . . The Sheriff apprehended a few of the simple sort, but he suffered the author of this evil to escape.

> **Portingale:** Portuguese

Source: Birt, Henry Norbert. *The Elizabethan Religious Settlement: A Study of Contemporary Documents.* London: George Bell and Sons, 1907, p. 461..

AFTERMATH

Sandys' raid on the Portuguese ambassador's residence led to the arrest of several individuals, who were committed to the Fleet Prison, but the ambassador himself repaired to the court and loudly complained to the Queen of what he considered an outrageous invasion. To Sandys' disgust, nothing was done to the ambassador, and, within a short time, English Catholics were once again secretly coming to his house to hear Mass. In the autumn of 1576, the bishop's officers again made forcible entry of the ambassador's residence and arrested another 13 Englishmen at Mass while several others escaped. The ambassador again complained to the Queen, who, to pacify him, ordered the arrest of Mr. Fleetwood, the recorder of London, who was immediately responsible for organizing the raid. However, Fleetwood's detention was merely for show, as his later description of his imprisonment for Burghley indicated, "I do beseech your Lordship thank Mr. Warden of the Fleet for his most friendly and courteous using of me, for surely (I thank God for it) I am quiet and lack nothing that he or his bedfellow are able to do for me. This is a place wherein a man may quietly be acquainted with God" (Birt 462–463).

ASK YOURSELF

1. Why do you think Bishop Sandys wrote also to the Earl of Leicester, who was a courtier and member of the royal council, but not the Queen's chief minister? Is there any difference in tone between the bishop's letter to Leicester and his letter to Burghley?
2. Why does Sandys find these services, which were held hurriedly in secret and often attended by few people, so dangerous? What reasons does he give for why they must be suppressed?
3. Why had the Elizabethan Church outlawed the Catholic Mass? How did it differ from the Anglican service? What about the Mass was objectionable to Protestants?

PENAL LAWS

The fear of Catholicism exhibited by Bishop Sandys in his letters found legal expression in the Elizabethan penal laws, which placed restrictions on the civil and political rights of Roman Catholics. In 1559, ELIZABETH's first Parliament made celebration of the Catholic mass illegal and required all subjects to attend Anglican services on Sundays and holy days (see "Elizabethan Parliaments," Document 11). Refusal to attend, known as recusancy, incurred a fine of 12 pence per absence. The Parliament of 1563 made upholding papal authority punishable by death for a second offense. Parliament also required clergymen and many laypersons to take the oath of supremacy, something most Catholics would not do because it meant denying papal authority.

In the 1560s, little active persecution of Catholics occurred in England, but the situation changed in the early 1570s with the discovery of the Ridolfi Plot (see "Ridolfi Plot," Document 16). Outright repression of English Catholics followed publication of the papal bull (papal letter, decree, or charter), *Regnans in Excelsis*, which excommunicated Elizabeth and declared her subjects absolved of their allegiance to her, and grew more intense with the discovery of political intrigues conducted by English Jesuits working secretly in England and English Catholic exiles working openly abroad. Publishing or implementing a papal bull in England became treason in 1571. In 1581, Parliament raised recusancy fines to a ruinous £20 per month and declared it treason to reconcile anyone to Rome, to become reconciled oneself, or to persuade anyone to withdraw allegiance from the Queen or the Anglican Church. In 1585, it became treason for a Catholic priest simply to be in England and a crime to send money overseas to support Catholic clergy. In 1593, Catholic recusants were forbidden to travel more than five miles from home without a special license.

TOPICS AND ACTIVITIES TO CONSIDER

- ↬ Access the definition and history of the principle of diplomatic immunity, found at http://www.ediplomat.com/nd/diplomatic_immunity.htm. Many of the standard practices of modern diplomacy were just developing in the sixteenth century, so diplomatic immunity, as observed today, did not exist in Elizabethan England. Write an account of what diplomatic repercussions might follow if a modern state allowed its police to forcibly enter a foreign embassy in which it believed illegal acts were occurring. Suggest how such a situation might be handled differently today.
- ↬ Read Document 19, which is written by John Gerard, a Catholic priest who was illegally saying Mass in England. Take the role of either an English official seeking to suppress illegal Masses or an English Catholic seeking to attend a secret Mass. Write a diary entry expressing why you believe you are right in doing what you do and why the other side is wrong.

Further Information

Beckingsale, B.W. *Burghley, Tudor Statesman*. New York: St. Martin's Press, 1967.

Bossy, John. *The English Catholic Community 1570–1850*. New York: Oxford University Press, 1976.

Gerard, John. *The Autobiography of a Hunted Priest*. Translated from Latin by Philip Caraman. New York: Pellegrini and Cudahy, 1952.

Haynes, Alan. *The White Bear: The Elizabethan Earl of Leicester*. London: Peter Owen, 1987.

Houliston, Victor. *Catholic Resistance in Elizabethan England: Robert Person's Jesuit Polemic, 1580–1610*. Farnham, Surrey: Ashgate, 2007.

Lunn, David. *The Catholic Elizabethans*. Bath: Downside Abbey, 1998.

Morey, Adrian. *The Catholic Subjects of Elizabeth I*. Totowa, NJ: Rowman and Littlefield, 1978.

Pritchard, Arnold. *Catholic Loyalism in Elizabethan England*. Chapel Hill: University of North Carolina Press, 1979.

Read, Conyers. *Lord Burghley and Queen Elizabeth*. New York: Alfred A. Knopf, 1960.

———. *Mr. Secretary Cecil and Queen Elizabeth*. London: Jonathan Cape, 1965.

Wilson, Derek: *Sweet Robin: A Biography of Robert Dudley*. London: Allen and Busby, 1981.

Web Site

"Elizabethan Catholics" by J.P. Sommerville: http://history.wisc.edu/sommerville/361/361-18.htm

16. CRITICIZING THE QUEEN: PETER WENTWORTH'S SPEECH IN THE HOUSE OF COMMONS (1576)

INTRODUCTION

On February 8, 1576, Peter WENTWORTH, member for the Cornish borough of Tregony, rose in the House of Commons to deliver a speech that he expected to result in his imprisonment. He was right. The speech did something that was simply not done in Elizabethan England—it directly criticized the Queen and her policies. Particularly angered by ELIZABETH's refusal in light of the Ridolfi Plot to execute MARY, Queen of Scots, as the Parliament of 1572 had urged, Wentworth declared that the Queen had overstepped her authority by attempting to limit debate on the subject in the House of Commons (see "Ridolfi Plot" below). A horrified House, utterly unaccustomed to open criticism of the Queen, stopped Wentworth in mid-speech and committed him to custody. Although later widely read in printed versions, the following excerpt comes from the undelivered portion of Wentworth's speech.

KEEP IN MIND AS YOU READ

1. As a PURITAN, Peter Wentworth saw parliamentary free speech as an act of conscience, whereby godly men could use Parliament to govern the realm in accordance with God's will should the monarch act clearly in opposition to that will, as Wentworth believed the Queen was doing (see "English Parliaments, " Document 11). This idea was revolutionary, for, if taken further, as it would be in coming centuries, it meant the eventual supplanting of the Crown by Parliament as head of the English body politic.

2. Reacting to the Ridolfi Plot, the Parliament of 1572 passed a bill condemning Mary, Queen of Scots, who was deeply implicated in the conspiracy, and removing her from the succession to the throne. Elizabeth, fearing that the execution of a divinely anointed monarch would undermine her own position, vetoed the bill, thus angering Wentworth, who believed the Queen, by her veto, was acting against the will of God and the best interests of the realm.

3. Because of the deference that was considered due a divinely sanctioned monarch, criticism of government policy was never aimed at the monarch personally, but at his or her ministers and advisors, whose ill-informed or ill-intentioned advice was held to be

responsible for the offending policies. Even rebels in arms, such as the PILGRIMAGE OF GRACE rebels in 1536–1537, directed their denunciations of the government's religious policies against the King's ministers, not against HENRY VIII himself.

Document: Excerpt from Peter Wentworth's 1576 Speech to the Commons

Well God, even the great and mighty God, whose name is the Lord of hosts . . . and who is the only good director of all hearts, was the last session [of Parliament] shut out of the doors. But what fell out of it? Forsooth his great indignation was therefore powered upon this House. How so? For he did put into the Queen's Majesty's heart to refuse good and wholesome laws for her own preservation, the which caused many faithful hearts for grief to burst out with sorrowful tears and moved all **papists**, traitors to God and her Majesty and every good Christian government, in their selves to laugh all the whole parliament house to scorn. And shall I pass over this weighty matter so lightly or so slightly? May I discharge my conscience and duty to God, my prince and country so? Certain it is, Mr. Speaker, that none is without fault, no, not our noble Queen. Since then that her Majesty has committed great faults, yea dangerous faults to herself and the state[,] love, even perfect love void of dissimulation, will not suffer me to hide them to her Majesty's peril but to utter them to her Majesty's safety. And these they are. It is a dangerous thing in a prince unkindly to entreat and abuse his or her nobility and people as her Majesty did the last parliament; and it is a dangerous thing in a prince to oppose or bend herself against her nobility and people, yea, against most loving and faithful nobility and people. And how could any prince more unkindly entreat, abuse and oppose herself against her nobility and people then her Majesty did the last parliament? Did she not call it of purpose to prevent traitorous perils to her person and for no other cause? Did not her Majesty send unto us two bills, willing to make a choice of what we liked best for her safety and thereof to make a law, promising her Majesty's royal consent thereto? And did we not first choose the one and her Majesty refused it, yielding no reason, nay, yielding great reasons why she ought to have yielded to it? Yet did not we nevertheless receive the other and agreeing to make a law thereof did not her Majesty in the end refuse all our travails? And did not we, he Majesty's faithful nobility and subjects, plainly and openly **decipher** ourselves unto her Majesty and our hateful enemy? And has not her Majesty left us all to her open revenge? Is this a just recompense in our Christian Queen for our faithful dealings? The heathen do requite good for good; then how much more is it dutiful in a Christian prince? And will not this her Majesty's handling, think you Mr. Speaker, make cold dealing in many of her Majesty's subjects toward her? Again, I fear it will.

> **decipher:** explain
> **papists:** Roman Catholics

Source: Hartley, T.E., ed. *Proceedings in the Parliaments of Elizabeth I: Volume I 1558–1581.* Leicester: Leicester University Press, 1981, pp. 430–31

RIDOLFI PLOT

Peter Wentworth's criticism of the Queen was an extreme expression of the fears that haunted many Protestant Englishmen, who saw Mary of Scotland as the focus of continual Catholic plotting to destroy their Queen and their Church. These fears were given particular substance in 1571 by discovery of the Ridolfi plot, a Catholic conspiracy against Elizabeth coordinated by Roberto Ridolfi, an Italian banker residing in England. A papal agent, Ridolfi brought *Regnans in Excelsis*, the papal bull excommunicating Elizabeth, into England in 1570.

In 1571, Ridolfi and the Spanish ambassador concocted a plan whereby Spanish troops from the Netherlands would invade England. Thomas HOWARD, Duke of Norfolk, whom Ridolfi persuaded to join the conspiracy, agreed to raise a revolt in conjunction with the invasion and either rescue Mary or seize Elizabeth. Catholicism would be restored, and Mary and Norfolk would jointly rule both Scotland and England. The plotters later decided that Elizabeth should be assassinated, an action to which both PHILIP II of Spain and the pope agreed.

The plot unraveled when one of Ridolfi's messengers was captured and confessed all. Norfolk was arrested and condemned for treason, and Parliament called for his and Mary's execution. The government expelled the Spanish ambassador, but Elizabeth was hesitant to execute either Mary or Norfolk. She finally consented to the duke's execution, which took place in June 1572, but the Queen spared Mary despite the outcry against her and the continuing demands, such as Wentworth's, that she be eliminated.

AFTERMATH

Immediately upon placing Wentworth in custody, the Commons appointed a committee to examine him regarding the meaning of and reasons for his speech. Wentworth stoutly defended himself (see Hartley 435–39 for a transcript of the interrogation) and then was committed to the Tower of London, where he remained in confinement for more than a month, until released by the Queen just before the end of the parliamentary session. Upon returning to the House, Wentworth was forced to make humble submission on his knees before being allowed to resume his seat. He was also lectured by Sir Walter Mildmay, who told him that parliamentary freedom of speech did not mean that "a man in this House may speak what and of whom he list" (Elton 347), and rebuked by the speaker, who reminded him that he was free only through the Queen's compassion.

In 1586, Wentworth again demanded wider freedom of speech for members of Parliament and was, as a consequence, again imprisoned. He entered the Tower a third time in 1591 for offending the Queen by writing a pamphlet that urged her to name a successor. Unrepentant, Wentworth remained in the Tower until his death in 1596.

ASK YOURSELF

1. Given the Elizabethan prohibition on criticizing the Queen, which line or statement in the above excerpt do you find the most shocking? Why? Do you think Wentworth's audience would have agreed with you? Why or why not?

2. How do you think Wentworth was viewed by subsequent generations? How do you think his speech, which was widely disseminated in full, was viewed by subsequent generations?

TOPICS AND ACTIVITIES TO CONSIDER

∾ Access the Glossary section of the British Parliament home page at http://www.parliament.uk/about/glossary.cfm?ref=unparli_9683, and read the brief definitions for "parliamentary privilege" and "unparliamentary language" to gain an understanding of the current definition of parliamentary free speech. Consider how modern views of free speech in Parliament differ from Elizabethan views on the subject.

∾ Access http://youtube.com, and search for videos of "prime minister's question period," which show the half-hour period every Wednesday reserved for members of the Commons to ask questions of the prime minister. View several of these videos to get a sense of the style, tone, and language of modern parliamentary debate and questioning.

Further Information

Elton, G.R. *The Parliament of England 1559–1581.* Cambridge: Cambridge University Press, 1986.

Graves, Michael A.R. *Elizabethan Parliaments 1559–1601.* London: Longman, 1987.

Hartley, T.E. *Elizabeth's Parliaments: Queen, Lords and Commons 1559–1601.* New York: St. Martin's Press, 1992.

Neale, J.E. *Elizabeth I and Her Parliaments.* 2 vols. New York: St. Martin's Press, 1958.

Web Sites

Peter Wentworth's 1576 Commons Speech: http://www.uark.edu/depts/comminfo/cambridge/wentworth.html

Sir Peter Wentworth: http://www.tudorplace.com.ar/Bios/PeterWentworth.htm

17. A Description of the New World: The First Expedition to Sir Walter Raleigh's Virginia (1584)

INTRODUCTION

On April 27, 1584, Philip AMADAS and Arthur BARLOWE, two young gentlemen in Sir Walter RALEIGH's household, left Plymouth in command of two small vessels bound for the New World. Raleigh, who had recently secured a grant from the Queen to establish an English settlement in North America, had charged the two gentlemen with reconnoitering the American coast to find a good settlement site and to learn something of the natives, climate, and products of the area. In July, after sailing along the coasts of the present-day states of Georgia, South Carolina, and North Carolina, Amadas and Barlowe landed on Hatteras Island and made friendly contact with the nearby Roanoke Indians. The following excerpt comes from the glowing account of the Roanoke region that Barlowe wrote shortly after the expedition's return to England in September.

KEEP IN MIND AS YOUR READ

1. Spain in the Elizabethan era controlled a huge overseas empire that included Mexico and other parts of North America, Central America, much of South America, and, in Europe, the Netherlands and parts of Italy. After 1580, Portugal and her vast trading and colonial empire in Africa, Brazil, and East Asia also fell under the control of Spain, which already dominated the Mediterranean trade.

2. While Spain grew rich on silver from Peru, spices from India, and gold from Africa, she strictly forbade foreign trade with her colonies and territories and jealously guarded her trade routes, such as the lucrative Southeast Passage around Africa to India and China. For almost a century, England had tried unsuccessfully to open trade with Spanish America and to discover a feasible northern passage to Asia.

3. American colonization was a daunting undertaking because the colonists had only those supplies they could carry with them. Resupply from England could take months or years, and the ships that brought the colonists quickly departed, leaving them without a good means of communication or return should problems arise. The first colonists thus found themselves heavily dependent on

the local Native Americans, whose initial willingness to help declined as the colonists became more needy and demanding, a situation that sometimes led to violence.

Document: Excerpt from Arthur Barlowe's "First Voyage to Roanoke"

[We] cast anchor about three **harquebus**-shots within the haven's mouth, on the left hand of the same: and after thanks given to God for our safe arrival thither, we manned our boats, and went to view the land next adjoining, and to take possession of the same, in the right of the Queen's most excellent Majesty, and rightful Queen, and Princess of the same, and after delivered the same over to your use, according to her Majesty's grant, and **letters patents**, under her Highness great seal. Which being performed, according to the ceremonies used in such enterprises, we viewed the land about us, being, whereas we first landed, very sandy and low towards the waters side, but so full of grapes, as the very beating and surge of the Sea overflowed them, of which we found such plenty, as well there as in all places else, both on the sand and on the green soil on the hills, as in the plains, as well on every little shrub, as also climbing towards the tops of high Cedars, that I think in all the world the like abundance is not to be found: and myself having seen those parts of Europe that most abound, find such difference as were incredible to be written.

We passed from the Sea side towards the tops of those hills next adjoining, being but of **mean** height, and from thence we beheld the Sea on both sides to the North, and to the South, finding no end any of both ways. This land lay stretching itself to the West, which after we found to be but an Island of twenty miles long, and not above six miles broad. Under the bank or hill whereon we stood, we beheld the valleys replenished with goodly Cedar trees, and having discharged our harquebus-shot, such a flock of Cranes (the most part white), arose under us, with such a cry redoubled by many echoes, as if an army of men had shouted all together.

This Island had many goodly woods full of Deer, **Conies**, Hares, and Fowl, even in the middle of Summer in incredible abundance. The woods are not such as you find in Bohemia [or] Muscovy . . . barren and fruitless, but the highest and reddest Cedars of the world, far bettering the Cedars of the Azores, of the Indies, or Lebanon, Pines, Cypress, Sassafras . . . Mastic . . . and many other of excellent smell and quality. . . .

[The brother of Wingina, the local chief] sent us every day a **brace** or two of fat Bucks, Conies, Hares, Fish the best of the world. He sent us **divers** kinds of fruits, Melons, Walnuts, Cucumbers, Gourds, Peas, and divers roots, and fruits very excellent good, and of their Country corn, which is very white, fair and well tasted,

brace: two of a kind; a pair
Conies: rabbits
divers: various
harquebus: a matchlock gun
letters patent: a royal letter conferring a public grant on a particular person
mattock: a digging tool with ax-like features
mean: low; little
underwoods: underbrush; undergrowth

and grows three times in five months: in May they sow, in July they reap, in June they sow, in August they reap: in July they sow, in September they reap: only they cast the corn into the ground, breaking a little of the soft turf with a wooden **mattock**, or pickaxe; ourselves proved the soil, and put some of our Peas in the ground, and in ten days they were of fourteen inches high: they have also Beans very fair of divers colors and wonderful plenty: some growing naturally, and some in their gardens, and so have they both wheat and oats.

The soil is the most plentiful, sweet, fruitful and wholesome of all the world: there are above fourteen several sweet smelling timber trees, and the most part of their **underwoods** are Bays and such like: they have those Oaks that we have, but far greater and better. . . .

[By the people] [w]e were entertained with all love and kindness, and with as much bounty, after their manner, as they could possibly devise. We found the people most gentle, loving and faithful, void of all guile and treason, and such as live after the manner of the golden age.

Source: Tarbox, Increase N., ed. *Sir Walter Ralegh and His Colony in America.* Boston: Printed for the Prince Society by John Wilson and Son, 1884, pp. 110–12, 119, 121.

ROANOKE COLONIES

In April 1585, an expedition of six vessels funded by Sir Walter Raleigh left the western port of Plymouth, carrying 600 men intent on establishing an English settlement in America. By July, the expedition had, with the aid of Manteo and Wanchese, two Indians who had sailed to England with Amadas and Barlowe, established friendly relations with the Roanoke chief Wingina, who allowed 100 Englishmen to settle on the northern end of Roanoke Island. The rest of the colonists returned to England. In spring, hostilities erupted with the Indians. Having arrived too late to plant crops, the colonists bartered for food with the Indians, whose willingness to trade declined with their own food supplies. In June, having learned through Manteo of Indian plans to attack the settlement, the colonists launched a preemptive raid on the Roanoke village, killing Wingina. One week later, a relief expedition under Sir Francis DRAKE arrived to take the surviving colonists back to England.

In May 1587, a second expedition of three vessels carrying 89 men, 17 women, and 11 children departed Plymouth, bound for Chesapeake Bay. Forced to settle on Roanoke when their ships' crews refused to take them to Chesapeake Bay, the settlers quickly suffered from the ill will the previous colonists had left among the Roanoke Indians, and attempts to reestablish good relations through Manteo failed. On August 18, Eleanor, the daughter of colony leader John WHITE and the wife of Ananias Dare, gave birth to a daughter. Virginia Dare was the first English child born in North America.

The unfriendliness of the Indians left the colony totally dependent on England for supplies, and the colonists decided that White should return to England to ensure regular provisions. Because the Armada crisis of 1588 tied up all shipping (see "Spanish Armada," Document 18), White did not return to Virginia until 1590. Landing on Roanoke, he found no trace of the colony, only the word "Croatoan" carved on a tree, which seemed to indicate the colony's removal to nearby Croatoan Island. However, storms prevented investigation, and White returned to England without ever knowing what became of the "lost colony" of Roanoke.

AFTERMATH

Hoping to secure the Queen's financial backing for his colonization scheme, Raleigh named the newly explored region Virginia, in honor of ELIZABETH, the "Virgin Queen." Although this ploy failed, Raleigh also widely distributed Barlowe's "First Voyage to Roanoke" to stimulate private investment in his colonial venture, and this effort was more successful. Barlowe's vivid description of the natural abundance of the region attracted private backers by convincing them that Virginia could supply England with all manner of products and commodities that were then only available from Spanish-controlled territories. As a result, Raleigh was able to raise the funding required to send his first colonization expedition to Roanoke in 1585 and a second in 1587 (see "Roanoke Colonies," p. 85).

ASK YOURSELF

1. What aspects of the Roanoke area does Barlowe emphasize in his report? Why do you think he does so?
2. Why do you think Wingina and the Roanoke Indians were so friendly to the English explorers? Barlowe ascribes it to their simplicity and lack of guile, but may there have been other reasons? How do you think the Roanoke people actually felt about these sudden strangers in their midst? Why?

TOPICS AND ACTIVITIES TO CONSIDER

- ☙ Access the American Journeys Web site at http://www.americanjourneys.org/index.asp, and read parts of the other accounts of Elizabethan explorations of America that are provided there, such as those by John Sparke, Ralph Lane, John White, or John Brereton. Compare these accounts to Barlowe's, and write an essay describing how they compare or how they differ. Explain what you believe to be the writer's reasons for setting down his account.
- ☙ Access the Virginia Historical Society Web site at http://www.vahistorical.org/cole/overview.htm and the Virtual Jamestown site at http://www.virtualjamestown.org to view the drawings of Raleigh's Virginia made by artist John White, a Roanoke colonist, and the engravings made from White's drawings by Theodor De Bry. From these images, write your own brief description of Virginia from the viewpoint of one of Raleigh's servants who has been charged with producing an account that will stimulate interest and investment in further colonization ventures.

Further Information

Coote, Stephen. *A Play of Passion: The Life of Sir Walter Raleigh*. London: Macmillan, 1993.

Durant, David N. *Raleigh's Lost Colony*. New York: Atheneum, 1981.

Kupperman, Karen Ordahl. *Roanoke: The Abandoned Colony*. New York: Barnes and Noble, 1993.

Lacey, Robert. *Sir Walter Ralegh*. New York: Atheneum, 1974.

Quinn, David B. *Set Fair for Roanoke: Voyages and Colonies, 1584–1606*. Chapel Hill: University of North Carolina Press, 1984.

Trevelyan, Raleigh. *Sir Walter Raleigh: Being a True and Vivid Account of the Life and Times of the Explorer, Soldier, Scholar, Poet, and Courtier. The Controversial Hero of the Elizabethan Age.* New York: Henry Holt, 2004.

Web Site

Arthur Barlowe's First Voyage to Roanoke: http://docsouth.unc.edu/nc/barlowe/menu.html
Richard Hakluyt's Principal Navigations, Voyages, Traffiques, and Discoveries of the English Nation: http://ebooks.adelaide.edu.au/h/hakluyt/voyages
Sir Walter Raleigh's American colonies: http://www.britishexplorers.com/woodbury/raleigh.html

18. THE DESTRUCTION OF THE SPANISH ARMADA: NEWS ACCOUNTS FROM IRELAND (1588)

INTRODUCTION

In late July and early August 1588, the Spanish Armada and the English navy fought a series of battles in the English Channel (see "Spanish Armada" below). Although the English generally got the better of these engagements, the Armada was still largely intact when, in mid-August, a strong southwest wind drove it into the North Sea. Low on ammunition and suffering serious shortages of food and water, the Spanish commander, the Duke of Medina Sidonia, realized that he could not resume the fight. A fifth of his men were dead or wounded, and morale plummeted as illness seized many of the rest. Unable to return to the Channel, the duke turned west, seeking to pass north of Scotland before making a wide southward arc around the west of Ireland and then to Spain. Although the Spanish sought to avoid Ireland, storms, hunger, thirst, and battle damage drove many vessels onto the Irish coast. Reproduced here are various reports sent to London from Ireland regarding the fate of the ships and men wrecked upon the shores of western Ireland in September 1588.

KEEP IN MIND AS YOU READ

1. The Irish, like the Spanish, were Roman Catholic, so, in most cases where Spanish castaways fell into the hands of native Irish, the survivors were fed, sheltered, and helped to escape the country. There is only one recorded instance of the killing of Spanish castaways by Irish not in the pay of the English government, and the act was widely condemned by other Irish.

2. Later stories about large numbers of stranded Spaniards settling in western Ireland and passing their physical features, such as dark eyes, hair, and complexions, on to their descendants are largely myths. A few seamen may have settled in isolated villages, but most of the Spanish who landed in Ireland either died there or escaped elsewhere. Several hundred armada seamen made their way safely to Scotland and then home with the help of friendly Irish. Any Spaniards who remained in Ireland were too few in number to affect the later appearance of the local population.

3. English authority in Ireland, particularly in the western districts, was always tenuous. From the perspective of the English government, any foreign presence in

Ireland, especially of Roman Catholics or Spaniards, constituted a serious threat to the security of England. Thus the government was quick to ensure that no Spanish landfall in the neighboring island, by men in whatever condition, was allowed to establish a foothold that PHILIP II could later exploit.

Document: Reports of the Destruction of Spanish Vessels Along the Irish Coast

Upon Saturday, the seventh of September, the bark which was in peril of wreck in the bay of Trayley, of between forty and fifty tons, did render themselves, in which there were twenty-four men, whereof two were the Duke's own servants, and two little boys.

On Tuesday the tenth of this September, there was a frigate cast off, as it seems, by this name, which, as Sir William Herbert says, wrecked upon the coast of Desmond.

On the same Tuesday, there wrecked, in the sound of the Bleskeys, a ship, called Our *Lady of Rosary*, of one-thousand tons. In this ship was drowned the Prince of Castile, the King's **base son**, one Don Pedro, Don Diego, and Don Francisco, with seven other gentlemen of account, that accompanied the Prince. There was drowned in her also Michael Oquendo, a principal seaman, chief governor of the ship; Ville Franca, of *Saint Sebastians*, captain of the same ship; Matute, captain of the infantry of that ship; Captain Suares, a Portuguese; Garrioncrie, Ropecho de la Vega, Montenese, and one Francisco Castilian, captains; one John Ryse, an Irish captain, Francis Roch, an Irishman, and about five-hundred persons, whereof one-hundred were gentlemen, but not of that **reckoning** as the former were; and only one John Anthonio de Monona, a Genoese, being the pilot's son of that ship, saved.

The same Tuesday, it was advertised to the vice-president of Munster, that there were lost, upon the coast of Thomond, two great ships, out of which there were drowned about seven-hundred persons, and taken prisoners about one-hundred and fifty.

About that Tuesday also, as appears by a letter written to Stephen White, of Limerick, the twelfth of this September, there was cast, upon the sands of Ballicrahihy, a ship of nine-hundred tons; thirteen of the gentlemen of that ship, as he writes, are taken; and so writes, that he heard the rest of that ship, being above four-hundred, have fought, for their defense, being much distressed, to entrench themselves.

He writes, also, of another ship which was cast away at the isle of Clare in Irrise, and that seventy-eight of the men of that ship are drowned and slain.

He writes also, that there was, about the same time, another great ship cast away in Tirawley, and that there are three noblemen, a bishop, and a friar, and sixty-nine other men taken by William Bourk, of Ardnerie, and all the residue of that ship are slain and drowned; insomuch, as he writes, that one Meleghlen MacCabb, a **Galloglass**, killed eighty of them with his Galloglass

bark: a small sailing ship

base son: illegitimate or bastard son

durst not: dare not

Galloglass: heavily armed Irish infantryman

reckoning: social stature or standing

ax. Wednesday the eleventh of this September, seven of those ships, that then remained within the Shannon, departed out of that road with an easterly wind, and, before their going forth, they set on fire one other very great ship of their company, which was one-thousand tons at least.

It was informed from the vice-president at Cork, upon this seventeenth of September last, that two other great ships of that fleet should be lost upon the coast of Connaught.

The admiral, called John Martin de Ricalde, came into the sound of Bleskcys, with one other great ship, and a **bark**, about the sixth day of this September, and remains there with one other ship, of four-hundred tons, and a bark which came in since that time, if they be not dispersed or lost, by the great tempest that was the seventeenth and eighteenth of this month: for the state of the admiral, at his coming in, was thus: the ship had been shot through fourteen or fifteen times, her main-mast so beaten with shot, as she **durst not** bear her full sail, and now not sixty mariners left in her, and many of them so sick, that they lie down, and the residue so weak, that they were not able to do any good service; and there are daily cast over the board, out of that ship, five or six of the company.

Source: *The Harleian Miscellany; or, a Collection of Scarce, Curious, and Entertaining Pamphlets and Tracts, as Well in Manuscript as in Print, Found in the Late Earl of Oxford's Library.* Vol. II. London: Printed for Robert Dutton, 1809, pp. 48–49.

AFTERMATH

A series of exceptionally severe storms, coupled with the effects of illness, ship deterioration, and lack of supply, caused at least 26 ships to wreck or founder on the Irish coast. Thousands of men drowned in the wrecks or were slain when they struggled ashore. Elizabeth's lord deputy in Ireland, Sir William FITZWILLIAM, had less than 2,000 ill-trained and ill-equipped soldiers at his disposal, so his policy was to kill all Spaniards who could be caught, including one group of Spanish gentlemen who surrendered only on receiving a promise that their lives would be spared. Many other castaways were eventually taken prisoner to England or escaped to Scotland, there to take service with Scottish lords or make their way to Europe. Of the 130 ships that had left Spain, more than a third never returned. Although Philip attempted other invasions of England in 1596 and 1597, the failure of 1588 was decisive.

ASK YOURSELF

1. The goal of the Armada was to transport Spanish troops from the Netherlands to England (see "Spanish Netherlands," Document 38). What do you think would have happened if the Armada had successfully landed those troops?
2. Would English Catholics have supported the invasion as the Spanish hoped and the English feared? Why or why not?
3. How important was affection for and loyalty to the Queen in rallying the English people to resist the Armada? Was it more or less important than simple fear of conquest or death? Was the fact that ELIZABETH was a woman a factor? (See Document 38 for Elizabeth's speech to her troops during the Armada crisis.)

SPANISH ARMADA

In the summer of 1588, Philip II of Spain sent an armada of 130 ships into the English Channel to transport Spanish troops from the Netherlands to England. The "Enterprise of England," as the invasion was called, aimed at restoring the English Catholic Church and overthrowing Elizabeth. The execution of MARY, Queen of Scots, in February 1587, when planning for the invasion had already begun, only strengthened Philip's resolve, but Sir Francis DRAKE's April 1587 raid on Cadiz, which destroyed ships and supplies, when combined with endless delays in procuring men, ships, and provisions, postponed the sailing of the Armada until May 1588.

On July 29, the Armada arrived in the Channel. The English fleet quickly gained the wind advantage and used the superior maneuverability of its ships and the greater range of its guns to outduel the Armada in skirmishes off Portsmouth, Plymouth, and the Isle of Wight. On August 6, the Armada anchored off Calais, but poor planning and communications made conjunction with Spanish troops in the Netherlands impossible. English fireships dispersed the Armada in confusion on the night of August 7, and the English had the better of a final skirmish off Gravelines the next day. The wind then drove the Armada into the North Sea and forced it to circumnavigate the British Isles. Only about two-thirds of the fleet returned home. Some 40 ships were destroyed, mostly by gales and reefs during the journey around Scotland and Ireland. The English victory gave confidence to English Protestants, soured English Catholics on foreign invasion schemes, and shattered belief in Spanish invincibility.

TOPICS AND ACTIVITIES TO CONSIDER

- ✿ Access the Spanish Armada section of the BritishBattles.com Web site at http://www.britishbattles.com/spanish-war/spanish-armada.htm. Review the text, images, and list provided regarding the Spanish Armada of 1588. From this and other sources, create a timeline for the Armada (its preparation, sailing, battles, and aftermath) that shows just how long this great threat loomed over the English Queen and people.

- ✿ In the twenty-first century, we are accustomed to receive news of events almost instantaneously. In the First Iraq War of 1991, for instance, television showed bombs and rockets exploding over Baghdad or Tel Aviv. We saw war as it happened. In the sixteenth century, news travelled more slowly. Using an online or atlas map of Ireland, locate some of the sites mentioned in the above reports. Then, using the Internet or an atlas, determine the distance from one of those sites to London. Then compile a list of steps and modes of transport by which news of a shipwreck in western Ireland had to travel to reach Elizabethan London, and estimate the length of time it would take.

Further Information

Hanson, Neil. *The Confident Hope of a Miracle: The True Story of the Spanish Armada*. New York: Vintage, 2006.

Kilfeather, T.P. *Ireland: Graveyard of the Spanish Armada*. Minneapolis: Irish Books and Media, 1979.

Martin, Colin, and Geoffrey Parker. *The Spanish Armada*. Revised edition. Manchester: Manchester University Press, 2002.

Mattingly, Garrett. *The Armada*. Boston: Mariner Books, 2005.

McDermott, James. *England and the Spanish Armada: The Necessary Quarrel*. New Haven, CT: Yale University Press, 2005.

19. Priest Hunters Search a House for Hidden Catholic Clergy: John Gerard's *Autobiography* (1591)

INTRODUCTION

In 1581, Parliament declared it treason to reconcile or convert anyone to Roman Catholicism (see "Elizabethan Parliaments," Document 11). In 1585, Parliament made the very presence of Catholic priests in England treason and declared anyone who sheltered or assisted a priest guilty of felony. Because treason and felony were capital crimes, anyone convicted of either offense was punishable by death (see "Penal Laws," Document 15). To enforce these statutes, the government relied on paid spies and zealous anti-Catholic informers to track and discover priests as they clandestinely entered and moved about the country.

Most priests found shelter with Catholic GENTRY, whose homes were often equipped with priest holes, specially built hiding places where priests could be secreted during searches of the house (see "Priest Holes" below). In the following excerpt from his *Autobiography*, the English Jesuit John GERARD described a search that occurred in October 1591 at Baddesley Clinton, a Warwickshire house that served as base for another prominent Jesuit, Henry GARNET. As Gerard described, he and nine other men, including Garnet and the Jesuits Robert SOUTHWELL and Edward OLDCORNE, eluded the searchers by hiding in a cave below the house.

KEEP IN MIND AS YOU READ

1. After 1570, various Catholic actions and intrigues generated real fear for the safety of the realm and the Queen and led directly to enactment of the Elizabethan Penal Laws against Catholics. Among the most serious of these actions were the papal excommunication of ELIZABETH in 1570, which formally absolved her subjects of their allegiance to her; the Ridolfi Plot of 1571 (see "Ridolfi Plot," Document 16), which included a plan to assassinate the Queen; and the arrival of the Jesuit Mission in 1580 (see "Jesuit Mission in England," Document 37), which established a secret network of politically active priests throughout the country.

2. An estimated 68 persons were executed under the Penal Laws during the reign of Elizabeth, 48 priests and 20 laypersons. Unlike the Protestants who were burned for heresy during the reign of Elizabeth's Catholic sister, MARY I, the Catholics who died under Elizabeth were executed for treason, not for religion.

3. The war with Spain that began in 1585; the presence in England of MARY, Queen of Scots, the Catholic claimant to the English throne; and the invasion of the

Spanish Armada in 1588 also increased tensions between England and the Catholic world, particularly Spain, and thus made more vigorous the enforcement of laws against Catholic clergy (see "Spanish Armada," Document 18).

Document: Excerpts from Gerard's Autobiography

It was about five o'clock [in the] morning. I was making my meditation, Father Southwell was beginning Mass and the rest were at prayer, when suddenly I heard a great uproar outside the main door. Then I heard a voice shouting and swearing at a servant who was refusing them entrance. It was the priest-hunters, or pursuivants, as they were called. There were four of them altogether, with swords drawn, and they were battering at the door to force an entrance. But a faithful servant held them back, otherwise we should have all been caught.

Father Southwell heard the din. He guessed what it was all about, and slipped off his vestments and stripped the altar bare. While he was doing this, we laid hold of all our personal belongings: nothing was left to betray the presence of a priest. Even our boots and swords were hidden away—they would have roused suspicions if none of the people they belonged to were to be found. Our beds presented a problem: as they were still warm and merely covered in the usual way preparatory to being made, some of us went off and turned the beds and put the cold side up to delude anyone who put his hand in to feel them.

Outside the ruffians were bawling and yelling, but the servants held the door fast. They said the mistress of the house, a widow, was not yet up, but was coming down at once to answer them. This gave us enough time to stow ourselves and all our belongings into a very cleverly built sort of cave.

At last these leopards were let in. They tore madly through the whole house, searched everywhere, pried with candles into the darkest corners. They took four hours over the work but fortunately they chanced on nothing. All they did was to show how dogged and spiteful they could be, and how forbearing Catholics were. In the end they made off, but only after they got paid for their trouble. Yes, that is the pitiful lot of Catholics—when men come with a warrant to upset their homes in this or any other way, it is they, the Catholics, not the authorities who send them, who have to pay. As if it were not enough to suffer, they are charged for suffering.

> **secular priests:** Catholic priests who were not members of any priestly order

When they had gone, and gone a good way, so that there was no danger of their turning back suddenly, as they sometimes do, a lady came and called us out of our den, not one but several Daniels. The hiding-place was below ground level; the floor was covered with water and I was standing with my feet in it all the time. Father Garnet was there; also Father Southwell and Father Oldcorne . . . Father Stanney and myself, two **secular priests** and two or three laymen.

So we were all saved that day.

Source: Gerard, John. *The Autobiography of a Hunted Priest*. Translated from Latin by Philip Caraman. New York: Pellegrini and Cudahy, 1952, pp. 41–42.

PRIEST HOLES

Priest holes were secret hiding places built into the country homes of Catholic gentry for the concealment from the authorities of Catholic clergymen. The English Penal Laws spurred the construction of small, secure places of concealment in the gentry homes where priests headquartered. The most skillful designer of priest holes was Nicholas Owen, who would work at night to construct hiding places that could foil even long and careful searches. Owen often devised hiding places within hiding places and usually contrived some sort of escape route and some means whereby the occupant of the hole might be fed during prolonged searches.

Not all priest holes were as clever or elaborate as Owen's constructions. Many were merely makeshift hiding places in attics, over ceilings, or behind walls. Many were dark, cramped, and airless. When a noted priest hunter named George Eliot invaded their house of refuge in July 1581, the Jesuit Edmund CAMPION and two other priests found themselves hurried into a dark, stifling hiding hole barely big enough for the three men to lay side by side. In a period without canned food and modern plumbing, extended stays in even the most cleverly designed priest holes were difficult. Nonetheless, such hiding places, some of which were only rediscovered in the twentieth century, made possible the work of Catholic priests in Elizabethan England.

AFTERMATH

The cave in which Gerard hid at Baddesley Clinton was originally the house sewer, a tunnel running under the entire west wing of the house. It was converted into a hiding place, probably by the most famous builder of priest holes, Nicholas Owen, by diverting the sewer and constructing cleverly concealed entrance shafts from the priests' rooms. In the 1590s, the house belonged to two women, the never-married, Anne Vaux, and her widowed sister, Eleanor Brooksby. Henry Garnet based himself at Baddlesley Clinton, which being but 90 miles from London, though in a remote area, had served before for meetings of Jesuits, like the one held in October 1591. Gerard escaped from England in 1606, but Garnet, Southwell, and Oldcorne were all later captured and executed.

ASK YOURSELF

1. Given the legal disabilities laid on Catholics and the repression of Catholic priests, why and how did Catholicism survive in England?
2. Who were the Jesuits? Why did the English government consider them a greater threat than secular priests, who were not attached to any Catholic order?

TOPICS AND ACTIVITIES TO CONSIDER

- ➾ Access the National Trust Web page on Baddesley Clinton at http://www.nationaltrust.org.uk/main/w-baddesleyclinton to see a description and pictures of the house. Use the Internet to find other still-existing Elizabethan houses that sheltered priests in priest holes. Compile a list of attributes that made a house a good base for Catholic priests in Elizabethan England.
- ➾ Create a timeline of major Catholic actions and English Protestant reactions during the reigns of Elizabeth and her successor JAMES I that

increased tensions on both sides. Be sure to include all important statutes, plots, conspiracies, executions, declarations, and rebellions.

    ✎ After the declaration of war against Japan at the start of World War II, the United States sent thousands of Japanese Americans living in California and on the West Coast to internment camps out of fear that they might support Japan. Like Catholics in Elizabethan England, they constituted a minority whose loyalty to the country was suspect. Access the Web site on the PBS documentary *Children of the Camps* at http://www.pbs.org/childofcamp/history/index.html and on the history of Japanese American internment at http://library.thinkquest.org/TQ0312008/Enter.html. Read the descriptions, documents, and timelines provided, and write an essay describing how the two historical situations were similar and how different. Decide whether or not the two are comparable, and conclude by giving reasons for your opinion.

Further Information

Bossy, John. *The English Catholic Community 1570–1850*. New York: Oxford University Press, 1976.

Gerard, John. *The Autobiography of a Hunted Priest*. Translated from Latin by Philip Caraman. New York: Pellegrini and Cudahy, 1952.

Houliston, Victor. *Catholic Resistance in Elizabethan England: Robert Person's Jesuit Polemic, 1580–1610*. Farnham, Surrey: Ashgate, 2007.

Lunn, David. *The Catholic Elizabethans*. Bath: Downside Abbey, 1998.

Morey, Adrian. *The Catholic Subjects of Elizabeth I*. Totowa, NJ: Rowman and Littlefield, 1978.

Pritchard, Arnold. *Catholic Loyalism in Elizabethan England*. Chapel Hill: University of North Carolina Press, 1979.

Web Site

"Elizabethan Catholics" by J.P. Sommerville: http://history.wisc.edu/sommerville/361/361-18.htm

20. Defending the Elizabethan Church: Richard Hooker's *Laws of Ecclesiastical Polity* (1593)

INTRODUCTION

Attacked by both Catholics and PURITANS, the Anglican Church, the official Church of England established by law in 1559, gradually acquired during ELIZABETH I's reign a set of philosophical principles by which it could both answer its critics and distinguish itself from them (see "Anglican Church" below). Reproduced here is a selection from the most comprehensive and influential statement of those principles, Richard HOOKER's eight-volume *Laws of Ecclesiastical Polity*. In the following excerpt, Hooker, a nephew of the Exeter chamberlain John HOOKER (see Documents 1 and 13), answered Puritan charges that the Anglican Church still preserved too many Catholic ceremonies and rituals.

KEEP IN MIND AS YOUR READ

1. While Roman Catholics considered the Elizabethan Church to be radically heretical and schismatic for what it rejected (e.g., papal authority, monasticism, and the sacrifice of the Mass), Puritans, who were in effect radical Anglicans, considered their Church to be too conservative because of what it retained (e.g., bishops, vestments, and popular rituals). As Catholics and Puritans sought to pull the Anglican Church in opposite directions, Elizabeth, as head of the Church, sought a *via media* (a middle way) between the two more extreme views.

2. Hooker based his arguments on natural law, a set of divine principles, knowable through the exercise of human reason, by which humans could properly and effectively order their lives, institutions, and societies. By this argument, Hooker countered the Puritan demand that Church and society be ordered strictly and solely according to the dictates of Scripture.

3. The proper form of Church government was one of the most vexing issues dividing Puritans and Anglicans. Puritans believed a Presbyterian form of government, which replaced bishops with assemblies of Church elders and ministers, to be mandated by Scripture. Hooker did not believe the Bible prescribed any form of ecclesiastical government and argued that the Church could be governed in

any manner that human reason found to be appropriate and convenient (see "Royal Supremacy," Document 13).

Document: Excerpts from Hooker's Ecclesiastical Polity

*The Fourth Book: concerning their [the Puritans'] third assertion, that our form of Church polity is corrupted with **Popish** orders, rites, and ceremonies, banished out of certain reformed Churches, whose example therein we ought to have followed.*

Popish: Roman Catholic

. . . Concerning rites and ceremonies, there may be fault either in the kind or in the number and multitude of them. The first thing blamed about the kind of ours is that in many things we have departed from the ancient simplicity of Christ and his Apostles, we have embraced more outward stateliness, we have those orders in the exercise of religion which they who best pleased God and served him most devoutly never had. For it is out of doubt that the first state of things was best, that in the prime of the Christian religion faith was soundest, the Scriptures of God were then best understood by all men, all parts of godliness did then most abound. . . . The glory of God and the good of his Church was the thing which the Apostles aimed at and therefore ought to be the mark whereat we also level. But seeing those rites and orders may be at one time more which at another time are less available unto that purpose, what reason is there in these things to urge the state of only one age as a pattern for all to follow? It is not, I am right sure, their meaning that we should now assemble our people to serve God in close and secret meetings; or that common brooks or rivers should be used for places of baptism; or that the Eucharist should be ministered after meat; or that the custom of Church-feasting should be renewed; or that all kinds of standing provision for the ministry should be utterly taken away and their estate made again dependent upon the voluntary devotion of men. In these things they easily perceive how unfit that were for the present, which was for the first age convenient enough.

Source: Hooker, Richard. "Of the Laws of Ecclesiastical Polity." In *The Works of Mr. Richard Hooker with an Account of His Life and Death by Isaac Walton.* 2 vols. Oxford: Clarendon Press, 1890, i., pp. 351–53.

AFTERMATH

By his death in 1600, Hooker had published five volumes of the *Laws of Ecclesiastical Polity.* The last three volumes were complete, but remained unpublished until the 1640s, giving rise to doubts about Hooker's authorship, although most modern scholars accept the volumes as authentic. Because Hooker's writing was so persuasive and articulate, the *Laws of Ecclesiastical Polity* became a powerful instrument in the seventeenth century against the political and theological attacks of Puritans, who dominated the state for over a decade after the abolition of the monarchy in 1649.

ANGLICAN CHURCH

As established under Elizabeth in 1559, the Church of England, or Anglican Church, was CALVINIST in doctrine, was episcopal (i.e., under bishops) in structure, and governed by the Crown through Parliament. Although they disappeared from the Calvinistic churches of Europe, bishops survived in the English Church because they served as useful instruments of royal control. Elizabeth was determined to have the English Church serve the needs of the English state as she defined those needs. Thus, she insisted on conformity to the manner of worship laid down by Parliament in the ACT OF UNIFORMITY and the *BOOK OF COMMON PRAYER*, but allowed a wide variety of beliefs and practices to exist within this mandated framework.

Englishmen and women could largely believe as they wished, so long as they outwardly conformed and kept unapproved opinions to themselves. The Anglican Church was thus based on the idea that matters of worship and church government not specifically outlined in the Bible and authorized by the state could be left to local practice and national custom as things indifferent to salvation and true belief. Conversely, Puritans maintained that almost all religious practices were strictly prescribed in Scripture and could not be left to local or national tradition.

At the Church's creation in 1559, Anglican doctrine and liturgy were vaguely defined, in part because the government sought to include as many people as possible, whether conservatives or advanced reformers, within the new church. But the parameters of Anglicanism became sharper during the course of the reign as Roman Catholics fell away and Puritans began to distinguish themselves from the national church through disputes over vestments, governance, and liturgy. Anglicanism also defined itself through the writings of its chief thinkers, the foremost of whom was Richard Hooker.

ASK YOURSELF

1. Why did Elizabeth prefer the Church to be governed through bishops rather than through Presbyterian assemblies?
2. Besides bishops, what other aspects of Anglican Church government and practice did Puritans object to and why?
3. Which group presented the most serious threat to the Anglican Church in the 1590s, the Catholics or the Puritans? Why?

TOPICS AND ACTIVITIES TO CONSIDER

- ~ Access the History section of the Church of England Web site at http://www.cofe.anglican.org/about/history. After reading and analyzing the section, write a brief essay describing how closely the modern Church of England still follows the Elizabethan idea of *via media*. From your reading, does it still stand between Roman Catholicism and Evangelical Protestantism, or does it seem to have shifted in one direction or the other? Give reasons for your opinion.
- ~ Draft a 10-question multiple choice quiz about the Elizabethan Anglican Church. Include questions about its governance, practices, rituals, and principles.

Further Information

Archer, Stanley. *Richard Hooker*. Boston: Twayne, 1983.

Atkinson, Nigel. *Richard Hooker and the Authority of Scripture, Tradition and Reason.* Vancouver, BC: Regent College Publishing, 2005.

Faulkner, Robert K. *Richard Hooker and the Politics of Christian England.* Berkeley: University of California Press, 1981.

Hooker, Richard. *Of the Laws of Ecclesiastical Polity.* Edited by A.S. McGrade. Cambridge: Cambridge University Press, 1989.

Web Sites

Works of Richard Hooker: http://anglicanhistory.org/hooker

Works of Richard Hooker: http://www.luminarium.org/renlit/hookbib.htm

LITERATURE AND HISTORY

21. CRITICIZING ELIZABETHAN PLAYGOERS: STEPHEN GOSSON'S *SCHOOL OF ABUSE* (1579)

INTRODUCTION

The following unflattering depiction of playgoing audiences is taken from Stephen GOSSON's *The School of Abuse* (1579), a satirical pamphlet that is famously critical of both plays and poetry. Himself a playwright and actor in the 1570s, Gosson later fell under PURITAN influence and renounced the theater. He eventually produced a number of polemics that attacked the manner in which he believed vulgar comedies and melodramas degraded and disordered London society (see "Elizabethan London," Document 7). The pamphlet's descriptive subtitle, *Containing a Pleasant Invective against Poets, Pipers, Players, Jesters and such like Caterpillars of a Commonwealth*, reflects the growing Puritan concern that plays and players promoted godlessness and immorality.

KEEP IN MIND AS YOU READ

1. In the Middle Ages, most theater had been religious in nature, using humor or cautionary tales to reinforce the teachings of the Church. With the Reformation (see "English Reformation," Document 14), the government, understanding that plays could be used to promote a particular religious or political point of view, gradually brought the theater under royal control. ELIZABETH banned the performance of unlicensed plays in 1559, restricted the sponsorship of troupes of players to noblemen in 1572, and empowered her master of revels to license all plays and acting companies in 1574.

2. Puritans objected to plays on religious grounds, and the government had political concerns, but there were also other reasons to regulate the public theater. In 1592, an outbreak of the plague caused the city of London to close all theaters and disband all acting companies. Theaters did not reopen until 1594.

3. In the 1570s, Robert DUDLEY, Earl of Leicester, the royal favorite, used plays and entertainments that his players performed for the Queen to promote his marriage to Elizabeth and to enhance his position at court.

Document: Excerpt from Gosson's The School of Abuse

deer takes soil: one hides or tries to throw off pursuers
narrowly: closely
pippins: apples
quetch: complain

In our assemblies at plays in London, you shall see such heaving, and shoving, such itching and shouldering to sit by women: such care for their garments, that they not be trod on: such eyes to their laps, that no chips light in them: such pillows to their backs, that they take no hurt: such masking in their ears, I know not what: such giving them **pippins** to pass the time: such playing at foot-saunt [footsie] without cards: such tickling, such toying, such smiling, such winking, and such manning them home, when the sports are ended, that it is a right comedy to mark their behavior, to watch their conceits, as the cat for the mouse, and as good as a course at the game itself, to dog them a little, or follow aloof by the print of their feet, and so discover by slot where the **deer takes soil**. If this were as well noted as ill seen, or as openly punished as secretly practiced, I have no doubt but the cause would be seared to dry up the effect, and these pretty rabbits very cunningly ferreted from their burrows. For they that lack customers all the week, either because their haunt is unknown or the constables and officers of their parish watch them so **narrowly** that they dare not **quetch**, to celebrate the Sabbath flock to theaters, and there keep a general market of bawdry. Not that any filthiness indeed is committed within the compass of that ground, as was done in Rome but that every wanton and his paramour, every man and his mistress, every John and his Joan, every knave and his queen, are there first acquainted and cheapen the merchandise in that place, which they pay for elsewhere as they can agree.

Source: Gosson, Stephen. *The School of Abuse, 1579, and A Short Apologie of The School of Abuse 1579*. Edited by Edward Arber. London: Alex Murray and Son, 1868, p. 35.

AFTERMATH

Although Gosson dedicated *The School of Abuse* to Sir Philip SIDNEY, that famous Elizabethan poet, not surprisingly, repudiated a work that opened with a lengthy denunciation of poetry. It also seems likely that Gosson's pamphlet motivated Sidney to write his "An Apology for Poetry" (see Document 23), which was published in 1581. In the early 1580s, Gosson published two more anti-theater tracts, *Ephemerides of Phialo* (1579) and *Plays Confuted in Five Actions* (1582), which in turn elicited many published refutations from poets and playwrights, including Thomas LODGE's *Defence of Plays* (1580), and many mocking revivals of Gosson's own plays. In the 1580s, Gosson became an Anglican clergyman, becoming rector on the Queen's appointment of Great Wigborough in Essex in 1591 and of St. Botolph's in Bishopsgate, London, in 1600. Meanwhile, the Puritan animosity toward players expressed by Gosson culminated in the closure of all theaters and the banning of all performances of stage plays by a Puritan-controlled Parliament in September 1642 at the start of the English Civil War.

GLOBE THEATER

Because it is closely associated with William SHAKESPEARE, the Globe Theater is the best-known theater of Elizabethan London and would likely have been a later site of many of the scenes Stephen Gosson describes in the excerpt above. In 1596, James BURBAGE sought unsuccessfully to renew the lease on his London theater. Burbage died in 1597, and, in 1598, his sons, Cuthbert and Richard BURBAGE, commissioned a carpenter to dismantle the entire theater and move it across the Thames to the southern suburb of Southwark. By late summer 1599, the new Globe Theatre was open for performances. Because the move was costly, the Burbages gathered a group of investors to finance the project, one of whom was Shakespeare.

The Globe was a round, wooden structure rising about 40 feet in height to accommodate three tiers of galleries that took up roughly 13 feet of the theater's 80-foot diameter. Thrusting into the uncovered central auditorium, which was about 65 feet in diameter, was a raised rectangular stage approximately 40 feet wide and partially covered by a thatched roof supported by two pillars. The stage could hold no more than 12 actors at a time, although the building could accommodate audiences of over 2,000. Actors' dressing rooms lay behind the stage. Rising above it were a gallery, which could be used for the audience or as part of the stage, and a balcony from which elaborate machinery caused gods and angels to descend to the stage. A trapdoor in the stage floor allowed the appearance of demons and the staging of burials.

Adorned with a globe on its roof, the theater had carved on its front a Latin quotation that translated roughly into Shakespeare's "All the world's a stage." When a play was in progress, the Globe flew a flag bearing its emblem. In June 1613, a blank volley fired as part of a performance of Shakespeare's *Henry VIII* started a fire that burned the Globe to the ground. It was rebuilt in 1614.

ASK YOURSELF

1. How did Puritans feel about the traditional celebrations surrounding Christmas and other major holidays? Why did they feel that way? How did these beliefs relate to their concerns regarding stage performances?
2. How, according to Gosson, do public performances of plays encourage immorality? Do Gosson's criticisms of Elizabethan theater mirror any modern criticisms, especially by religious groups, of modern forms of music or entertainment?

TOPICS AND ACTIVITIES TO CONSIDER

- Access the Renascence Editions Web site, and read an excerpt from Thomas Lodge's reply to Gosson's *The School of Abuse* at http://www.uoregon .edu/~rbear/lodge.html. List some of the arguments Lodge makes to counter those of Gosson. Write a brief essay giving your opinion as to which of the two writers was more persuasive and why.
- In the early twenty-first century, there is much discussion in the United States over the role of Hollywood in national politics. Should movie and television stars and other celebrities use their fame to endorse candidates and promote their political or social agendas? Many people say no, just as many people in Elizabethan England worried, for religious reasons, about the influence of stage actors, the celebrities of the day. Use the Internet to search for recent articles, essays, and editorials on this issue. Then write your own essay giving your opinion on the subject and your reasons for believing as you do.

Further Information

Gosson, Stephen. *School of Abuse, Containing a Pleasant Invective Against Poets, Pipers, Players, Jesters, &*. Charleston, SC: BookSurge Publishing, 2001.

Ringler, William A. *Stephen Gosson: A Biographical and Critical Study*. London: Octagon Press, 1972.

Web Site

The Schoole of Abuse: http://www.uoregon.edu/~rbear/gosson1.html

22. A Contemporary Description of Elizabethan England: John Lyly's Novel *Euphues and His England* (1580)

INTRODUCTION

Reproduced here is a description of England taken from John LYLY's *Euphues and His England*, the sequel to his immensely popular romance novel, *Euphues, the Anatomy of Wit*. Because they are considered its highest expression, these novels gave their name to a style of writing and mode of speaking, Euphuism, which was fashionable in late Elizabethan England. Euphuism was an elaborate, artificial style characterized by balance, alliteration, and extensive use of historical, philosophical, and mythological allusions. Lyly purposely undertook to develop an ornate, witty style that would contrast with the dense, heavy style of contemporary scholarship and be especially attractive to female readers. Addressing himself to "the gentle-women of England," Lyly declared that he would prefer his works "lie shut in a lady's casket than open in a scholar's study" (http://www.luminarium.org/renlit/euphuism.htm).

KEEP IN MIND AS YOU READ

1. In the 1570s, Lyly was secretary to the poet Edward de VERE, Earl of Oxford, who some scholars argue was the real writer of the plays ascribed to William SHAKESPEARE (see Document 28).
2. In the 1580s, Lyly managed a company of child actors known as Paul's Boys. The company performed a series of comedies by Lyly, the first to be written in prose, at the Blackfriars Theater.
3. Lyly involved himself on the side of the bishops in the MARTIN MARPRELATE controversy of 1589. This involvement may have been part of Lyly's efforts to ingratiate himself at court.
4. Lyly's style influenced many other Elizabethan writers, including Shakespeare and Thomas LODGE, who wrote several works in the euphuic style.

Document: Excerpt from Lyly's Euphues and His England

Euphues Glass for Europe.

There is an Isle lying in the Ocean Sea, directly against that part of France, which contains Picardy and Normandy, called now England, heretofore named

Britain, it has Ireland upon the West side, on the North the Main Sea, on the East side, the German Ocean. This Island is in circuit 1720 miles, in form like unto a Triangle, being broadest in the South part, and gathering narrower and narrower till it come to the farthest point of Caithness Northward, where it is narrowest, and there ends in manner of a Promontory. To repeat, the ancient manner of this Island, or what sundry nations have inhabited there, to set down the Giants, which in bigness [highness] of bone have passed the common size, and almost common credit, to rehearse what diversities of Languages have been used, into how many kingdoms it has been divided, what Religions have been followed before the coming of Christ, although it would breed great delight to your ears [eyes], yet might it happily seem tedious: For that honey taken excessively cloys the stomach though it be honey.

But my mind is briefly to touch such things as at my being there I gathered by mine own study and inquiry, not meaning to write a Chronicle, but to set down in a word what I heard by conference.

It has in it twenty and six Cities, of the which the chiefest is named London, a place both for the beauty of building, infinite riches, variety of all things, that excels all the Cities in the world: insomuch that it may be called the Storehouse and Mart of all Europe. Close by this City runs the famous River called the Thames, which from the head where it rises . . . unto the full midway it is thought to be an hundred and fourscore miles. What can there be in any place under the heavens, that is not in this noble City either to be bought or borrowed?

It hath divers Hospitals for the relieving of the poor, six-score faire Churches for divine service, a glorious Borse which they call the Royal Exchange, for the meeting of Merchants of all countries where any traffic is to be had. And among all the strange and beautiful shows, me thinks there is none so notable, as the Bridge which crosses the Thames, which is in manner of a continual street, well replenished with large and stately houses on both sides, and situate upon twenty Arches, whereof each one is made of excellent free stone squared, every one of them being three-score foot in height, and full twenty in distance one from another.

To this place the whole Realm has his recourse, whereby it seems so populous, that one would scarce think so many people to be in the whole Island, as he shall see sometimes in London.

This makes Gentlemen brave, and Merchants rich, Citizens to purchase, and sojourners to mortgage, so that it is to be thought, that the greatest wealth and substance of the whole Realm is couched within the walls of London, where they that be rich keep it from those that be riotous, not detaining it from the lusty youths of England by rigor, but increasing it until young men shall favor of reason, wherein they **mew** themselves treasurers for others, not borders for themselves, yet although it be sure enough, would they had it, in my opinion, it were better to be in the Gentleman's purse, then in the Merchant's hands.

There are in this Isle two and twenty Bishops, which are as it were superintendants over the church, men of great zeal, and deep knowledge, diligent Preachers of the word, earnest followers of their doctrine, careful watchmen that the Wolf devour not the Sheep, in civil government politique, in ruling the spiritual sword

---

Corselets: a piece of armor covering the trunk of the body

Fustian: a strong cotton and linen fabric

mew: to shut up; confine

physicke: medicine

visitation: an official inspection of a diocese or clerical jurisdiction to uncover and root out heresy or improper doctrine or ritual (as far as to [in] them under their Prince appertains) just, cutting off those members from the Church by rigor, that are obstinate in their heresies, and instructing those that are ignorant, appointing godly and learned Ministers in every of their Sees, that in their absence may be lights to such as are in darkness, salt to those that are unflavored, leaven to such as are not seasoned.

Visitations are held oftentimes, whereby abuses and disorders, either in the laity for negligence, or in the clergy for superstition, or in all, for wicked living there are punishments, by due execution whereof the divine service of God is honored with more purity, and followed with greater sincerity.

There are also in this Island two famous Universities, the one Oxford, the other Cambridge, both for the profession of all sciences, for Divinity, **physicke**, Law, and all kind of learning, excelling all the Universities of Christendom.

I was myself in either of them, and like them both so well, that I mean not in the way of controversy to prefer any for the better in England, but both for the best in the world, saving this, that Colleges in Oxford are much more stately for the building, and Cambridge much more sumptuous for the houses in the town, but the learning neither lies in the free stones of the one, nor the fine streets of the other, for out of them both do daily proceed men of great wisdom, to rule in the commonwealth, of learning to instruct the common people, of all singular kind of professions to do good to all. And let this suffice, not to enquire which of them is the superior, but that neither of them have their equal, neither to ask which of them is the most ancient, but whether any other be so famous.

But to proceed in England, their buildings are not very stately unless it be the houses of noble men and here and there, the place of a Gentleman, but much amended, as they report that have told me. For their munitions they have not only great store, but also great cunning to use them, and courage to practice them, there armor is not unlike unto that which in other countries they use, as **Corselets** . . . shirts of mail, jackets quilted and covered over with Leather, **Fustion** or Canvas, over thick plates of iron that are sewed into the same.

The ordinance they have is great, and thereof great store.

Their navy is divided as it were into three sorts, of the which the one serves for wars, the other for burthen, the third for fishermen. And some vessels there be (I know not by experience, and yet I believe by circumstance) that will sail nine hundred miles in a week, when I would scarce think that a bird could fly four hundred.

Source: Arber, Edward, ed. *English Reprints: John Lyly. Euphues. The Anatomy of Wit; Euphues and His England*. London: Alexander Murray and Son, 1868, 433–436.

AFTERMATH

A playwright, pamphleteer, and member of Parliament, Lyly received instant acclaim for his novels and tried to turn that popularity into a position at court, where he sought to obtain the office of master of revels. However, he was frustrated in this by the longevity of the incumbent, Edmund TILNEY, who held the office from 1579 until his death in 1610. In 1597, when the mastership was promised to another man upon Tilney's death, a disappointed Lyly wrote a letter of complaint to the Queen and his minister, Sir Robert CECIL. Lyly's fame and the popularity of Euphuism declined in the 1590s, and the writer's ongoing search for court patronage, which lasted until his death in 1606, proved largely unsuccessful.

ENGLISH UNIVERSITIES

In the excerpt above, John Lyly provides a glowing description of England's two universities—Oxford and Cambridge. The medieval universities educated lower-class boys for careers in the church. By ELIZABETH I's reign, the Reformation had brought the universities, like the church itself, under royal control (see "English Reformation," Document 14). With the teaching of canon (Church) law prohibited after 1535, most of the universities' original purpose disappeared, and attendance declined sharply in the 1530s and 1540s. But, in the 1550s, the universities revived as training centers for the well-born sons of the GENTRY. By 1603, most JUSTICES OF THE PEACE, members of Parliament, and royal officials had received some university training.

In the 1590s, the yearly number of incoming freshmen at Oxford was about 360, over three times the number of the 1510s. Many incoming students did not complete the full four-year course of study for a degree, leaving after two or three years to tour Europe or begin legal studies in the COMMON LAW at the INNS OF COURT. The Elizabethan curriculum was sufficiently influenced by HUMANISM to place heavier emphasis on the study of Greek and Latin. The expansion of Elizabethan trade and exploration also created a demand for more courses in geography and history and for more training in such practical skills as navigation. Many Elizabethan clergymen took advanced degrees in divinity. Cambridge, in particular, acquired a reputation as a PURITAN school. By 1603, the English universities were increasingly secular institutions providing education for the sons of gentlemen (see "Elizabethan Education," Document 2).

ASK YOURSELF

1. Do you think the euphuic style is difficult for a modern reader? Why do you believe as you do? Why do you think the style was so popular in the 1580s but has not been popular since?

2. Access Shakespeare's *Hamlet* at http://shakespeare.mit.edu/hamlet/full.html, and read the speeches of the character Polonius, especially the longer ones in Act I, Scene 3. Do these speeches seem to mirror Lyly's style? Why or why not? Read also the speeches of the character Moth in *Love's Labour's Lost* and the repartees of the characters Beatrice and Benedick in *Much Ado About Nothing*. Is there any hint of the euphuic style in these Shakespearean lines?

TOPICS AND ACTIVITIES TO CONSIDER

- ☙ Access the digitized edition of Lyly's *Euphues, the Anatomy of Wit* and *Euphues and His England* at http://books.google.com/books, and read a representative section of either work. From your reading, try to identify the main features of the euphuic style, and then write a brief description of something that happened to you in that style. Rewrite the description in your own modern style. Compare the two, and see how they differ.

- ☙ Analyze Lyly's description of England, and list what you see as his praises of England and his criticisms of it. Access Shakespeare's *Richard II* at http://books.google.com/books, and read the famous description of England given there by the character of John of Gaunt in Act II, Scene 1. Gaunt is lamenting the state of England during the Hundred Years War, but his description of what it was and could be is soaring. Write a brief essay comparing Lyly's description with Shakespeare's.

Further Information

Houppert, Joseph W. *John Lyly*. Boston: Twayne, 1975.

Hunter, G.K. *John Lyly: The Humanist as Courtier*. Cambridge, MA: Harvard University Press, 1962.

Lyly, John. *The Complete Works of John Lyly*. Edited by R. Warwick Bond. Reprint ed. Whitefish, MT: Kessinger Publishing, 2006.

———. *"Euphues: The Anatomy of Wit" and "Euphues and His England": An Annotated, Modern-Spelling Edition*. Edited by Leah Scragg. Manchester: Manchester University Press, 2002.

Web Site

Biography of Lyly and Discussion of Euphuism: http://www.luminarium.org/renlit/lylybio.htm

Selected Works of John Lyly: http://www.luminarium.org/renlit/lylybib.htm

23. An Elizabethan Defense of Poets and Their Work: Sir Philip Sidney's Treatise "An Apology for Poetry" (1581)

INTRODUCTION

Sir Philip SIDNEY, the nephew of Robert DUDLEY, Earl of Leicester, the Queen's favorite, and the godson of PHILIP II of Spain, was accepted in his own time as the archetypical Elizabethan courtier-poet. In the 1580s, Sidney, to express his passion for Lady Penelope RICH, wrote the first English sonnet cycle, *Astrophel and Stella*, which influenced many other English poets, including William SHAKESPEARE (see "Shakespearean Sonnet," Document 28). This selection is drawn from Sidney's "An Apology for Poetry" (or the "The Defence of Poetry"), which was meant, at least in part, as a response to Stephen GOSSON's attack on poets and players in his *The School of Abuse* (see Document 21). In this excerpt, Sidney defended poets from charges that their work was of lesser value than other endeavors.

KEEP IN MIND AS YOU READ

1. Without asking permission, Gosson dedicated his *The School of Abuse* to Sidney, an act that is thought to have particularly angered Sidney and motivated his writing of the "Apology."
2. Sidney was a member of a group of court poets and philosophers known as the "Aeropagus," which sought to elevate both the quality and appreciation of English poetry and literature.
3. Most of Sidney's works, such the "Apology" and his popular prose romance *Arcadia*, were published after his death. Thus, unlike Gosson and other writers not of the nobility or GENTRY, poetry for Sidney was a pastime, not a livelihood.
4. The Elizabethan period was a time of transition from a system of private literary patronage, where a poet or writer relied on a wealthy nobleman for financial support, to the appearance of professional authors who relied on the sale of their works to earn a livelihood. During the reign of ELIZABETH I, the old system was by no means dead, but the new system was clearly developing.

Document: Excerpt from Sidney's "An Apology for Poetry"

Now then we go to the most important imputations laid to the poor Poets, for aught I can yet learn, they are these: first, that here being many other more fruitful knowledges, a man might better spend his time in them than in this. Secondly, that it is the mother of lies. Thirdly, that it is the Nurse of abuse, infecting us with many pestilent desires: with a Siren's sweetness drawing the mind to the Serpent's tale of sinful fancy. And herein especially comedies give the largest field to err, as Chaucer says: how both in other Nations and in ours, before poets did soften us, we were full of courage, given to martial exercises; the pillars of manlike liberty, and not lulled asleep in the shady idleness with Poets' pastimes. And lastly, and chiefly, they cry out with an open mouth, as if they outshot Robin Hood, that Plato banished them out of his Commonwealth. Truly, this is much, if there be much truth in it. First to the first: that a man might better spend his time, is a reason indeed: but it does (as they say) but *petere principium*: for if it be as I affirm, that no learning is so good as that which teaches and moves to virtue; and that none can both teach and move thereto so much as Poetry: then is the conclusion manifest, the Ink and Paper cannot be to a more profitable purpose employed. And certainly, though a man should grant their first assumption, it should follow (methinks) very unwillingly that good is not good because better is better. But I still and utterly deny that there is sprung out of earth a more fruitful knowledge. To the second therefore, that they should be the principal liars, I answer paradoxically, but truly—I think truly—that of all writers under the sun the Poet is the least liar: and though he would, as a Poet can scarcely be a liar, the Astronomer, with his cousin the Geometrician, can hardly escape, when they take upon them to measure the height of the stars.

How often, think you, do the Physicians lie, when they aver things good for sickness which afterwards send Charon a great number of souls drowned in a potion before they come to his Ferry? And no less of the rest which take upon them to affirm. Now, for the Poet, he nothing affirms, and therefore never lies. For, as I take it, to lie is to affirm that to be true which is false. So as the other Artists, and especially the Historian, affirming many things, can in the cloudy knowledge of mankind hardly escape from many lies. But the Poet (as I said before) never affirms. The Poet never makes any circles about your imagination to conjure you to believe for true what he writes. He cites not authorities of other Histories, but, even for his entry, calls the sweet Muses to inspire into him a good invention: in truth, not laboring to tell you what is, or is not, but what should or should not be: and therefore, though he recount things not true, yet because he tells them not for true, he lies not . . . . Which as a wicked man dares scare say, so think I none so simple would say that Aesop lied in the tales of his beasts: for who thinks that Aesop wrote it for actually true were well worthy to have his name chronicled among the beasts he writes of.

What child is there that, coming to a Play, and seeing Thebes written in great letters upon an old door, does believe that it is Thebes? If then a man can arrive at that child's age to know that the Poets' persons and doings are but pictures what should be, and not

---

groundplot: ground plan
petere principium: beg the question

---

stories what have been, they will never give the lie to things not affirmatively but allegorically and figuratively written. And therefore, as in History, looking for truth, they go away full fraught with falsehood: so in Poetry, looking for fiction, they shall use the narration but as an imaginative **groundplot** of a profitable invention.

But hereto is replied that the Poets give names to men they write of, which argues a conceit of an actual truth, and so, being true, proves a falsehood. And does the Lawyer lie then, when under the names of *John-a-stile* and *John-a-noakes* he puts his case? But that is easily answered. There naming of men is but to make their picture the more lively, and not to build any history: painting men, they cannot leave men nameless. We see we cannot play at Chess but that we must give names to our Chess-men; and yet methinks he were a very partial Champion of truth that would say we lied for giving a piece of wood the reverend title of a Bishop. The Poet names Cyrus or Aeneas no other way than to show what men of their fames, fortunes and estates should do.

Their third is how much it abuses men's wit, training it to wanton sinfulness and lustful love: for indeed that is the principal, if not the only abuse I can hear alleged. They say the Comedies rather teach than reprehend amorous conceits. They say, the Lyric is larded with passionate Sonnets. The Elegiac weeps the want of his mistress. And that even to the Heroical Cupid has ambitiously climbed. Alas, Love! I would you could as well defend yourself as you can offend others. I would those on whom you do attend could either put you away or yield good reason why they keep you. But grant love of beauty to be a beastly fault (although it be very hard, since only man, and no beast, has that gift, to discern beauty); grant that lovely name of Love to deserve all hateful reproaches (although even some of my Masters the Philosophers spent a good deal of their Lamp-oil in setting forth the excellence of it); grant, I say, whatsoever they will have granted; that not only love, but lust, but vanity, but (if they list) scurrility possesses many leaves of the Poets' books; yet think I, when this granted, they will find their sentence may with good manners put the last words foremost: and not say that Poetry abuses man's wit, but that man's wit abuses Poetry.

Source: Sidney, Sir Philip. "An Apology for Poetry." In Laurie Magnus, ed. *Documents Illustrating Elizabethan Poetry.* London: George Routledge and Sons Ltd., 1906, pp. 77–81.

AFTERMATH

Firmly committed to the Protestant cause, Sidney deplored the Queen's proposed marriage to Francis VALOIS, Duke of Anjou, the brother of the French king (see Documents 32 and 33). To protest the match, he sent a bold letter of remonstrance to the Queen and quarreled violently with Edward de VERE, Earl of Oxford (see Document 28), who supported the marriage. These actions brought Sidney into royal disfavor and led him to exile himself from court. During this exile, Sidney wrote his most famous works, the *Astrophel and Stella* sonnet sequence, the romance *Arcadia*, and the "Apology." He was readmitted to favor in 1582, but again angered the Queen in the following year when he made an unapproved marriage with the daughter of Sir Francis WALSINGHAM. Denied royal employment, Sidney was about to sail for the New World with Sir Francis DRAKE when Elizabeth appointed him governor of the Dutch town of Flushing. A year later, in 1586, Sidney died of wounds received in battle against the Spanish in the Netherlands (see "Spanish Netherlands," Document 38).

ELIZABETHAN POETRY

The reign of Elizabeth was one of the most creative and prolific periods in the history of English poetry. This poetic flowering began in the quarter century between 1550 and 1575, when humanist scholars and Protestant reformers used English, long considered inferior to Latin and Greek, as a literary language to teach and to preach. Prose works of scholarship, like Roger ASCHAM's *The Schoolmaster* (1570) (see Document 2) and religious works like John FOXE's "Book of Martyrs," illustrated the strength and flexibility of Elizabethan English. Poetry, the pastime of courtiers in earlier decades, reached a wider audience in the 1560s with the publication of Richard TOTTEL's anthology *Songs and Sonnets* (1557), a work generally known as "Tottel's Miscellany." By popularizing the court poetry of HENRY VIII's time and the work of unknown contemporary poets, Tottel inspired a host of similar poetry collections that helped build demand for English verse.

This growing interest in poetry was illustrated by the popularity of *A Mirror for Magistrates*, a collection of poetic laments supposedly spoken by participants in the Wars of the Roses. The plainer, simpler poetry published by Tottel and the *Mirror* in the 1560s was superseded in the next two decades by the more ornate and innovative lyric poetry written by Edmund Spenser and Sir Philip Sidney. Spenser was the first English poet to use print to deliberately disseminate his work to a wider public. His *The Faerie Queen* was a lyric epic of Protestant nationalism, casting Elizabeth as the Faerie Queen herself. Sidney's work was also fused with Protestant fervor and tied to the cult of the Virgin Queen. Where Spenser inspired every English poet of the 1590s to try lyric poetry, Sidney, through his *Astrophel and Stella* cycle, initiated a flood of sonnet sequences, including William Shakespeare's.

ASK YOURSELF

1. What arguments against the writing of poetry does Sidney refute? What arguments does he make to support the writing of poetry?
2. Do you agree with Sidney's views on poetry and literature? Why or why not?

TOPICS AND ACTIVITIES TO CONSIDER

- Access the digitized edition of Clara Gebert's *An Anthology of Elizabethan Dedications and Prefaces* at http://books.google.com/books. View Gosson's dedication to Sidney from his The *School of Abuse* at http://darkwing.uoregon.edu/~rbear/gosson1.html. From reading and analyzing a selection of these dedications and prefaces, make of list of what appear to be the various reasons for including them. Draft your own short dedication, in the Elizabethan style, for a current work, including a book, poem, movie, etc. to a current public or popular figure.
- Access the digitized edition of *England in Shakespeare's Day* by G.B. Harrison at http://books.google.com/books. On pages 8–11 are reproduced two of the many tributes written to Sidney after his death. Read and analyze these tributes by Edmund SPENSER and Fulke GREVILLE and any others that you might find online. Greville and Spencer were friends of Sidney, but many other poets and writers who lamented him could hardly have known him. Write a brief essay explaining why you think most every Elizabethan with literary pretensions felt obliged to pay tribute to Sidney.

Further Information

Duncan-Jones, Katherine. *Sir Philip Sidney*. New Haven, CT: Yale University Press, 1991.

Greville, Fulke, Baron Brooke. *Sir Fulke Greville's Life of Sir Philip Sidney*. Folcroft, PA: Folcroft Press, 1971.

Hamilton, A.C. *Sir Philip Sidney: A Study of His Life and Works*. Cambridge: Cambridge University Press, 1977.

Howell, Roger. *Sir Philip Sidney: The Shepherd Knight*. Boston: Little, Brown and Company, 1968.

Sidney, Sir Philip. *An Apology for Poetry*. Edited by Forrest G. Robinson. New York: Macmillan, 1970.

———. *Sir Philip Sidney: The Major Works*. Edited by Katherine Duncan-Jones. Oxford World's Classics. Oxford: Oxford University Press, 2002.

———. *Sir Philip Sidney's Apology for Poetry and Astrophil and Stella: Texts and Contexts*. Edited by Philip C. Herman. Glen Allen, VA: College Publishing, 2001.

Stewart, Alan. *Philip Sidney: A Double Life*. New York: St. Martin's Press, 2000.

Web Site

Sidney's "An Apology for Poetry": http://books.google.com/books

Works of Sir Philip Sidney: http://www.luminarium.org/renlit/sidbib.htm

24. WILLIAM SHAKESPEARE AND HIS SOURCES: THE SECOND EDITION OF HOLINSHED'S *CHRONICLE* (1587) AND *RICHARD III* (C. 1592–1593)

INTRODUCTION

Reproduced below are two descriptions of the same event, a meeting of the royal Council held at the Tower of London on June 13, 1483. The meeting is famous as the starting point of Duke Richard of Gloucester's usurpation of the throne of his young nephew, Edward V. Once his uncle became King as Richard III, Edward and his younger brother, who were lodged in the Tower, disappeared, thus creating one of the greatest mysteries in English history.

The first version of the meeting given here comes from the second edition of Raphael HOLINSHED's *Chronicles of England, Scotland, and Ireland*, a popular history of Britain published in 1587 (see "Holinshed's *Chronicles*" below). William SHAKESPEARE used the second edition of Holinshed as source material for many of his history plays, such as *Richard III*, from which the second excerpt is taken. Although Holinshed and his editors were writing a history and Shakespeare a drama, it is from the latter that many modern readers learn their history of fifteenth-century England.

KEEP IN MIND AS YOU READ

1. Shakespeare wrote two major four-play cycles, known as tetralogies, covering the history of England from the deposition of Richard II in 1399 to the accession of HENRY VII, Elizabeth's grandfather, in 1485. These eight plays view the first of those events as an overthrow of the divine order and the second as the restoration of that order, thus the rise of the Tudor dynasty was sanctioned by God, a very politic opinion to hold with a Tudor Queen on the throne.

2. *Richard III* is one of the most popular of Shakespeare's plays in large part because of the playwright's striking depiction of the wicked king, whose witty enthusiasm for villainy makes the character a perfect contrast to Shakespeare's virtuous Henry VII. Since 1485, Tudor propaganda had depicted Richard III as a man so ambitious for the throne that he would murder anyone who stood in his way of achieving it. Shakespeare's character is the culminating expression of that depiction. Only in the last century have there been serious efforts to rehabilitate the reputation of the historical Richard III.

3. Although popular with the public, both editions of Holinshed's *Chronicles* angered the Queen, who ordered the deletion of various passages that she found offensive. In the first edition, ELIZABETH objected to the characterization of recent events in Ireland. In the second edition, she disliked the descriptions of the Babington Plot (see "Babington Plot," Document 35) and the Netherlands expedition of her favorite, Robert DUDLEY, Earl of Leicester.

Document 1: Holinshed's Chronicle: Account of the Tower Council Meeting of 13 June 1483

[O]n the Friday [being the thirteenth of June], many lords assembled in the Tower, and there sat in council, devising the honorable solemnity of the king's coronation; of which the time appointed then so near approached, that the pageants and subtleties were in making day & night at Westminster, and much **vittles** killed therefore, that afterward was cast away. These lords so sitting together communing of this matter, the protector came in amongst them, first about nine of the clock, saluting them courteously, and excusing himself that he had been from them so long; saying merrily that he had been a sleeper that day.

After a little talking with them, he said unto the bishop of Ely: "My lord, you have very good strawberries at your garden in Holborn, I require you let us have a mess of them." "Gladly, my lord" (quoth he) "would God I had some better thing as ready to your pleasure as that I!" And therewithal in all the haste he sent his servant for a mess of strawberries. The protector set the lords fast in communing, & thereupon, praying of them to spare him for a little while, departed thence. And soon after one hour, between ten & eleven, he returned into the chamber amongst them, all changed, with a wonderful sour angry countenance, knitting the brows, frowning, and fretting and gnawing on his lips: and so sat him down in his place.

All the lords were much dismayed, and sore marveled at this manner of sudden change, and what thing should him ail. Then, when he had sat still a while, thus he began: "What were they worthy to have that compass and imagine the destruction of me, being so near of blood unto the king, and protector of his royal person and his realm?" At this question, all the lords sat sore astonished, musing much by whom this question should be meant, of which every man wished himself clear. Then the lord chamberlain (as he that for the love between them thought he might be boldest with him) answered and said, that they were worthy to be punished as heinous traitors, whatsoever they were. And all the other affirmed the same. "That is" (quoth he) "yonder sorceress my brother's wife, and other with her" (meaning the Queen.)

At these words many of the other lords were greatly abashed, that favored her. But the lord Hastings was in his mind better content, that it was moved by her, than by any other whom he loved better: albeit his heart somewhat grudged, that he was not afore made of counsel in this matter, as he was of the taking of her kindred, and of their putting to death, which were by his assent before devised to be beheaded at Pomfret this self same day; in which he was not [aware] that it was by other devised, that he him-self should be beheaded the same day at London. Then said the protector: "Ye shall all see in what wise that sorceress, and that other witch of her counsel, Shore's wife, with their affinity, have, by their sorcery and witchcraft, wasted my body." And therewith he plucked up his **doublet** sleeve to his elbow, upon his left arm, where he showed a **weerish** withered arm, and small; as it was never other.

Hereupon every man's mind sore misgave them, well perceiving that this matter was but a quarrel. For they well knew that the Queen was too wise to go about any such folly. And also, if she would, yet would she, of all folk least, make Shore's wife of her counsel; whom of all women she most hated, as that concubine whom the king her husband had most loved. And also, no man was there present, but well knew that his arm was ever such since his birth. Nevertheless, the lord chamberlain (which from the death of king Edward kept Shore's wife, on whom he somewhat doted in the kings life . . .) answered and said: "Certainly my lord, if they have so heinously done, they be worthy heinous punishment."

"What" (quoth the protector) "you serve me, I see, with 'ifs' and with 'ands': I tell you they have so done, and that I will make good on thy body, traitor!" and therewith, as in a great anger, he clapped his fist upon the board a great rap. At which token one cried, "Treason!" Therewith a door clapped, and in come there rushing men in **harness**, as many as the chamber might hold. And anon the protector said to the lord Hastings: "I arrest thee, traitor!" "What me, my lord?" (quoth he.) "Yea, you, traitor!" quoth the protector. . . .

Then were they all quickly bestowed in diverse chambers, except the lord chamberlain, whom the protector bade speed and shrive him apace, "for, by saint Paul" (quoth he) "I will not to dinner till I see your head off." It **booted** him not to ask why, but heavily he took a priest at adventure, and made a short shrift: for a longer would not be suffered, the protector made so much haste to dinner, which he might not go to, until this were done, for saving of his oath.

> **booted:** availed; profited
> **doublet:** a man's close-fitting jacket
> **harness:** armor; military gear
> **vittles (usually spelled victuals):** provisions; food supplies
> **weerish:** weak; shrunken

Source: Boswell-Stone, W.G. *Shakespeare's Holinshed: The Chronicle and the Historical Plays Compared.* London: Chatto and Windus, 1907, pp. 370–373.

Document 2: Shakespeare's Richard III, *Act III, Scene 4: The Tower Council Meeting of June 13, 1483*

Enter Gloucester
Bishop of Ely: In happy time, here comes the Duke himself.
Gloucester: My noble lords and cousins all, good morrow.
    I have been long a sleeper, but I trust
    My absence doth neglect no great design
    Which by my presence might have been concluded.

Buckingham: Had you not come upon your cue, my lord,
    William Lord Hastings had pronounc'd your part—
    I mean, your voice for crowning of the King.
Gloucester: Than my Lord Hastings no man might be bolder;
    His lordship knows me well and loves me well.
    My lord of Ely, when I was last in Holborn
    I saw good strawberries in your garden there.
    I do beseech you send for some of them.
Bishop of Ely: Marry and will, my lord, with all my heart.
Exit
Gloucester: Cousin of Buckingham, a word with you.
[Takes him aside]
    Catesby hath sounded Hastings in our business,
    And finds the testy gentleman so hot
    That he will lose his head ere give consent
    His master's child, as worshipfully he terms it,
    Shall lose the royalty of England's throne.
Buckingham: Withdraw yourself awhile; I'll go with you.
Exeunt Gloucester and Buckingham
Derby: We have not yet set down this day of triumph.
    To-morrow, in my judgment, is too sudden;
    For I myself am not so well provided
    As else I would be, were the day prolong'd.
Re-enter the Bishop of Ely
Bishop of Ely: Where is my lord the Duke of Gloucester?
    I have sent for these strawberries.
Hastings: His Grace looks cheerfully and smooth this morning;
    There's some conceit or other likes him well
    When that he bids good morrow with such spirit.
    I think there's never a man in Christendom
    Can lesser hide his love or hate than he;
    For by his face straight shall you know his heart.
Derby: What of his heart perceive you in his face
    By any livelihood he show'd to-day?
Hastings: Marry, that with no man here he is offended;
    For, were he, he had shown it in his looks.
Re-enter Gloucester and Buckingham
Gloucester: I pray you all, tell me what they deserve
    That do conspire my death with devilish plots
    Of damned witchcraft, and that have prevail'd
    Upon my body with their hellish charms?
Hastings: The tender love I bear your Grace, my lord,
    Makes me most forward in this princely presence
    To doom th' offenders, whosoe'er they be.
    I say, my lord, they have deserved death.
Gloucester: Then be your eyes the witness of their evil.
    Look how I am bewitch'd; behold, mine arm
    Is like a blasted sapling wither'd up.

And this is Edward's wife, that monstrous witch,
Consorted with that harlot strumpet Shore,
That by their witchcraft thus have marked me.
Hastings: If they have done this deed, my noble lord—
Gloucester: If?—thou protector of this damned strumpet,
Talk'st thou to me of ifs? Thou art a traitor.
Off with his head! Now by Saint Paul I swear
I will not dine until I see the same.
Lovel and Ratcliff, look that it be done.
The rest that love me, rise and follow me.
Exeunt all but Hastings, Lovel, and Ratcliff

Source: *Richard III.* Renascence Editions Web site: http://www.uoregon.edu/
~rbear/shake/riii.html. Text in public domain.

AFTERMATH

The second edition of Holinshed's *Chronicles* was hugely successful. It was superior to the first edition in many ways, having better pagination, better indexing, and even higher quality paper. For Elizabethan poets and playwrights, the edition was a wealth of source material, being full of legends, anecdotes, and dramatic depictions of historical events. By comparing the plays of Shakespeare to the text of the second edition, a nineteenth-century scholar uncovered keywords and phrases in the former that only appear in the latter, thus proving that Shakespeare used the second edition as a source. Although Holinshed was superseded as a work of history in the seventeenth century when various more modern chronicles and histories appeared, Holinshed remained important for its link to the works of Shakespeare and other Elizabethan literary figures. Revival of interest in Shakespeare in the late eighteenth century resulted in the eventual publication of new editions of Holinshed from which any post-1587 accretions had been removed, thus making the exact text used by Shakespeare available to scholars.

HOLINSHED'S *CHRONICLES*

The Chronicles of England, Scotland, and Ireland, now known popularly as Holinshed's *Chronicles* because it was written and compiled under the editorship of Raphael Holinshed, was one of the most popular Elizabethan histories of Britain and the source for Shakespeare's history plays. Collaborating with a distinguished team of writers and compilers, Holinshed combined new material written by himself and his associates with material drawn from a wide variety of other chronicles and sources. Working largely on his own on the first volume, which covered the history of England, Holinshed reproduced, almost verbatim, large sections from the works of various other sixteenth-century chroniclers. He also included selections from writers like Sir Thomas More and from various medieval and classical chroniclers and writers.

The first edition of Holinshed's *Chronicles* appeared in two volumes in 1577 and was immediately popular with Elizabethan readers. After Holinshed's death in 1580, John HOOKER (see Documents 1 and 13), a writer and Exeter civic magistrate, collaborated with another editorial team to produce a three-volume second edition published in 1587. The new edition updated the *Chronicles* to 1586 and provided source material for 13 of Shakespeare's plays—the 10 English history plays and *King Lear, Cymbeline,* and *Macbeth.*

ASK YOURSELF

1. How does Shakespeare's depiction of the June 1483 Council meeting differ from the account in Holinshed's *Chronicles*? Why might Shakespeare have chosen to alter the story at some points? What parts of Holinshed's account has Shakespeare retained in his play? Why do you think he did so?
2. Does the depiction of Richard III in Holinshed differ in any way from the depiction of the king in the play? If so, how?

TOPICS AND ACTIVITIES TO CONSIDER

- After reading the two excerpts above, identify words and phrases from Shakespeare's play that seem to come from the account in Holinshed's *Chronicles*.
- The University of Pennsylvania has placed its copy of the 1587 edition of Holinshed online at http://dewey.lib.upenn.edu/sceti/PrintedBooksnew/index.cfm?TextID=holinshed_chronicle&PagePosition=1. Spelling, type style, and wording in this volume are very different from modern printing, so a contemporary reader unaccustomed to Elizabethan volumes may have trouble reading this site. Nonetheless, go to the site, and try to read a page of the *Chronicles* to get a sense of what the actual edition used by Shakespeare looked like.
- Write your own brief description of Richard III from what you read of him in the above account in Holinshed. Then write another brief description of the king based on the above depiction of him in *Richard III*. Compare your two accounts to see if they differ.

Further Information

Greenblatt, Stephen. *Will in the World: How Shakespeare Became Shakespeare*. London: W.W. Norton & Company, 2004.

Hosley, Richard, ed. *Shakespeare's Holinshed*. New York: Putnam Sons, 1968.

Kay, Dennis. *Shakespeare: His Life, Work, and Era*. New York: William Morrow, 1992.

Levi, Peter. *The Life and Times of William Shakespeare*. New York: Henry Holt and Company, 1988.

Norwich, John Julius. *Shakespeare's Kings: The Great Plays and the History of England in the Middle Ages, 1337–1485*. New York: Scribner, 2001.

O'Connor, Garry. *William Shakespeare: A Popular Life*. New York: Applause, 2000.

Patterson, Annabel. *Reading Holinshed's Chronicles*. Chicago: University of Chicago Press, 1994.

Wells, Stanley, Gary Taylor, John Jowett, and William Montgomery, eds. *William Shakespeare: The Complete Works*. The Oxford Shakespeare. Oxford: Clarendon Press, 1991.

Web Sites

Complete Works of Shakespeare: http://shakespeare.mit.edu

Holinshed's *Chronicles*: http://www.gutenberg.org/browse/authors/h#a5166

Holinshed Project at Oxford: http://www.cems.ox.ac.uk/holinshed/news.shtml

Richard III: http://www.uoregon.edu/~rbear/shake/riii.html

Shakespeare's Sources: http://www.shakespeare-online.com/sources/macbethsources.html

25. EXTOLLING THE REIGN OF GLORIANA: INTRODUCTION TO BOOK IV OF EDMUND SPENSER'S *FAERIE QUEENE* (1596)

INTRODUCTION

Edmund SPENSER was among the foremost poets of the Elizabethan age. His highly innovative *The Shepheardes Calendar*, a long poem dedicated to fellow poet Sir Philip SIDNEY (see Document 23), was enthusiastically received, especially at court, and led to Spenser's appointment as secretary to the lord deputy of Ireland. The following excerpt comes from Spenser's masterpiece, his grand epic poem *The Faerie Queene*, which was dedicated to Elizabeth and contained sonnets addressed to prominent courtiers (see "Shakespearean Sonnet," Document 28). *The Faerie Queene* won Spenser an annuity of £50 for life, thus providing him with the kind of royal recognition and patronage that eluded John LYLY (see Document 22). Eventually comprising six books, *The Faerie Queene* relates the adventures of the knights of the great Queen Gloriana (i.e., ELIZABETH I). Reproduced here are five stanzas from the Introduction to Book IV, which express the hope that the great Queen will enjoy and often read this work.

KEEP IN MIND AS YOU READ

1. Sir Walter RALEIGH, a neighbor and friend of Spenser's in Ireland, where Spenser began writing *The Faerie Queene*, persuaded him to present the first three books of the epic to the Queen herself and then to publish them in London.
2. Like most great epics, *The Faerie Queene* is an expression of national pride. The poem praises the Tudor dynasty by connecting it to the glorious history of King Arthur, the legendary hero of early Britain. Elizabeth herself is clearly Gloriana, the manifestation of national glory, but many other characters in the epic can be identified, in full or in part, with prominent Elizabethans.
3. Spenser deliberately employed outmoded and outdated words and phrases in *The Faerie Queene* to heighten the mythological and magical effect of the text.

Document: Excerpt from Spenser's
Faerie Queene

I.

The rugged forehead, that with grave foresight
Welds kingdoms, causes and affairs of state,

My looser rimes (I **wote**) doth sharply **wite**
For praising love as I have done of late,
And magnifying lovers dear debate;
By which frail youth is oft to folly led,
Through false allurement of that pleasing bait,
That better were in virtues discipled,
Then with vain poems weeds to have their fancies fed.

II

Such ones ill judge of love, that cannot love,
Ne in their frozen hearts feel kindly flame:
Forthy they ought not thing unknown reprove,
Ne natural affection faultless blame,
For fault of few that have abused the same.
For it of honor and all virtue is
The root, and brings forth glorious flowers of fame,
That crown true lovers with immortal bliss,
The **meed** of them that love, and do not live amiss.

III

Which whoso list look back to former ages,
And call to count the things that then were done,
Shall find that all the works of those wise sages,
And brave exploits which great Heroes won,
In love were either ended or begun:
Witness the father of Philosophic,
Which to his Critias, shaded oft from sun,
Of love full many lessons did apply,
The which these . . . censors cannot well deny.

IV

To such therefore I do not sing at all,
But to that sacred Saint my sovereign Queen,
In whose chaste breast all bounty natural
And treasures of true love enlocked been,
Bove all her sex that ever yet was seen;
To her I sing of love, that loveth best,
And best is lov'd of all alive I **ween**:
To her this song most fitly is addrest,
The Queen of love, and Prince of peace from heaven blest.

V

Which that she may the better deign to hear,
Do thou dread infant, Venus dearling dove,
From her high spirit chase imperious fear,
And use of awful Majestic remove:
Instead thereof with drops of melting love,
Dewed with ambrosial kisses, by thee gotten
From thy sweet-smiling mother from above,
Sprinkle her heart, and haughty courage soften,
That she may hark to love, and read this lesson often.

forthy: therefore
meed: reward
ween: imagine
wite: blame
wote: know

Source: Warren, Kate M., ed. *The Faerie Queene: By Edmund Spenser*. Book IV. Westminster: Archibald Constable and Company, 1899, pp. 1–2.

THE VIRGIN QUEEN

On Elizabeth's accession in 1558, her gender was thought to be her greatest weakness as a monarch. Ruling a kingdom was considered a man's job, and everyone accepted the belief that the Queen must have a husband both to help her govern and to maintain order among her male advisors. The great achievement of Elizabeth's reign was her success in turning the supposed weakness of her sex into an instrument for controlling, disciplining, and directing the men who formed her court, Council, and military command. Elizabeth accomplished this transformation by remaining unmarried and making herself the center of a secular, political cult of devotion that, in some ways, replaced the medieval religious cult of the Virgin Mary, which the Reformation had destroyed (see "English Reformation," Document 14). Spenser's portrayal of Elizabeth as the Faerie Queen was but one expression of this cult of devotion.

Where the knightly ideal of chivalry had dedicated itself to the Virgin and the devotion and protection of chaste femininity, Elizabethan courtiers dedicated themselves to the service and protection of a ruler who was not only a woman, but also a virgin. The cult of the Virgin Queen allowed Elizabeth to identify herself with the state and to channel the touchy pride and ready violence of her courtiers away from disorder and into controlled competition for her favor. Beginning with an element of romance, as when the young Elizabeth showed favor to Robert Dudley, Earl of Leicester, the cult of the Virgin Queen became almost a form of worship by Elizabeth's later years, with the name and idea of Elizabeth inspiring men to achievement in many fields. By using her femininity as a focus of devotion and service, Elizabeth became one of the strongest and most effective rulers in English history.

AFTERMATH

According to a 1589 letter from Spencer to Raleigh, which is usually printed as a preface to most modern editions of *The Faerie Queene*, the poem was to have 24 books, 12 focusing on the Queen's knights, each of whom personified a particular virtue, and 12 focusing on King Arthur, who likewise represented various good qualities. However, Spenser never followed this outline fully, and the final organization of the work, had Spenser lived to finish it, is uncertain. Spencer published only six books before his death in 1599. Book I depicts the virtue of "Holiness"; Book II, "Temperance"; Book III, "Chastity"; Book IV, "Friendship"; Book V, "Justice"; and Book VI, "Courtesy." According to legend, parts of Books VII–IX were destroyed in 1598 when Irish rebels burned the castle in which Spenser was then living.

ASK YOURSELF

1. How does Spenser address the Queen in the above excerpt? What qualities does he impart to her, and what role does he see her play in the life of the kingdom?
2. How important do you think the obtaining of royal patronage was to Spenser? Do you think *The Faerie Queene* was undertaken primarily to win rewards, in terms of money and office, from the Queen, or do you think the need to seek such patronage was simply part of literary life in the period and not Spenser's primary motivation?

TOPICS AND ACTIVITIES TO CONSIDER

- The excerpt above is written in Spenserian stanzas, a verse form especially devised by Spenser for *The Faerie Queene*. The nine-line stanzas use a particular meter, that is, the rhythm the words of each line establish, and a specific rhyme scheme. As to meter, the first eight lines of each stanza use iambic pentameter while the last line uses iambic hexameter. The rhyme scheme for each stanza is *ababbcbcc*. In all printed editions of *The Faerie Queene*, all lines of each stanza, except for the first and last, are indented. Use the Internet to read more of *The Faerie Queene* and to research iambic pentameter and hexameter. Then try your hand at writing a Spenserian stanza.

∾ *The Faerie Queene* is an allegory, that is, the story and adventures it narrates are a symbolic representation of something else. In this case, the long struggle between good and evil and the political reality, as Spencer saw it, of Elizabethan England. Google one of the many online editions of *The Faerie Queen*, and read a selection from one of the books. Then make a list of various characters, events, and ideas that appear, identifying for each the symbolical meaning that you think Spenser assigned to it. For instance, the dragon that the Redcrosse Knight fights in Book I is a symbol of evil.

Further Information

Hales, John W. *A Biography of Edmund Spenser*. London: Dodo Press, 2007.

Spenser, Edmund. *Edmund Spencer's Poetry*. Edited by Hugh Maclean and Anne Lake Prescott. Norton Critical Editions. New York: W.W. Norton and Company, 1993.

———. *The Faerie Queene*. Edited by Thomas P. Roche and C. Patrick O'Donnell. New York: Penguin Classics, 1979.

Waller, Gary F. *Edmund Spenser: A Literary Life*. London: Macmillan, 1994.

Web Sites

The Faerie Queene: http://www.uoregon.edu/~rbear/fqintro.html

Works of Edmund Spenser: http://www.luminarium.org/renlit/spensbib.htm

26. William Shakespeare's Commentary on Contemporary Acting: *Hamlet*, Act III, Scene 2 (c. 1600–1601)

INTRODUCTION

The following excerpt, lines 1–45 from the start of Act III, Scene 2 of William SHAKESPEARE's *Hamlet*, is famous because it is believed to reflect Shakespeare's own views on the art of acting. The excerpt contains Hamlet's advice to a company of travelling actors on how to deliver their lines in a play they are about to perform at the Danish court. Hamlet's opinions of what he does and does not like in a stage performance are usually taken to be an expression of Shakespeare's own views on his craft.

In the play, Hamlet proposes that the players perform a work entitled, "The Murder of Gonzago," a brief drama that depicts a killing similar to the murder of the late king, Hamlet's father. Hamlet hopes that his uncle, the new king, whom he suspects of the crime, will, upon seeing the performance of this "play within a play," react in such a way as to confirm his guilt. Hamlet reveals his plan to the audience with the famous lines that end his long soliloquy at the close of Act II, "The play's the thing/Wherein I'll catch the conscience of the King."

KEEP IN MIND AS YOU READ

1. Earlier in Act II, the characters of Rosencrantz and Guildenstern report to Hamlet that the popularity of this troupe of adult players has suffered recently due to the growing success of a company of child actors. For this reason, the players have left their theater and taken to traveling. This passage is an allusion to a contemporary event in London, the so-called War of the Theaters, an ongoing rivalry between several playwrights that involved the production of various satirical plays by companies of child actors between 1599 and 1602.

2. There is some dispute as to how truly Hamlet's opinions mirror those of Shakespeare himself. In the play, Hamlet is depicted as a university man who has studied at Wittenberg in Germany. In three plays written and performed for students at St. John's College, Cambridge (see "English Universities," Document 22) between 1598 and 1601, Shakespeare was satirized for not being a university-educated playwright whose works followed the formal rules of poetry advocated by Sir Philip SIDNEY. They were, like most popular plays of the time, less formal and

ornate. It is possible then that Hamlet's advice was itself meant to be satirical, a response to the university playwrights.

Document: Excerpt from Shakespeare's Hamlet

Enter Prince Hamlet and two or three of the Players.

Hamlet: Speak the speech, I pray you, as I pronounced it to you—trippingly on the tongue; but if you mouth it, as many of our players do, I had as **lief** the town crier had spoke my lines. Nor do not saw the air too much with your hand, thus, but use all gently; for in the very torrent, tempest, and as I may say the whirlwind of your passion, you must acquire and beget a temperance that may give it smoothness. O, it offends me to the soul to hear a **robustious periwig-pated** fellow tear a passion to tatters, to very rags, to split the ears of the groundlings, who for the most part are capable of nothing but inexplicable **dumb shows** and noise. I would have such a fellow whipped for o'erdoing Termagant. It out-Herods Herod. Pray you avoid it.

First Player: I warrant your honour.

Hamlet: Be not too tame neither; but let your own discretion be your tutor. Suit the action to the word, the word to the action; with this special observance: that you o'erstep not the modesty of nature. For anything so overdone is from the purpose of playing, whose end, both at the first and now, was and is to hold, as 'twere the mirror up to nature; to show virtue her own feature, scorn her own image, and the very age and body of the time his form and pressure. Now this overdone, or come tardy off, though it make the unskillful laugh, cannot but make the judicious grieve; the censure of the which one must in your allowance o'erweigh a whole theatre of others. O, there be players that I have seen play, and heard others praise, and that highly, not to speak it profanely, that neither having the accent of Christians nor the gait of Christian, pagan, nor no man, have so strutted and bellowed that I have thought some of nature's journeymen had made men, and not made them well, they imitated humanity so abominably.

First Player: I hope we have reformed that indifferently with us, sir.

Hamlet: O, reform it altogether. And let those that play your clowns speak no more than is set down for them; for there be of them that will themselves laugh to set on some quantity of barren spectators to laugh too, though in the mean time some necessary question of the play be then to be considered. That's villainous and shows a most pitiful ambition in the fool that uses it. Go make you ready.

Exeunt Players

Source: Wells, Stanley, Gary Taylor, John Jowett, and William Montgomery, eds. *William Shakespeare: The Complete Works.* Oxford: Clarendon Press, 1988, p. 671.

---

dumb show: scene, usually from a tragedy, performed in pantomime

lief: rather

periwig-pated: wearing a wig on one's head

robustious: rough; boisterous; unrefined

CHAMBERLAIN'S MEN

The Chamberlain's Men were a London acting company whose membership included William Shakespeare after 1594. In the early 1590s, Shakespeare was a member of Lord Strange's Men, a troupe under the patronage of Ferdinando STANLEY, Lord Strange. However, in 1592, a violent outbreak of the plague caused the city authorities to close all theaters and disband all acting companies. Lord Strange died in 1594. When the theaters reopened later that year, his acting company came under the patronage of Henry CAREY, Lord Hunsdon, lord chamberlain of England. The Chamberlain's Men was a partnership with the company's six main actors, including Richard BURBAGE, William KEMPE, and Shakespeare, receiving profits from the performances according to the amount of their investment in the company.

In 1598, the company moved to the Globe Theatre in Southwark, in which the company's principals were also shareholders (see "Globe Theater," Document 21). The shareholders' investment bought and maintained costumes and props while their profits came from a division of half the receipts from the gallery seats at the Globe. The other half of the gallery income went toward the costs and upkeep of the theater, which included the hiring of actors for minor roles and the paying of watchmen, wardrobe keepers, copyists, and musicians. Shakespeare remained a member of the company for the rest of his career, acting and writing an average of two plays per year until about 1608. The company performed frequently at court for the Queen and, in 1603, came under the patronage of JAMES I and thus became known as the King's Men. By 1604, the number of company shareholders had increased to 12. By Shakespeare's death in 1616, the King's Men had 26 permanent actors.

AFTERMATH

The performance of "The Murder of Gonzago" has the desired effect, causing the king to rise in distress and anger and stalk out of the room in the middle of the play, which is never completed. His suspicions confirmed, Hamlet rejoices at the success of his plan. In a soliloquy, the king reveals his guilt, lamenting that he has been unable to pray for forgiveness because he knows he is still benefiting from the crime; he still holds his brother's throne and is still married to his brother's widow. As the king tries again to pray, Hamlet comes upon his uncle and seriously considers killing him on the spot. However, fearing that a man killed in the act of prayer would be sent to heaven, Hamlet holds his hand and vows to kill the king only when he can catch him engaged in some sin or misdeed, thus ensuring his immediate dispatch to hell.

ASK YOURSELF

1. What advice does Hamlet offer to the players? How does he think lines should be delivered? What does he see as a particular fault in an actor?
2. Who are the groundlings that Hamlet mentions in the first speech of the excerpt? What does Hamlet say about the groundlings? Is this a complimentary allusion to them? How do you think the groundlings would have reacted to these lines about them? Why?

TOPICS AND ACTIVITIES TO CONSIDER

- ➢ Reread the excerpt above, and then recast Hamlet's advice to the players in your own words, covering every point Hamlet makes regarding how a player should and should not deliver his lines.

    ➶ Because Hamlet is one of the most complex and tragic figures in the Shakespearean canon, the character has been a favorite role of actors for over 400 years. Using books and the Internet, research one of the following famous Shakespearean performers, all of whom played Hamlet at some time in their careers: Richard Burbage (likely the original Hamlet), Thomas Betterton, David Garrick, John Philip Kemble, William Henry West Betty, and Sarah Bernhardt. Write a brief essay describing how the actor you chose approached the role of Hamlet and how his or her approach altered public perception of the role.

    ➶ If possible, view one or more of the modern film versions of *Hamlet* available on DVD, such as the following:

        ➶ *Hamlet* (2007) starring Kenneth Branagh, Julie Christie, Billy Crystal, and Kate Winslet

        ➶ *Hamlet* (2004) starring Mel Gibson, Glenn Close, Allen Bates, and Ian Holm

        ➶ *Hamlet* (2000) starring Ethan Hawke, Kyle MacLachlan, Sam Shepard, and Bill Murray

        ➶ *Hamlet: Criterion Collection* (2000) starring Sir Laurence Olivier in the 1948 film

        ➶ *Richard Burton's Hamlet* (1999) starring Richard Burton in a 1964 performance

Pay particular attention to how each actor in the role of Hamlet delivered the lines quoted above. Do you think he took Shakespeare's advice to heart in his performance?

    ➶ View the DVDs of the 1998 film *Shakespeare in Love* or the 1977 miniseries *William Shakespeare: His Life and Times*, paying particular attention to the theater scenes.

Further Information

Greenblatt, Stephen. *Will in the World: How Shakespeare Became Shakespeare*. London: W.W. Norton & Company, 2004.

Kay, Dennis. *Shakespeare: His Life, Work, and Era*. New York: William Morrow, 1992.

Levi, Peter. *The Life and Times of William Shakespeare*. New York: Henry Holt and Company, 1988.

O'Connor, Garry. *William Shakespeare: A Popular Life*. New York: Applause, 2000.

Wells, Stanley, Gary Taylor, John Jowett, and William Montgomery, eds. *William Shakespeare: The Complete Works*. The Oxford Shakespeare. Oxford: Clarendon Press, 1991.

Web Sites

Complete Works of Shakespeare: http://shakespeare.mit.edu

Hamlet: http://www.online-literature.com/shakespeare/hamlet

27. The Changing Character of Elizabethan Theater: Playwright Thomas Middleton from the Introduction to His Play *The Roaring Girl* (1611)

INTRODUCTION

The following excerpt is from Thomas MIDDLETON's "Epistle to the Comic Play-Readers," a brief introduction to the printed edition of *The Roaring Girl*, a play that Middleton is thought to have written in collaboration with fellow playwright Thomas DEKKER. In this passage, Middleton compared changes in the tastes of Elizabethan and Jacobean audiences to changes in popular fashions. The mention of fashion, however, had another meaning here because *The Roaring Girl* is about a notorious figure of the London underworld, the cross-dressing female thief Mary Frith, who was widely known as Moll Cutpurse (see also Document 7). Middleton's mention in the excerpt of a woman who "passes through the play in doublet and breeches" was a reference to Frith. Note also that Middleton addressed his introduction to "Play-Readers," an indication that he, unlike most other playwrights of the period, intended his plays to be read as well as performed.

KEEP IN MIND AS YOU READ

1. Unlike modern playhouses and theater companies, Elizabethan theaters and acting troupes did not offer a succession of performances of one play. No play was ever performed two days in a row. This rule held true even for the most popular works of the most popular playwrights, such as William SHAKESPEARE and Christopher MARLOWE. The practice of rotating different plays seems to have been an attempt to keep a limited London audience from drifting off to a rival theater after they had seen a particular play. The first recorded instance of a play being performed on successive days was the nine-day run of Middleton's *A Game at Chess* in August 1624.

2. The title of *The Roaring Girl* derived from the Elizabethan slang term "roaring boys," which referred to young men who drank, caroused, and generally led dissolute or even criminal lives.

3. Because Elizabethan society frowned upon unconventionality in women, a woman's wearing of male attire, for which Mary Frith was well known, was considered scandalous. Such a woman was thought to be outrageously and indecently sexual. Frith seems to have enjoyed more leeway in her choice of attire simply because her entire lifestyleshe was an admitted thief and pimp was disreputable. Such unconventional attire seemed almost expected.

Document: Excerpt from Middleton's The Roaring Girl

To the Comic Play-Readers, **Venery** and Laughter

> **bombasted:** pompous; overblown
> **codpiece:** flap or bag concealing an opening in the front of men's breeches
> **crop-doublet:** a particular style of doublet or a man's close-fitting jacket
> **nineness:** elegance
> **spruceness:** neatness; spareness
> **termers:** persons who come to London during the legal term when the courts are in session
> **Venery:** pursuit of sexual pleasure or indulgence

The fashion of play-making I can properly compare to nothing so naturally as the alteration in apparel. For, in the time of the great **crop-doublet**, your huge bombasted plays, quilted with mighty words to lean purpose, was only then in fashion. And as the doublet fell, neater inventions began to set up. Now in the time of **spruceness**, our plays follow the **niceness** of our garments: single plots, quaint conceits, lecherous jests, dressed up in hanging sleeves, and those are fit for the times and the **termers**. Such a kind of light color summer stuff, mingled with diverse colors, you shall find this published comedy, good to keep you in an afternoon from dice at home in your chambers. And for venery you shall find enough for sixpence, but well couched an [if] you mark it. For Venus, being a woman, passes through the play in doublet and breeches, a brave disguise and a safe one, if the statute untie not her **codpiece** point. The book I make no question but is fit for many of your companies, as well as the person itself, and may be allowed both gallery room at the playhouse and chamber room at your lodging. Worse things, I must needs confess, the world has taxed her for than has been written of her. But 'tis the excellency of a writer to leave things better than he finds 'em though some obscene fellow (that cares not what he writes against others yet keeps a mystical bawdy-house himself, and entertains drunkards to make use of their pockets and rent his private bottle-ale at midnight) though such a one would have ripped up the most nasty vice that ever hell belched forth, and presented it to a modest assembly. Yet we rather wish in such discoveries, where reputation lies bleeding, a slackness of truth than fullness of slander.

Source: Bullen, A.H., ed. *The Works of Thomas Middleton.* vol. 4. Boston: Houghton, Mifflin and Company, 1885, pp. 7–8.

AFTERMATH

In 1611, Mary Frith, as usual dressed in men's clothes, took the stage of the Fortune Theater in London, where she joked with the audience and sang (a probably bawdy) song while accompanying herself on the lute. In an age when women did not wear male attire or perform on stage (all women's roles were performed by men), Frith's performance did not go unpunished. She was subsequently arrested and forced to do public penance for her "evil living" at Paul's Cross, the pulpit outside London's St. Paul's Cathedral. Although eyewitnesses claimed that Frith wept bitterly and expressed sincere repentance, later rumors claimed that she was drunk and that her repentance was merely another performance.

In the 1620s, Frith, by her own account, was making a good living as a fence for stolen goods and as a pimp, procuring young women for male clients and young men for the wives of London citizens. Frith died in 1659 and, three years later, was the subject of a popular biography, *The Life of Mrs. Mary Frith*, which perpetuated many of the myths that eventually clung to her memory.

ELIZABETHAN THEATER

The last two decades of ELIZABETH I's reign witnessed the writing and production of some of the finest plays in the English language. The Reformation (see "English Reformation," Document 14) and the political turmoil that attended it freed English drama from religious themes and provided playwrights with secular plots while English nationalism, stimulated by the break with Rome, caused writers to mine English history for stories and characters. The development of English humanism put Elizabethan writers in touch with classical Greek and Roman styles and imbued them with a love of drama and literature. Wary of the political and religious purposes for which drama could be used, Elizabeth banned the performance of unlicensed plays in 1559 and suppressed religious play cycles in the 1570s. In 1572, she forbade anyone but peers to sponsor professional troupes of players and, in 1574, empowered her master of revels to license all plays and acting companies. These actions placed the English theater under royal control and accelerated the secularization of Elizabethan drama.

Beginning with Leicester's Men, an acting troupe sponsored by Robert DUDLEY, Earl of Leicester, numerous professional companies arose under the patronage of important courtiers. Along with the development of groups of professional players came the building of permanent theaters. The first was James BURBAGE's The Theatre, constructed across the Thames from London in 1576. Many company actors became shareholders in particular theaters. For example, William Shakespeare and the other principals of the Chamberlain's Men were part owners of the Globe (see "Globe Theater," Document 21). The development of a professional theater meant that playwrights no longer had to attach themselves to a noble patron and limit themselves to the themes and forms he favored, but could do well by writing for a theater or troupe on themes that, within government guidelines, interested them and their audiences.

ASK YOURSELF

1. What was the purpose of this introduction? To what would you compare it in modern theater or literature?
2. Remember that Middleton, who was born in 1580, was writing in the reign of JAMES I, when the accession of a new male monarch with very different tastes and interests from the late Queen was changing popular tastes and fashion. What does Middleton say about changing fashions in plays and in audiences' tastes? What does he say plays were like before, and how have they changed?

TOPICS AND ACTIVITIES TO CONSIDER

- Access the text of *The Roaring Girl* at http://books.google.com/books. Read selections from Act I, which is attributed to Thomas Dekker. Then read selections from Act II, which is attributed to Middleton. Can you discern differences in style between the two acts that would lead one to believe they were written by different playwrights? Make a list of reasons why you believe the acts are by different playwrights or why you think they are the work of the same person. Read other passages of the play and try to determine who might have written them.
- Access the text of Middleton's *The Witch* at http://www.tech.org/~cleary/witch.html, and read a selection. Then access one of the online editions of Shakespeare's *Macbeth* and read Act III, Scene 5, Lines 39–43, and Act IV, Scene 1, Lines 125–132, which are believed to be later additions from *The Witch*. Do you agree that Shakespeare incorporated part of *The Witch* into *Macbeth*?

❧ Middleton was arrested and briefly imprisoned in 1624 for writing *A Game at Chess*, a boldly anti-Spanish and anti-Catholic work that openly criticized the King's efforts to ally with Spain by marrying his son to a Spanish princess. Access the text of *A Game at Chess* at http://books.google.com/books and read a selection. Identify passages that, in your opinion, may have led to Middleton's confinement.

Further Information

Heinemann, Margot. *Puritanism and Theatre: Thomas Middleton and Opposition Drama Under the Early Stuarts*. Cambridge: Cambridge University Press, 1982.
Mulryne, J.R. *Thomas Middleton*. New York: Longman Publishing Group, 1979.
Taylor, Gary, and John Lavagnino, eds. *Thomas Middleton: The Collected Works*. Oxford: Oxford University Press, 2008.

Web sites

Life of Thomas Middleton: http://www.luminarium.org/sevenlit/middleton/thomasbio.htm
Plays of Thomas Middleton: http://www.tech.org/~cleary/middhome.html

28. ELIZABETHAN SONNETS: THE EARL OF OXFORD'S "LOVE THY CHOICE" (C. 1576) AND WILLIAM SHAKESPEARE'S SONNETS 116 AND 150 (1609)

INTRODUCTION

This selection reproduces three Elizabethan sonnets (see "Shakespearean Sonnets" below), the first by Edward de VERE, the seventeenth Earl of Oxford, and the other two by William SHAKESPEARE. Some people, known as Oxfordians, consider these two men to be one and the same, arguing that the works ascribed to Shakespeare were actually written by Oxford, who, as a prominent nobleman and courtier, could not publicly acknowledge his authorship of plays for the common theater. Although rejected by most Shakespeare scholars, the theory, which was first proposed in 1920, has gained many adherents and generated much scholarship on the identity of Shakespeare.

Oxford is known to have been a patron of the theater and to have written plays for a juvenile acting company called Oxford's Boys, but none of his plays survive. "Love Thy Choice" is one of only a small body of surviving poems and songs that can be definitely attributed to the earl. Sonnets 116 and 150 are part of a collection of 154 sonnets published in 1609 under the title *Shake-speares Sonnets*. Sonnet 116 echoes the themes of constancy and truth found in "Love Thy Choice." Because of its powerful description of ideal romantic love, it is one of the most famous and quoted poems in the Shakespeare sonnet cycle. Sonnet 150, in its series of questions, echoes in wording and meaning some of the questions in Oxford's poem.

KEEP IN MIND AS YOU READ

1. The 1609 edition of Shakespeare's sonnets is dedicated to a mysterious "Mr. W.H.," who is described as "the onlie [only] begetter" of the poems. No one is certain to whom these initials refer, although scholars have proposed numerous candidates, including William HERBERT, Earl of Pembroke, a noted theater patron to whom the FIRST FOLIO was dedicated; Henry WRIOTHLESLEY, Earl of Southampton (reversing the initials), Shakespeare's patron; William Harvey, Southampton's stepfather; or William Hall, a London printer. Other theories are that "W.H." is merely a printer's error for Shakespeare's initials "W.S." or "W. SH" or that "W.H." simply stands for "William Himself."

2. Oxfordians theorize that the man from Stratford-upon-Avon whom we know as William Shakespeare may have been an actor who fronted for Oxford, an acceptable public face of authorship for works actually written by the earl. Another theory is

that the works of Shakespeare were produced by a group of writers, with Oxford the lead author and William Shakespeare of Stratford one of the group members.

3. Many noblemen, such as Sir Philip SIDNEY, were well known as poets and writers, but they did not publish their works for mass consumption. They instead circulated them privately among aristocratic and court circles. Although some scholars dispute this, most accept the idea that it would have been considered degrading and inappropriate for a nobleman to publish his plays and allow them to be performed on the public stage.

4. Two other mysterious figures that appear in the sonnets of Shakespeare are the "fair youth," an unnamed young man to whom Sonnets 1–126 are addressed, and the "dark lady," so-called because her hair is said to be "black" and her skin "dun," to whom sonnets 127–152 are addressed. Many candidates have been suggested for both, including Southampton, Pembroke, and Southampton's wife, Elizabeth VERNON. However, no definitive conclusion can be reached from the evidence of the sonnets.

Document 1: "Love Thy Choice" by Edward de Vere, Earl of Oxford

Who taught thee first to sigh, alas! my heart?
Who taught thy tongue the woeful words of **plaint**?
Who filled your eyes with tears of bitter smart?
Who gave thee grief and made thy joys to faint?
Who first did paint with colors pale thy face?
Who first did break thy sleeps of quiet rest?
Above the rest in court who gave thee grace?
  Who made thee strive in honor to be best?
  In constant truth to bide so firm and sure,
  To scorn the world regarding but thy friends?
  With patient mind each passion to endure,
  In one desire to settle to the end?
    Love then thy choice wherein such choice thou bind
    As **nought** but death may ever change thy mind.

> **nought:** nothing
> **plaint:** complaint; protest

Source: Looney, J. Thomas. *"Shakespeare" Identified in Edward de Vere the Seventeenth Earl of Oxford.* New York: Frederick A. Stokes Company, Publishers, 1920, p. 387.

Document 2: Sonnet 116 by William Shakespeare

Let me not to the marriage of true minds
Admit impediments. Love is not love
Which alters when it alteration finds,
Or bends with the remover to remove:
O no; it is an ever-fixed mark,
That looks on tempests, and is never shaken;
It is the star to every wandering bark,

Whose worth's unknown, although his height be taken.
Love's not Time's fool, though rosy lips and cheeks
Within his bending sickle's compass come;
Love alters not with his brief hours and weeks,
But bears it out even to the edge of doom.
　　If this be error, and upon me proved,
　　I never writ, nor no man ever loved.

Source: Tyler, Thomas, ed. *Shakespeare's Sonnets*. London: David Nutt, 1890, p. 275.

Document 3: Sonnet 150 by William Shakespeare

O from what power hast thou this powerful might,
With insufficiency my heart to sway,
To make me give the lie to my true sight,
And swear that brightness doth not grace the day?
Whence hast thou this becoming of things ill,
That in the very refuse of thy deeds
There is such strength and **warrantise** of skill
That in my mind thy worst all best exceeds?
Who taught thee how to make me love thee more,
The more I see and hear just cause of hate?
O, though I love what others do abhor,
With others thou shouldst not abhor my state;
If thy unworthiness raised love in me,
More worthy I to be beloved of thee.

> **warrantise:** guarantee; surety

Source: Rolfe, William J., ed. *Shakespeare's Sonnets*. New York: Harper and Brothers, Publishers, 1891, p. 122.

SHAKESPEAREAN SONNET

The English sonnet, a sixteenth-century English variation on a popular Italian verse form, is one of the most common poetic forms in English and American poetry. Because the English form was associated so closely with William Shakespeare, it has become widely known as the Shakespearean sonnet. The Italian sonnet comprised 14 lines, an eight-line octave rhyming *abbaabba* and a six-line sestet usually rhyming *cdecde*, although variations were possible. The octave usually defined a problem or described an experience that was reacted to in the sestet.

Sir Thomas WYATT, who wrote poetry for Anne BOLEYN, and Henry HOWARD, Earl of Surrey, a cousin of Queen ELIZABETH, imported the sonnet into England in the 1530s and 1540s. They modified the sonnet by ending the sestet with a rhyming two-line couplet (e.g., *cddcee*), a common device in English poetry, and by using pentameter, the most common English rhythm scheme (see "Elizabethan Poetry," Document 23). Elizabethan poets, including Shakespeare, further altered the rhyme scheme to produce the standard Shakespearean form: *ababcdcdefefgg*. However, the sonnet form was flexible, and variations in rhyme and meter were common.

Themes varied greatly as well. Early English sonnets explored courtly love and other amorous themes, but Elizabethan poets reacted against this trend by writing anti-love sonnets that complained of courtly pretense and the fickleness of lovers. In his collection of 154 sonnets, Shakespeare wrote on both themes.

AFTERMATH

Oxford led an extravagant and adventurous life that included a conversion to Catholicism, which put him at odds with his wife and father-in-law, William Cecil, Lord Burghley, and a famous quarrel with Sir Philip Sidney, which earned him royal disfavor. The strongest objection to Oxford's authorship is his death in 1604, which is well before many of the plays of Shakespeare are thought to have been written and 12 years before the death of William Shakespeare of Stratford. Oxfordians counter this by arguing that none of Shakespeare's plays can definitely be said to have been written after 1604, nor can any be proved to be based on a source published after that date. They also argue that regular publication of works by Shakespeare ceased around 1604 and that certain evidence points to the death of Shakespeare prior to the accepted date of 1616, most notably the dedication to the 1609 edition of the sonnets, which calls Shakespeare "our ever-living poet."

ASK YOURSELF

1. What is Oxford saying in "Love Thy Choice"? What is Shakespeare saying in Sonnets 116 and 150? Are there similarities between the themes and ideas presented? Are there similarities in the wording? If so, are they sufficient to make you believe all three poems were written by the same poet? Why or why not?

2. Access an online edition of Shakespeare's sonnets, and read a selection of poems between 18 and 126. What do you think is the nature of the love the poet expresses for the "fair youth," who is addressed in this series of poems? Is it friendship, admiration, platonic love, or something more, a romantic or even sexual attraction? What are your reasons for believing as you do?

3. Read a selection of Shakespeare's sonnets between 127 and 152. What do you think is the nature of the relationship between the poet and the "dark lady," to whom these poems are addressed? How does the "fair youth" figure in this series of sonnets?

TOPICS AND ACTIVITIES TO CONSIDER

- Access the Web site of the Shakespeare Oxford Society at http://www.shakespeare-oxford.com. The Society is dedicated to researching the Shakespeare authorship question and to presenting evidence that the Earl of Oxford was the true author of the works of Shakespeare. Read the Society's arguments in favor of Oxford's authorship and decide whether you find them persuasive or not. Write an essay giving the reasons why you accept or reject the Oxfordian theory.

- Read the "Shakespearean Sonnet" sidebar on the previous page to gain an understanding of the sonnet form. Then write your own sonnet on any topic or idea you wish.

- In March 2009, Shakespeare scholar Stanley Wells announced that he had discovered the only portrait of Shakespeare painted during his lifetime. The portrait, which was publicly unveiled at London's National Portrait Gallery, is owned by an Irish descendant of the Earl of Southampton, Shakespeare's patron. Search the Internet for recent articles on the unveiling and view the portrait as well as other portraits that are thought to be of Shakespeare. How do they relate to the popular image of Shakespeare?

   ∾ Access the site of the Folger Shakespeare Library at http://www
.folger.edu/index.cfm. Review their list of Shakespeare FAQs regarding the
life and works of Shakespeare. Which of these facts do you find surprising? Why?

Further Information

Anderson, Mark. *Shakespeare by Another Name: A Biography of Edward de Vere, Earl of Oxford, the Man Who Was Shakespeare*. New York: Gotham Books, 2005.

Duncan-Jones, Katherine, ed. *Shakespeare's Sonnets*. The Arden Shakespeare. London: Thomas Nelson and Sons Ltd., 1998.

Greenblatt, Stephen. *Will in the World: How Shakespeare Became Shakespeare*. London: W.W. Norton & Company, 2004.

Kay, Dennis. *Shakespeare: His Life, Work, and Era*. New York: William Morrow, 1992.

Levi, Peter. *The Life and Times of William Shakespeare*. New York: Henry Holt and Company, 1988.

Love Poems and Sonnets of William Shakespeare. New York: Doubleday, 1957.

Nelson, Alan H. *Monstrous Adversary: The Life of Edward de Vere, 17th Earl of Oxford*. Liverpool: Liverpool University Press, 2003.

O'Connor, Garry. *William Shakespeare: A Popular Life*. New York: Applause, 2000.

Vere, Edward de. *The Poems of Edward de Vere*. Chapel Hill: University of North Carolina Press, 1981.

Wells, Stanley, Gary Taylor, John Jowett, and William Montgomery, eds. *William Shakespeare: The Complete Works*. The Oxford Shakespeare. Oxford: Clarendon Press, 1991.

Web Sites

Complete Works of Shakespeare: http://shakespeare.mit.edu

Oxford Authorship Site: http://www.oxford-shakespeare.com/marprelate.html

Shakespeare's Sonnets: http://www.shakespeares-sonnets.com/sonn01.htm

29. Accounts of Performances of William Shakespeare's *Macbeth* (1610) and *A Winter's Tale* (1611): The Diary of Dr. Simon Forman

INTRODUCTION

Reproduced here are two excerpts from a manuscript titled the "Book of Plays," which was found among the papers of Simon FORMAN, a noted Elizabethan healer, astrologer, and occultist. The document contains descriptions of four theatrical performances attended by Forman, who also noted the moral lessons he drew from the plays. The selections below describe performances at the Globe Theater in 1610 and 1611 of two of William SHAKESPEARE's plays, *Macbeth* and *A Winter's Tale* (see "Globe Theater," Document 21). The other plays mentioned in the document are an April 1611 performance at the Globe of *Richard II* and a performance of *Cymbeline* at an unspecified time and place. If genuine, the "Book of Plays" is one of the earliest extant descriptions of performances of the plays of Shakespeare.

KEEP IN MIND AS YOU READ

1. The "Book of Plays" was discovered in 1836 by John Payne Collier, a Shakespearean critic and scholar whom contemporaries accused of forging various Shakespeare texts and documents. For this reason, questions were raised regarding the authenticity of Forman's "Book of Plays," which exhibited odd spellings and mentioned characters in *Macbeth* "riding through a wood," which, given the nature of Elizabethan stagecraft, seemed most unlikely. Although some present-day scholars still dismiss the document as a forgery, defenses of Collier were published in the 1980s, and most now accept the "Book of Plays" as genuine.

2. The full title of the document is "The Book of Plays and Notes hereof per Forman—for Common Policy," with the term "common policy" meaning, in Elizabethan parlance, "practical use." For Forman, who was interested in astrology, prophecy, and magic and had a thriving consulting practice for clients interested in such things as discovering treasure, finding missing persons, and starting or maintaining a love affair, practical matters included the many magical and supernatural happenings in a play like *Macbeth*.

Document 1: A Performance of Macbeth *(20 April 1610)*

In Macbeth at the Globe, 1610, the 20 of April, Saturday, there was to be observed, first how Macbeth and Banquo, two noblemen of Scotland, riding through a wood, there stood before them three women fairies or **nymphs**, and saluted Macbeth, saying three times unto him, Hail, Macbeth, King of Codon; for thou shalt be a king, but shall beget no kings, etc. Then said Banquo, what all to Macbeth, and nothing to me? Yes, said the nymphs, hail to thee, Banquo, thou shalt beget kings, yet be no king; and so they departed and came to the court of Scotland to Duncan, King of Scots, and it was in the days of Edward the Confessor. And Duncan bade them both kindly welcome, and made Macbeth forthwith Prince of Northumberland, and sent him home to his own castle, and appointed Macbeth to provide for him, for he would sup with him the next day at night, and did so. And Macbeth contrived to kill Duncan and through the persuasion of his wife did that night murder the king in his own castle, being his guest; and there were many **prodigies** seen that night and the day before. And when Macbeth had murdered the king, the blood on his hands could not be washed off by any means, nor from his wife's hands, which handled the bloody daggers in hiding them, by which means they became both much amazed and affronted. The murder being known, Duncan's two sons fled, the one to England the [other to] Wales to save themselves. They being fled, they were supposed guilty of the murder of their father, which was nothing so. Then was Macbeth crowned king; and then he, for fear of Banquo, his old companion, that he should beget kings but be no king himself, he contrived the death of Banquo, and caused him to be murdered on the way as he rode. The next night, being at supper with his noblemen who he had bid to the feast, to the which also Banquo should have come, he began to speak of noble Banquo, and to wish that he were there. And as he thus did, standing up to drink a **carouse** to him, the ghost of Banquo came and sat down in his chair behind him. And he, turning about to sit down again, saw the ghost of Banquo, which fronted him so, that he fell into a great passion of fear and fury, uttering many words about his murder, by which, when they heard that Banquo was murdered, they suspected Macbeth. Then MacDuff fled to England to the king's son, and so they raised an army and came into Scotland, and at Dunsinane overthrew Macbeth. In the meantime, while MacDuff was in England, Macbeth slew MacDuff's wife and children, and after in the battle MacDuff slew Macbeth. Observe also how Macbeth's queen did rise in the night in her sleep, and walked and talked and confessed all, and the doctor noted her words.

> **carouse:** toast
> **nymphs:** female magical or mystical beings
> **prodigies:** wonders

Document 2: A Performance of A Winter's Tale *(15 May 1611)*

In the Winter's Tale at the Globe, 1611, the 15 of May, Wednesday.— Observe there how Lyontes, the King of Cicillia, was overcome with jealousy of his wife with the King of Bohemia, his friend, that came to see him, and how he contrived his death, and would have had his cupbearer to have poisoned, who gave the King of Bohemia warning thereof and fled with him to Bohemia.—Remember also how he sent to the oracle of Apollo, and the answer of Apollo that she was guiltless, and that the king was jealous, etc., and how, except the child was found again that was lost, the king should die without issue; for the child was carried into Bohemia, and there laid in a forest, and brought up by a shepherd, and the King of Bohemia his son married that wench; and how they fled into Cicillia to Leontes, and the shepherd, having showed the letter of the nobleman by whom Leontes sent as [sic] was that child, and these jewels found about her, she was known to be Leontes' daughter and was then 16 year old.—Remember also the rogue that came in all **tottered** like Coll Pipci, and how he feigned him sick and to have been robbed of all that he had, and how he **couzzened** the poor man of all his money; and after came to the sheep-sher with a pedler's pack, and there couzzened them again of all their money; and how he changed apparel with the King of Bohemia his son, and then how he turned courtier, etc. Beware of trusting feigned beggars or fawning fellows.

couzzened: tricked
tottered: unsteady; wobbling

Source: Lambert, D.H., ed. *Cartae Shakespeareanae: Shakespeare Documents: A Chronological Catalogue of Extant Evidence Relating to the Life and Works of William Shakespeare.* London: George Bell and Sons, 1904, pp. 69, 71–72.

WORKS OF WILLIAM SHAKESPEARE

William Shakespeare wrote, or has had attributed to him, 37 plays. Although the complete lack of any manuscripts makes the dating of the plays highly conjectural, most are thought to have been written in London between about 1592 and ELIZABETH I's death in 1603. Dates are assigned by a careful reading of both internal evidence (e.g., allusions to datable events, nature, and type of rhyme, imagery, or vocabulary) and external evidence (e.g., actual date of publication and the date the work was entered in the Stationers' Register) (see "Stationers' Register," Document 12). Several classic tragedies, such as *Othello*, *King Lear*, and *Macbeth*, were likely written in the first years of JAMES I, and the last few works, including *Tempest* and *Henry VIII*, were probably written in Stratford about 1611–1613.

The plays break down into four categories: the history plays, such as *Henry V* and *Richard III*, which draw on English history for their themes; the comedies, such as *Two Gentlemen of Verona* and *Taming of the Shrew*, which employ extensive rhyme and wordplay and borrow heavily from Roman and other comic traditions; the tragedies, such as *Hamlet*, *Macbeth*, and *King Lear*, which, in their powerful explorations of human conflict, are often considered the greatest dramas ever written; and the romances or tragicomedies, such as *Cymbeline* and *A Winter's Tale*, which were written late in the playwright's career and explore themes of reconciliation.

Shakespeare also published the love poems *Venus and Adonis* and *The Rape of Lucrece* in the early 1590s and a collection of 154 sonnets, entitled simply *Shake-speares Sonnets*, in 1609. Scholars have searched the sonnets for biographical information on Shakespeare himself, looking intently, but so far unsuccessfully, for the identities of "Mr. W.H.," to whom the poems are dedicated, and the "dark lady," who is mentioned in a number of sonnets (see "Shakespearean Sonnet," Document 28).

AFTERMATH

Forman was so popular and well known in London that he was mentioned by name in several works by the playwright Ben JONSON, who likely included the references as a way to engage audiences by using real persons with whom they were familiar. According to his diary, Forman was a frequent theater attender and would, on occasion, meet old or pick up new lovers at a performance, thus giving some credence to Stephen GOSSEN's moralistic criticisms of theater audiences in *School of Abuse* (see Document 21). Forman's diaries and casebooks indicate that he had connections to London literary circles. His clients included James and Richard BURBAGE, associates of Shakespeare, and the poet Emilia LANIER, who has been suggested as the "dark lady" of Shakespeare's sonnets (see Document 28). Forman has thus been an invaluable source of information for modern social historians.

ASK YOURSELF

1. What kinds of things does Forman notice in the plays? What do these tell you about Forman's interests? Is there anything about Forman's descriptions of the two plays that surprises you? If so, why?
2. What do you think of the moral conclusions that Forman draws? Do they make sense to you, or do they seem far-fetched? Why do you think as you do?

TOPICS AND ACTIVITIES TO CONSIDER

- Modern mystery writer Judith Cook has published *The Casebooks of Simon Forman*, a series of mystery novels in which Simon Forman, "Elizabethan doctor and solver of mysteries," is the central character. The novels are in part based on events and passages mentioned in Forman's original casebooks. Titles in the series include *Death of a Lady's Maid* (1997), *Murder at the Rose* (1998), *School of the Night* (2000), *Kill the Witch* (2000), and *Blood on the Borders* (2004). Read one of the Cook mysteries. If you enjoy the novels and are interested in learning more about Forman, Cook also wrote a biography of him entitled *Dr. Simon Forman: A Most Notorious Physician* (2001).
- Access an online edition of any one of Shakespeare's plays that interests you. Then write your own description of the action of the play, selecting, like Forman, the scenes and incidents that most interest you. Draw your own conclusions as to what in particular the scenes are trying to say or teach.

Further Information

Cook, Judith. *Dr. Simon Forman: A Most Notorious Physician*. London: Chatto & Windus, 2001.
Kassell, Lauren. *Medicine and Magic in Elizabethan London: Simon Forman, Astrologer, Alchemist, and Physician*. Oxford: Oxford University Press, 2005.
Rowse, A.L. *Sex and Society in Shakespeare's Age: Simon Forman the Astrologer*. New York: Charles Scribner's Sons, 1974.
Traister, Barbara Howard. *The Notorious Astrological Physician of London: Works and Days of Simon Forman*. Chicago: University of Chicago Press, 2001.

Web Site

Dr. Simon Forman: http://www.mysteriousbritain.co.uk/occult/dr-simon-forman.html

30. Writing the History of Elizabeth's Reign: William Camden's *The History of the Most Renowned and Victorious Princess Elizabeth* (1615)

INTRODUCTION

William CAMDEN, the Elizabethan antiquary and historian, is known for two major Latin works: *Britannia*, a historical/topographical survey of Britain dedicated to William CECIL, Lord Burghley, and the *Annales rerum Anglicarum et Hibernicarum regnante Elizabetha*, a history of the reign of ELIZABETH I proposed by Burghley (see "Elizabethan Antiquarianism" below). Reproduced here is a selection from the latter work, the title of which in English is usually rendered as *The Annals or the History of the Most Renowned and Victorious Princess Elizabeth*. In this excerpt, Camden describes how he came to undertake the work, what he sought to achieve with the work, and the sources from which he drew his information.

KEEP IN MIND AS YOU READ

1. Medieval English chronicles were annalistic in form, meaning they were arranged by year with all the events of a particular year under one entry. The chroniclers also took an uncritical approach to their sources, very often copying large parts of previous chronicles verbatim. By the sixteenth century, however, Italian historical writers, such as Polydore VERGIL, who wrote the *Anglica Historia* (1534), a comprehensive, humanist history of England, had abandoned the annalistic approach for a chronological/biographical organization and adopted a critical approach to sources. Vergil, for instance, rejected the legendary accounts of Brutus and King Arthur that had been repeated as fact by most medieval chroniclers. Camden was influenced in his work by both the medieval chronicles and the new Italian critical history.

2. Tudor chroniclers, such as Raphael HOLINSHED (see Document 24), Edward HALL, Richard GRAFTON, and John STOW, had created a market for contemporary history by producing popular English-language works that covered recent events and people still living. Although increasing critical attention was paid to sources, these works were written in a lively, engaging style. They were strongly patriotic and Protestant in tone, and they were meant to celebrate the glories and achievements of Tudor/Elizabethan England.

3. Camden had a very different purpose from the popular Tudor chroniclers. Although he adopted the familiar annalistic organization, he chose to write in Latin, which signaled his intention to address an international and scholarly, rather

than popular, audience. Although he certainly felt devotion to the late Queen and undertook his work as a patriotic duty, Camden also sought to achieve an impartial tone to remove his own bias from the work. He also based his history on state documents to which he was given unprecedented access and not on the uncritical use of legends and early chronicles.

Document: Excerpt from Camden's History of the Most Renowned and Victorious Princess Elizabeth

Above eighteen Years since William Cecil, Baron of Burghley, Lord Treasurer of England, (when full little I thought of any such business) imparted to me, first his own, and then the Queen's Rolls, Memorials and Records, willing me to compile from thence an Historical Account of the first Beginnings of the Reign of Queen Elizabeth: with what Intent I know not, unless, while he had a desire to **eternize** the Memory of that Renowned Queen, he would first see an Introduction thereinto by my Pains in this kind. I obeyed him, and not unwillingly, lest I might seem either to neglect the Memory of that most Excellent Princess, or to fail his Expectation and (which I prized as dear as them both) the Truth itself. For in these Papers, if anywhere, I had confident Hopes to meet the real Truth of Passages lodged, as it were, in so many Repositories.

But at my first entrance upon the Task, an intricate Difficulty did in a manner wholly discourage me. For I lighted upon great Piles and Heaps of Papers and Writings of all sorts, reasonably well digested indeed in respect of the Times, but in regard of the Variety of the Arguments very much confused. In searching and turning over whereof whist I labored till I sweat again, covered all over with Dust, to gather fit Matter together, (which I diligently sought for, but more rarely found than I expected,) that Noble Lord died, and my Industry began to flag and wax cold in the Business. Not long after that Incomparable Princess also rendered her celestial Soul to God: when I stood in expectation for some time, full of Hope that some other Person . . . would render her this due and deserved piece of Gratitude [but finding none] . . . I buckled myself afresh to my intermitted Study, and plied it harder than before. I procured all the Helps I possibly could for writing it: Charters and Grants of Kings and great Personages, Letters, Consultations in the council-Chamber, Ambassadors' Instructions and Epistles, I carefully turned over and over; Parliamentary Diaries, Acts and Statutes, I thoroughly perused, and read over every Edict or Proclamation. For the greatest part of all which as I am beholden to that most Excellent Gentleman Sir Robert Cotton, Knight and Baronet, who has with great cost and successful Industry furnished himself with the choicest things relating to History and Antiquity; (for he readily and willingly gave me Light and Direction in my Business . . .) so, Reader, if I shall in anything profit or delight thee in this Undertaking, though are deservedly obliged to give him Thanks for the same.

Mine own Cabinets and Writings I also searched into: who though I have been a studious Regarder and Admirer of venerable Antiquity, yet have I not been altogether careless of later . . . Occurrences; but then have myself seen and observed many things, and received others from credible Persons.

eternize: make eternal

ELIZABETHAN ANTIQUARIANISM

William Camden was approached to write a history of Elizabeth's reign in part because he was a well-known antiquarian. Elizabethan England witnessed a rise of interest in collecting and cataloging artifacts of British history, as well as a growing enthusiasm for studying the history, natural and human, of the various counties and localities of Britain. This passion for preserving the literary and material artifacts of the British past was known as antiquarianism and its practitioners as antiquaries. Elizabethan antiquaries were amateur scholars, such as wealthy gentlemen or country clergymen, who had the money or leisure to collect, research, and write. Elizabethan antiquarianism was stimulated by the destruction of medieval art and artifacts caused by the Reformation and the dissolution of the monasteries in the 1530s and 1540s (see "English Reformation," Document 14). The loss of these antiquities, combined with the accelerating pace of change in the Elizabethan world, generated an interest in preserving and understanding as much of the past as still remained.

Because antiquaries could delve most easily into the past of their own neighborhoods, antiquarian studies rapidly developed a focus on local history, topography, and genealogy. Camden was a member of the Society of Antiquaries, which was founded in London around 1573. Members discussed ideas at meetings, corresponded with one another about their researches and discoveries, and wrote papers and dissertations on topics of mutual interest. The work of Elizabethan antiquaries resulted in the creation of a whole new historical genre, the county survey, such as Richard CAREW's *Survey of Cornwall*. Besides Camden's *Annals*, Elizabethan antiquarianism also produced broader histories such as Holinshed's *Chronicles* (see Document 24).

Source: Camden, William. *The History of the Most Renowned and Victorious Princess Elizabeth Late Queen of England.* Edited by Wallace T. MacCaffrey. Chicago: University of Chicago Press, 1970, pp. 3–4.

AFTERMATH

Burghley first suggested a history of Elizabeth's reign to Camden in about 1597 when the minister put his own papers and those of the Queen at the writer's disposal. With the death of Burghley in 1598 and that of the Queen in 1603, Camden's interest in the work waned, and he did not begin in earnest until about 1608. The first half of the *Annals*, covering events up to 1588, appeared in 1615, and the second half was complete by 1617, but was not published until 1625, two years after Camden's death. A complete English translation of the work did not appear until 1630, with various other new editions and translations appearing over the next century.

ASK YOURSELF

1. What does Camden say his purpose is in undertaking this history of Elizabeth's reign? Access the online edition of the *Annals* at http://www.philological.bham.ac.uk/camden, and read a selection. From your reading, would you say that Camden achieved his purpose? Why or why not?
2. What types of sources does Camden say he consulted? Where does he say he obtained these sources? What kind of different information do you think these sources would provide? How would it differ from the information available in popular chronicles like Holinshed's?

TOPICS AND ACTIVITIES TO CONSIDER

∾ Access the online edition of the *Annals* at http://www.philological.bham .ac.uk/camden, and read selections from several of the annual entries. Following Camden's organization and style, write your own annalistic history of the United States since 2000, noting important political, social, economic, and cultural events and personalities. Or write your personal history of the last 10 years, noting the events and people who were important in your life.

∾ Access the online edition of the *Annals* at http://www.philological.bham .ac.uk/camden and the online excerpts from Holinshed's *Chronicles* on the Richard III Society Web site at http://www.r3.org/bookcase/holinshed/ index.html. Read selections from each, noting the differences in tone and style between the two. Write a chronicle entry for a recent year in the tone and style of Camden. Then write an entry for the same year in the tone and style of Holinshed.

∾ Access the online edition of Camden's *Britannia* at http://www.philological .bham.ac.uk/cambrit, and read a selection. Describe how this work differs from the *Annals*.

∾ Who was Sir Robert COTTON, the gentleman mentioned by Camden? Use books and the Internet to find out more about Cotton and why Camden seemed so indebted to him.

Further Information

Camden, William. *The History of the Renowned and Victorious Princess Elizabeth Late Queen of England: Selected Chapters*. Edited by Wallace T. MacCaffrey. Chicago: University of Chicago Press, 1970.

Herendeen, Wyman H. *William Camden: A Life in Context*. Rochester, NY: Boydell Press, 2007.

Web Sites

Thomas Smith, Life of Camden (1691): http://www.philological.bham.ac.uk/smith

William Camden, *Annales Rerum Gestarum Angliae et Hiberniae Regnante Elizabetha* (English and Latin): http://www.philological.bham.ac.uk/camden

THE QUEEN

31. THE QUEEN ON PROGRESS: ROBERT LANEHAM'S ACCOUNT OF THE QUEEN'S ENTERTAINMENT BY THE EARL OF LEICESTER AT KENILWORTH CASTLE (1575)

INTRODUCTION

For 19 days in July 1575, Queen ELIZABETH visited Kenilworth Castle in Warwickshire as the guest of her favorite, Robert DUDLEY, Earl of Leicester. Seeking to impress both Queen and court with his merits as a possible husband for Elizabeth, Leicester spared no expense in providing a lavish and spectacular round of feasts and entertainments for his royal guest. One guest who was certainly dazzled by what he saw was Robert LANEHAM, a London merchant who owed his presence at Kenilworth to the patronage of Leicester. Laneham later described the visit in enthusiastic detail in a letter to another London merchant, Humfrey Martin. In the following excerpt from that letter, Laneham described the welcome accorded the Queen upon her arrival at Kenilworth on Saturday, July 9.

KEEP IN MIND AS YOU READ

1. About the same age as the Queen, Robert Dudley was the only man Elizabeth probably gave serious consideration to marrying. Like Elizabeth, Dudley had been imprisoned in the Tower of London during the reign of Elizabeth's Catholic half-sister, MARY I. Upon her accession in 1558, Elizabeth showed immediate favor to Dudley, who received many rewards and offices and was frequently in her company. Although Dudley was married, rumors soon spread that he intended to marry the Queen and that Elizabeth was not unreceptive.

2. In September 1560, Dudley's wife was found dead under mysterious circumstances, leading to charges that Dudley had murdered her to have the Queen. An investigation ruled the death an accident, but the resulting scandal caused Elizabeth to cool her relationship with Dudley, who became Earl of Leicester in 1563. Although the Queen continued to love him and he continued to press for her hand, Elizabeth decided that she could not marry Dudley and never did.

3. Tradition states that an 11-year-old William SHAKESPEARE, who lived nearby in Stratford, was among the crowd of local commoners who were permitted to view some of the entertainments at Kenilworth in 1575 and that memories of what he saw there were later reflected in his play *A Midsummer Night's Dream*.

4. The entertainments staged during the Queen's visit included a spectacular fireworks display, a grand waterborne pageant on a great lake, a bear-baiting, and

numerous plays and masques (a musical play similar to opera). A large tower was built to house the guests and provide views of the lake and its entertainments, and a large Pleasance, a magnificent pleasure garden, was laid out for the Queen's use along the north side of the castle. The entire visit is said to have cost Leicester £1,000 per day, an enormous sum for the time.

Document: Excerpt of Laneham's Account of the Queen's Progress of 1575

[H]er Majesty pleasantly so passed from thence toward the Castle gate; whereunto, from the base Court over a dry valley, cast into a good form, was there framed a fair Bridge of a twenty foot wide, and a seventy foot long, graveled for treading, railed on either part with seven posts on a side, that stood a 12 foot asunder, thickened between with well-proportioned pillars turned. Upon the first pair of posts were set too **comely** square wire cages, each a three foot long, two foot wide; and . . . in them live . . . dainty birds, of the presents of Sylvanus the god of Foul.

On the second pair, too great silvered bowls, neatly **apted** to the purpose, filled with apples, pears, cherries, filberts, walnuts, fresh upon their branches, and with oranges, pomegranates, [and] lemons . . . all for the gifts of Pomona goddess of Fruits.

The third pair of posts, in two such silvered bowls, had (all in ears green and old) wheat, barley, oats, beans, and peas, as the gifts of Ceres.

The fourth post on the left hand, in a like silvered bowl, had grapes in clusters white and red, **gracified** with their vine leaves. The match post against it had a pair of great white silver . . . pots for wine: and before them, two glasses of good capacity filled full: the one with white wine, the two other with **claret**: so fresh of color, and of look so lovely, smiling to the eyes of many, that by my faith me thought, by their leering, they could have found in their hearts (as the evening was hot) to have kissed them sweetly, and thought it no sin: and these for the potential presents of Bacchus, the god of Wine.

The fifth pair had each a fair large trey strewn with fresh grass; and in them conger, burt, mullet, fresh herring, oysters, salmon . . . and such like, from Neptunus, god of the sea.

On the sixth pair of posts were set two ragged staves of silver, as my Lord gives them in arms, beautifully glittering of armor, thereupon depending, bows, arrows, spears, shield, head-piece, **gorget**, corselets, swords, targets, and such like, for Mars' gifts, the god of war. And the aptlier (me thought) was it that those ragged staves supported these martial presents, as well because these staves by their tines seem naturally meet for the bearing of armor, as also that they chiefly in this place might take upon them principal protection of her Highness' parson, that so benignly pleased her to take harbor.

On the seventh posts, the last and next to the Castle, were there pitched two . . . Bay branches of a four foot high, adorned on all sides with lutes, viols . . . cornets, flutes, recorders, and harps, as the presents of Phoebus the god of Music, for rejoicing the mind, and also of physic, for health to the body.

Over the Castle Gate was there fastened a table beautifully garnished above with her Highness' Arms, and neatly with ivy wreaths bordered about, of a ten foot square: The ground black, whereupon in large white capital Roman fair written, a poem mentioning these gods and their gifts, thus presented unto her Highness . . . :

But the night well spent, for that these Verses by torch light could not easily be read; by a Poet, therefore in a long **ceruleus** garment, with a die and wide sleeves Venetian wise drawn up to his elbows, his **doublet** sleeves under that crimson, nothing but silk; a bay garland on his head, and a scroll in his hand, making first a humble obeisance at her Majesty's coming, and pointing unto every present as he spoke; the same was pronounced; pleasantly thus viewing the gifts, as she passed, and how the posts might agree with the speech of the Poet. At the end of the bridge and entry of the gate, was her Highness received with a fresh delicate harmony of flutes, in performance of Phoebus presents.

So passing into the inner Court, her Majesty . . . there set down from her **palfrey**, was conveyed up to chamber: When after did follow so great a peal of guns, and such lightning by firework a long space together, as Jupiter would show himself to be no further behind with his welcome than the rest of his gods; and that would he have all the country to know; for indeed the noise and flame were heard and seen a twenty mile off. Thus much, Master Martin, (that I remember me,) for the first day's **bien-venu**. Be you not weary, for I am scant in the midst of my matter.

Source: Nichols, John, ed. *The Progresses and Public Processions of Queen Elizabeth.* vol. I. London: Printed by and for John Nichols and Son, 1823, pp. 432–435.

---

apted: suited; designed
bien-venu: welcome
ceruleus: blue
claret: a dark red wine
comely: attractive; handsome
doublet: a close-fitting jacket worn by men
gorget: piece of armor designed to protect the throat; ornamental collar
gracified: graced; decorated
palfrey: a small, easy-gaited horse for a woman to ride

ROYAL PROGRESSES

No English monarch made better or more extensive political use of royal progresses than Elizabeth I. Progresses were formal summer tours of the kingdom conducted by the Queen and a portion of the court, usually between the months of August and October when the weather was generally good and the harvest was being gathered. For Elizabeth, royal progresses were always first and foremost an opportunity for her to see and be seen by her subjects. Following an itinerary published well in advance, a progress would carry the Queen to various of the more distant royal residences, to the country homes of the local nobility or gentry, or to lodgings provided by a town. Traveling on horseback or in an open litter, Elizabeth stopped frequently to talk to the people who crowded the roadside to watch her pass.

If the Queen enjoyed progresses, her household officials did not, since they were responsible for loading and transporting hundreds of carts stuffed with the Queen's household goods and those of her attendants. Finding lodging for the Queen's followers could also be a nightmare, both for those seeking lodging and those expected to supply it. While a great honor, entertaining the Queen on progress in one's home or town was also a crushing expense and a source of much anxiety lest the quality of accommodations or entertainment fall short of court expectations. William CECIL, Lord Burghley, spent over £1,000 to host the Queen for 10 days in 1591, and Leicester spent a fortune for the Kenilworth entertainments in 1575. Competition to host the Queen led to an Elizabethan architectural phenomenon known as prodigy houses—large and splendid aristocratic country homes built specifically to attract a royal progress.

AFTERMATH

Despite the spectacular display at Kenilworth in 1575, the Queen refused to marry Leicester, who, in 1578, secretly married Lettice KNOLLYS, the widowed countess of Essex and Elizabeth's cousin. When the Queen learned of the marriage from the French ambassador, who was seeking to discredit Leicester's opposition to the Queen's proposed marriage to the French Duke of Anjou (see Documents 31 and 32), she angrily sent Leicester to the Tower. Although the Queen soon forgave Leicester and restored him to favor, she never forgave her cousin, who was banished from court for the rest of her life and hounded for payment of debts to the Crown that her husband left at his death in 1588.

ASK YOURSELF

1. What symbolism do you see in the pageants that welcomed the Queen? What message was Leicester trying to convey with these pageants? To whom do you think they were addressed?
2. How do you think Laneham feels about his patron, the Earl of Leicester? Does he seem pleased to be at Kenilworth or not? Give reasons for your opinion.

TOPICS AND ACTIVITIES TO CONSIDER

- ॐ Access the English Heritage site for Kenilworth Castle at http://www.english-heritage.org.uk/server.php?show=nav.16873 and the History of Kenilworth Castle site at http://hearteng.110mb.com/kenilworth.htm. View the many images of the castle at these sites, and read about the castle's long history and its appearance in various films and DVD histories of Britain.
- ॐ Access Laneham's letter at http://books.google.com/books, and read a selection from it. Following Laneham's style, write an account of a noteworthy event that you recently witnessed.
- ॐ Access Laneham's letter at http://books.google.com/books, and read excerpts from the descriptions of each day's entertainments. Create a brief timeline for the length of the Queen's visit, summarizing the highlights of each day's events.

Further Information

Archer, Elisabeth Jayne, Elizabeth Goldring, and Sarah Knight, eds. *The Progresses, Pageants, and Entertainments of Queen Elizabeth I.* Oxford: Oxford University Press, 2007.
Dovey, Zillah. *An Elizabethan Progress.* Herndon, VA: Sutton Publishers, 1996.
Gristwood, Sarah. *Elizabeth and Leicester: Power, Passion, Politics.* New York: Viking, 2007.
Haynes, Alan. *The White Bear: The Elizabethan Earl of Leicester.* London: Peter Owen, 1987.
Osborne, Jane. *Entertaining Elizabeth: The Progresses and Great Houses of Her Time.* London: Bishopsgate Press, 1998.
Wilson, Derek: *Sweet Robin: A Biography of Robert Dudley.* London: Allen and Busby, 1981.

Web Site

Robert Laneham's Letter: http://books.google.com

32. The Queen's Marriage: Pros and Cons of the Proposed Match with the Duke of Anjou (1579)

INTRODUCTION

During the course of her reign, Elizabeth I entertained a variety of marriage suits from foreign princes, including her former brother-in-law Philip II of Spain, Charles IX and Henri III of France, Archduke Charles of Austria, and Eric XIV of Sweden. Because of religious differences, age differences, or the Queen's indifference, none ever progressed very far. The only foreign suitor who came close to marrying Elizabeth was the younger brother of Henri III of France, Francis Valois, Duke of Anjou (who is better known in English history by his former title, Duke of Alençon). Although first proposed as a husband for the Queen in 1572, Anjou did not become a serious suitor for her hand until 1579. In 1581, he came to England to press his suit in person. He charmed Elizabeth, but horrified English Protestants, who feared their 48-year-old Queen would die in childbed, leaving them to be ruled by a French Catholic. The following document is a list of reasons both for and against the marriage that were raised and discussed by the listed commissioners—all leading royal ministers and advisors—at a meeting held at Westminster in 1579.

KEEP IN MIND AS YOU READ

1. Although the duke was said to be ugly, short, and pockmarked, his chief representative, Jean de Simier, was a handsome, accomplished courtier who was said to be "thoroughly versed in Love-fancies, pleasant conceits, and Court-dalliance (Camden 227). Simier wooed the Queen, in effect courting her on his master's behalf. Elizabeth initiated the marriage discussion to cement a firm alliance with France against Spain, but she maintained the talks in part because of the pleasure she derived from Simier's attentions.

2. Although a Catholic and heir to the throne of France, Anjou, in 1578, concluded an agreement with the Dutch Protestants, then in rebellion against Philip II, to be their protector and assist them militarily against Spain. Thus, obtaining the Queen's financial and military assistance in securing his position in the Netherlands was at least as important to Anjou as securing the Queen's hand in marriage (see "Spanish Netherlands," Document 38). For him and his brother the king, the latter was largely a means to achieving the former.

3. By 1579, the belief that Elizabeth had to marry to secure the succession and the help of a husband in governing the realm was giving way to a new patriotism that

viewed the Queen's unmarried virginity as the symbol of the realm's independence and inviolability. The image of the Virgin Queen was becoming the focus of national pride, and the country's Protestant majority began to turn strongly against any marriage (see "The Virgin Queen," Document 25).

Document: List of Reasons For and Against the Queen's Marriage to the Duke of Anjou

The sum of the principal heads remembered in the conference at Westminster touching the Q. marriage with the Duke of Anjou, the Fr[ench]. K[ing]'s Brother.

The Commissioners,

> The L. of Burghley, L. Treasurer.
> The Earl of Sussex
> The Earl of Leicester
> The L. of Hunsdon.
> Sir Christ. Hatton.
> Sir Fr. Walsingham. [Secretary]
> Doctor Wilson. [Secretary]

The means to assure her Majesty of peace, and to preserve her person and state from danger.

1. Assistance of the Religion in France.

> To give help in the case of the Low Countries.
> To maintain our Religion, Laws and Justice inviolably.
> To concert with Scotland and their King fast and lovingly, with plausible terms and good and commodious actions.
> To make an Act of Parliament to disable all such persons from the claim of the Crown as shall by any means interrupt her Majesty's quiet or endanger her person.

Perils growing by the marriage

The difficulty of the continuance of our Religion.

The fear that may be justly conceived that he will bring the Realm into his own possession.

The danger of separation, if he should be called by his brother's decease into his own kingdom.

England will abide no Viceroy.

The great charge that this Realm shall be at for his maintenance.

2. The discontentment of the people to be governed by a **stranger**.

The suspicion of treason in seeking her Majesty, to profess [possess?] another afterwards.

The danger of falling into foreign wars by maintaining at her Majesty's great charges this prince's quarrels wheresoever.

The encouragement that the Scots might take against us in hope of the favor of the French, with whom they have always had ancient league and alliance, greatly to our prejudice and disquiet.

The Low Countries will be jealous of the match, the Germans will be displeased, and Spain will not abide the greatness of these two kingdoms, grown so mightily by this alliance.

The people shall be more taxed than heretofore, which they will murmur at, the rather because it is by the means of a stranger.

The Commodities growing by the marriage.

The gaining of the French by this alliance.

The suppressing of sedition, which may otherwise ensue by **popery** in this Realm.

Spain will not dare to trouble or offend her Majesty.

Her Majesty may, by this Prince's help, win to her the possession of the Low Countries.

3. The comfort which may redound to the Realm by the blessed fruit of her Majesty's body.

Spain shall be glad to take reasonable conditions of the Low Countries.

Perils ensuing by leaving this Alliance.

Their griefs already conceived against us.

The alienating of Scotland from us.

Monsieur will seek the King of Spain's daughter, whereby his faction should cease in France, and he should happily have the Low Countries for his wife's dower.

Spain and France would then set up the Q[ueen]. of Scots.

They would reduce the Low Countries to obedience.

They would practice to win the King of Scots to them, and then marry him at their pleasure.

They would supplant the Religion in Europe, and begin at the root.

If the **Papists** in England had but one of these Kings to back them, they would be ready to rebel.

The Q[ueen]. of Scots being in England would further the motion.

When hope of issue shall fail, her subjects will begin to ***adorare solem orientem***.

Source: Collier, J. Payne, ed. *The Egerton Papers: A Collection of Public and Private Documents, Chiefly Illustrative of the Times of Elizabeth and James I, from the Original Manuscripts, the Property of the Right Hon. Lord Francis Egerton, M.P.* London: Printed for the Camden Society by John Bowyer Nichols and Son, 1840, pp. 79–80.

> ***adorare solem orientem:*** follow the rising sun, that is, Englishmen would begin to look for favor with the King of Scots, Elizabeth's likely heir if she remained childless
> **Papists:** Roman Catholics
> **popery:** Roman Catholicism
> **stranger:** here meaning "foreigner"

AFTERMATH

The English PRIVY COUNCIL was bitterly divided over the marriage and thus could give the Queen no clear or consistent advice. Popular opinion, however, was solidly against the match. By the summer of 1579, numerous pamphlets and ballads appeared, denouncing the duke for his religion and nationality and suggesting that the Queen was being deceived. John STUBBS, the writer of the most virulent pamphlet, was arrested, convicted of seditious libel, and had his right hand struck off.

Nonetheless, Elizabeth drew back. Although negotiations for an alliance continued, the marriage seemed dead. Then, in October 1581, the duke came himself to England, ostensibly to obtain financial support for his campaigns in the Netherlands. However, Elizabeth

THE QUESTION OF THE QUEEN'S MARRIAGE

When Elizabeth came to the throne at age 25 in 1558, her need to marry quickly was almost universally acknowledged. This urgency arose from a practical need to secure the succession. Elizabeth required an undisputed heir to succeed her. The heir apparent in 1558 was MARY, Queen of Scots, a foreign and pro-French Catholic, whose possible succession greatly troubled Protestants. Beyond the succession, the assumption of the age was that a woman could not rule a kingdom and required a husband to rule for her.

Complicated by the question of religion and the need for a useful alliance, foreign marriages could make England a mere pawn to another country's interests. Marriage to a subject deprived England of a valuable foreign alliance and threatened the creation of internal political factions. Even though Elizabeth's Privy Council urged her to marry in 1559 and Parliament repeatedly petitioned her to marry, both councilors and MPs were seriously divided over which of the Queen's many suitors would make the best husband (see "Elizabethan Parliaments," Document 11). Thus, although there was strong agreement with the general principle that the Queen must marry, there was much contradictory advice offered her as to whom she should marry in particular. Many candidates were proposed, but Elizabeth's two most serious marriage suits involved Robert DUDLEY, Earl of Leicester, in the 1560s and Anjou in the late 1570s. Anjou's suit prompted the list of pros and cons reproduced above. For political and personal reasons, neither marriage occurred, and Elizabeth defied the expectations of her times and remained unmarried to her death.

confounded all by treating the duke as a suitor, kissing him and flirting with him before the court. When she drew a ring from her finger and presented it to him, it seemed that a marriage was concluded.

The apparently impulsive act drew a decidedly negative reaction from the Privy Council and the ladies of the Queen's household. After a sleepless night, the Queen took the duke aside and broke off the match, leaving Anjou to "rail on the lightness of women and the inconstancy of islanders" (Camden iii 12). Whether the whole episode was a diplomatic ploy designed to wring concessions from the French on the military alliance or a genuinely unguarded act quickly regretted is now unclear (see Document 33). Anjou left England, apparently satisfied with Elizabeth's agreement to financially support his campaigns in the Netherlands, and the marriage of the Queen was never again seriously contemplated.

ASK YOURSELF

1. From the list above, what would you surmise to be the majority opinion of the marriage? Does the list seem to lean one way or the other? What are your reasons for believing as you do?
2. Which of the pros and cons listed above carries the most weight with you? From these lists of reasons for and against the marriage, how would you decide the question? Would you favor the marriage or oppose it? Why?

TOPICS AND ACTIVITIES TO CONSIDER

- ⮞ Choose a current political issue or controversy about which you do not have a definite or settled opinion, such as abortion, stem cell research, gun control, or the death penalty. Devise your own list of reasons supporting each side in the debate. From the list, does it seem like you lean in one direction or the other?

- The Duke of Anjou was said to be physically unattractive. Access the French Web site *Les Derniers Valois* at http://derniersvalois.canalblog .com/archives/francois_d_alencon/index.html, which offers a series of portraits of the duke. What is your opinion of Anjou's physical appearance?
- Access the YouTube video Web site at http://youtube.com. Search for "Elizabeth I and the Duke of Anjou" and view the two or three short video clips that dramatize the marriage suit.

Further Information

Camden, William. *The History of the Most Renowned Princess Elizabeth, Late Queen of England.* London, 1688.

Doran, Susan. *Monarchy and Matrimony: The Courtships of Elizabeth I.* London: Routledge, 1996.

Johnson, Paul. *Elizabeth I: A Biography.* New York: Holt, Rinehart and Winston, 1974.

Loades, David. *Elizabeth I.* London: Hambledon Continuum, 2006.

MacCaffrey, Wallace. *Elizabeth I.* London: Edward Arnold, 1993.

———. *Queen Elizabeth and the Making of Policy, 1572–1588.* Princeton, NJ: Princeton University Press, 1981.

Neale, J.E. *Elizabeth I and Her Parliaments 1584–1601.* New York: St. Martin's Press, 1958.

33. ELIZABETH THE POET LAMENTS THE FINAL LEAVE-TAKING OF THE DUKE OF ANJOU: "ON MONSIEUR'S DEPARTURE" (1582)

INTRODUCTION

A number of poems written by ELIZABETH I have survived, including two lines of verse that Elizabeth scratched into a window with a diamond while she was a prisoner under suspicion of treason in 1554–1555 during the reign of her sister, MARY I. That poem reads simply as follows:

> Much suspected by me,
> Nothing proved can be.
> > Elizabeth the prisoner

Reproduced here is perhaps the most famous poem attributed to Elizabeth, a lament on unrequited love that has been titled "On Monsieur's Department" because it is believed to refer to the final departure from England in 1582 of her last and most serious foreign suitor, Francis VALOIS, Duke of Anjou (the "Monsieur" of the title) (see Document 32).

KEEP IN MIND AS YOU READ

1. Elizabeth was fluent in several languages and wrote poetry not only in English, but in French and Latin as well.
2. This poem does not exist in any manuscript dating to Elizabeth's lifetime. The earliest extant (i.e., existing) copy dates to the 1630s and titles the poem "Elizabeth: On Monsieur's Departure." There is thus no definitive evidence, beyond the title of later copies, that the poem refers to Anjou.
3. Unrequited love is one of the central themes of Elizabethan poetry. Such a love is idealized as a symbol of pure and perfect devotion. By expressing the poet's deep feelings for an unnamed individual with whom she can never be united, "On Monsieur's Departure" fits well within this poetic tradition.

Document: "On Monsieur's Departure" by Elizabeth I

On Monsieur's Departure
I grieve and dare not show my discontent,

prate: chatter

I love and yet am forced to seem to hate,
I do, yet dare not say I ever meant,
I seem stark mute yet inwardly do **prate**.
I am and not, I freeze and yet am burned,
Since from myself my other self I turned.
My care is like my shadow in the sun,
Follows me flying, flies when I pursue it,
Stands and lies by me, doth what I have done.
His too familiar care doth make me rue it.
   No means I find to rid him from my breast
   Till by the end of things it be suppressed.
Some gentler passions slide into my mind,
For I am soft and made of melting snow;
Or be more cruel, love, and so be kind.
Let me float or sink, be high or low.
   Or let me live with some more sweet content,
   Or die and so forget what love ere meant.

Source: Nichols, John, ed. *The Progresses and Public Processions of Queen Elizabeth.* vol. 2. London, 1823, p. 346.

AFTERMATH

Although few modern scholars dispute that the poem was written by Elizabeth and that it is in some way autobiographical, there is debate as to just when the poem was written and whether it actually refers to the departure of the Duke of Anjou or not. Some historians date the poem to the late 1560s rather than to 1582 and argue that it refers instead to

MARRIAGE IN ELIZABETHAN ENGLAND

The question of the Queen's marriage was a matter of high policy, but, for other English men and women in the Elizabethan era, marriage was an important social milestone because it marked the official passage to adult independence. To be a householder, a man had to be married. Few economically independent bachelors existed, even within the nobility. The average age of marriage was high—27 for men and 24 for women among the lower classes and about three to four years younger among the upper classes. Parental permission was required for anyone under 21 to marry, but many marriages were arranged by parents. Such arrangements were particularly common among the nobility, where landed estates were involved and where political alliances were as important as social and economic considerations.

The bride's parents provided her with a dowry, a settlement of money or property that came under her husband's control. Betrothal was a legally binding contract, and any breach of a promise to marry was prosecuted in church courts. Prior to the wedding, marriage banns were called in the parish church on three successive Sundays. The banns provided time and opportunity for uncovering impediments to the match, such as the existence of a prior betrothal or marriage or the fact that the couple was too closely related. The wedding was celebrated in the parish church with an exchange of rings and was legally recognized by being recorded in the parish register. Women took their husband's surname. Once married, a couple was legally required to live together, with separations permitted only by court order and then only for such extreme circumstances as cruelty and adultery. Divorce was rarely granted, although annulment could be granted for good cause, such as discovery of a prior marriage.

the Queen's feelings for her longtime favorite, Robert DUDLEY, Earl of Leicester. Others argue that the poem, whatever the original impetus for its writing, was later made public as a deliberate attempt by the Queen to enhance her image with her people, showing them all she had given up to devote herself to their welfare. While this interpretation is certainly possible—Elizabeth was very careful of her public image and the poem creates a clear division between how the poet feels and how she must act—most historians accept the poem's connection with the end of Anjou's marriage suit.

ASK YOURSELF

1. What is Elizabeth saying in this poem? What is she grieving? Why?
2. In your opinion, does this poem display a true romantic attachment to the Duke of Anjou and sorrow at Elizabeth's inability to marry him for political reasons, or is the Queen lamenting something else or even simply engaging in a melancholy poetic exercise? What are your reasons for believing as you do?
3. Given the personal feelings it express, why do you think Elizabeth allowed this poem to be published during her lifetime?
4. What are the mood and tone of the poem? What literary devices did Elizabeth use to establish them?

TOPICS AND ACTIVITIES TO CONSIDER

- ❧ "On Monsieur's Departure" is often called a sonnet. Compare the poem to the sonnets by William SHAKESPEARE and Edward de VERE, Earl of Oxford in Document 28. Write a brief essay explaining why, in your opinion, the Queen's poem is or is not a sonnet. Give reasons supporting your opinion.
- ❧ Watch one of the following recent films of Elizabeth's life, and view the depictions of Anjou and his marriage suit presented in each:
  - ❧ *Elizabeth I* (2005) starring Helen Mirren
  - ❧ *Elizabeth R* (1971) starring Glenda Jackson
- ❧ In *Elizabeth I*, Anjou's visit is depicted in Part 1. Here the Queen gives the poem to Anjou as he boards the boat to depart. He silently reads the poem as the boat pulls away while Elizabeth's recitation of the poem is heard in voiceover. In the third episode of *Elizabeth R*, which is titled "Shadow in the Sun" from a line of the poem, Elizabeth mentally composes the verses as Anjou takes his leave. Which depictions of Elizabeth and Anjou did you find most credible? Why?
- ❧ Access online versions of other poems by Elizabeth at http://rpo.library .utoronto.ca/poet/112.html and http://www.tudorhistory.org/poetry/elizabeth.html or printed versions in *Elizabeth I: Collected Works* by Marcus et al. Choose your favorite, and use it as a guide for writing your own poem in the same style and on the same subject.

Further Information

Doran, Susan. *Queen Elizabeth I*. New York: New York University Press, 2003.
Marcus, Leah S., Janel Mueller, and Mary Beth Rose, eds. *Elizabeth I: Collected Works*. Chicago: University of Chicago Press, 2000.

Web Sites

Luminarium: Anthology of English Literature: http://www.luminarium.org/renlit/elizabib
.htm
Selected Poetry of Elizabeth I: http://rpo.library.utoronto.ca/poet/112.html
Tudor History: Poetry of Elizabeth I: http://www.tudorhistory.org/poetry/elizabeth.html
Voices of English Renaissance Women: http://www.albertrabil.com/projects2000/walters/
part%206.html

34. Protecting the Protestant Queen: The Bond of Association (1584–1585)

INTRODUCTION

In 1583, the Elizabethan government uncovered and thwarted a Catholic conspiracy, known as the THROCKMORTON PLOT, which aimed at murdering Elizabeth and replacing her with MARY, Queen of Scots. In 1584, a Spanish Catholic agent assassinated WILLIAM, Prince of Orange, the leader of the Dutch Protestant revolt against Spain (see "Spanish Netherlands," Document 38). Alarmed by these events, William CECIL, Lord Burghley, the lord treasurer, and Sir Francis WALSINGHAM, secretary of state, drafted the document reproduced below, the Bond of Association, which bound its signers to resist, pursue, and destroy any persons who threatened the Queen's life. Signers also agreed that any attempt on ELIZABETH's life would bar any person who benefitted by the attempt from the Crown and would obligate the signers to kill both that person and his or her heirs. Sent around the country, the Bond was signed by thousands who thereby committed themselves to taking murderous vengeance on anyone whose interests might lead to the formation of plots and conspiracies against the Queen.

KEEP IN MIND AS YOU READ

1. Although her name was never mentioned in it, the Bond of Association was aimed squarely at Mary, Queen of Scots, in whose interest various Catholic conspiracies were devised to murder Elizabeth, such as the Ridolfi and Throckmorton Plots (see "Ridolfi Plot," Document 16). The provision regarding heirs was an attempt to prevent Mary's Protestant son, James VI of Scotland (see JAMES I), from succeeding to the English throne.
2. Some English Protestants, although loyal to Elizabeth and alarmed by the continual plotting of Mary's supporters, refused to sign the Bond because they could not in good conscience commit themselves to a pact that endorsed murder.

Document: The Bond of Association

The Instrument of an Association for the Preservation of Her Majesty's Royal Person, by the Lords of Her Majesty's Privy Council, binding themselves under a vow and promise before the Majesty of Almighty God, with their whole powers, bod-

ies, lives, lands, and goods, and with their children and servants, faithfully to serve and obey the Queen, and to defend her against all Estates, Dignities, and earthly Powers whatsoever, and to pursue to utter extermination all that shall attempt by any act, counsel, or consent to anything that shall tend to the harm of Her Majesty's Royal Person, or claim succession to the Crown by the untimely death of Her Majesty; vowing and protesting in the presence of the Eternal and Everliving God to prosecute such persons to the death. Dated at Hampton Court on the 19th October 1584. Signed and sealed by thirteen of the Privy Council then present.

Forasmuch as Almighty God hath ordained kings, queens, and princes, to have dominion and rule over all their subjects, and to preserve them in the possession and observation of the true Christian religion, according to his holy word and commandment: and, in like sort, that all subjects should love, fear, and obey their sovereign princes, being kings or queens, to the utmost of their power; at all times, to withstand, pursue, and suppress, all manner of persons, that shall by any means intend and attempt anything dangerous or hurtful to the honor, states, or persons of their sovereigns.

Therefore, we whose names are or shall be subscribed to this writing, being natural-born subjects of this realm of England, and having so gracious a lady our Sovereign Elizabeth, by the ordinance of God, our most rightful Queen, reigning over us these many years with great felicity, to our inestimable comfort: and finding lately by **divers** depositions, confessions, and sundry advertisements, out of foreign parts, from credible persons, well known to her Majesty's council, and to divers others; that, for the furtherance and advancement of some pretended title to the crown, it hath been manifested, that the life of our gracious sovereign lady, Queen Elizabeth, hath been most dangerously exposed to the peril of her person, if Almighty God, her perpetual defender, of his mercy, had not revealed and withstood the same: by whose life we, and all other her Majesty's true and loyal subjects, do enjoy an inestimable benefit of peace in this land; do, for the reasons and causes before alleged, not only acknowledged ourselves most justly bound with our lives and goods for her defense, in her safety, to prosecute, suppress, and withstand, all such pretenders, and all other her enemies, of what nation, condition, and degree whatsoever they shall be, or by what council or title they shall pretend to be her enemies, or to attempt any harm upon her person; but do farther think it our bounden duties, for the great benefit of peace and wealth, and godly government, we have more plentifully received these many years, under her Majesty's government, than any of our fore-fathers have done in any longer time of any other **progenitors**, kings of this realm:

Do declare, and by this writing make manifest, our bounden duties to our said Sovereign Lady for her safety: and, to that end, we, and every of us, first calling to witness the name of Almighty God, and most willingly bind ourselves, every one of us to the other, jointly and severally, in the band of one firm and loyal society; and do hereby vow and promise by the Majesty of Almighty God, that with our whole powers, bodies, lives, and goods, and with our children and servants, we, and every of us, will faithfully serve and humbly obey our said Sovereign Lady Queen Elizabeth, against all states, dignities, and earthly powers whatsoever; and will, as well with our joint and particular forces, during our lives, withstand, offend, and pursue, as well by force of arms, as by all other means of revenge, all manner of persons, of what state soever they shall be, and their abettors, that shall attempt any act, council, or consent, to anything that shall tend to the harm of her Majesty's royal person, and will never desist from all manner of forcible pursuit against such persons, to the utter extermination of them, their counsellors, aiders, and abettors.

divers: various
progenitors: ancestors; forefathers

And if any such wicked attempt against her most royal person shall be taken in hand and procured, whereby any that have, may, or shall pretend title to come to this crown, by the untimely death of her Majesty, so wickedly procured (which God for his mercy sake forbid) may be avenged: we do not only bind ourselves, both jointly and severally, never to allow, accept, or favor any such pretended successor, by whom, or for whom, any such detestable act shall be attempted or committed, as unworthy of all government in any Christian realm or civil state:

But do also further vow and protest, as we are most bound, and that in the presence of the eternal and everlasting God, to prosecute such person and persons to death with our joint and practical forces, and to ask the utmost revenge upon them, that by any means we or any of us can devise or do, or cause to be devised and done, for their utter overthrow and extirpation.

And, to the better corroboration of this our royal bond and association, we do also testify by this writing, that we do confirm the contents hereof by our oaths corporally taken upon the Holy Evangelists, with this express condition: that no one of us shall for any respect of persons or causes, or for fear or reward, separate ourselves from this association, or fail in the prosecution thereof, during our lives, upon pain of being by the rest of us prosecuted, and suppressed as perjured persons, and public enemies to God, our Queen, and our native country. To which punishments and pains we do voluntarily submit ourselves, and every of us, without benefit of any color and pretence:

In witness of all which promises to be inviolably kept, we do to this writing put our hands and seals; and shall be most ready to accept and admit any others, hereafter, to this society and association.

QUEEN'S SAFETY ACT

The Act for the Queen's Safety, passed by Parliament in 1585, extended throughout the kingdom the protections erected around the Queen by the Bond of Association. Patterned after the Bond of Association, the act declared that anyone supporting a claimant to the throne who sought to advance his or her claim by assassination of the Queen was guilty of treason. The act also authorized loyal subjects to pursue and kill both those who had attempted the murder and the claimant on whose behalf they had acted. The act differed from the Bond in that it did not empower subjects to also seek out and kill the claimant's heirs. Although it mentioned no one by name, the act, like the Bond, was clearly aimed at Mary Stuart. Elizabeth intervened in December 1584 while the bill was being debated to object to the provision allowing for destruction of heirs, which was an attempt to include Mary's Protestant son, James VI of Scotland, in the consequences of any Catholic plot on his mother's behalf.

In March 1585, a new bill, devised in consultation with the Queen, was introduced into Parliament. This bill excluded heirs from vengeance unless the heirs' involvement in the assassination plot could be conclusively proven. The act also created a mechanism for determining who was involved in any assassination attempt and who was thus subject to the penalty of treason as meted out by the Queen's subjects. Should any rebellion, invasion, or murder plot be undertaken against Elizabeth, a commission would be created to investigate the deed and determine the guilty. Upon passage of the act, the Bond of Association was amended to conform to it.

Source: *The Harleian Miscellany; or, a Collection of Scarce, Curious, and Entertaining Pamphlets and Tracts, as Well in Manuscript as in Print, Found in the Late Earl of Oxford's Library.* Vol. II. London: Printed for Robert Dutton, 1809, pp. 5–7. The preamble is taken from the *Calendar of State Papers, Domestic Series, of the Reign of Elizabeth, 1581–1590.* London: Her Majesty's Stationery Office, 1865, p. 210.

AFTERMATH

In late 1584, the PRIVY COUNCIL sought to have the main provisions of the Bond of Association enacted into law by Parliament (see "English Parliaments," Document 11). The Queen, however, objected to the clause calling for the destructions of heirs, which, if passed, would have included James VI in the consequences arising from any Catholic plot undertaken on his mother's behalf but without his knowledge. Thus, the statute subsequently passed, known as the Queen's Safety Act (see "Queen's Safety Act," p. 169), excluded heirs unless their involvement in an assassination plot could be definitely proven.

In 1586, following Mary's conviction for treason for her endorsement of the Babington conspirators' plan to assassinate Elizabeth (see "Babington Plot," Document 35), the Queen demanded that Mary be killed privately by a signer of the Bond of Association, who, under terms of the Bond, was empowered to commit such a deed. Burghley wanted the Queen to sign a warrant authorizing a public execution under the Queen's Safety Act. The Queen wished Mary's death to be the private act of a private citizen. A public beheading would create a legal precedent for the execution of an anointed monarch, and use of the Queen's Safety Act as the basis for the execution would cede some of the monarch's power over the disposition of traitors to Parliament. As Document 35 illustrates, Mary was eventually publicly executed.

ASK YOURSELF

1. How do you view the Bond of Association? Is it a legitimate response to a serious threat, or is it an extreme overreaction? Why do you believe as you do?
2. What alternative steps do you think the government might have taken to protect the Queen and discourage Catholic plots?
3. Compare the signing of the Bond of Association with the passage of the PATRIOT Act by the U.S. Congress after the bombing of the Twin Towers in New York City on September 11, 2001. Were they motivated by similar or different considerations?

TOPICS AND ACTIVITIES TO CONSIDER

- Access the Papal Encyclicals Web site at http://www.papalencyclicals.net/ Pius05/p5regnans.htm, and read the text of the papal bull, *Regnans in Excelsis*. List all the actions the pope took against Elizabeth in this document and the reasons given for doing so. Write an essay explaining how you think this bull might have contributed to the atmosphere of fear and suspicion of Catholics in England. Or write an essay explaining how you think issuance of this bull affected the life of Catholics in England.
- Access the Hanover Historical Texts Web site at http://history.hanover .edu/texts/ENGref/er85.html, and read the text of the 1585 Act Against Jesuits and Seminarists (see "Penal Laws," Document 15). Passed at the

same time the Bond of Association was being circulated, this statute sought to protect the Queen from another Catholic threat, the activities of English Jesuits (see "Jesuit Mission in England," Document 37). After reading the act, write an encyclopedia entry of several hundred words that clearly explains what the act was meant to do and why. Your entry should clearly explain the act and its provisions to someone who has no previous knowledge of it.

Further Information

Johnson, Paul. *Elizabeth I: A Biography.* New York: Holt, Rinehart and Winston, 1974.

Loades, David. *Elizabeth I.* London: Hambledon Continuum, 2006.

MacCaffrey, Wallace. *Elizabeth I.* London: Edward Arnold, 1993.

Neale, J.E. *Elizabeth I and Her Parliaments 1584–1601.* New York: St. Martin's Press, 1958.

Web Site

Bond of Association: http://ccat.sas.upenn.edu/~jmcgill/bond.html

35. THE DEATH OF A QUEEN: RICHARD WIGMORE'S DESCRIPTION OF THE EXECUTION OF MARY, QUEEN OF SCOTS (1587)

INTRODUCTION

After 19 years in confinement in England, MARY, Queen of Scots was brought to trial for treason in October 1586. Although speedily convicted, Mary was not executed until February 8, 1587. Unwilling to take responsibility for ordering the death of a kinswoman and an anointed Queen, ELIZABETH tried to convince Mary's jailer, Sir Amias PAULET, to murder Mary privately. Horrified by the suggestion, Paulet refused. Elizabeth finally signed Mary's death warrant on February 1, but again hinted, this time to Secretary William DAVISON, the minister who brought the warrant to her, that she wanted Mary killed quietly. Instead of arranging this, as Elizabeth apparently hoped, Davison took the signed warrant to William CECIL, Lord Burghley, and Sir Francis WALSINGHAM, who issued orders for the execution to be carried out. Reproduced below is the description of Mary's execution, written by Burghley's agent that day at Fotheringhay Castle, Richard Wigmore.

KEEP IN MIND AS YOU READ

1. Mary and Elizabeth were cousins. Mary's grandmother was Margaret TUDOR, the sister of Elizabeth's father, HENRY VIII, and the mother of Mary's father, JAMES V of Scotland. Thus Elizabeth and Mary were both descended from HENRY VII, the founder of the Tudor dynasty, Elizabeth being his granddaughter and Mary his great-granddaughter. Because Elizabeth's siblings were dead and she herself was childless, Mary was, by right, next heir to the English throne. Because Mary was staunchly Catholic and pro-French, the prospect of Mary's accession terrified English Protestants.
2. Although Mary never sat upon the English throne, her son reigned after Elizabeth as JAMES I, and all succeeding English monarchs, including the current Queen, Elizabeth II, are descended from Mary, Queen of Scots, and not from Elizabeth I.
3. Protestants had been calling for the execution of Mary since at least 1572 (see Document 14 for one of the first of these calls).

Document: Excerpt from Wigmore's Description of the Death of Queen Mary of Scots

It may please your Lordship to be advertised, that, according as your honor gave me in Command, I have here set down in writing the true order and manner of the execution of the Lady Mary last Q[ueen]. of Scots, the 8 of February last, in the great hall within the Castle of Fotheringhay . . . .

The said 8 day of February being come, and time and place appointed for the execution, the said Queen being of stature tall, of body corpulent, round shouldered, her face fat and broad, double chinned, and hazel eyed, her **borrowed hair aborne**, her attire was this. On her head she had a dressing of **lawn** edged with bone lace, a pomander chain and an **Agnus dei** about her neck, a Crucifix in her hand, a pair of beads at her girdle, with a silver cross at the end of them. A vale of lawn fastened to her **caule** bowed out with wire, and edged round about with bone lace. Her gown was of black satin painted, with a train and long sleeves to the ground, set with acorn buttons of Jett trimmed with pearl, and short sleeves of satin black cut, with a pair of sleeves of purple velvet whole under them. Her **kirtle** whole, of figured black satin, and her petticoat skirts of Crimson velvet, her shoes of Spanish leather with the rough side outward, a pair of green silk garters, her nether stockings worsted . . . clocked with silver, and edged on the tops with silver, and next her leg, a pair of Jersey hose, white, &c. Thus appareled she departed her chamber, and willingly bended her steps towards the place of execution. . . .

Then said Mr. Deane [Mr. Doctor Fletcher, Deane of Peterborough], "Madam, change your opinion, and repent you of your former wickedness. Settle your faith only upon this ground, that in Christ Jesus you hope to be saved." She answered again and again, with great earnestness, "Good Mr. Deane, trouble not yourself any more about this matter, for I was born in this religion, have lived in this religion, and am resolved to die in this religion." Then the earls, when they saw how far unconformable she was to hear Mr. Deane's good exhortation, said, "Madam, we will pray for your grace with Mr. Deane, that you may have your mind lightened with the true knowledge of God and his word." My lords," answered the queen, "if you will pray with me, I will even from my heart thank you, and think myself greatly favored by you; but to join in prayer with you in your manner, who are not of one religion with me, it were a sin, and I will not." Then the lords called Mr. Deane again, and bade him save on, or what he thought good else. The dean kneeled and prayed . . . . during which prayer, the queen sat upon her stool, having her Agnus Dei, crucifix, beads, and an **office** in Latin. Thus furnished with superstitious trumpery, not regarding what Mr. Deane said, she began very fastly with tears and a loud voice to pray in Latin, and in the midst of her prayers, with overmuch weeping and mourning, slipped off her stool, and kneeling presently said **divers** other Latin prayers. Then she rose, and kneeled down again, praying in English, for Christ's afflicted church, an end of her troubles, for her son, and for the queen's majesty, to God for forgiveness of the sins of them in this island: she forgave her enemies with all her heart that had long sought her blood. This done she desired all saints to make intercession for her to the Savior of the world, Jesus Christ. Then she began to kiss her crucifix, and to cross herself, saying these words, "Even as thy arms, oh, Jesu Christ, were spread here upon the cross, so receive me into the arms of mercy." Then the two executioners kneeled down unto her, desiring her to forgive them her death. She answered, "I forgive you with all my heart. For I hope this death shall give an end to all my troubles." They, with her two women helping, began to disrobe her, and then she laid the crucifix upon the stool. One of the executioners took from her neck the Agnus Dei, and she laid hold of it, saying, she would give it to one of her women, and, withal, told the executioner that he should have money for it. Then they took off her chain. She made herself unready with a kind of gladness, and smiling, putting on a pair of sleeves with her own hands, which the two executioners before had rudely put off, and with such speed, as if she had longed to be gone out of the world.

During the disrobing of this queen, she never altered her countenance, but smiling said she never had such grooms before to make her unready, nor ever did put off her clothes before such a company. At lengths unattired and unapparelled to her petticoat and kirtle, the two women burst out into a great and pitiful shrieking, crying, and lamentation, crossed themselves, and prayed in Latin. The queen turned towards them . . . crossed and kissed them, and bade them pray for her. Then with a smiling countenance she turned to her men servants, Melvin and the rest, crossed them, bade them farewell, and pray for her to the last. One of the women having a Corpus Christi cloth, lapped it up three corner wise, and kissed it, and put it over the face of her queen, and pinned it fast upon . . . her head. Then the two women departed. The queen kneeled down upon the cushion resolutely, and, without any token of fear of death, said aloud in Latin [a] psalm . . . . Then groping for the block, she laid down her head, putting her chain over her back with both her hands, which, holding their still, had been cut off, had they not been espied. Then she laid herself upon the block most quietly, and stretching out her arms and legs cried out: *In manus tuas, domine, commendo spiritum meum*, three or four times. At last, while one of the Executioners held her straitly with one of his hands, the other gave two strokes with an Axe before he did cut off her head, and yet left a little gristle behind.

She made very small noise, no part stirred from the place where she lay. The Executioners lifted up the head, and bade God save the Queen. Then her dressing of lawn fell from her head, which appeared as gray as if she had been **three score and ten** years old, pulled very short. Her face much altered, her lips stirred up and down almost a quarter of an hour after her head was cut off. Then said Mr. Deane: "So perish all the Queen's enemies."

Source: Strickland, Agnes, ed. *Letters of Mary, Queen of Scots*. Vol. II. London: Henry Colburn, 1848, pp. 261–262, 268–271.

Agnus dei: an image of a lamb with a cross and banner symbolizing Christ as the "lamb of God"
borrowed hair aborne: wearing a wig
caule: type of feminine headdress
divers: various
lawn: a fine, sheer linen or cotton fabric
In manus tuas, domine, commendo spiritum meum: "Into your hands, Lord, I commend my spirit"; the last words of Jesus on the cross
kirtle: a long gown or dress worn by women
office: prayerbook
three score and ten: 70; Queen Mary was 44 at her death

BABINGTON PLOT

In 1586, a young Catholic gentleman named Anthony Babington became involved in a Jesuit plot to assassinate Elizabeth, put Mary Stuart on the English throne, and restore English Catholicism. In 1580, while in Paris, Babington met Thomas Morgan, Mary's agent in France. On his return to England, Babington involved himself with a clandestine group of English gentlemen engaged in hiding members of the Jesuit Mission in England. Babington's pro-Catholic activities caused John Ballard, a Jesuit priest, to recruit him for a plot against Elizabeth. Babington and his co-conspirators secretly communicated with Mary. On July 12, 1586, Babington wrote to the Queen of Scots, outlining the entire plan for her, including the murder of Elizabeth.

Unbeknownst to Mary and the plotters, Sir Francis Walsingham, Elizabeth's secretary of state, had discovered and tapped into Mary's secret system of correspondence by means of a renegade Catholic spy. Walsingham thus knew of the plot even before Babington wrote his letter to Mary. Because the secretary's chief aim was to prove Mary's complicity in a plot to kill Elizabeth and so force the Queen to consent to her cousin's execution, he did nothing and waited for Mary's reply to Babington's letter. On July 17, Mary, in her response, seemed to endorse the plan, including Elizabeth's murder. Some modern historians argue that Mary said nothing about the assassination plan, that the deciphered version of her letter was altered, on Walsingham's orders, to make it seem that she had consented to the plan and thus convince Elizabeth of the need for her cousin's trial and execution. In any event, Babington and his co-conspirators were arrested and executed in September 1586. Mary was tried for treason the following month and executed in February 1587.

AFTERMATH

When Elizabeth learned of Mary's death, she raged at her ministers, accusing them of acting without her orders. Davison was even arrested and imprisoned, becoming, in fact, the scapegoat for Elizabeth's unwillingness to take responsibility for her cousin's death. Although James VI of Scotland strongly protested his mother's execution, he took no further action, being more interested in maintaining his position in the English succession than standing up for a mother he never knew (see Document 36). News of the execution spurred Philip II of Spain to move forward with plans for the invasion of England (see Document 38 and "Spanish Armada," Document 18). Meanwhile, the execution was popular in England, removing the specter of a Catholic succession and preventing any future Catholic plots or invasions from using the crowning of Mary as justification.

ASK YOURSELF

1. Why do you think Elizabeth was so hesitant to order Mary's execution, even though most of her ministers and many of her subjects had urged her to do so for years?
2. What is the tone of Wigmore's description of the execution—sympathetic to Mary, hostile to Mary, or neutral? Why?
3. From this description, how do you think Mary met her death—bravely, fearfully, or foolishly? Why?
4. What do you think is the most striking or surprising part of Wigmore's description? Why?

TOPICS AND ACTIVITIES TO CONSIDER

- ⮞ Access the University of Pennsylvania's "Mary Queen of Scots and the Babington Plot" Web site at http://ccat.sas.upenn.edu/~jmcgill/project

.html. Click the links for Sir Anthony BABINGTON's letter to Mary and Mary's reply. These letters provided the English government with proof of Mary's approval of the assassination of Elizabeth and led to her trial and execution. Using the letters, write in your own words a brief description of the plot, as described by Babington's and Mary's response to Babington's plans (see "Babington Plot," p. 176). Identify which passage you believe sealed Mary's fate.

❧ Some historians (see, for instance, Warnicke, Chapter 9) believe that on Walsingham's instructions, his agent, Thomas Phelippes, who deciphered the coded letters for Walsingham, altered or added to the text of Mary's July 1586 reply to Babington to strengthen the evidence that Mary had agreed to Elizabeth's assassination. These historians argue that Mary would never have consented to the murder of another monarch, whose activities, like her own, she believed could only be judged by God. Access the University of Pennsylvania's "Mary Queen of Scots and the Babington Plot" Web site at http://ccat.sas.upenn.edu/~jmcgill/project.html and read Mary's reply to Babington. Do you see any evidence in the tone, organization, flow, or wording of Mary's letter to indicate possible tampering? If so, explain what you found and why you believe it indicates tampering.

❧ Watch one of the following recent films of Elizabeth's and Mary's lives, and view the depictions of Mary's confinement, trial, and execution as presented in each:
  ❧ Elizabeth I (2005) starring Helen Mirren
  ❧ Elizabeth R (1971) starring Glenda Jackson
  ❧ Mary, Queen of Scots (1971) starring Vanessa Redgrave and Glenda Jackson

❧ In Elizabeth I, Mary's execution is covered in Part 1. In Elizabeth R, the story of Mary is covered in the fourth episode, "Horrible Conspiracies." Mary, Queen of Scots covers the Scottish Queen's life from 1560 to her death. Keeping in mind that, in real life, Elizabeth and Mary likely never met one another, which depictions of the two Queens did you find most credible? Why?

❧ Access the online edition of William CAMDEN, Annales Rerum Gestarum Angliae et Hiberniae Regnante Elizabetha at http://www.philological.bham .ac.uk/camden (see also Document 30). Read Camden's description of Mary's execution, and compare it to Wigmore's. Write a brief essay comparing and contrasting the two descriptions, and give your reasons for believing why one of the other description is more credible.

Further Information

Dunn, Jane. *Elizabeth and Mary: Cousins, Rivals, Queens*. New York: Alfred A. Knopf, 2004.

Guy, John. *Queen of Scots: The True Life of Mary Stuart*. Boston: Houghton Mifflin, 2004.

Johnson, Paul. *Elizabeth I: A Biography*. New York: Holt, Rinehart and Winston, 1974.

Loades, David. *Elizabeth I*. London: Hambledon Continuum, 2006.

MacCaffrey, Wallace. *Elizabeth I*. London: Edward Arnold, 1993.

Marcus, Leah S., Janel Mueller, and Mary Beth Rose, eds. *Elizabeth I: Collected Works*. Chicago: University of Chicago Press, 2000.

Neale, J.E. *Queen Elizabeth I: A Biography*. Chicago: Academy Chicago Publishers, 1992 (originally published in 1934).

Warnicke, Retha M. *Mary Queen of Scots*. London: Routledge, 2006.

Wormald, Jenny. *Mary, Queen of Scots: Pride, Passion, and a Kingdom Lost*. Revised ed. London: Tauris Parke Paperbacks, 2001.

Web Sites

Execution of the Queen of Scots: http://www.eyewitnesstohistory.com/maryqueenofscots.htm

Tudor History: Execution of the Queen of Scots: http://www.tudorhistory.org/primary/exmary.html

36. "The Serpent That Poisons Me": Elizabeth's Letters to James VI of Scotland on the Execution of His Mother (1587–1588)

INTRODUCTION

Reproduced here is a series of letters from Elizabeth I to James VI of Scotland regarding the execution of James' mother, Mary, Queen of Scots, then a prisoner in England condemned for treason. The first two letters, dating to January and the beginning of February 1587, were written before Mary's execution on February 8. In the first letter, Elizabeth informed James of a new conspiracy against her life, which only heightened the danger of keeping Mary alive both to herself and the realm. In the second letter, Elizabeth responded to a proposal from James' commissioners that Mary be transferred to the custody of a neutral prince and that he and others agree on Mary's behalf that she should henceforth abstain from any interference in the affairs of England. Elizabeth flatly rejected this plan and argued that necessity demanded Mary's death. In the third letter, dated to May 1588, over a year after the execution, Elizabeth proclaimed her innocence in the death of Mary, desired to forget any bad feeling that had arisen because of it, and offered her firm friendship.

KEEP IN MIND AS YOU READ

1. Mary was tried and convicted of treason in October 1586. In November and again in January 1587, James sent commissioners to England to plead for his mother's life. However, the force of these intercessions was severely undercut by the fact that each commission was also charged with making inquiries regarding the succession to the English throne. Public opinion in both England and Scotland was convinced that James was far more interested in ensuring his position as Elizabeth's heir than in saving his mother.
2. The conspiracy mentioned in the letter of January 1587 supposedly implicated the French ambassador in a new attempt to assassinate Elizabeth. However, when confronted by the man who had informed the government of the plot, the ambassador flatly denied it, and nothing further came of the incident. It is today unclear whether or not an actual conspiracy existed.
3. After Mary's execution, Elizabeth sent an ambassador to Scotland to personally assure James of her innocence in bringing about his mother's death. However, the feeling in Scotland against Elizabeth was so hostile that James did not feel able to guarantee the ambassador's safety. He therefore had him stopped at the border, where the ambassador delivered his message in writing to James' representatives before returning to the English court.

4. Mary had left Scotland when James was little more than two years old. He had not seen his mother since and had been brought up a Protestant. What's more, with Mary's death, his own path to the English throne was considerably eased.

Document 1: Letter of Queen Elizabeth to King James VI of Scotland (January 1587)

To my very good brother and cousin, the king of Scots.

I find myself so troubled lest sinister tales might delude you, my good brother, that I have willingly found out this messenger, whom I know most sincere to you and a true subject to me, to carry unto you my most sincere meaning toward you, and to request this just desire, that you never doubt my entire good will in your behalf; and do protest, that, if you knew, even since the arrival of your commissioners . . . the extreme danger my life was in, by an ambassador's honest silence, if not invention, and such good accomplices as have themselves, by god's permission, unfolded the whole conspiracy, and have **avouched** it before his face, though it be the peril of their own lives, yet voluntarily, one of them never being suspected broke it with a councilor to make me acquainted therewith. You may see whether I keep the serpent that poisons me, when they confess to have reward. By saving of her life, they would have had mine. Do I not, think you, make myself a goodly prey for every wretch to devour? Transfigure yourself into my state, and suppose what you ought to do, and thereafter weigh my life, and reject the care of murder, and shun all baits that may untie our amities, and let all men know, that princes know best their own laws, and misjudge not that you know not.

> **avouched:** affirmed; avowed; declared
> **meanest:** lowest; most humble

For my part, I will not live to wrong the **meanest**. And so I conclude you with your own words, you will prosecute or mislike as much those that seek my ruin as if they sought your heart's blood, and would I had none in mine if I would not do the like; as God knows, to whom I make my humble prayers to inspire you with best desires.

Your most affectionate sister and cousin,
Elizabeth R.

Document 2: Letter of Queen Elizabeth to King James VI of Scotland (c. February 1, 1587)

To my dear brother and cousin, the king of Scots.

Be not carried away, my dear brother, with the lewd persuasions of such, as instead of informing you of my needful and helpless cause of defending the breath that God has given me, to be better spent than spilled by the bloody invention of traitor's hands, may perhaps make you believe, that either the offense was not so great, or if that cannot serve them, for the over-manifest trial which in public and by the greatest and most in this land has been manifestly proved, yet they will make that her life may be saved and mine safe, which would God were true, for when you make view of my long danger endured these four—well **nye** five—months time . . . the greatest wits among my own, and then of French, and last of you, will grant with me, that if need were not more than my malice she should not have her merit.

. . . Your commissioners tell me, that I may trust her in the hand of some indifferent prince, and have all her cousins and allies promise she will no more seek my ruin. Dear brother and cousin, weigh in true and equal balance whether there lack not much good ground when such stuff serves for their building. Suppose you I am so mad to trust my life in another's hand and send it out of my own? . . . Let your councilors, for your honor, discharge their duty so much to you as to declare the absurdity of such an offer; and, for my part, I do assure myself to much of your wisdom, as, though like a most natural good son you charged them to seek all means they could devise with wit or judgment to save her life, yet I cannot, not do not, allege my fault to you of these persuasions, for I take it that you will remember, that advice or desires ought ever agree with the surety of the party sent to and the honor of the sender, which when both you weigh, I doubt not but your wisdom will excuse my need, and wait my necessity, and not accuse me either of malice or of hate. . . .

Your most assured loving sister and cousin,
Elizabeth R.

> **nye:** near; almost

Document 3: Letter of Queen Elizabeth to King James VI of Scotland (May 15, 1588)

To our good brother and cousin, the king of Scotland.

My pen, my dear brother, has remained so long dry as I suppose it hardly would have taken ink again, but, mollified by the good justice that with your own person you have been pleased to execute, together with the large assurance that your words have given to some of my ministers, which all does make me ready to drink most willingly a large draught of the **river of Lethe,** never minding to think of unkindness, but to turn my eyes to the making up of that sure amity and staunch good will which may be presently concluded in ending our league, that so unhappily, to my heart's grief, was delayed and deferred, assuring you, on the faith of a Christian and word of a king, that my heart cannot accuse my conscience of one thought that might infringe our friendship, or let so good a work. God the searcher of all hearts ever so have **misericorde** of my soul as my innocency in that matter deserves, and no otherwise; which invocation were too dangerous for a guilty conscience . . . . And for your part, my dear brother, think, and that with most truth, that, if I find you willing to embrace it, you shall find of me the carefulest prince of your quiet government, ready to assist you with force, with treasure, counsel, or any thing you shall have need of, as much as in your honor you can require, or upon cause you shall need. You may the more soundly trust my vows, for never yet were they stained, neither will I make you the first on whom I shall bestow untruth, which God will not suffer me live unto. . . .

Your most assured loving sister and cousin,
Elizabeth R.

> **misericorde:** mercy
> **river of Lethe:** in Greek mythology, the river of forgetfulness in Hades; the Queen is expressing her desire to forget any discord arising between her and James over the execution of his mother

SCOTLAND IN THE SIXTEENTH CENTURY

During the course of Elizabeth's reign, Scotland went from being a Catholic kingdom allied with France to a Protestant kingdom allied with England. The most important factor in Anglo-Scottish relations under Elizabeth was the fact that Mary, the Catholic Queen of Scotland, was the next heir to the English throne. In 1559, only months after Elizabeth's accession, Mary Stuart also became Queen of France, thus placing the power of France behind her claim to the English Crown. However, the 1560 Scottish Reformation, by giving England and Scotland a shared religion on which to base a political alliance, led to the Treaty of EDINBURGH, whereby Scotland was freed of French troops and influence. In 1561, Mary, recently widowed, returned to Scotland, where her spectacular misrule was marked by the murder of her secretary, the murder of her second husband, and her mysterious third marriage to her late husband's likely killer.

Deposed in favor of her infant son James VI in 1567, Mary failed to regain her throne in 1568. Driven into England, she was confined by her cousin Elizabeth for the next 19 years. Elizabeth could neither give Mary her freedom nor bring herself to order Mary's death. Raised a Protestant, James VI was more highly motivated by the promise of eventual succession to the English throne than by affection for a mother he never knew. By concluding the Treaty of Berwick with Elizabeth in 1586, James signaled his willingness to sacrifice the latter to have the former. In 1587, when Mary was finally executed, James did no more than protest, though, as the letters reproduced above indicate, Elizabeth was concerned about what James' attitude would be. Nonetheless, on Elizabeth's death in 1603, James succeeded peacefully to the Crown of England.

Source: Bruce, John, ed. *Letters of Queen Elizabeth and King James VI of Scotland.* London: Printed for the Camden Society by J.B. Nichols and Son, 1849, pp. 42–44, 47–48.

AFTERMATH

Despite frequent urgings from James, Elizabeth refused to name a successor, remembering how, in the reign of her sister, MARY I, opponents of the regime had made Elizabeth herself an unwilling focus of discontent. Although relations between the two monarchs fluctuated with events, over time, James' accession seemed increasingly inevitable. In 1601, with the Queen nearing 70, Robert CECIL, Elizabeth's chief minister, came to a secret agreement with James, promising to bring the Scottish king to the throne when Elizabeth died, but affirming his loyalty to Elizabeth until that happened. Cecil then became only one of many Elizabethan ministers and courtiers who maintained a secret correspondence with the Scottish court. On her deathbed in March 1603, Elizabeth is said to have finally acknowledged James as her successor, and his subsequent accession to the English throne as JAMES I was peaceful and uncontested.

ASK YOURSELF

1. What in your opinion is Elizabeth's tone in each of the letters—frightened, imperious, angry, friendly, worried, or something else?
2. What reasons does Elizabeth give to support the necessity of Mary's execution? Do these reasons seem credible to you?

TOPICS AND ACTIVITIES TO CONSIDER

- ⮞ Access the online edition of John Bruce's *Letters of Queen Elizabeth and King James VI of Scotland* at http://books.google.com/books. Read a selection of other letters between the two in the years 1588–1602. Create a list of what appears from the letters to be Elizabeth's chief expectations and concerns regarding James and the succession.

- ⮞ Access the online edition of John Bruce's *Correspondence of King James VI of Scotland with Robert Cecil and Others in England During the Reign of Queen Elizabeth* at http://books.google.com/books. Read a selection of letters between the King and Cecil, as well as a few letters from other correspondents. Write an encyclopedia entry of several hundred words describing the correspondence for an encyclopedia user who knows nothing about it. Be sure to comment upon the nature, tone, purpose, and importance to history of the correspondence.

- ⮞ Watch the following modern films depicting the reigns of Elizabeth and James:
  - ⮞ *Elizabeth I* (2005) starring Helen Mirren
  - ⮞ *William Shakespeare: His Life and Times* (1977) starring Tim Curry

  Pay particular attention to the depictions of James I, Robert Cecil, and Elizabeth's attitude toward the succession.

Further Information

Dunn, Jane. *Elizabeth and Mary: Cousins, Rivals, Queens.* New York: Alfred A. Knopf, 2004.

Guy, John. *Queen of Scots: The True Life of Mary Stuart.* Boston: Houghton Mifflin, 2004.

Johnson, Paul. *Elizabeth I: A Biography.* New York: Holt, Rinehart and Winston, 1974.

Loades, David. *Elizabeth I.* London: Hambledon Continuum, 2006.

MacCaffrey, Wallace. *Elizabeth I.* London: Edward Arnold, 1993.

Marcus, Leah S., Janel Mueller, and Mary Beth Rose, eds. *Elizabeth I: Collected Works.* Chicago: University of Chicago Press, 2000.

Neale, J.E. *Queen Elizabeth I: A Biography.* Chicago: Academy Chicago Publishers, 1992 (originally published in 1934).

Stewart, Alan. *The Cradle King: The Life of James VI and I, the First Monarch of a United Great Britain.* New York: St. Martin's Press, 2003.

Warnicke, Retha M. *Mary Queen of Scots.* London: Routledge, 2006.

Willson, D. Harris. *King James VI and I.* New York: Henry Holt and Company, 1956.

Wormald, Jenny. *Mary, Queen of Scots: Pride, Passion, and a Kingdom Lost.* Revised ed. London: Tauris Parke Paperbacks, 2001.

Web Site

Bruce, *Letters of Queen Elizabeth and James VI of Scotland*: http://books.google.com/books

37. TURNING ENGLISH CATHOLICS AGAINST THE QUEEN: CARDINAL WILLIAM ALLEN'S *AN ADMONITION TO THE NOBILITY AND PEOPLE OF ENGLAND* (1588)

INTRODUCTION

William ALLEN was a leader of the Elizabethan English Catholic community. He fled to Europe in 1561 after refusing the oath of supremacy to the Queen as head of the English Church and later founded colleges for English missionary priests in Rome and the Netherlands. He also wrote a series of tracts and pamphlets defending the rights of English Catholics. In 1588, the pope asked Allen to encourage English Catholics to support PHILIP II's planned invasion of England (see "Spanish Armada," Document 18). The result was *An Admonition to the Nobility and People of England*, from which the following excerpt is drawn.

The work was a radical departure for Allen, whose earlier polemics had been scholarly pieces that criticized the policies of the English government or the Queen's ministers. The *Admonition*, seeking to destroy all loyalty that English Catholics felt for the Queen, was a direct and bitter personal attack on ELIZABETH herself, calling her, among other things, "the bane of Christendom" and "an incestuous bastard" and even suggesting that she had condoned the murder of the wife of her favorite, Robert DUDLEY, Earl of Leicester (see Document 31). In the following excerpt, Allen listed the many crimes he believed Elizabeth had committed.

KEEP IN MIND AS YOU READ

1. Because the *Admonition* is so different in tone from Allen's earlier works, some modern historians have suggested that it was not written by him, but was actually the work of another writer that Allen merely signed.
2. Because the *Admonition* ran to 60 pages, Allen believed it might be too long for the common people he was seeking to reach and thus issued an abbreviated version of the work entitled *A Declaration of the Sentence and Deposition of Elizabeth, the Usurper and Pretensed Queen of England*, which was also widely disseminated in England and abroad.
3. By showing the enormity of Elizabeth's crimes and the depravity of her personal life, Allen hoped to convince English Catholics and those English people not strongly committed to any religion to support the Spanish invasion and the overthrow of the Queen and her government.

Document: Excerpts from Allen's An Admonition to the Nobility and People of England

She usurped by Luciferian pride, the title of supreme Ecclesiastical government, a thing in a woman, in all men's memory unheard of, nor tolerable to the masters of her own sect, and to Catholics in the world most ridiculous, absurd, monstrous, detestable, and a very fable to the posterity.

She unlawfully intruded herself . . . into possession of the crown of England, and the annexed dominions not by any descent of inheritance or other lawful title, but only by enforced unjust laws partly made by her supposed father being then an excommunicated person, and partly co-acted by herself and her [ac]complices in the beginning of her pretended reign, being indeed taken and known for an incestuous bastard, begotten and borne in sin, of an infamous courtesan Anne Bullen [Boleyn], afterward executed for adultery, treason, heresy and incest, amongst others with her own natural brother, which Anne, her said supposed father kept by pretended marriage, in the life of his lawful wife, the most renowned and blessed lady Queen Katherine, daughter of Castile and Aragon, as he did before unnaturally know and keep both the said Anne's mother and sister.

She is guilty of perjury and high impiety for that she did break, violate, and deride the solemn oath and promise made in her coronation, for defense of the Ecclesiastical liberties and privileges granted by the ancient Christian kings of our realm, and for the contempt of the holy ceremony used in anointing and investing of all faithful princes: wherein her wickedness was so notorious, that the principal Prelate that then was in the realm, and to whom by ancient order (the Cardinal of Canterbury then being dead) that function appertained, durst not for fear of God, and respect of his conscience, nor did not anoint her.

She did immediately upon her said intrusion violently against all law and order . . . to the perdition of infinite souls, abolish the whole Catholic Religion, and faith, that all the former faithful kings of our country honorably lived and died in; repealing at the same time all the godly acts that Queen Maries (Mary I) the only lawful daughter of King Henry the eighth, made for the reconcilement of the realm, to the unity of God's universal Church again; and revived all the impious statutes, made by her foresaid supposed father and brother against God, the Church, the See Apostolic, and all innocency, by which she severed herself and subjects violently from the society of all Catholic countries, and from the fellowship of all faithful princes and priests in the world.

She did at the same time abolish or profane all the holy sacraments of Christ's Church, and above other in particular, the very blessed and sovereign sacrifice of Christ's body and blood, erecting for the same, and in disgrace thereof, high idolatry, and polluted bread of schism and abominable desolation.

She did shut up both pulpits and Churches from all Catholic priests, preachers, and people, caused all God's public true ancient honor, service, solemnity, through the whole realm of England (a most lamentable case) and not long after in Ireland, to cease upon one day, constraining by great penalties and extreme punishment many thousand poor and Christian souls of every degree and sex, to forsake that faith and religion, in which they and all their forefathers were baptized and brought up, ever since the realm was first converted to Christ, to the great torment of their minds and consciences and shortening of their days.

Source: Allen, William. *An Admonition to the Nobility and People of England and Ireland Concerning the Present Warres made for the execution of his Holines Sentence by the highe and mightie Kinge Catholike of Spaine.* Antwerp, 1588, pp. xi–xiii.

AFTERMATH

When shown the *Admonition*, Elizabeth flew into a rage and ordered the immediate suppression of the work, which she believed to be both treasonous and slanderous. A PROCLAMATION issued on July 1, 1588, prohibited anyone from possessing or distributing any papal bull or any other libelous writing printed overseas. Those who came upon such works were to immediately surrender them to the PRIVY COUNCIL or the local sheriff and to report the name and location of the person from whom they obtained them. To stop overseas distribution of the *Admonition*, Elizabeth ordered her ambassadors to insist that local magistrates find and destroy all copies. She even threatened to break diplomatic relations with the Dutch if they did not assist in suppressing the work within their borders.

Despite these efforts, the *Admonition* was widely disseminated both in England and in Europe. However, it did not have the desired effect on English Catholics, many of whom were repelled and embarrassed by its vituperative tone. Most English Catholics considered the Spanish Armada a political rather than a religious undertaking and remained loyal to their Queen and country.

JESUIT MISSION TO ENGLAND

In 1580, three English Jesuits, members of the Society of Jesus, an order of Catholic priests founded in 1540, were dispatched to England by William Allen to begin the process of restoring the country to Roman Catholicism. Before 1580, the Jesuits had 69 English members serving throughout the world. Jesuit interest in a mission to England developed in the 1570s as English priests began entering England in increasing numbers. In 1579, when Allen founded the English College in Rome, the school's management was given to the Jesuits. The next year, the English Jesuits, Edmund CAMPION and Robert PARSONS, led the first Jesuit Mission to England.

The Elizabethan government, well aware of the Jesuits' tendency to involve themselves in political plots, publicized the mission as an invasion. The Jesuits themselves promoted the mission as the beginning of a Catholic revival. The publicity increased government persecution of English Catholics and won the Jesuits the distrust of many secular priests, who sought only to minister to their flocks and not to engage in political activities. In the 1580s, the Jesuit Mission led to the passage of new penal laws against Catholics and to the stricter enforcement of existing laws (see "Penal Laws," Document 15). In the last decades of Elizabeth's reign, the Jesuit Mission in England rarely numbered above 12 members. Several Jesuits were executed for their work, including Campion and Robert SOUTHWELL. Another well-known English Jesuit, John Gerard, escaped from the Tower in 1597 and left behind an autobiographical account of his missionary work in England. Although the Jesuit Mission made little progress in restoring England to Catholicism, its members did help preserve and strengthen a small English Catholic community (see also Document 19).

ASK YOURSELF

1. How do you feel about the tone of Allen's work? If you were an Elizabethan reader of the *Admonition*, would you find the work persuasive? Why or why not?
2. What are the major crimes and wicked acts of which Elizabeth is accused? What are the consequences to ordinary subjects that Allen sees as flowing from Elizabeth's misdeeds?

TOPICS AND ACTIVITIES TO CONSIDER

- Today, talk radio programs, Web sites, and television news programs are the media through which editorial and political opinion pieces are disseminated. Pamphlets and tracts like the *Admonition* were the Elizabethan media for disseminating particular political and religious points of view. While few modern media employ the venomous tone of the *Admonition*, opportunities for instant response to modern opinion pieces, particularly on the Internet, are growing. Access the Web site of a modern news organization, such as FOXNews, CNN, the BBC, ABC, NBC, or CBS, or the Web site of a political party or group. Read a selection of editorials and the response blogs from readers. Do you see more echoes of Allen's tone in the responses?

- Compare the criticism of Elizabeth in this excerpt of the *Admonition* to the criticism leveled at her in the excerpt from Peter WENTWORTH's speech in Document 16. The one is written by a Catholic critic; the other is written by a PURITAN critic. Write a brief essay analyzing the differences in tone and approach between the two. Give your explanations for the difference.

- Access the online edition of Thomas Knox's *Letters and Memorials of William Cardinal Allen* at http://books.google.com/books. Read a selection of Allen's letters. Did you see in your reading any expression of the harsh tone Allen used in the *Admonition*?

Further Information

Knox, Thomas Francis, ed. *The Letters and Memorials of William Cardinal Allen*. London: David Nutt, 1882.

Martin, Colin, and Geoffrey Parker. *The Spanish Armada*. Rev. ed. Manchester: Manchester University Press, 2002.

Mattingly, Garrett. *The Armada*. Boston: Mariner Books, 2005.

Web Site

Knox, *Letters and Memorials of William Cardinal Allen*: http://books.google.com/books

38. ELIZABETH DEFIES THE KING OF SPAIN: DR. LIONEL SHARP'S VERSION OF THE QUEEN'S SPEECH TO HER ARMY AT TILBURY CAMP (1588)

INTRODUCTION

On August 9, 1588, in the midst of the Armada crisis (see "Spanish Armada," Document 18), Queen ELIZABETH, accompanied by her general Robert DUDLEY, Earl of Leicester, visited her troops in camp at Tilbury and is said to have delivered the following address. According to tradition, rumors were circulating that the Armada was still in the Channel and might yet carry Spanish troops in the Netherlands to England. Moving out among the men with but a small escort, the Queen sought to hearten her army by appealing to their pride and patriotism and to their affection for her. By 1588, the cult of the Virgin Queen was turning Elizabeth herself into the symbol of the nation (see "The Virgin Queen," Document 25). In this way, Elizabeth turned the supposed disadvantage of her sex into a strength and explained for her people the special connection that she felt with them. The following version of the speech was recorded by Dr. Lionel Sharp, the Queen's chaplain, who was present at Tilbury.

KEEP IN MIND AS YOU READ

1. No one is quite certain exactly what Elizabeth said at Tilbury Camp or exactly when or how she might have said it. The best-known version of the speech is attributed to Dr. Lionel Sharp, who wrote the Queen's words and described the circumstances of their delivery in a letter sent to the Duke of Buckingham in the 1620s. Sharp declared that he was ordered to record the speech. The next day, it was read again from his notes to the assembled men, many of whom had been unable to hear the Queen on the previous day. Other less well-known versions of the speech also exist.

2. The aim of the Spanish Armada was to transport Spanish troops from the Netherlands across the English Channel to England. The landing of Spanish soldiers was to be the signal for English Catholics to rise in rebellion and aid the invaders in overthrowing Elizabeth and initiating the restoration of Catholic worship in England.

3. According to traditional descriptions, Elizabeth appeared in Tilbury Camp on either August 8 or 9, riding a white horse and wearing a white velvet gown. Across her chest was a silver cuirass (an armored breastplate). A page went before her, carrying her

silver helmet. It is unclear whether events actually unfolded in this way, but Elizabeth was very image-conscious and the theatricality of this description accords well with that, leading most historians to accept the description as credible.

Document: "Queen's Speech at Tilbury Camp"

My loving people, we have been persuaded by some that are careful of our safety to take heed how we commit ourself to armed multitudes for fear of treachery. But I assure you I do not desire to live to distrust my faithful and loving people. Let tyrants fear; I have always so behaved myself that, under God, I have placed my chiefest strength and safeguard in the loyal hearts and goodwill of my subjects. And therefore I am comes amongst you as you see at this time not for my recreation and disport, but being resolved in the midst and heat of the battle to live or die amongst you all, to lay down for my God and for my kingdom and for my people, my honor and my blood even in the dust.

I know I have the body but of a weak and feeble woman, but I have the heart and stomach of a king, and a king of England too, and think foul scorn that Parma, or Spain, or any prince of Europe should dare to invade the borders of my realm, to which rather than dishonor shall grow by me, I myself will take up arms, I myself will be your general, judge, and rewarder of every one of your virtues in the field. I know already for your forwardness you have deserved rewards and crowns, and we do assure you in the word of a prince they shall be duly paid to you. In the mean time my lieutenant general shall be in my stead, than whom never prince commanded a more noble or worthy subject. Not doubting but your obedience to my general, by your concord in my camp, and your valor in the field, we shall shortly have a famous victory over those enemies of my God, my kingdoms, and of my people.

Source: *Cabala: Mysteries of State, in Letters of the Great Ministers of King James and King Charles.* 1654, sig. 2L2v. Reprinted in May, Steven W., ed. *Queen Elizabeth I: Selected Works.* New York: Washington Square Press, 2004, pp. 77–78.

AFTERMATH

By August 9, the Armada was already in the North Sea, and any danger of invasion had passed. Whether Elizabeth knew this on August 9 is unclear, even though the speech, as recorded above, seems to indicate that she did not. Nonetheless, two days later, the army at Tilbury was discharged. A thanksgiving service was held at St. Paul's Cathedral in the autumn with the Queen in attendance, even though she was in mourning for the Earl of Leicester, who had died in early September. A commemorative medal was struck with the words "Afflavit Deus et dissipati sunt" (God blew and they were scattered) inscribed upon it. Although the defeat of the Armada brought great joy and relief to England and to the Protestant cause throughout Europe, the Anglo-Spanish war continued until 1604.

SPANISH NETHERLANDS

The war with Spain that led to the Armada expedition against England had numerous causes, but one of the most important was the Spanish control of the Netherlands across the Channel from England. Ruled since 1556 by PHILIP II of Spain, the 17 provinces of the Netherlands were of vital political and economic importance to Elizabethan England. Bound together only by the Habsburg dynasty, the provinces had different histories, political institutions, languages, and economies. The southern provinces spoke French dialects while the northern provinces spoke Dutch or German dialects. The north was less urbanized, but more heavily influenced by reformist religious ideas. By 1560, a growing minority of the northern population had accepted the ideas of John Calvin, despite the efforts of the Catholic Habsburgs to repress Protestantism.

The political state of the Netherlands was of vital concern to England because, whoever ruled the Netherlands, controlled the opposite shore of the English Channel, the most direct route for invasion. Habsburg rule meant the coast opposite Protestant England was controlled by Catholic Spain, the greatest power in Europe. The economic state of the Netherlands was also of great importance to England because the economies of the two countries were bound together by the cloth industry. English wool growers and cloth manufacturers sold their products to textile makers in the Netherlands, who processed English wool and cloth for resale throughout Europe. Any disruption of trade hurt both states.

When the Protestant Dutch rebelled against Spain in the 1560s, Elizabeth reluctantly, but increasingly, sent financial aid to the Netherlands. This English intervention convinced Philip of Spain that his rule in the Netherlands would never be secure until he had dealt with the Protestant regime in England, a belief that led to the dispatching of the Spanish Armada.

ASK YOURSELF

1. How does the Queen make use of her gender in the speech? What does she say about being a woman and a monarch? How does she use that to encourage her troops?
2. From the speech above, what do you think was the mood in the camp when the Queen delivered it—fearful, hopeful, or uncertain? Why do you believe as you do?
3. Is there anything in the speech that leads you to believe it might contain material added later by Dr. Sharp or that it might indeed mainly be the work of Dr. Sharp writing long after 1588 when the meaning of events in that year had become settled tradition? If so, what are they?

TOPICS AND ACTIVITIES TO CONSIDER

- ✍ Watch one of the following recent films of the life of Elizabeth, and view the depictions of the Tilbury speech:
  - ✍ Elizabeth I (2005) starring Helen Mirren
  - ✍ Elizabeth R (1971) starring Glenda Jackson
- ✍ Alternatively, access the YouTube Web site at http://youtube.com, and search for "Elizabeth I Tilbury" to find clips of those scenes. After viewing the scenes, list how the depictions differ from one another.
- ✍ Search the Internet for pictures of the "Armada portrait," an allegorical painting of a richly gowned Elizabeth standing before a depiction of the defeat of the Armada. Tradition says the pearls she wore in this painting were given to her by her late favorite, the Earl of Leicester. The portrait

is believed to be the work of George GOWER and to have been done in late 1588. Carefully review the several versions of the portrait. Write a brief essay explaining what it is meant to symbolize and what Elizabeth was trying to say to her people and to the world by the way she is depicted here.

Further Information

Johnson, Paul. *Elizabeth I: A Biography*. New York: Holt, Rinehart and Winston, 1974.

Loades, David. *Elizabeth I*. London: Hambledon Continuum, 2006.

MacCaffrey, Wallace. *Elizabeth I*. London: Edward Arnold, 1993.

Marcus, Leah S., Janel Mueller, and Mary Beth Rose, eds. *Elizabeth I: Collected Works*. Chicago: University of Chicago Press, 2000.

Neale, J.E. *Queen Elizabeth I: A Biography*. Chicago: Academy Chicago Publishers, 1992 (originally published in 1934).

Web Sites

Luminarium: Anthology of English Literature: http://www.luminarium.org/renlit/tilbury.htm

Modern History Sourcebook: http://www.fordham.edu/halsall/mod/1588elizabeth.html

39. The Queen's Valedictory: Elizabeth's "Golden Speech" (1601)

INTRODUCTION

On November 30, 1601, a deputation of the House of Commons came to Whitehall Palace at Westminster near London to thank ELIZABETH I for her recent PROCLAMATION promising to reform the abuse of monopolies (see "Monopolies" below). The speech she delivered that day, made poignant by the unspoken belief of her hearers that it was the last time the aging Queen would address her people, was to be cherished for generations as the "Golden Speech," for, said one member of Parliament, it was worthy "to be written in gold." The Parliament of 1601, Elizabeth's last, had angrily demanded that the Queen keep her promise to the previous Parliament to reform monopolies. Because Parliament's demands constituted, in effect, an attempt to limit or modify the powers inherent in the Crown, the issue precipitated one of the few serious political disputes to occur between Queen and Parliament during Elizabeth's reign (see "English Parliaments," Document 11).

Realizing from the intensity of Parliament's anger how great was the outrage over monopolies, Elizabeth issued a proclamation promising remedy. This action transformed the angry mood of the Commons to joy. When the speaker of the Commons tried to name a deputation to deliver the Commons' thanks to the Queen, he was met by cries of "All! All! All!" When the Queen responded that all were welcome, the speaker and some 140 members of the Commons came to Whitehall to hear Elizabeth give the following address.

KEEP IN MIND AS YOU READ

1. Members of the House of Commons were not noblemen accustomed to being at court or in the presence of the Queen. They were, for the most part, country landowners and merchants or professional men from the towns.
2. Even though both Elizabeth and her hearers believed that she ruled England as God's chosen representative, the Queen, knowing the hesitancy many had about being governed by a woman, strove always to assure her people that their well-being was her sole concern.
3. Only nine months before this speech was delivered, Elizabeth had sanctioned the execution of Robert DEVEREUX, the popular and charismatic Earl of Essex, who had,

at the time, believed there was sufficient dissatisfaction with the Queen's rule to support an uprising aimed at placing him in control of both her and her government.

4. Despite the Queen's personal popularity, the 1590s had been a period of plague (London theaters were closed for two years for fear of contagion), poor harvests, and general economic distress, all of which led to increasing dissatisfaction with the government.

Document: The "The Golden Speech" of Elizabeth I

In the afternoon, about three of the clock, some seven score of the House met at the great chamber before the Council Chamber in Whitehall. At length the Queen came into the Council Chamber, where, sitting under the **cloth of state** at the upper end, the Speaker with all the company came in, and after three low **reverences** [delivered his speech]. . . . And after three low reverences made, he with the rest knelled down, and her Majesty began thus to answer herself, *viz.* . . .

Mr. Speaker. We have heard your declaration and perceive your care of our estate , by falling into the consideration of a grateful acknowledgment of such benefits as you have received; and that your coming is to present thanks unto us, which I accept with no less joy than your loves can have desire to offer such a present.

I do assure you that there is no prince that loves his subjects better, or whose love can countervail our love. There is no jewel, be it of never so rich a prize, which I prefer before this jewel, I mean your love, for I do more esteem it than any treasure or riches, for that we know how to prize, but love and thanks I count inestimable. And though God has raised me high, yet this I count the glory of my crown, that I have reigned with your loves. This makes me that I do not so much rejoice that God has made me to be a queen as to be a queen over so thankful a people. Therefore I have cause to wish nothing more than to content the subject, and that is a duty which I owe. Neither do I desire to live longer days than that I may see your prosperity, and that is my only desire. And as I am that person that still, yet under God, has delivered you, so I trust, by the almighty power of God, that I still shall be His instrument to preserve you from envy, peril, dishonor, shame, tyranny, and oppression, partly by means of your intended helps, which we take very acceptably, because it manifests the largeness of your loves and loyalties unto your sovereign. Of myself I must say this: I never was any greedy, scraping grasper, nor a strait fast-holding prince, nor yet a waster; my heart was never set on worldly goods, but only for my subjects' good. What you do bestow on me I will not hoard up, but receive it to bestow on you again. Yea, mine own properties I count yours, to be expended for your good. Therefore render unto them, I beseech you, Mr. Speaker, such thanks as you imagine my heart yields, but my tongue cannot express.

[*Up to this point the entire assemblage had knelt before the queen.*]

Mr. Speaker, I would wish you and the rest to stand up, for I shall yet trouble you with longer speech.

Mr. Speaker, you give me thanks, but I doubt me I have more cause to thank you all than you me; and I change you to thank them of the House of Commons from me, for had I not received a knowledge from you, I might have fallen into the lap of an error only for lack of true information. Since I was queen yet never did I put my pen to any grant, but that upon pretext and semblance made unto me that it was both good and beneficial to the subjects in general, though a private profit to some of my ancient servants who had deserved well. But the contrary being found by experience, I am exceedingly beholding to such subjects as would move the same at first. And I am not so simple to suppose but that there be some of the Lower House whom these grievances never touched, and for them I think they speak our of zeal to their countries and not out of spleen or malevolent affection, as being parties grieved. And I take it exceedingly grateful from them because it gives us to know that no respects or interests had moved them, other than the minds they bear to suffer no diminution of our honor and our subjects' love unto us. The zeal of which affection, tending to ease my people and knit their hearts unto me, I embrace with a princely care. Far above all earthly treasure I esteem my people's love, more than which I desire not to merit.

That my grants should be grievous to my people and oppressions to be privileges under color of our patents, our kingly dignity shall not suffer it. Yea, when I heard it, I could give no rest to my thoughts until I had reformed it. Shall they think to escape unpunished that have thus oppressed you and have been respectless of their duty and regardless of our honor? No, Mr. Speaker, I assure you, were it more for conscience' sake than for any glory or increase of love that I desire these errors, troubles, vexations, and oppressions done by these varlets and lewd persons, not worthy the name of subjects, should not escape without condign punishment. But I perceive they dealt with me like physicians who, ministering a drug, make it more acceptable by giving it a good aromatical savour, or when they give pills, do gild them all over.

I have ever used to set the last judgment day before mine eyes and so to rule as I shall be judged to answer before a higher Judge. To Whose judgment seat I do appeal that never thought was cherished in my heart that tended not to my people's good. And if my kingly bounty have been abused and my grants turned to the hurt of my people, contrary to my will and meaning, of if any in authority under me have neglected or perverted what I have committed to them, I hope God will not lay their **culps** and offenses to my charge. And though there were danger in repealing our grants, yet what danger would not I rather incur for your own good, than I would suffer them still to continue?

I know the title of king is a glorious title, but assure yourself that the shining glory of princely authority has not so dazzled the eyes of our understanding but that we well know and remember that we also are to yield an account of our actions before the Great Judge. To be a king and wear

cloth of state: a cloth sumptuously embroidered with the arms of England and hung over the throne for state occasions

countries: counties

culps: faults

enticed: charmed or impressed

Mr. Secretary: Sir Robert Cecil, Elizabeth's secretary of state in 1601

Mr. Speaker: John Crooke, speaker of the 1601 House of Commons

reverences: a gesture of respect such as a deep bow

a crown is more glorious to them that see it than it is pleasure to them that bear it. For myself, I was never so much **enticed** with the glorious name of a king or royal authority of a queen as delighted that God has made me this instrument to maintain His truth and glory, and to defend this kingdom, as I said, from peril, dishonor, tyranny, and oppression. There will never queen sit in my seat with more zeal to my country or care to my subjects, and that will sooner with willingness yield and venture her life for your good and safety than myself. And though you have had and may have many princes more mighty and wise sitting in this seat, yet you never had or shall have any that will be more careful and loving.

Should I ascribe anything to myself and my sexly weakness, I were not worthy to live then, and of all most unworthy of the mercies I have had from God, Who has ever yet given me a heart which never yet feared foreign or home enemies? I speak it to give God the praise as a testimony before you, and not to attribute anything unto myself. For I, O Lord, what am I, whom practices and perils past should not fear? O what can I do that I should speak for any glory? God forbid. This, Mr. Speaker, I pray you deliver unto the House, to whom heartily recommend me. And so I commit you all to your best fortunes and further counsels. And I pray you, Mr. Comptroller, **Mr. Secretary**, and you of my council, that before these gentlemen depart into their **countries**, you bring them all to kiss my hand.

Source: D'Ewes, Sir Simonds. *The Journals of All the Parliaments during the Reign of Queen Elizabeth, both of the House of Lords and House of Commons.* London, 1682, pp. 658–660.

MONOPOLIES

Elizabeth delivered her "Golden Speech" in response to a Commons deputation come to thank her for addressing the issue of monopolies. The Crown had the power to regulate trade by granting certain monopolistic rights to individuals. The recipients of such grants were licensed to import prohibited goods or were exempted from statutes that regulated the manufacture of important commodities. Beginning in the 1580s, the Crown's extreme need for money to carry on the war with Spain led Elizabeth to grant monopolies as favors to courtiers, officials, and servants. Such monopolies acted as a cheap form of Crown patronage and as a ready source of revenue. Some monopolies, for instance, were sold for cash to individuals or groups. The grantees received a monopoly on the manufacture, sale, or import of a specified commodity or were empowered to license others to engage in such manufacture or sale.

By the 1590s, patents had been granted on iron, steel, glass, vinegar, coal, salt, and soap. Because such monopolies usually led to higher prices for consumers, discontent over the grants was soon intense. Patentees also enjoyed wide search and seizure rights to protect their monopolies, and persons with grievances against monopolists had no remedy at law because the actions of monopolists arose from the royal prerogative. The Parliament of 1597 complained of monopolies, but the Queen promised reform, and Parliament took no action. When Parliament met again in 1601, the Queen had still not acted, and an angry House of Commons sought to legislate on monopolies. Rather than risk a fight with Parliament, the Queen agreed to review all monopolies and to cancel any that were harmful. Elizabeth then issued a PROCLAMATION revoking certain monopolies. In response to this action, the Commons sent to the Queen the deputation that heard her deliver the "Golden Speech."

AFTERMATH

The speech exists in various versions. The version reprinted above is taken from the *Journal of Parliament*, but an official version of the speech, somewhat edited and elaborated by the Queen, was quickly issued by the royal printer. The Queen and her chief minister, Sir Robert CECIL, had quickly recognized the publicity value of the speech. But an unofficial version, closer to the speech as delivered on November 30 because it was drawn from the rough notes the Queen handed that day to Henry Saville, provost of Eton, was soon circulating under the title "The Golden Speech of Queen Elizabeth." Another version, drawn from the account left in his diary by Hayward Townshend, one of the men kneeling before the Queen as the speech was delivered, became the one to be reprinted many times over the next two centuries, appearing any time England was threatened or perceived to be in danger.

As relations between Parliament and Elizabeth's Stuart successors—JAMES I and Charles I—deteriorated in the early seventeenth century, descending eventually into civil war, Elizabeth's speech was instrumental in erasing the turmoil of her age from the national memory and turning the reign into a seeming golden age.

ASK YOURSELF

1. How did Elizabeth stage-manage her appearance to make it even more memorable in the minds of her hearers? How do modern leaders do the same thing?
2. Although Elizabeth was much concerned with public opinion, she was not an elected leader and could not be removed from office through electoral defeat or constitutional action, such as impeachment. How does Elizabeth's position as head of state compare to that of an American president or other leader of a modern democracy?
3. How does the relationship between the legislature (Parliament) and head of state (Elizabeth) in the sixteenth century differ from that between Congress and the president in the United States in the twenty-first century? How much, in terms of procedure and tradition, did the American Congress and presidency inherit from their ancestors—the British Parliament and Crown?

TOPICS AND ACTIVITIES TO CONSIDER

- The sixteenth century saw a number of other important female rulers, including MARY I (Elizabeth's sister) in England; MARY, Queen of Scots; and CATHERINE DE MEDICI in France. Write an essay describing how sixteenth-century society viewed women in general and women rulers in particular. Compare sixteenth-century views of women's roles to twenty-first century views.
- Search the Internet for portraits of Elizabeth I (see "Portraits of Queen Elizabeth," Document 40). Portraits of the Queen were much valued during her reign, and she kept careful control of the likenesses that were made of her, even ordering the destruction of images that she felt were not flattering. As she got older, she hid wrinkled skin under thick makeup, gray and thinning hair under a bright red wig, and stained and decaying teeth behind her hand as she talked. Over 130 contemporary portraits of the Queen survive, and many of them are available for viewing online. Consider how the portraits dated to later in the reign differ from those

made earlier in the reign, if, in fact, they do. Consider also how the portraits may reflect the events of the years in which they were created.

- ✍ Watch one of the following recent films of the life of Elizabeth, and view the depictions of the Golden Speech:
  - ✍ Elizabeth I (2005) starring Helen Mirren
  - ✍ Elizabeth R (1971) starring Glenda Jackson
- ✍ Alternatively, access the YouTube Web site at http://youtube.com, and search for "Elizabeth I Golden Speech" to find clips of the speech from various sources. After viewing the scenes, list how the depictions differ from one another.

Further Information

Johnson, Paul. *Elizabeth I: A Biography.* New York: Holt, Rinehart and Winston, 1974.

Loades, David. *Elizabeth I.* London: Hambledon Continuum, 2006.

MacCaffrey, Wallace. *Elizabeth I.* London: Edward Arnold, 1993.

Marcus, Leah S., Janel Mueller, and Mary Beth Rose, eds. *Elizabeth I: Collected Works.* Chicago: University of Chicago Press, 2000.

Neale, J.E. *Queen Elizabeth I: A Biography.* Chicago: Academy Chicago Publishers, 1992 (originally published in 1934).

Web Sites

Modern History Sourcebook: http://www.fordham.edu/halsall/mod/elizabeth1.html#The%20Farewell%20Speech,%201601

Renascence Editions, "The Golden Speech": http://www.uoregon.edu/~rbear/eliz1.html

40. A Look Back at Elizabeth's Coronation: Sir John Hayward's *Annals of the First Four Years of the Reign of Queen Elizabeth* (1612)

INTRODUCTION

Reproduced here is a description of ELIZABETH I as she appeared and behaved at her coronation as Queen in January 1559. The description is not an eyewitness account, but the work of the historian Sir John HAYWARD, who, like William CAMDEN (see Document 30), made careful use of documentary sources and eyewitness testimony to write his contemporary histories. In about 1612, Hayward, while talking with his patron, Prince Henry, the eldest son of JAMES I, responded to the prince's question about what he had done to write the history of England by saying, "I did principally bend and bind myself to the times wherein I should live." The prince approved this focus on contemporary events, which led Hayward to write and present to Henry a manuscript entitled "Certain Years of Queen Elizabeth's Reign." It is from this manuscript, which was not published until 1840 as the *Annals of the First Four Years of the Reign of Queen Elizabeth*, that the following excerpt is taken.

KEEP IN MIND AS YOU READ

1. Hayward was imprisoned by Elizabeth in 1599–1600 because the Queen disliked Hayward's recently published *The First Part of the Life and Reign of King Henry IV*. Hayward dedicated the book to Robert DEVEREUX, Earl of Essex, the stepson of the late Robert DUDLEY, Earl of Leicester, and the Queen's new favorite. Because Essex was then in disfavor and under suspicion of treason for his actions in Ireland and because the history of Henry IV described the deposition of one monarch in favor of another, the Queen believed the work was treasonous, a veiled call for Essex to supplant her on the throne.

2. When the Queen asked Sir Francis BACON to read Hayward's *Henry IV* and find passages on which a charge of treason could be based, Bacon is said to have responded that he could find none for treason, "but for felony very many." When Elizabeth asked what he meant, Bacon replied, "[T]he author had committed very apparent theft; for he had taken most of the sentences of [the Roman historian] Cornelius Tacitus, and translated them into English, and put them in his text," a charge that had some truth because Hayward was much enamored of Roman historians and tried to emulate them in his works.

3. Already in the reign of her successor, James I, Elizabeth's reign was being looked upon as a past golden age. Depictions of the Queen, which had already been mostly favorable in her lifetime, were beginning to cast her as the model of princely virtue.

Document: Excerpt from Hayward's Annals of the First Four Years of the Reign of Queen Elizabeth

Now, if ever any person had either the gift or the style to win the hearts of people, it was this Queen; and if ever she did express the same, it was at that present, in coupling mildness with majesty as she did, and in stately stooping to the meanest sort. All her faculties were in motion, and every motion seemed a well guided action; her eye was set upon one, her ear listened to another, her judgment ran upon a third, to a fourth she addressed her speech; her spirit seemed to be everywhere, and yet so entire in herself, as it seemed to be nowhere else. Some she pitied, some she commended, some she thanked, at others she pleasantly and wittily jested, condemning no person, neglecting no office; and distributing her smiles, looks, and graces, so artificially, that thereupon the people again redoubled the testimonies of their joys; and afterwards, raising everything to the highest strain, filled the ears of all men with immoderate extolling their Prince.

She was a Lady, upon whom nature had bestowed, and well placed, many of her fairest favors; of stature **mean**, slender, straight, and amiably composed; of such state in her carriage, as every motion of her seemed to bear majesty: her hair was inclined to pale yellow, her forehead large and fair, a seemly seat for princely grace; her eyes lively and sweet, but short-sighted; her nose somewhat rising in the middle; the whole compass of her countenance somewhat long, but yet of admirable beauty, not so much in that which is termed the flower of youth, as in most delightful composition of majesty and modesty in equal mixture. But without good qualities of mind, the gifts of nature are like painted flowers, without either virtue or sap; yea, sometimes they grow horrid and loathsome. Now her virtues were such as might suffice to make an Ethiopian beautiful, which, the more a man knows and understands, the more he shall admire and love. In life, she was most innocent; in desires, moderate; in purpose, just; of spirit, above credit and almost capacity of her sex; of divine wit, as well for depth of judgment, as for quick conceit and speedy expedition; of eloquence, as sweet in the utterance, so ready and easy to come to the utterance: of wonderful knowledge both in learning and affairs; skillful not only in Latin and Greek, but also in **divers** other foreign languages: none knew better the hardest art of all others, that is, of commanding men, nor could more use themselves to those cares without which the royal dignity could not be supported. She was religious, magnanimous, merciful and just; respective of the honor of others, and exceeding tender in the touch of her own. She was lovely and loving, the two principal bands of duty and obedience. She was very ripe and measured in counsel and experience, as well not to let go occasions, as not to take them when they were green. She maintained justice at home, and arms abroad, with great wisdom and authority in either place. Her majesty seemed to all to shine through courtesy: but as she was not easy to receive any to especial grace, so was she most constant to those whom she received; and of great judgment to know to what point of greatness men were fit to be advanced. She was rather liberal than magnificent, making good choice of the receivers; and for this cause was thought weak by some against the desire of money. But it is certain that beside the want of treasure which she found, her continual affairs in Scotland, France, the Low Countries, and in Ireland, did occasion great provision of money, which could not be better supplied, than by cutting off either excessive or unnecessary expense at home. Excellent Queen! what do my words but wrong thy worth? what do I but guild gold?

> **divers:** various
> **mean:** average; of middling height

Source: Hayward, Sir John. *Annals of the First Four Years of the Reign of Queen Elizabeth.* Edited by John Bruce. London: Printed for the Camden Society by John Bowyer Nichols and Son, 1840, pp. 6–8.

AFTERMATH

Hayward did not continue his history of Elizabeth because his patron, Prince Henry, died in 1612 and the prince's brother, the future Charles I, showed little interest in history and did not extend his patronage to the historian. Unable to make a living writing history, Hayward turned to works of religious devotion, such as "The Sanctuary of a Troubled Soul" and "Christ's Prayer on the Cross for His Enemies," which won him a wider audience. Hayward's best-known work of history is his *Life and Reign of King Edward the Sixt*, which describes the reign of Elizabeth's brother. It was found among his papers and published in 1630, three years after Hayward's death.

ASK YOURSELF

1. What is the overall tone of this excerpt? What description does Hayward provide of Elizabeth's character and her mental abilities? Is there any hint of rancor in the description for the woman who imprisoned him?
2. What is the physical description that Hayward provides of Elizabeth, who was 25 at the time of her coronation? What does he say are her most striking physical features?

TOPICS AND ACTIVITIES TO CONSIDER

- Watch one historian David Starkey's History Channel series *Elizabeth* (2003), and view the depiction of Elizabeth's coronation. Alternatively, the scene can be accessed at http://youtube.com by searching for "Elizabeth I coronation." Also search on the YouTube site for "Elizabeth II coronation" to find a clip of the 1952 coronation ceremony of the current Queen of England. Note the similarities between the forms of the two ceremonies, which occurred almost 400 years apart.
- Access the online edition of Hayward's *Annals* at http://books.google .com/books, and read an extended selection. Write an encyclopedia entry of several hundred words about the *Annals,* describing for a nonspecialist reader what the work covers, how it is organized, and how it reads.

PORTRAITS OF QUEEN ELIZABETH

Hayward's description of the Queen fed a growing nostalgia for her reign that developed in the decades following her death; however, even during Elizabeth's lifetime, there was great interest among the populace in her deeds and person, as illustrated by the keen interest in royal portraits. Pictures of Elizabeth were in high demand from the beginning of the reign. A 1563 PROCLAMATION regulated production of Elizabeth's likeness by proposing the distribution to painters of one portrait commissioned and approved by the Queen as the pattern for all royal images. But Elizabeth's excommunication in 1570, the start of war with Spain in 1585, and the Armada crisis in 1588 made displaying the royal likeness an act of patriotism, and the demand for royal portraits soon exceeded the time and talent needed to produce them in the form and quality demanded by the Queen.

In 1596, when the PRIVY COUNCIL ordered the destruction of poor quality portraits that were causing Elizabeth "great offense," a large number were collected and burned. Among the most famous surviving portraits of Elizabeth I are the "Armada Portrait," painted by George GOWER around 1588 and showing the Queen wearing an elaborate bow-covered gown and standing before a depiction of the defeat of the Armada, and Nicholas HILLIARD's 1585 "Ermine Portrait," named for the white ermine, a symbol of chastity, that curls around the Queen's left wrist. The "Ditchley Portrait" from 1592 is the largest surviving image of Elizabeth, and one of the few to suggest her age. Almost all other portrayals of the Queen, including the "Rainbow Portrait," painted when Elizabeth was nearing 70, give her the face of a young woman, a convention dictated by the propaganda needs of the state and the Queen's vanity.

Further Information

Haigh, Christopher. *Elizabeth I*. London: Longman, 1988.

Hayward, John. *Annals of the First Four Years of the Reign of Queen Elizabeth*. Edited by John Bruce. Reprint ed. Whitefish, MT: Kessinger Publishing, 2008.

Johnson, Paul. *Elizabeth I: A Biography*. New York: Holt, Rinehart and Winston, 1974.

Loades, David. *Elizabeth I*. London: Hambledon Continuum, 2006.

MacCaffrey, Wallace. *Elizabeth I*. London: Edward Arnold, 1993.

Neale, J.E. *Queen Elizabeth I: A Biography*. Chicago: Academy Chicago Publishers, 1992 (originally published in 1934).

Web Site

Hayward's *Annals of the First Four Years of the Reign of Queen Elizabeth*: http://books .google.com/books

APPENDIX 1: BIOGRAPHICAL SKETCHES OF IMPORTANT INDIVIDUALS MENTIONED IN TEXT

Listed here are brief biographies of the authors of documents reproduced in this volume as well as of individuals mentioned in connection with those documents. The first mention of any of these individuals in any section are highlighted as cross-references.

Allen, William (1532–1594): An English scholar, polemicist, and priest, Allen was founder and director of the mission for reconverting Elizabethan England to Catholicism. He founded colleges for the training of English missionary priests at Douai in the Netherlands in 1568 and at Rome in 1575. He organized the first Jesuit Mission to England in 1580 and was named a cardinal of the Catholic Church in 1587. He wrote many tracts and pamphlets supporting the restoration of Catholicism in England by political means.

Amadas, Philip: (1550–1618): Amadas and Arthur Barlowe (see below) were two young gentlemen in the household of Sir Walter Raleigh (see below), who, in 1584, commissioned the pair to lead a voyage of exploration to the North American coast, where Raleigh had been authorized by the Queen to found a colony. Commanding two vessels, Amadas and Barlowe left England in April and reconnoitered the coasts of present-day Georgia and the Carolinas, making friendly contact with the Roanoke Indians and returning safely in September. The expedition brought back much information on the region, as well as two Roanoke Indians. Beyond the fact that he returned to America in 1585 with Raleigh's first colonization expedition, little else is known of Amadas.

Ascham, Roger (1515–1568): A Protestant humanist scholar, Ascham was Latin secretary to both Edward VI and Mary I (see both below) and private tutor to Elizabeth. He taught Greek at Cambridge, where he helped develop the university's Greek studies program. Despite this, Ascham argued for the use of English as a scholarly language and wrote his major works in that tongue rather than Latin. His best-known writings are *Toxophilus*, a treatise on archery, and the *Schoolmaster*, a treatise on education that criticized the harsh discipline employed in most Tudor schools.

Babington, Sir Anthony (1561–1586): A member of a wealthy gentry family, Babington was a secret Catholic who outwardly conformed to the Anglican church. As a youth, he served as page to the Earl of Shrewsbury, the jailer of Mary, Queen of Scots (see below) and may have met Mary, to whose cause he was later devoted. In 1586, he became leader of a plot to free Mary and assassinate Elizabeth. When Babington's secret correspondence with Mary was intercepted, it provided the government with the proof needed to proceed against both Mary and Babington for treason. Babington was executed in September 1586.

Bacon, Sir Francis (1561–1626): The nephew of William Cecil, Lord Burghley (see below), Bacon was one of the most influential philosophers and scientists in Elizabethan England. Intensely ambitious, Bacon sought advancement at court, but received little support from his uncle or his cousin, Sir Robert Cecil (see below), and his political career did not flourish until after Cecil's death in 1612. Thereafter, Bacon became attorney general, lord keeper, and chancellor in rapid succession. In 1621, he was impeached by Parliament for bribery and stripped of the chancellorship. His most important writings include the *Novum Organum*, a treatise on scientific method; the *History of the Reign of Henry the Seventh*, an attempt to regain favor; and *New Atlantis*, a utopian fable.

Barlowe, Arthur (1550–1620): A member of Sir Walter Raleigh's (see below) household, Barlowe was co-leader with Philip Amadas (see above) of the two-ship expedition Raleigh sent to reconnoiter the eastern coast of North America in 1584. Licensed by the Queen to plant a colony in the New World, Raleigh charged Barlowe and Amadas with learning as much as they could about the climate, products, and natives of the region. Upon the expedition's return in September, Barlowe wrote a glowing account of the Roanoke region of present-day North Carolina, where the expedition had made contact with the local Indians. Entitled *The First Voyage to Roanoke, 1584*, the report encouraged investment and participation in Raleigh's colonization schemes. It is unclear whether Barlowe, like Amadas, retuned to Roanoke in 1585 with the first colonization expedition.

Boleyn, Anne (c. 1501–1536): Anne Boleyn was the second wife of Henry VIII (see below) and the mother of Elizabeth I. The daughter of a prominent courtier and the sister of Henry's former mistress, she captured the amorous interest of the King in about 1526, just as Henry VIII was beginning to question the validity of his marriage. In love with Anne and in need of a new wife to bear the son he lacked, Henry sought an annulment of his marriage from the pope, who denied the request for political reasons. Henry broke with Rome and had Parliament declare him head of the English Church, which then granted the annulment without reference to the pope. Anne gave birth to Elizabeth in 1533, but later pregnancies, one of a son, ended in miscarriage, and Henry soon grew weary of a wife he found outspoken and difficult. Anne was accused of adultery with various men, including her brother, and was beheaded in May 1536. Elizabeth, who was only two at the time of Anne's death, is said to have never mentioned her mother's name as an adult.

Burbage, James (c. 1530–1597): Burbage was the owner and builder of the first theater in Elizabethan England. A member of the Earl of Leicester's acting company, he likely took part in the entertainments performed for the Queen at Kenilworth Castle in 1575. Burbage opened a playhouse called The Theater in London in 1576. Besides managing the theater, Burbage hired and trained the actors. His venture was highly successful, and, in 1596, he sought to open an indoor playhouse at the former Blackfriars monastery, but died before the Blackfriars Theater could open. Burbage was the father of the famous actor Richard Burbage (see below).

Burbage, Richard (c. 1567–1619): The son of theater owner James Burbage (see above), Richard Burbage was one of the most popular dramatic actors in Elizabethan England. A close associate of William Shakespeare (see below), Burbage was co-owner with his brother of The Theater, a playhouse that the brothers later moved across the Thames to Southwark, where it was renamed the Globe Theater. Burbage is believed to be the originator of many of Shakespeare's most famous characters, including Hamlet, Macbeth, Othello, King Lear, and Richard III. As majority owner of the Globe, in which Shakespeare was also a shareholder, Burbage grew wealthy and was later able to acquire other playhouses.

Camden, William (1551–1623): A noted Elizabethan historian and antiquary, Camden wrote *Britannia*, the first topographical survey of the British Isles. *Britannia* was well received, going through six editions in twenty years and inspiring a whole series of county surveys, such as Richard Carew's (see below) *Survey of Cornwall*. In 1608, Camden, following up on a suggestion from the late William Cecil, Lord Burghley (see below), undertook a history of the reign of Elizabeth, the *Annales Rerum Anglicarum et Hibernicarum Regnante Elizabetha*, which was published in two parts in 1615 and 1627, with an English translation appearing in 1630.

Campion, Edmund (1540–1581): Campion was a member of the first English Jesuit Mission to land in England in 1580. In 1571, Campion fled to the Netherlands, where he entered William Allen's (see above) seminary at Douai. He later joined the Jesuit Order in Rome, and, in 1580, he and Robert Parsons (see below) were selected by Allen to become the first Jesuit missionaries working in England. Basing himself in the homes of Catholic gentry, Campion worked in the northern and western counties, where he said Mass and ministered to lapsed and practicing Catholics. Arrested in July 1581, he was convicted of treason and executed in December.

Carew, Sir Peter (c. 1514–1575): Born into a Devon gentry family, Carew was an important figure in the Elizabethan conquest and colonization of Ireland. Carew had served Elizabeth's father and brother in various military and diplomatic capacities, but had suffered exile and imprisonment under Mary I (see below) for opposing the Queen's Spanish marriage. In the 1560s, he instituted legal proceedings seeking to recover long-lost family estates in Ireland. His lawsuits disaffected the former landholders, triggering the Butler Wars and leading Elizabeth to order a halt to his efforts. He spent his last years seeking to revive his Irish causes and arguing that stability and peace in Ireland required more English settlers, stronger military efforts, and more repressive government.

Carew, Richard (1555–1620): Carew was a prominent Elizabethan scholar and antiquary who was noted for his mastery of languages and his study of natural history and literature. A friend of William Camden (see above) and a member of the Society of Antiquaries, Carew translated various works from European languages and wrote a verse fantasy entitled *A Herring's Tail*. His best-known work is his *Survey of Cornwall*, a detailed study of his own county that he dedicated to Sir Walter Raleigh (see below).

Carey, Henry, Lord Hunsdon (1525–1596): A cousin of Queen Elizabeth, Hunsdon, in 1583, became lord chamberlain of England, a position that gave him responsible for the functioning of the royal household. In the 1590s, an acting company known as the Chamberlain's Men, which included Richard Burbage (see above) and William Shakespeare (see below), came under his patronage. He was a commissioner at the trial of Mary of Scotland (see below) in 1586 and was then sent north to explain the necessity of executing Mary to her son, James VI of Scotland (see James I below). In 1588, during the Armada crisis, he was one of the commanders of the army camp at Tilbury.

Catherine de Medici (1519–1589): As the wife of Henri II, Catherine was queen of France from 1547 to 1559. Following the brief reign of her son Francis II, she became regent for her young son Charles IX (see below). She dominated the king, but was unable to impose either peace or order on a kingdom increasingly divided by religion. In 1572, she was one of the chief instigators of the St. Bartholomew's Massacre of French Protestants, known as Huguenots. Seeking to eliminate the Huguenot leadership, Catherine only turned Protestants against the monarchy and destroyed her own credibility with Protestant rulers like Elizabeth. After the accession of her son Henri III (see below) in 1574, Catherine's political influence gradually waned.

Cecil, Sir Robert (1563–1612): As secretary of state since 1596, Robert Cecil, the son of William Cecil, Lord Burghley (see below), was the Crown's chief minister and advisor during the last years of Elizabeth and the first of James I (see below). His influence at court was opposed by Robert Devereux, Earl of Essex (see below), the Queen's favorite, but became paramount after Essex's execution for treason in 1601. Cecil was instrumental in securing the accession of James I in 1603, having secretly corresponded with the Scottish king for some time before the Queen's death. James elevated Cecil to the peerage as Earl of Salisbury in 1605.

Cecil, William, Lord Burghley (1520–1598): Cecil was Elizabeth's closest and most trusted advisor, being named principal secretary at the Queen's accession and lord high treasurer in 1572 when he was raised to the peerage as Lord Burghley. Burghley tended to serve as a moderate counterbalance in both religion and foreign policy to the more extreme Protestant and aggressive foreign policies of the royal favorite, Robert Dudley, Earl of Leicester (see below). Cecil involved himself in all aspects of government, directing the Privy Council, managing Parliament, supervising finance, and advising on foreign affairs. In the 1590s, he was succeeded as chief minister by his son, Sir Robert Cecil (see above).

Charles IX (1550–1574): The son of Henri II and Catherine de Medici (see above), Charles IX succeeded his brother Francis II as king of France in 1560 at the age of 10. Both physically and emotionally weak, Charles was dominated by his mother, who served as regent during his minority. In August 1572, Catherine convinced her son that the Huguenots were plotting to assassinate him, leading him to authorize attacks on the Huguenot leadership that grew into the St. Bartholomew's Day Massacre and the deaths of thousands. Haunted by this event, Charles IX died of tuberculosis just a month short of his twenty-fourth birthday in 1574. He was succeeded by his brother Henri III (see below).

Cotton, Sir Robert (1571–1631): A prominent Elizabeth antiquary, Cotton is best known for using his wife's inheritance to build the most extensive collection of books and manuscripts in Elizabethan England. A close friend of Ben Jonson (see below), John Donne, and many other writers and scholars, Cotton opened his library to anyone who required access to it for research. In 1622, he moved his collection to a house in Westminster near the meeting place of Parliament, which became the unofficial library for members of Parliament. When the library became a meeting place for opposition members, who searched Cotton's collections for arguments and historical precedents to fill their speeches, Charles I closed the library and banned Cotton from using it.

Crowley, Robert (c. 1518–1588): A printer, writer, and preacher, Crowley published numerous works that satirized clerical corruption, expounded Protestant doctrine, and promoted social justice. He fled to Europe during the reign of the Catholic Queen Mary I (see below), returning after Elizabeth's accession in 1558. Crowley acquired a number of livings in the Elizabethan Church, but resigned most in 1567 when he refused to wear the vestments required by the Queen. He thereafter became increasingly Puritan in his preaching and writing and spent much time attempting to convert Catholic clergy imprisoned in the Tower of London. His most famous literary undertaking was his publication of the first printed edition of *The Vision of Piers Plowman*, a fourteenth-century allegorical poem by William Langland.

Davison, William (c. 1541–1608): A privy councilor and assistant secretary of state, William Davison became Elizabeth's scapegoat for her refusal to accept responsibility for the execution of Mary, Queen of Scots (see below). Prior to his appointment to the council in 1586, Davison had successfully undertaken a number of diplomatic missions. After the trial and conviction of Mary in October 1586, William Cecil, Lord Burghley (see above), gave the death warrant to Davison to obtain the Queen's signature. Elizabeth finally signed the warrant on February 1, 1587, but hinted to Davison that he should arrange to have Mary quietly murdered. Davison took the warrant to Burghley and the council, who authorized the execution. When Elizabeth heard of Mary's death, she ordered Davison's arrest for contempt and improper performance of an official duty. He was convicted and imprisoned in the Tower until 1589, his career at an end.

Dekker, Thomas (1572–1632): A playwright and pamphleteer, Dekker began his writing career in the 1590s, producing plays for Philip Henslowe's acting company, the Admiral's Men. Many of his early plays were collaborations with other playwrights, such as Ben Jonson (see below) and John Marston. Between 1599 and 1602, Dekker was a participant in the so-called "War of the Theaters," during which Dekker and Marston wrote a series of plays satirizing the work of Jonson, who, in turn, wrote plays satirizing his rivals. Dekker's chief contribution to war was the play *Satiromastix*, which mocked Jonson as arrogant and hypocritical. Although imprisoned for debt for seven years in 1612, Dekker resumed writing plays on his release, often in collaboration with younger writers.

Devereux, Robert, Earl of Essex (1567–1601): The stepson of Robert Dudley, Earl of Leicester (see below), Essex succeeded the earl in Elizabeth's affections in the years after Leicester's death. The most prominent courtier and English military figure of the 1590s, Essex was co-leader of the highly successful Cadiz Raid of 1596, which won him great popularity. High-strung and emotionally volatile, Essex's relationship with the Queen was stormy, and his political rivalry with other courtiers and ministers, such as Sir Robert Cecil (see above) and Sir Walter Raleigh (see below), were increasingly hostile. In 1599, the Queen appointed him lord lieutenant of Ireland. But fearing for his position at home, Essex arranged an unauthorized truce with the rebel leader and returned home without permission. Accused of dereliction of duty, he was stripped of his offices and monopolies. In 1601, he led a failed uprising in London that aimed at imprisoning the Queen. For this, he was tried and executed for treason.

Drake, Sir Francis (c. 1543–1596): The most famous seaman, explorer, and privateer of Elizabethan England, Drake is best known for his successful circumnavigation of the world in 1577–1580. This voyage and his many daring privateering expeditions against Spain and Spanish America made Drake a hero in both England and Europe. In 1587, Drake led a raid on Cadiz, Spain, where his destruction of naval stores delayed the sailing of the Spanish Armada. Drake was one of the leaders of the English fleet during the naval battles that defeated the Armada in 1588. In the 1590s, Drake retired from naval service, but, in 1595, joined a new expedition to Spanish America, which ended in his death.

Dudley, Robert, Earl of Leicester (1532–1588): The lifelong favorite of Queen Elizabeth, Robert Dudley was the only man she seriously consider marrying. Appointed master of horse at the Queen's accession, Dudley was so frequently in Elizabeth's company and so high in her favor that rumors began circulating that accused him of planning to poison his wife to marry the Queen. When Dudley's wife was found dead under mysterious circumstances in 1560, Elizabeth cooled the relationship, and the possibility of a marriage gradually faded. Nonetheless, Dudley, who was created Earl of Leicester in 1563, continued to press the Queen to marry him by scheming with foreign ambassadors, creating a domestic political following, and staging plays and entertainments, such as those performed at Kenilworth Castle in 1575, that promoted his merits as a husband. Leicester commanded the English expedition to the Netherlands in the 1580s and was commander of the army at Tilbury during the Armada crisis of 1588. When he died in September 1588, Elizabeth carefully preserved his last letter to her as a cherished keepsake.

Edward IV (1442–1483): King of England from 1461–1470 and again from 1471 to his death, Edward IV, the first ruler of the House of York, was the great-grandfather of Elizabeth I. Edward won the throne during the series of civil conflicts known as the Wars of the Roses. A successful military leader, he secured his dynasty on the throne and restored the power and prestige of the monarchy. At his death in 1483, he was succeeded by his 12-year-old son Edward V, who was within months dethroned and possibly murdered by Edward IV's brother, the Duke of Gloucester, who became King as Richard III (see below). Edward IV's daughter, Elizabeth of York, later married Richard's supplanter, Henry VII (see below), by whom she became the mother of Henry VIII (see below) and the grandmother of Elizabeth.

Edward VI (1537–1553): The son of Henry VIII (see below) and his third Queen, Jane Seymour, Edward VI, the half-brother of Elizabeth, was King of England from 1547 to 1553. Given an intensive humanist education by his father, Edward, who ascended the throne at the age of nine, developed into a strong Protestant. During his reign, the English Church embraced Calvinist doctrine. His government was led first by his maternal uncle, Edward Seymour, Duke of Somerset, who acted a lord protector, and then by John Dudley, Duke of Northumberland, who engineered Somerset's overthrow and eventual execution. When Edward's health began to deteriorate in 1553, Northumberland and the King devised a plan to prevent Edward's Catholic sister Mary (see below) from succeeding. This plan, which put Edward's Protestant cousin Jane Grey on the throne for nine days, failed, and Mary became Queen.

Elizabeth I (1533–1603): The daughter of Henry VIII (see below) and his second wife, Anne Boleyn (see above), Elizabeth, the last monarch of the Tudor dynasty, was Queen of England from 1558 to 1603. Succeeding her Catholic sister Mary I (see below), Elizabeth returned England to Protestantism, having Parliament declare her head of a moderate Calvinist church. Although Catholics opposed the break with Rome and radical Protestants, later known as Puritans, demanded further reform, Elizabeth maintained her Church, as ordained by Parliament in 1559, throughout her reign. Frugal, shrewd, and a good judge of character, Elizabeth strove to avoid war and promote trade until Catholic plots forced her to consent to the execution of her Catholic cousin and heir, Mary of Scotland (see below). Mary's death, English intervention in the Netherlands, and English privateering raids on Spanish America led to war with Spain and to dispatch of the Spanish Armada against England in 1588. The defeat of the Armada enhanced Elizabeth's reputation in Europe and among her people, who began to view their Virgin Queen as the symbol of English pride and identity. In this way, Elizabeth was able to confound the expectations of the time and avoid marriage, becoming, despite the supposed limitations of her gender, one of England's most effective and beloved monarchs.

Fitzwilliam, Sir William (1526–1599): Fitzwilliam was twice lord deputy of Ireland, from 1572 to 1575 and again from 1588 to 1594. During his first posting, he was charged with failing to support the Irish colonization ventures of Sir Thomas Smith (see below) and the Earl of Essex and asked to be recalled. During his second appointment, he conducted operations, leading to the capture and execution of Spanish seamen who had washed up on the Irish coast during the defeated Armada's return voyage to Spain. His subsequent involvement in the quarrels of Irish chieftains opened him to charges of provoking the rebellion known as the Nine Years War. After his second recall, Fitzwilliam was forced to defend himself against charges of corruption leveled at him by his many enemies in Ireland and England.

Forman, Simon (1552–1611): An astrologer and healer, Forman is best known through his diaries and casebooks, which provide detailed descriptions of his life and medical practice. Forman secured his fortune and his reputation as a healer by successfully treating himself and others during the 1592-1593 London visitation of the plague. Thereafter, any time the Royal College of Physicians sought to shut him down, he was rescued by the intervention of highly placed friends. Forman was frequently consulted not only on medical matters, but by women seeking to start or maintain a love affair, people seeking hidden treasure, or those seeking stolen property or missing relatives. As he records in his diaries, Forman commenced sexual relationships with many of his female clients. His practice in both astrology and medicine flourished until his death.

Foxe, John (1516–1587): A Protestant scholar and cleric, Foxe is best known as the author of the *Book of Martyrs*, the most influential and widely read book in Elizabethan England. While in exile during the reign of the Catholic Queen, Mary I (see below), Foxe wrote a Latin work describing the sufferings of the English Protestants being martyred by the

Marian regime. In 1563, after having returned to England to be ordained into the Elizabethan church, Foxe republished his work in an expanded English edition entitled *Acts and Monuments of These Latter and Perilous Days*, which became popularly known as the *Book of Martyrs*. The book was so popular and so widely read that, in 1571, the bishops ordered every English cathedral church to own a copy. Foxe continued to revise and expand the work, and many new editions appeared after his death.

Garnet, Henry (1555–1606): Garnet was head of the Jesuit Mission in England from 1587 to his death. He landed in England with fellow priest Robert Southwell (see below) in 1587 and was sheltered in the homes of Catholic gentry as he ministered to Catholics about the kingdom, even coming secretly to London to comfort Catholic prisoners. Under his leadership, the size of the English Jesuit Mission and the number of Catholics who left the country to join the Jesuit Order greatly increased. Garnet was captured in 1605 after a four-day search of the house in which he was hiding forced him to leave his priest hole. Because he had learned through the confessional of the Gunpowder Plot, a conspiracy of Catholic gentry to blow up both King and Parliament, Garnet was convicted of treason and executed.

Gerard, John (1563–1637): A prominent member of the Jesuit Mission to England, Gerard is best known for his autobiography, which provides the most vivid and detailed surviving description of Jesuit activity in Elizabethan England. Ordained a Jesuit in 1588, Gerard left immediately for England, where he ministered to English Catholics until he was arrested and imprisoned in the Tower of London. Severely tortured, he saved his life by engineering a daring escape, swinging himself out across the Tower moat on a rope. After returning to his ministry, Gerard refused to support any political plots, believing that the new King, James I (see below), would suspend the Penal Laws; however, this did not happen. He fled the country in 1606 after he was implicated in the Gunpowder Plot, a Catholic conspiracy to blow up the King and Parliament.

Gosson, Stephen (1554–1624): An Elizabethan playwright and moralist, Gosson is best known for his *School of Abuse*, a 1579 pamphlet that attacked the stage as immoral and harmful to the public order. Gosson had himself written plays and worked as an actor in the 1570s, but he turned against his former life after falling under the influence of Puritanism. Both the *School of Abuse* and a later similar tract were dedicated to Sir Philip Sidney (see below), who rejected Gosson's work and is thought to have written his *An Apology for Poetry* as a response to Gosson. His works provoked many responses from London playwrights, including Thomas Lodge's *Defence of Plays*. Gosson later took holy orders and was presented by the Queen to various livings in the Anglican Church.

Gower, George (c. 1540–1596): One of the most successful portrait painters in England, Gower became serjeant-painter to the Queen in 1581 and thus was much in demand for his services at court. Gower is believed to have painted the famous "Armada Portrait" of Elizabeth, which shows the Queen standing before a depiction of the English victory over the Spanish Armada. With the famous miniaturist Nicholas Hilliard (see below), Gower tried unsuccessfully to obtain a monopoly on the production of royal portraits, which were much in demand. In 1593, Gower became the official painter of the English navy. Although many existing paintings of Elizabethan courtiers and nobles are attributed to Gower, few can now be definitely identified as his.

Grafton, Richard (c. 1513–c. 1572): A London printer and chronicler, Grafton is best known for his original works of English history, including his *A Chronicle at Large and Mere History of the Affairs of England* (1568). In the 1530s, Grafton was involved in the attempt to print a revised edition of Miles Coverdale's English Bible. In 1543, Grafton published an updated edition of *The Chronicle of John Hardynge*, and, in 1547, he produced a new edition of *Hall's Chronicle*. Under Edward VI (see above), Grafton printed the first *Book of Common Prayer* and an edition of the Acts of Parliament, but his printing of the proclamation that announced Jane Grey as Queen led to his imprisonment by Mary I (see below) and the loss of his printing business. In the 1560s, he returned to printing, producing three original chronicles of English history.

Greene, Robert (1558–1592): A prolific and popular writer of prose, Greene wrote many works for the stage, including *The Comical History of Alphonsus King of Aragon*; *The Scottish History of James the Fourth, Slain at Flodden*; and his most successful play, *The Honorable History of Friar Bacon and Friar Bungay*. His is also well known for a series of pamphlets describing the characters and life of the London underworld, with Greene, as a frequenter of taverns and brothels, was well acquainted. These cony-catching pamphlets—from the Elizabethan slang for scam or confidence game—included *The Defence of Cony-Catching*, *A Notable Discovery of Cozenage*, *The Second Part of Cony-Catching*, *The Third and Last Part of Cony-Catching*, and *A Disputation Between a He Cony-Catcher and a She Cony-Catcher*. In his autobiographical work entitled *A Groatsworth of Wit*, Greene criticized William Shakespeare (see below) as an "upstart crow."

Gregory XIII (1502–1585): Pope of the Roman Catholic Church from 1572 to 1585, Gregory XIII (born Ugo Buoncompagni) is best known for his 1582 reform of the calendar. The Gregorian calendar, which remedied defects in the Julian calendar, thus rendering it more accurate, was immediately adopted by Catholic Europe, but not accepted by Protestant England until 1752. As pope, Gregory enacted many of the reforms proposed by the Council of Trent, attacking clerical abuses, establishing a list of forbidden books, and initiating aggressive missionary campaigns in Protestant Europe, such as the first Jesuit Mission to England in 1580, which Gregory strongly endorsed.

Greville, Fulke (1554–1628): An Elizabethan poet and courtier, Greville is best known as the biographer of his friend Sir Philip Sidney (see below). Greville was a member of the Areopagus, the group of court poets that included Sidney, Edmund Spenser (see below), and Gabriel Harvey. In 1590, he supervised the publication of Sidney's *Arcadia* and, after 1603, began his life of Sidney, which was not published until 1652. In 1612, after the death of his rival, Robert Cecil, Earl of Salisbury (see above), he resumed a political career, becoming chancellor of the exchequer and holding various other posts until ill health forced him to retire. *Caelica*, a collection of his poetry, was published after his death.

Hall, Edward (1497–1547): Hall was a popular Tudor chronicler best known for his *The Union of the Two Noble and Illustrious Families of Lancaster and York*, a history of fifteenth- and early sixteenth-century England. Published in 1548, Hall's chronicle traced the history of England from the deposition of Richard II in 1399 to the death of Henry VIII (see below) in 1547. Hall viewed history as a means of teaching moral lessons. Edifying or cautionary stories of the behavior of past princes were thought useful for teaching proper action in the present. In his chronicle, Hall projected the fears of his own times unto the fifteenth century, which he portrayed as a period of intense and terrible civil strife. His portrayal of the Wars of the Roses influenced the history plays of William Shakespeare (see below), who used Hall's chronicle as a source.

Harrison, William (1534–1593): An Elizabethan historian, topographer, and antiquary, Harrison is best known as the author of *The Description of England*, the most important surviving account of life in Elizabethan times. A cleric in the Church of England, Harrison was a member of the team of writers assembled by Raphael Holinshed (see below) to compile his *Chronicles of England, Scotland, and Ireland*, for which Harrison produced an introduction entitled "An Historical Description of the Island of Britain." For the second edition of Holinshed's *Chronicle*, published in 1587 by an editorial team under John Hooker (see below), Harrison revised his treatise, renaming it "The Description of England," which focused on the social organization and physical resources of England and Wales.

Hayward, Sir John (c. 1560–1627): Hayward was an Elizabethan historian best known for his *Life and Reign of King Edward the Sixt*, a biography of Queen Elizabeth's brother. In 1599, Hayward published *The First Part of the Life and Reign of King Henry IV*, which he dedicated to his patron Robert Devereux, Earl of Essex (see above). Disliking the tone of the work, which depicted the deposition of an English monarch, and the dedication, Essex, then being under suspicion at court, the Queen had Hayward briefly imprisoned. After 1603, Hayward wrote several works of history for his new patron Prince Henry, eldest son of James I (see below), including the biography of Edward VI (see above) and a manuscript entitled "Certain Years of Queen Elizabeth's Reign," which was not published until 1840 as the *Annals of the First Four Years of the Reign of Queen Elizabeth*.

Henri III (1551–1589): The third son of Henri II and Catherine de Medici (see above), Henri III was king of France from 1574 to 1589. Commencing two years after the St. Bartholomew's Day Massacre, of which he is considered an instigator, Henri's reign was marred by ongoing civil war between Catholics and Huguenots. Once himself a proposed suitor for Elizabeth's hand, Henri later encouraged the suit of his younger brother Francis Valois, Duke of Anjou (see below), who nearly married Elizabeth in 1581. A weak man caught in the intensifying rivalry between Henri, Duke of Guise, leader of the Catholic party, and Henri of Bourbon, leader of the Huguenots, the king arranged the murder of Guise and was himself murdered by a fanatical Catholic friar several months later. Henri's assassination led to the accession of Bourbon as Henri IV (see below).

Henri IV (1553–1610): A cousin of the last Valois kings, Henri IV, first ruler from the House of Bourbon, was king of France from 1589 to 1610. Raised a Protestant, Henri became heir to his childless Catholic cousin Henri III (see above) in 1584 upon the death of the king's brother, Francis Valois, Duke of Anjou (see below). Because of his royal blood and his marriage to Henri III's sister, Margaret of Valois, his life was spared during the St. Bartholomew's Day Massacre of Huguenots in 1572. Opposed by his

Catholic subjects, Henri, upon his accession, appealed to Elizabeth for military and financial aid, which she provided. However, to end the French civil wars and secure his Crown, Henri was forced to accept Catholicism in July 1593. In 1598, he made peace with Spain and issued the Edict of Nantes, which guaranteed the rights of Huguenots. Henri was assassinated by a Catholic fanatic in 1610.

Henry VII (1457–1509): The founder of the Tudor dynasty and grandfather of Elizabeth I, Henry VII was King of England from 1485 to 1509. As heir to the House of Lancaster, Henry ended the civil wars of the fifteenth-century by defeating and killing the last Yorkist King, Richard III (see below), at the Battle of Bosworth Field, and then married Richard's niece, Elizabeth of York, to unite the two royal houses. By avoiding war and suppressing the violence and ambition of the nobility, Henry restored the Crown's power and solvency. Although he faced many threats to his rule from Yorkist pretenders, Henry married his children into the royal houses of Spain and Scotland and secured his dynasty on the English throne.

Henry VIII (1491–1547): The second son of Henry VII (see above) and Elizabeth of York, Henry VIII, who became heir to the throne upon the death of his elder brother in 1502, was King of England from 1509 to 1547. By his second wife, Anne Boleyn (see above), Henry was the father of Elizabeth I. In seeking to annul his first marriage to Catherine of Aragon, the mother of his daughter, Mary I (see below), Henry broke with Rome when the pope, for political reasons, refused to dissolve the marriage. Henry proclaimed himself head of the English Church, a title officially declared by Parliament, and initiated a series of ecclesiastical reforms that led to the publication of an English Bible and the dissolution of the monasteries. After the failure of his first two wives to bear a living son, Henry finally got a male heir, the future Edward VI (see above), from his third wife, Jane Seymour. In the last years of his reign, Henry, who was conservative in doctrine, moved away from religious reform, maintaining many Catholic rituals and practices within an English Church divorced from Rome. After marrying three more wives but fathering no more children, Henry died in 1547.

Herbert, William, Earl of Pembroke (1580–1630): A poet and possible patron of William Shakespeare (see below), Pembroke is a popular candidate for the "fair youth" who is addressed by the poet in many of Shakespeare's sonnets. Pembroke is also believed by many to be the "Mr. W.H." to whom Shakespeare's sonnets are dedicated. Around age 20, Pembroke had a brief sexual relationship with Mary Fitton, who is considered by some scholars to be a candidate for the "dark lady," who is addressed in other Shakespearean sonnets and, with whom, according to the poet, the "fair youth" had an affair.

Hillard, Nicholas (c. 1547–1619): Hilliard was the most famous miniaturist in Elizabethan England. In 1572, the Queen appointed Hillard to be royal limner (i.e., miniature painter) and goldsmith. His refined, idealized style was much to the Queen's liking, especially as she grew older, and he executed many portraits of her and of many prominent courtiers. Because his miniatures were often designed as jewels, he also worked as a goldsmith and jeweler, making the pendants and lockets on which the miniatures could be worn or displayed. He also painted some large-scale works, but few now survive. At his death, he left uncompleted his *Treatise on the Art of Limning*.

Holinshed, Raphael (c. 1498–1580): Holinshed was the editor and co-author of one of the most popular and influential sixteenth-century histories of England, *The Chronicles of England, Scotland, and Ireland*, popularly known as Holinshed's *Chronicles*. Although Holinshed wrote most of the first volume of the *Chronicles*, the first edition, which was published in 1577, was really the work of a team of writers and compilers that included William Harrison (see above), Edmund Campion (see above), and Richard Stanyhurst. The *Chronicles* were immediately successful, although the Queen ordered some deletions in passages she found offensive. After Holinshed's death, another team of writers headed by John Hooker (see below) published a second edition of Holinshed's *Chronicles* in 1587. The second edition was widely used as source material by other writers, including William Shakespeare (see below) in his history plays.

Hooker, John (1525–1601): A writer and chamberlain of the city of Exeter, Hooker is best known as the editor of the second edition of Holinshed's *Chronicles*, for which he wrote most of Book VI on Ireland, and as the author of *The Order and Usage of the Keeping of a Parliament in England*, one of the most valuable sources on the functioning of Elizabethan Parliaments. Hooker sat in the Irish Parliament of 1569 and the English parliament of 1571, both of which experiences he recorded in journals of the two parliamentary sessions. Hooker also wrote a biography of his patron, Sir Peter Carew (see above); a *Description of the City of Exeter*; and a "Synopsis Chorographical of Devonshire," an antiquarian description of his native county.

Hooker, Richard (c. 1554–1600): Hooker is the author of the *Laws of Ecclesiastical Polity*, a brilliant defense of the Anglican Church against Puritan criticisms and the most important Elizabethan statement of Anglican philosophy. Recognizing Hooker's ability as a writer and teacher, Archbishop John Whitgift obtained for him various Church livings that allowed him the time to research and write. Although all eight books of the *Laws* were completed by Hooker's death in 1600, the last three were not published until the 1640s.

Howard, Henry, Earl of Surrey (c. 1516–1547): Surrey was one of the most important poets of early Tudor England and deeply influenced the development of Elizabethan poetry. With Thomas Wyatt (see below), Surrey is credited with introducing the sonnet and other Italian verse forms into England. He also influenced the composition of much future English poetry by translating Vergil's *Aeneid* into English blank verse, unrhymed lines of iambic pentameter that were entirely Surrey's own invention. By taking the unprecedented step of publishing his elegy on the death of Wyatt, Surrey elevated the work of his fellow poet to heroic stature and invested the writing of poetry with a status it had never held before. Sir Philip Sidney (see below) considered Surrey's poetry to be among the finest in English literature and viewed the earl as the ideal courtier poet. A proud and volatile man, Surrey fell afoul of Henry VIII (see above), who considered Surrey dangerously ambitious and had him executed for treason in 1547.

Howard, Thomas, Duke of Norfolk (1536–1572): The son of the poet Henry Howard, Earl of Surrey (see above), Thomas Howard, the fourth Duke of Norfolk, was a kinswoman of Elizabeth and the only duke in Elizabethan England. In 1569, feeling shut out from power by William Cecil (see above), the Queen's chief minister, Norfolk suggested himself as a husband for the imprisoned Mary of Scotland (see below). When Elizabeth rejected this proposal, Norfolk withdrew from court, issuing threats against

Cecil and his supporters. After a brief imprisonment, Norfolk involved himself in the Ridolfi Plot, a conspiracy to free Mary and dethrone Elizabeth. The plot also included plans for a Spanish invasion, the restoration of Catholicism, and the marriage of Norfolk to the Scottish queen. The plot was discovered, and Norfolk was tried for treason and executed in 1572.

James I (1566–1625): The son of Mary, Queen of Scots (see below), James was king of Scotland as James VI from 1567 and King of England as James I from 1603. Only a year old when his mother was forced to abdicate the Scottish Crown on his behalf, James was raised a Protestant. Although Elizabeth refused to name a successor, she gave James money and advice and promised not to oppose his claim to the English Crown so long as he followed policies in Scotland that met her approval. When Elizabeth executed Mary in 1587, James showed that he was more concerned for the succession than for the mother he never knew by limiting his response to a formal protest. Assisted by the Queen's chief minister, Sir Robert Cecil (see above), with whom he had been conducting a secret correspondence, James succeeded peacefully to the English Crown on Elizabeth's death in 1603.

James V (1512–1542): The son of James IV and Margaret Tudor (see below), the sister of Henry VIII (see above), and the father of Mary, Queen of Scots (see below), James V was king of Scotland from 1513. Although urged by his uncle to break with Rome and seek closer ties with England, James remained an orthodox Catholic and followed largely pro-French policies. In 1541, he failed to show for a planned meeting with Henry VIII in York, a slight that enraged his uncle, who revived English claims to suzerainty over Scotland and initiated a series of English invasions of the northern kingdom. Depressed by a Scottish defeat by the English at Solway Moss, James fell ill and died in December 1542, only six days after the birth of his only surviving child, Mary, who thus became queen of Scotland as an infant.

Jonson, Ben (1572–1637): Jonson is usually ranked with William Shakespeare and Christopher Marlowe (see both below) as the most talented playwrights of Elizabethan England. Jonson wrote several plays for Shakespeare's acting company, the Chamberlain's Men, who performed them at the Globe Theater. Among Jonson's most famous works are *Catiline*, *Volpone*, *The Alchemist*, *Bartholomew Fair*, *The Devil Is an Ass*, and *The Staple of News*. During the reign of James I (see above), Jonson wrote many of the masques performed at court, achieving great popularity and unofficial recognition as the court poet laureate. He was responsible for a large body of literary criticism and, in 1616, published a collected edition of his poems, plays, and masques. In 1623, Jonson wrote some dedicatory verses for the First Folio edition of Shakespeare's plays.

Kempe, William (d. 1609): Kempe was the leading comic actor of Elizabethan England and an associate of William Shakespeare (see below), with whom he was a shareholder in the Chamberlain's Men. Kempe was widely known for his popular (and often obscene) song-and-dance sketches, known as jigs. Kempe originated many comedic roles in Shakespeare's plays, including Peter in *Romeo and Juliet* and Dogberry in *Much Ado About Nothing*. He was an original shareholder in the Globe Theater, but left the company in 1600 to undertake his most famous exploit, a monthlong morris dance from London to Norwich, which netted Kempe a large profit in bets and gifts. He derived further income from the venture through publication of a book describing the dance, entitled *Kempe's Nine Days Wonder*.

Kiechel, Samuel (1563–1619): Kiechel was a German Lutheran merchant who visited England in the late 1580s. His account of the visit, later published in *Die Reisen des Samuel Kiechel* (The Travels of Samuel Kiechel), is a valuable source of information on Elizabethan social customs and practices, including London play-going.

Knollys, Lettice (1540–1634): A cousin of Queen Elizabeth, for whom she was maid of honor, Lettice Knollys is best known for her secret marriage in 1578 to the Queen's favorite, Robert Dudley, Earl of Leicester (see above). When the French ambassador Jean Simier revealed the marriage to the Queen in 1579 to forestall Leicester's opposition to Elizabeth's proposed marriage to Francis Valois, Duke of Anjou (see below), the Queen banished both Leicester and his wife from court. Although the earl was soon forgiven, the countess was never readmitted to royal favor, even when her son by her first marriage, Robert Devereux, Earl of Essex (see above), became the Queen's new favorite in the 1590s.

Kyd, Thomas (1558–1594): Kyd was one of the most popular tragic poets and playwrights of Elizabethan England. A friend of the playwright Christopher Marlowe (see below), Kyd made his literary reputation through repeated production of his immensely popular drama, *The Spanish Tragedy*, which was performed several times in London in 1592 by Lord Strange's Men and revived later by the Chamberlain's Men, the acting company of which William Shakespeare (see below) was a shareholder. Kyd shared lodgings with Marlowe and was a member of a group of young playwrights, including Marlowe, Thomas Lodge (see below), and Thomas Nashe, who were notorious for their dissolute lifestyle. Kyd was eventually arrested on suspicion of treason and heresy and apparently forced to confess under torture to the atheistic opinions of his late friend, Marlowe. Kyd died shortly thereafter in December 1594.

Laneham, Robert (fl. 1570s): A client of Robert Dudley, Earl of Leicester (see above), who got him appointed doorkeeper of the royal council chamber, Laneham is best known for his detailed account of the lavish entertainments his patron provided for the Queen on her visit to Kenilworth Castle in July 1575. Contained in a long letter to a London merchant friend, Laneham's vivid description of the Kenilworth visit is one of the best surviving descriptions of an Elizabethan royal progress.

Lanier, Emilia (1569–1645): The first Englishwoman to publish her own volume of poetry, Emilia Lanier has been proposed by some scholars as the "dark lady" who appears in some of William Shakespeare's (see below) sonnets. Her collection of poetry, entitled *Salve Deus Rex Judaeorum*, was published in 1611. The longtime mistress of Henry Carey, Lord Hunsdon (see above), Elizabeth's cousin and master of revels, Lanier was Italian by birth, and scholars have speculated that she had dark hair and a dark complexion and thus would fit the description of the "dark lady." Other aspects of her life, including her membership in a musical family, also fit the descriptions in the sonnets. Lanier appears frequently in the diaries of Simon Forman (see above), whom she often consulted, but little else is known of her personal life.

Lodge, Thomas (c. 1558–1625): An Elizabethan dramatist and romance writer, Lodge was part of the circle of young London writers and playwrights that included Christopher Marlowe (see below) and Thomas Kyd (see above). Lodge's first work was the pamphlet *A Defence of Plays*, which was a response to Stephen Gosson's (see above) attack on the theater in *School of Abuse*. Lodge wrote several well-received romances, including *The Delectable History of Forbonius and Priscilla; Scylla's Metamorphosis*, which inspired William Shakespeare's (see below) later poem "Venus and Adonis"; and *Rosalynde*, which may have been a source for Shakespeare's *As You Like It*. Lodge also wrote several other pamphlets and a collection of sonnets and lyric poems. In the 1590s, Lodge converted to Catholicism and started a new career as a physician, studying at a French university and opening a practice in London.

Lyly, John (c. 1554–1606): Lyly was a popular Elizabethan writer whose works and style strongly influenced other writers, including Robert Greene and Thomas Lodge (see both above). Secretary for several years to the poet Edward de Vere, Earl of Oxford (see below), Lyly published *Euphues, the Anatomy of Wit*, the first part of his great romance novel, in 1579. The second part, *Euphues and His England*, appeared in 1580. These two works were widely acclaimed, making Lyly the most popular writer in England. Written in an elaborate, artificial style marked by the use of much alliteration and many historical and mythological allusions, Lyly's "euphuic" style heavily influenced many later Elizabethan writers. Lyly also wrote a series of plays, mainly for a company of child actors known as Paul's Boys. His popularity waned after 1590 as literary tastes changed, and Lyly spent his last years in a largely unsuccessful effort to win court patronage.

Marlowe, Christopher (1564–1593): Marlowe is often considered to be the greatest Elizabethan dramatist after William Shakespeare (see below), whose works some modern scholars attribute to Marlowe. Marlowe's first play, *Tamburlaine the Great*, was performed by the Admiral's Men in 1587 and was an immediate success. His plays, such as *The Jew of Malta*, which later inspired Shakespeare's *Merchant of Venice*; *Edward II*; *The Tragical History of Doctor Faustus*; and the *Tragedy of Dido, Queen of Carthage*, were soon in high demand by actors, theater owners, and audiences. Marlowe led a riotous life and was often in trouble with the law. He also was employed by Francis Walsingham (see below), the secretary of state, as a government spy. In 1593, he was summoned before the Privy Council and questioned about several atheistic writings found in his lodgings, though otherwise not punished. Shortly thereafter, he was stabbed to death in a mysterious tavern brawl.

Mary I (1516–1558): The daughter of Henry VIII (see above) and his first wife, Catherine of Aragon, Mary was the half-sister of Elizabeth and Queen of England from 1553 to 1558. A staunch Catholic, Mary began her reign by repealing her father's and brother's religious legislation and restoring the English Church to papal allegiance. Anxious to remove heresy from the realm, she sanctioned the burning of hundreds of Protestants, actions that earned her the name "Bloody Mary" and ingrained a deep fear of Catholicism into the English people. Her marriage to Philip of Spain (see below) provoked a rebellion in which Elizabeth was implicated, though nothing could be proved against her and she was eventually released from confinement. Prevented by age and poor health from bearing children, she died childless in 1558 when she was succeeded by Elizabeth.

Mary, Queen of Scots (1542–1587): The daughter of James V (see above) of Scotland and the granddaughter of Margaret Tudor (see below), Mary, Queen of Scots was cousin to Queen Elizabeth and heir to her throne. Because Mary was staunchly Catholic and pro-French (having grown up at the French court), most Englishmen feared her possible succession to the throne, thus the continual urging from Parliament that Elizabeth marry and have children. Upon the death of her first husband, Francis II of France in 1560, Mary returned to Scotland, where she soon clashed with the Protestant nobility. Her second husband, Henry Stuart, Lard Darnley, proved to be weak, dissolute, and unstable. When he was murdered by persons unknown in 1567, most people accused Mary and her favorite, James Hepburn, Earl of Bothwell, of the crime. When the Queen subsequently married Bothwell, a confederation of nobles forced Mary to abdicate in favor of her infant son. In 1568, Mary fled to England, where she was kept in confinement for the next 19 years. Implicated in various plots against Elizabeth, Mary was finally tried and executed for treason in 1587, despite Elizabeth's reluctance to kill a kinswoman and anointed monarch.

Middleton, Thomas (1580–1627): A popular London dramatist, Middleton wrote plays for the Admiral's Men, Paul's Boys, and other acting companies. His most famous surviving plays are the comedies *A Chaste Maid in Cheapside* and *A Fair Quarrel* and the tragedies *The Changeling* and *The Witch*, several of which were written in collaboration with other playwrights. One of his most popular works, *A Game at Chess*, criticized the proposed Spanish marriage of Prince Charles, son of James I (see above), and was banned by the Privy Council. Middleton's play, *The Witch*, contains passages mirrored in William Shakespeare's (see below) *Macbeth*. Middleton also wrote pageants and plays for entertainments put on by the city of London.

Oldcorne, Edward (1561–1606): Oldcorne was a member of the English Jesuit Mission, arriving in England with John Gerard (see above) in 1589. He focused his ministry in Worcestershire, where he frequently headquartered at Hinslip Hall, which contained a priest hole designed by Nicholas Owen. In 1605, Oldcorne was implicated in the Gunpowder Plot, a conspiracy by Catholic gentlemen to blow up the King and Parliament. Forced to remain eight days in the priest hole at Hinslip due to a prolonged search of the house, Oldcorne finally surrendered along with Henry Garnet (see above). Taken to London and tortured, Oldcorne was finally executed in April 1606.

O'Neill, Hugh, Earl of Tyrone (c. 1550–1616): Tyrone was leader of the Irish forces during the Nine Years War (1593–1602). Raised in Dublin and perhaps in England, the English government recognized O'Neill as Earl of Tyrone in the 1580s and assisted him in extending his authority throughout Ulster in northern Ireland. In 1595, Tyrone seized an English fort on the Blackwater and then defeated an English army sent to recover it at Yellow Ford in 1598. His authority now extended into central Ireland, and the Elizabethan government sent Robert Devereux, Earl of Essex (see above), to Ireland to subdue Tyrone, but Essex, fearing the loss of his influence at home, made an unauthorized truce with Tyrone, which allowed the Irish earl time to negotiate for troops from Spain, which arrived in Ireland in 1601. However, Tyrone's attempt to join his forces with the Spaniards failed, and the Irish rebellion was crushed. Tyrone submitted to the government in 1603 and fled to Rome in 1607.

Parsons, Robert (1546–1610): Parsons was a leader and organizer of the English Jesuit Mission to England, where he landed with fellow Jesuit Edmund Campion (see above) in 1580. Parsons worked mainly in the western counties, but was also responsible for setting up a secret press in London that printed and distributed Catholic tracts, including his own *Decem Rationes*. Parsons left England in 1581 and traveled to Spain, where he worked with William Allen (see above) to convince Philip II (see below) and the pope to undertake an invasion of England. He soon assumed full direction of the English Jesuit Mission and became rector of the English College in Rome. After defeat of the Spanish Armada in 1588, Parsons urged another invasion and wrote a series of tracts advocating the right of English Catholics to overthrow their heretical Queen, though most English Catholics eventually repudiated Parson's arguments.

Paulet, Sir Amias (c. 1536–1588): From 1585, Paulet, a Puritan gentleman, was the official custodian of Mary, Queen of Scots (see above). Ordered to keep Mary closely confined, Paulet inspected her correspondence, restricted her spending, and monitored her visitors. Mary demanded a less severe jailor, but the Queen refused. Paulet worked closely with Sir Francis Walsingham (see below) in uncovering the Babington Plot, which led to Mary's trial and execution. When Elizabeth hinted that he should murder Mary privately to relieve her of responsibility for ordering her cousin's execution, Paulet returned a horrified refusal, even though he fully agreed with her public execution.

Philip II (1527–1598): The son of the Holy Roman Emperor, Charles V, and the husband of Elizabeth's sister, Mary I (see above), Philip II was king of Spain from 1556. After Mary's death, Philip unsuccessfully offered himself as a husband to his former sister-in-law, Elizabeth. Over the three decades following Elizabeth's accession in 1558, relations between England and Spain deteriorated due to religious differences, English privateering raids in Spanish America, and English support for the Netherlands Revolt. War erupted in 1585 when Elizabeth sent troops to the Netherlands. Philip, who was now convinced that he would never subdue the Netherlands until he had overthrown Elizabeth, began making preparations for an invasion of England. The failure of the Spanish Armada in 1588 heartened Protestant Europe and shattered the Spanish aura of invincibility, but the Anglo-Spanish war continued for the rest of Philip's reign.

Raleigh, Sir Walter (c. 1552–1618): A prominent courtier, soldier, poet, and historian, Raleigh did more than any other Elizabethan to promote English exploration and colonization of North America. In the 1570s, Raleigh and his half-brother Sir Humphrey Gilbert fought rebels in Ireland and outfitted privateering expeditions against Spanish shipping. In the 1580s, Raleigh, who was a royal favorite, obtained license from the Queen to plant colonies in America. Although he funded and organized six colonizing expeditions and was responsible for introducing such American products as tobacco and potatoes to England, he was unsuccessful in establishing a permanent colony. He fell into disfavor for secretly marrying Elizabeth Throckmorton, one of the Queen's ladies and became a bitter rival of Robert Devereux, Earl of Essex (see above). Upon the accession of James I (see above) in 1603, Raleigh was arrested for treason and imprisoned in the Tower, where he wrote much poetry and his *History of the World*. After a failed expedition to South America, Raleigh was re-arrested and executed at the insistence of the king of Spain.

Rich, Penelope (1563–1607): The sister of Robert Devereux, Earl of Essex (see above), Penelope Rich was the inspiration for "Stella" in Sir Philip Sidney's (see below) sonnet cycle *Astrophel and Stella* and has been suggested by some modern scholars as the "dark lady" of William Shakespeare's (see below) sonnets. Penelope was proposed as a bride for Sidney, but her father died before he could arrange the match. She then married the wealthy, but unattractive, Robert Rich, Lord Rich. Sidney, meanwhile, fell deeply in love with his lost bride and poured his unrequited passion for her into his poetry. Lady Rich later became the mistress of Charles Blount, Lord Mountjoy. Her identification as the "dark lady" rests on her reputation for great beauty, sensuality, and promiscuity, all of which qualities could be attributed to the woman in Shakespeare's sonnets.

Richard III (1452–1485): The brother of Edward IV (see above) and the last ruler of the House of York, Richard III was King of England from 1483 to 1485. Richard is at the heart of one of the greatest mysteries in English history, the disappearance of his 12-year-old nephew Edward V and his younger brother in the Tower of London. Because Richard had declared his nephew illegitimate and supplanted him on the throne, rumors soon spread throughout England that Richard had ordered the murders of the two boys. These rumors generated much opposition to his rule, and, in 1485, Richard was defeated and killed by Henry Tudor, Earl of Richmond, heir to the Lancastrian claim to the throne, at the Battle of Bosworth Field. Richmond, who took the throne as Henry VII (see above), was the grandfather of Elizabeth and the founder of the Tudor dynasty. Today, the question of whether or not Richard had anything to do with the deaths of his nephews is hotly debated.

Sackville, Sir Richard (d. 1566): Sackville served successive Tudor monarchs as an administrator and financial officer. During his career, he held the posts of under-treasurer of the Exchequer, chancellor of the Court of Augmentations, and escheator of Surrey and Sussex. He was a distant cousin of Elizabeth's mother, Anne Boleyn (see above).

Sandys, Edwin (c. 1516–1588): Sandys was bishop of London from 1570 and archbishop of York from 1576. Sandys fled the Catholic regime of Mary I (see above) in the 1550s, but returned upon Elizabeth's accession to become Bishop of Worcester. A Puritan, Sandys believed the Anglican religious settlement was too conservative. He particularly opposed the vestments clerics were required to wear and the suppression of Puritan prophesyings ordered by the Queen. In the 1560s, Sandys was one of the translators of the Bishops' Bible.

Shakespeare, William (1564–1616): Shakespeare is considered by many to be the greatest poet and playwright in the English language. The son of a glover and grain dealer in Stratford-on-Avon, Shakespeare seems to have had little formal education beyond grammar school. He came to London in about 1592, joining the Chamberlain's Men acting company and eventually becoming a shareholder in Richard Burbage's (see above) Globe Theater, where he was known as both playwright and actor. His wife and children continued to live in Stratford, where he returned in about 1610. Shakespeare wrote 37 plays, a cycle of 154 sonnets, and several other longer poems. Because no manuscripts of Shakespeare's works survive and because his education seems to have been brief, many other Elizabethan figures have been proposed as the true author of the works of Shakespeare, including Edward de Vere, Earl of Oxford (see below), Christopher Marlowe, and Sir Francis Bacon (see both above). Most Shakespeare scholars reject these theories. The First Folio edition of Shakespeare's plays appeared in 1623, seven years after his death.

Sidney, Sir Philip (1554–1586): The nephew of the royal favorite Robert Dudley, Earl of Leicester (see above), and the godson of Philip II of Spain (see above), Sidney was considered in his own time to be the archetypal Elizabethan courtier-poet. Sidney's first works included *Discourse on Irish Affairs*, which defended his father's actions as Irish lord deputy, and *The Lady of May*, a play performed for the Queen. In the 1580s, he wrote a prose romance, *Arcadia* and the first English sonnet cycle, *Astrophel and Stella*, both of which greatly influenced later writers, including William Shakespeare (see above). Sidney became head of a circle of poets and writers that included Fulke Greville (see above), Gabriel Harvey, and Edmund Spenser (see below), who dedicated his popular *Shepheardes Calendar* to Sidney. In likely response to Stephen Gossen's (see above) attack on poetry in *School of Abuse*, Sidney wrote his treatise, *An Apology for Poetry*. A strong Protestant who fell into disfavor for his opposition to the Queen's proposed marriage to Francis Valois, Duke of Anjou (see below), Sidney accompanied his uncle Leicester on campaign in the Netherlands and died of wounds received in battle.

Smith, Sir Thomas (1513–1577): Smith was a classical scholar and experienced civil servant who rose to the office of secretary of state. His most important work was *De Republica Anglorum* (1584), a detailed description of the working of Elizabethan government and is a valuable resource for modern historians. He also wrote many other political and scholarly tracts, including several urging the Queen to marry. In the 1570s, Smith won the Queen's permission to plant an English colony in Ulster in northern Ireland, but the venture collapsed when Smith's only son was murdered by his Irish servants in 1573.

Southwell, Robert (1561–1595): Southwell was a member of the Jesuit Mission to England and a leading Catholic poet. He landed in England in 1586 with Henry Garnet (see above) and headquartered at the London home of the Countess of Arundell, whom he served as chaplain. He wrote (and had surreptitiously published and distributed) a series of letters and tracts intended for the comforting and encouraging of English Catholics. His best-known works are the pamphlet, *An Epistle of Comfort*; the poem, "The Burning Babe"; and *St. Peter's Complaint*, St. Peter's narration of the last days of Christ. He was arrested in 1592 and executed in 1595 after suffering torture in the Tower. His collection of poems entitled *Maeoniae* was published in 1595, and his *Fourfold Meditation of the Four Last Things* appeared posthumously in 1606.

Spenser, Edmund (c. 1552–1599): Considered by contemporaries to be one of the foremost poets and writers of his time, Spenser is best known for his grand epic poem, *The Faerie Queen*. His first work, *The Shepheardes Calendar*, a series of highly innovative eclogues dedicated to Sir Philip Sidney (see above), was well received and brought Spenser to the attention of the court. *The Faerie Queen*, a long allegory depicting the adventures of the knights of the brilliant Queen Gloriana (i.e., Elizabeth), was dedicated to the Queen and earned Spenser a generous annuity. He also produced a sonnet cycle, *Amoretti*; a lament on the death of Sidney, *Astrophel*, and a tract denigrating the Irish and supporting English conquest of Ireland, *A View of the Present State of Ireland*.

Stanley, Ferdinando, Lord Strange (1559–1594): Strange was patron and namesake of an acting company known as Lord Strange's Men, which, in the 1590s, included such important theatrical figures as William Kempe (see above), Edward Alleyn, and William Shakespeare (see above). The company performed at Philip Henslowe's Rose

Theater, at James Burbage's (see above) The Theater, and at court and may have been the first acting troupe to perform the works of Shakespeare. After Strange's death in 1594, Lord Strange's Men were reconstituted as the Chamberlain's Men under the patronage of the lord chamberlain, Henry Carey, Lord Hunsdon (see above).

Stow, John (c. 1525–1605): Stow was an important and popular chronicler of English history and a member of the editorial team that produced the second edition of Holinshed's *Chronicle* in 1587. His best-known work, *The Chronicles of England*, which was later popularly known as the *Annals*, was first published in 1580 and reissued in 1592. Stow's work, which took English history up to the present day, borrowed extensively from Holinshed's *Chronicles*. In the 1590s, Stow compiled his *Survey of London*, which was a valuable study of the origins, development, and customs of the city.

Stubbs, John (c. 1543–1591): An English Puritan pamphleteer, Stubbs is best known for his pamphlet, *The Discovery of a Gaping Gulf Whereinto England Is Like to Be Swallowed by Another French Marriage*, which attacked the Queen's proposed marriage with Francis Valois, Duke of Anjou (see below). Stubbs argued that the match was unnecessary because the Queen was too old for children and detrimental to the freedom of Englishmen because it could lead to French rule and the restoration of Catholicism. Stubbs' blunt language angered the Queen, who ordered his arrest and the confiscation and burning of his pamphlet. Tried and convicted of seditious writing, Stubbs was punished by having his right hand cut off.

Stubbs, Philip (c. 1555–c. 1610): A Puritan moralist who may have been the brother or close relative of pamphleteer John Stubbs (see above), Philip Stubbs is best known for his pamphlet, *The Anatomy of Abuses*, which attacked as immoral such popular activities as play-going, dancing, and holiday festivities. In another of his writings, *A Motive to Good Works*, Stubbs lamented the failure of the government to prevent and control the licensing of plays, books, and other writings that he found irreligious and indecent.

Tilney, Edmund (d. 1610): Tilney was royal master of the revels from 1579 until his death. Tilney gradually expanded the scope of his office to include the oversight of all acting companies and all London theaters. He licensed all actors, censored plays, and exercised increasing control over what plays were and were not performed. He also organized all court entertainments and arranged all court appearances by acting companies.

Tottel, Richard (d. 1594): Tottel was a London printer who is best known for his publication, in 1557, of a collection of poetry entitled *Songs and Sonnets*, popularly known as *Tottel's Miscellany*. *Songs and Sonnets* introduced a broad English readership to the new verse forms coming out of Italy, such as sonnets and canzones. The collection included works by Italian poets and works by English poets writing in the Italian style and was thus the first publication of poems by Thomas Wyatt (see below) and Henry Howard, Earl of Surrey (see above), the most important English poets of the early Tudor period. By popularizing this poetry, *Tottel's Miscellany* had an important influence on the development of Elizabethan poetry.

Tudor, Margaret (1489–1541): The elder sister of Henry VIII (see above) and wife of James IV of Scotland, Margaret was the grandmother of Mary of Scotland (see above), and it was through her that the Stuarts eventually came to the English throne in the person of James I (see above). After the death of her husband, Margaret, who had a poor relationship with her brother, Henry VIII, served several times as regent for her young son James V (see above). In the 1540s, Henry removed Margaret's descendants from the succession because of their Catholicism, but, failing other heirs, Margaret's great-grandson, James VI of Scotland, who was a Protestant, peacefully succeeded Elizabeth in 1603.

Valois, Francis, Duke of Anjou (1554–1584): Francis Valois, Duke of Anjou, was the fourth son of Henri II of France and Catherine de Medici (see above). He became heir to the throne upon the accession of his brother, Henri III (see below), in 1574. He was first proposed as a husband for Elizabeth in 1572 when he was 18, but only became a serious suitor for her hand after 1578 when he became protector of the Netherlands and thus responsible for military leadership of the rebellion against Spain. In 1579, Anjou visited England and charmed the Queen, who entered into serious marriage talks as part of a general Anglo-French alliance in the Netherlands. Public opinion in England was strongly against the match, with many fearing that the 46-year-old Queen would die in childbed, leaving the country under the rule of a French Catholic. In 1581, Elizabeth gave the duke a ring and startled everyone by announcing their engagement. However, influenced perhaps by the negative reaction of her court, she quickly changed her mind, and the marriage never occurred.

Van Meteren, Emanuel (1535–1612): Born in Antwerp in the Netherlands, Van Meteren was brought by his father to England in 1550. He spent most of his life in London, where he died in 1612. Van Meteren served for many years as the trade consul in London for Netherlands merchants, representing their interests to the English government. His publications as a historian included the *Historia Belgica; Historie der Nederlanden*, which drew upon the journals and logbooks of Henry Hudson, whom van Meteren may have persuaded to join the Dutch East India Company; and *Belgische ofte Nederlandsche Historie van onzen Tijden*, a survey and, in some parts, a firsthand account of the early part of the long war between the Netherlands and Spain.

Vere, Edward de, Earl of Oxford ((1550–1604): Oxford was an Elizabethan courtier and poet who, in the twentieth century, became a leading candidate for authorship of the plays and poems traditionally attributed to William Shakespeare (see above). Oxford, who was the ward and later the son-in-law of William Cecil, Lord Burghley (see above), fell in and out of royal favor. His skill at poetry and dancing attracted the Queen, but his extravagant lifestyle, sudden conversion to Catholicism, and frequent misadventures, such as a violent quarrel with Sir Philip Sidney (see above) and his seduction of one of the Queen's ladies estranged him from his family and cost him a spell of imprisonment. Oxford is known to have written plays for a juvenile acting company and to have been patron to an adult company, but none of his plays has survived. Most scholars reject the theory that he authored the works of Shakespeare.

Vergil, Polydore (1470–1555): Vergil was an Italian historian and papal official who wrote the *Anglica Historia*, the first comprehensive humanist history of England. Vergil came to England in 1502 and entered the service of his kinsman, who was Bishop of Hereford. Later, he undertook diplomatic missions at the papal court for the English Crown. In 1517, he retired from public service to devote himself to his scholarly studies. His *Anglica*

Historia was different from all previous histories of England in that it abandoned the year-by-year listings of medieval chronicles for the chronological/biographical organization of the new Italian humanist history and it made critical use of sources, rejecting the traditional tales of English and British legend. Vergil's account of fifteenth-century English history influenced most sixteenth-century depictions of the period, including the history plays of William Shakespeare (see above).

Vernon, Elizabeth (1573–1655): A maid of honor at court, Elizabeth Vernon incurred the Queen's wrath when she became pregnant by her lover, Henry Wriothesley, Earl of Southampton (see below), the patron of William Shakespeare (see above). The couple married secretly, but, when Elizabeth Vernon's condition became apparent, the Queen imprisoned Southampton and so abused his wife that she fled the court to have her child at the country home of Penelope Rich, Lady Rich (see above). In 1601, the earl involved himself in Essex's rebellion and was thus imprisoned in the Tower for the rest of the reign. In 1603, upon the accession of James I (see above), the Earl and Countess of Southampton were both received back into royal favor. Elizabeth Vernon has been suggested as a candidate for the "dark lady" of Shakespeare's sonnets.

Walsingham, Sir Francis (1532–1590): As secretary of state from 1573, Walsingham built and directed an extensive intelligence network by which he tracked the activities of Catholic priests and potential Catholic plotters at home and abroad. A Puritan, Walsingham undertook various diplomatic missions and was English ambassador in Paris during the St. Bartholomew's Day Massacre of 1572 when he offered sheltered to Huguenots. He repeatedly urged the death of Mary of Scotland (see above), and it was his discovery of the Babington Plot in 1586 that led to Mary's trial and execution.

Wentworth, Peter (c. 1524–1596): Wentworth was a parliamentary critic of the royal prerogative and a staunch advocate for wider freedom of speech in Parliament. He is most famous for a speech he tried to deliver in the House of Commons in February 1576, which personally criticized the Queen for "great faults" in her failure to settle the succession and her actions limiting debate on the matter in the House. In an era when direct attacks on the monarch were unheard of, a horrified House stopped Wentworth in mid-speech and committed him to custody. The Queen released him after a month, but he was forced to make humble submission on his knees at the bar of the House before being allowed to resume his seat in Parliament. His continued opposition to royal policies and actions led to further imprisonments. He was imprisoned for the last time in 1593 when his tract on the succession question again angered Elizabeth. Wentworth died in the Tower in 1596.

White, John (d. 1593): An Elizabethan painter and cartographer, White is most famous for his vivid drawings of Native American life in sixteenth-century Virginia. A member of Sir Walter Raleigh's (see above) first American colonization expedition in 1585, White made many drawings of the flora and fauna and of Indian life, as well as many maps of the North American coast. In 1587, Raleigh named White governor of the second colonization expedition, which also included members of his family. In August, White's granddaughter, Virginia Dare, became the first English child born in North America. In need of supplies, the colonists sent White back to England to ensure their dispatch. However, thanks to the Armada crisis, White could not return to America for three years. When White finally did return in 1590, he could find no trace of the colony, which thereafter passed into legend as the "lost colony."

William, Prince of Orange (1533–1584): Orange was leader of the Dutch revolt against Spain and a founder of the independent United Provinces of the Netherlands. Holder of the German principality of Orange, the prince, a Protestant, also held vast estates in the Spanish Netherlands. Originally the chief of a group of nobles who believed Philip II (see above) was denying them their rightful part in running the country, Orange later took up arms against Spain after the Netherlands erupted in revolt in 1566. Assuming military leadership of the rebellion, Orange also sought financial and military assistance for the rebels from England and elsewhere. Outlawed by Philip in 1580, Orange was assassinated by a Spanish agent in 1584.

Wilson, Thomas (c. 1560–1629): Wilson succeeded his uncle, the rhetorician Thomas Wilson, as keeper or clerk of the State Paper Office in 1581. Wilson studied civil law at Cambridge, but failed to be a fellow of Trinity Hall and found employment as a government negotiator and intelligencer (i.e., agent) in Ireland and elsewhere. In 1600, while in the service of Sir Robert Cecil (see above), Wilson wrote his well-known treatise entitled *On the State of England Anno Dom. 1600*, which is a valuable source for modern historians.

Wriothesley, Henry, Earl of Southampton (1573–1624): A prominent supporter of Elizabethan literature, Southampton is most famous for being the only known patron of William Shakespeare (see above). Young and wealthy and a frequenter of London playhouses, Southampton had many literary works dedicated to him by writers seeking his patronage. Shakespeare dedicated his poems "Venus and Adonis" and "The Rape of Lucrece" to the earl, who may also have been the young man to whom many of Shakespeare's sonnets are addressed. Southampton was involved in Essex's rebellion in 1601 and narrowly escaped execution, spending the rest of Elizabeth's reign in the Tower of London. Released upon the accession of James I (see above) in 1603, the earl remained in favor at court for most of James' reign.

Wyatt, Sir Thomas (c. 1503–1542): Wyatt was one of the most important poets of early Tudor England and is best known for a supposed relationship with Anne Boleyn (see above), Elizabeth's mother, prior to her marriage to Henry VIII (see above). Although the idea is controversial, several of Wyatt's poems are believed to have been addressed to Anne. Wyatt is credited with introducing the Italian sonnet into England and with reinvigorating English poetry through his experimentation with Italian verse forms. He wrote much fine lyric poetry, as well as elegies, epigrams, and satire. Along with fellow court poet, Henry Howard, Earl of Surrey (see above), he laid the foundations for the growth and development of Elizabethan poetry. Arrested at the time of Anne Boleyn's fall in 1536, Wyatt was never brought to trial and eventually released.

Appendix 2: Glossary of Terms Mentioned in Text

Listed here are brief definitions of terms mentioned in connection with the documents reproduced in this volume. The first mention of any of these terms in any section are highlighted as cross-references.

Act of Uniformity: Acts of Parliament that mandated the use of a uniform liturgy throughout the English Church. Three Acts of Uniformity were enacted in the sixteenth century. The first two, passed during the reign of Edward VI in 1549 and 1552, enjoined the use of the first and second *Books of Common Prayer* (see below), English services that replaced the Catholic Latin Mass. The third was enacted in 1559 under Elizabeth I, who thereby abolished the Catholic Mass restored by her sister Mary I and enjoined the uniform use of a revised *Book of Common Prayer*.

Anglo-Irish: The descendants of Norman and English invaders who overran and settled parts of Ireland in the twelfth and thirteenth centuries. Because the Anglo-Irish tended to be Catholic, to speak Irish as well as English, and to practice many Irish customs, they became known as the "Old English" in the seventeenth century to distinguish them from Protestant, English-speaking colonists of Elizabethan and early Stuart times, who were known as the "New English." Under Elizabeth I and James I, the New English gradually replaced the Anglo-Irish as the island's political and military elite.

Berwick, Treaty of (1560): An agreement between Elizabeth I and Scottish Protestant nobles to act in concert against the expansion of French Catholic influence in Scotland. Under its terms, Elizabeth, who entered into the treaty reluctantly, sent troops into Scotland to assist the Scots in besieging the French fortress at Leith. This English intervention led later in the year to the Treaty of Edinburgh (see below) and the subsequent withdrawal of both English and French forces from Scotland.

Book of Common Prayer: The parliamentary-sanctioned English liturgy of the Protestant Church of England under Edward VI and Elizabeth I. The official service book of the Anglican Church, the Elizabethan Prayer Book, contained the prescribed forms of all ceremonies, rites, and rituals used in Anglican worship. Use of the *Book of Common Prayer* was enjoined on all Elizabethan clergy by the Act of Uniformity (see above), passed in 1559.

Butler Wars (1569): An uprising against the government led by the younger brothers of Thomas Butler, Earl of Ormond, in the Carlow region of southeastern Ireland in the summer of 1569. Although it occurred at the same time as other religious and politically motivated rebellions elsewhere in Ireland, the Butler uprising arose mainly from the dissatisfaction of the Butler family over the outcome of lawsuits initiated by Sir Peter Carew to regain lands from the Butlers that his family had held in Ireland some 200 years previously.

Calvinist/Calvinism: The doctrines and practices that arose out of the teachings of the French religious reformer John Calvin in the Protestant Churches that developed in England, Scotland, France, and the Netherlands. At the core of Calvinist thought were the doctrines of predestination and election, which declared all humans sinful and worthy of damnation, but some humans (the Elect) were chosen by God for salvation through the divine gift of grace freely given.

Catholic League: A union of French Catholics who opposed the extension of civil rights and religious freedom to French Huguenots (see below). In the 1570s, small local unions of Catholics formed a national organization under the leadership of the Guise family. The League opposed the rule of the Protestant king, Henri IV, continuing the civil war in alliance with Spain until the king converted to Catholicism in 1593.

Common Law: The body of English legal principles evolved since the twelfth century by judges from custom and precedent and administered, in Elizabethan times, in the main royal courts sitting at Westminster Hall near London. The chief courts of the common law were the Court of Queen's (King's) Bench, which dealt with matters affecting the Crown and criminal complaints; the Court of Common Pleas, which dealt with civil disputes between subjects on a variety of matters; and the Exchequer, which handled matters of royal finance.

Dissolution of the Monasteries: The dissolution and transfer to the Crown of the property held by over 800 English religious houses in the late 1530s. Supervised by Thomas Cromwell as deputy for Henry VIII, who had recently declared himself head of the English Church, the dissolution was undertaken to reform English monasticism and to increase royal revenue. In 1536, Parliament dissolved all houses with incomes under £200 per year, and, in 1539, another statute formally abolished all monasteries and religious houses. By Henry VIII's death in 1547, over half of the former monastic property had been sold or granted away, mainly to local gentlemen, Crown officers, and merchants and professional men seeking landed estates in the country.

Edinburgh, Treaty of (1560): An agreement that ended both French and English military intervention in Scotland and civil war between Scottish Protestants and Catholics for control of the regency government of Mary, Queen of Scots. The treaty broke the ancient Franco-Scottish alliance and laid the foundation for better Anglo-Scottish relations on the basis of a shared Protestantism.

Enclosure: An act of hedging or fencing land, whether arable, pasture, or waste, that had previously been common land open to the use of an entire village or parish community. Enclosers reserved the land for their own use and prevented all other residents of the community from exploiting the land or its resources. Because contemporary opinion perceived enclosure as widespread and harmful to local economies and social structures, the practice was highly controversial and frequently criticized.

Equity: The custom and practice of law that arose outside the English common law (see above) to remedy deficiencies and inequities in the common law. The chief courts of equity were the court of Chancery and the courts that arose in the late Middle Ages from the judicial function of the royal council, such as the Courts of Star Chamber and Requests.

First Folio (1623): The first collected edition of the plays of William Shakespeare, which appeared in 1623 under the editorial direction of Shakespeare's friends and fellow actors, John Heminges and Henry Condell. The First Folio contained 36 of Shakespeare's 37 plays, lacking only *Pericles, Prince of Tyre*. The First Folio was the first appearance in print and today is the sole authority for 18 of the plays, including *As You Like It*, *Julius Caesar*, *Macbeth*, and *Twelfth Night*.

Gentry: The Elizabethan social class comprising those landowners who lacked titles of nobility but exercised extensive, social, political, and economic influence in their localities. By the end of Elizabeth's reign in 1603, the gentry are estimated to have made up about 3 percent of the English population.

Huguenots: Members of the Protestant communities of sixteenth-century France. The movement spread rapidly throughout all French social classes, acquiring great political influence and generating strong opposition. From the 1560s to the 1590s, the Huguenots struggled to gain civil rights and religious freedom. Although their leadership was decimated by the St. Bartholomew's Day Massacre (see below) in 1572, Huguenots gained official toleration in 1598 when King Henri IV, a former Huguenot, issued the Edict of Nantes.

Humanism: An educational program based on the moral and intellectual value of studying the languages and literatures of ancient Greece and Rome. Humanism arose in Italy in the fourteenth century and reached the universities of England in the late fifteenth and early sixteenth centuries. Humanism often encouraged the impulse for religious reform, both within Catholic and Protestant contexts.

Inns of Court: Several inns in London that became residences for apprentices learning the common law (see above) that later were empowered to license practitioners of the law. This licensing system led to development at the Inns of Court of a formal educational system for preparing young men for a legal career. The four Inns of Court were Gray's Inn, Lincoln's Inn, the Inner Temple, and the Middle Temple.

Justices of the Peace (JPs): The principal administrative and judicial officials of local government in Elizabethan England. The JPs were local gentlemen with an annual income of at least £20 and some measure of political and social influence in their county. The JPs supervised local government, tried local criminal cases, and enforced in the county the directives of the Privy Council and the statutes of Parliament, in which many JPs sat.

Lutheran/Lutheranism: The doctrine and practices that arose out of the teachings of the German reformer Martin Luther in Germany, Scandinavia, and elsewhere. In England, the theological reformation begun under Henry VIII was initiated and advanced by reformers influenced by the ideas of Luther. Under Edward VI and Elizabeth I, Calvinism gradually superseded Lutheranism as the basis of English Protestantism.

Martin Marprelate Tracts: A series of seven pamphlets secretly printed and distributed between 1587 and 1589 that attacked the bishops of the Anglican Church. Published under the pseudonym "Martin Marprelate," the tracts aimed at thoroughly discrediting bishops and clergy who were opposing Puritan reforms in the Church. The tracts ridiculed the learning of the bishops, mocked their writing style, and taunted them with their inability to discover "Martin Marprelate." The writers and printers of the tracts were eventually found and arrested.

Nine Years War (1593–1602): The longest and costliest Irish uprising of Elizabeth's reign. Led by Hugh O'Neill, Earl of Tyrone, the rebellion saw the defeat of an English army at Yellow Ford in 1598; an unauthorized truce arranged between Tyrone and Robert Devereux, Earl of Essex, in 1599; and the landing in Ireland of Spanish troops to support the rebellion in 1601. The failure of the rebellion led to the exile of Tyrone and the extension of English rule throughout most of the island.

Pilgrimage of Grace (1536–1537): An armed uprising of the common people of northern England against the religious policies of Henry VIII, especially the dissolution of the monasteries (see above). For a time, the rebel army numbered almost 30,000 and controlled the city of York and most of Yorkshire. The Pilgrimage was eventually suppressed with great severity.

Privy Council: The select body of royal councilors, ministers, and advisors who served as the chief instrument of Elizabethan government. The Privy Council handled daily administration, acted as a judicial board for cases of various types, oversaw the defense of the realm, regulated trade, managed royal finance, and enforced religious statutes. Under Elizabeth, the Council never had more than 20 members, with most meetings attended by less than a dozen members.

Proclamation: A legislative order, administrative regulation, or formal policy announcement issued by the Crown without the consent of either Parliament or the Privy Council. Proclamations were inferior to parliamentary statutes, which could be neither modified nor contradicted by proclamation. Proclamations expired upon the death of the monarch who had issued them.

Puritans: Members of the Elizabethan Church who demanded further Protestant reform or purification of worship, more and better preaching, and stricter adherence to the dictates of Scripture. Although the term covered a variety of doctrines, attitudes, and positions, Puritans were united in their demand that the Anglican Church be purged of any ideas, doctrines, rituals, or other elements that they regarded as Catholic, superstitious, or unscriptural.

St. Bartholomew's Day Massacre: The murder of thousands of Huguenots (see above) in Paris and throughout France on August 24, 1572, the feast of St. Bartholomew. Fearing that the Huguenots might kidnap the king and murder the royal family, the French queen mother, Catherine de Medici, and her sons, King Charles IX and Henri, Duke of Anjou, approved the murders of the Huguenot leaders, who were then assembled in

Paris for a royal wedding. However, when these killings began, strongly Catholic Paris erupted in anti-Huguenot violence that led to the deaths of all Huguenots who could be caught by the mob.

Star Chamber: A formal court of equity that evolved in the sixteenth century from informal meetings of the royal council in the Star Chamber at Westminster to hear petitions made directly to the King. Star Chamber was separated from the council and formally constituted in 1540. Under Elizabeth I, Star Chamber narrowed its focus to misdemeanor criminal matters, such as assaults, riots, unlawful assemblies, perjury, corruption, and seditious libel.

Throckmorton Plot (1583): An English Catholic conspiracy to murder Elizabeth and replace her on the throne with Mary, Queen of Scots. Led by two young Catholic gentlemen, the brothers Francis and Thomas Throckmorton, the plot, which was thwarted by the government, led to the creation of the Bond of Association for the protection of the Queen.

Tithes: Traditional payments in kind made for the support of priests and clergy by the local parish community. Consisting of grain, eggs, fish, poultry, and other commodities in the Middle Ages, tithes by the Elizabethan period had usually been converted to a cash payment. After the Reformation, many of the new lay owners of former monastic properties kept a large portion of the tithe payment for themselves, thus forcing the clergyman to subsist on an inadequate stipend.

BIBLIOGRAPHY

PRINTED WORKS

Primary Sources and Contemporary Works

Allen, William. *An Admonition to the Nobility and People of England and Ireland Concerning the Present Warres made for the execution of his Holines Sentence by the highe and mightie Kinge Catholike of Spaine*. Antwerp, 1588.

Arber, Edward, ed. *English Reprints: John Lyly. Euphues. The Anatomy of Wit: Euphues and His England*. London: Alexander Murray and Son, 1868.

Archer, Elisabeth Jayne, Elizabeth Goldring, and Sarah Knight, eds. *The Progresses, Pageants, and Entertainments of Queen Elizabeth I*. Oxford: Oxford University Press, 2007.

Ascham, Roger. *The Scholemaster*. Edited by Edward Arber. Birmingham, 1870.

———. *The Scholemaster*. Edited by R.J. Schoeck. Don Mills, Ontario: Dent, 1966.

Bell, Robin, ed. *Bittersweet Within My Heart: The Love Poems of Mary, Queen of Scots*. San Francisco: Chronicle Books, 1992.

Birt, Henry Norbert. *The Elizabethan Religious Settlement: A Study of Contemporary Documents*. London: George Bell and Sons, 1907.

Blacker, Irwin R., ed. *The Portable Hakluyt's Voyages*. New York: Viking Press, 1965.

Bland, A.E., P.A. Brown, and R.H. Tawney, eds. *English Economic History: Select Documents*. New York: Macmillan Company, 1919.

Boswell-Stone, W.G. *Shakespeare's Holinshed: The Chronicle and the Historical Plays Compared*. London: Chatto and Windus, 1907.

Bruce, John, ed. *Letters of Queen Elizabeth and King James VI of Scotland*. London: Printed for the Camden Society by J.B. Nichols and Son, 1849.

Bullen, A.H., ed. *The Works of Thomas Middleton*. Vol. 4. Boston: Houghton, Mifflin and Company, 1885.

Camden, William. *The History of the Most Renowned and Victorious Princess Elizabeth Late Queen of England*. Edited by Wallace T. MacCaffrey. Chicago: University of Chicago Press, 1970.

Christie, Richard Copley, ed. *Letters of Sir Thomas Copley of Gatton, Surrey, and Roughey, Sussex, Knight and Baron in France, to Queen Elizabeth and Her Ministers*. Reprint ed. New York: Burt Franklin, 1970 (originally published 1897).

Collier, J. Payne, ed. *The Egerton Papers: A Collection of Public and Private Documents, Chiefly Illustrative of the Times of Elizabeth and James I, from the Original Manuscripts, the Property of the Right Hon. Lord Francis Egerton, M.P.* London: Printed for the Camden Society by John Bowyer Nichols and Son, 1840.

Crowley, Robert. *The Select Works of Robert Crowley.* Edited by J.M. Cowper. English Text Society, extra series, vol. 15. London: Trubner, 1872 (reprint ed. 1987).

D'Ewes, Sir Simonds. *The Journals of All the Parliaments during the Reign of Queen Elizabeth, both of the House of Lords and House of Commons.* London, 1682.

Duncan-Jones, Katherine, ed. *Shakespeare's Sonnets.* The Arden Shakespeare. London: Thomas Nelson and Sons Ltd., 1998.

Edwards, Philip, ed. *Last Voyages: Cavendish, Hudson, Ralegh, the Original Narratives.* Oxford: Clarendon Press, 1988.

The First and Second Prayer Books of Edward VI. New York: E.P. Dutton, 1949.

Foxe, John. *Fox's Book of Martyrs.* Edited by William Byron Forbush. Grand Rapids, MI: Zondervan, 1980.

Gerard, John. *The Autobiography of a Hunted Priest.* Translated from Latin by Philip Caraman. New York: Pellegrini and Cudahy, 1952.

Gosson, Stephen. *School of Abuse, Containing a Pleasant Invective Against Poets, Pipers, Players, Jesters, &.* Charleston, SC: BookSurge Publishing, 2001.

———. *The School of Abuse, 1579, and A Short Apologie of The School of Abuse 1579.* Edited by Edward Arber. London: Alex Murray and Son, 1868.

Greene, Robert. *The thirde and last part of Cony-catching. With the newly devised knauish Art of Foole-taking. The like Cosenages and Villenies neuer before discouered. A Dispvtation Betweene a Hee Cony-catcher and a Shee Cony-catcher.* Edited by G.B. Greville, Fulke, Baron Brooke. *Sir Fulke Greville's Life of Sir Philip Sidney.* Folcroft, PA: Folcroft Press, 1971.

Harrison. New York: E. P. Dutton and Co., 1923.

Halliday, F.E., ed. *Richard Carew of Antony: The Survey of Cornwall.* London: Andrew Melrose, 1953.

The Harleian Miscellany; or, a Collection of Scarce, Curious, and Entertaining Pamphlets and Tracts, as Well in Manuscript as in Print, Found in the Late Earl of Oxford's Library. Vol. II. London: Printed for Robert Dutton, 1809.

Harriot, Thomas. *A Brief and True Report of the New Found Land of Virginia.* Facsimile ed. Introduced by Randolph G. Adams. New York: History Book Club, 1951.

Harrison, William. *The Description of England: The Classic Contemporary Account of Tudor Social Life.* Edited by Georges Edelen. Washington, DC: Folger Shakespeare Library; New York: Dover Publications, 1994.

———. *Harrison's Description of England in Shakspere's Youth.* Edited by Frederick Furnivall. London: Published for The New Shakspere Society by N. Trübner and Co., 1877.

Hartley, T.E., ed. *Proceedings in the Parliaments of Elizabeth I. Volume I: 1558–1581.* Leicester: University of Leicester Press, 1981.

Hayward, Sir John. *Annals of the First Four Years of the Reign of Queen Elizabeth.* Edited by John Bruce. London: Printed for the Camden Society by John Bowyer Nichols and Son, 1840.

Hooker, John. "Life of Sir Peter Carew." In John Maclean, ed. *The Life and Times of Sir Peter Carew, Kt.* London: Bell and Daldy, 1857.

Hooker, Richard. "Of the Laws of Ecclesiastical Polity." In *The Works of Mr. Richard Hooker with an Account of His Life and Death by Isaac Walton.* 2 vols. Oxford: Clarendon Press, 1890.

———. *Of the Laws of Ecclesiastical Polity.* Edited by A.S. McGrade. Cambridge: Cambridge University Press, 1989.

Hurstfield, Joel, and Alan G.R. Smith, eds. *Elizabethan People: State and Society.* London: Edward Arnold, 1972.

Jones, Emrys, ed. *The New Oxford Book of Sixteenth Century Verse.* Oxford: Oxford University Press, 1992.

Kempe, William. *Kemps Nine Daies Wonder: Performed in a Daunce from London to Norwich.* Edited by Alexander Dyce. London: Printed for the Camden Society by John Bowyer Nichols, 1840.

Kinney, Arthur F., ed. *Elizabethan Backgrounds: Historical Documents of the Age of Elizabeth I.* Hamden, CT: Archon Books, 1990.

———. *Rogues, Vagabonds, and Sturdy Beggars: A New Gallery of Tudor and Early Stuart Literature.* Amherst: University of Massachusetts Press, 1990.

Knox, Thomas Francis, ed. *The Letters and Memorials of William Cardinal Allen.* London: David Nutt, 1882.

Lambert, D.H., ed. Cartae *Shakespeareanae: Shakespeare Documents; A Chronological Catalogue of Extant Evidence Relating to the Life and Works of William Shakespeare.* London: George Bell and Sons, 1904.

Looney, J. Thomas. *"Shakespeare" Identified in Edward de Vere the Seventeenth Earl of Oxford.* New York: Frederick A. Stokes Company, Publishers, 1920.

Love Poems and Sonnets of William Shakespeare. New York: Doubleday, 1957.

Lyly, John. *The Complete Works of John Lyly.* Edited by R. Warwick Bond. Reprint ed. Whitefish, MT: Kessinger Publishing, 2006.

———. *"Euphues: The Anatomy of Wit" and "Euphues and His England": An Annotated, Modern-Spelling Edition.* Edited by Leah Scragg. Manchester: Manchester University Press, 2002.

Magnus, Laurie, ed. *Documents Illustrating Elizabethan Poetry.* London: George Routledge and Sons Ltd., 1906.

Marcus, Leah S., Janel Mueller, and Mary Beth Rose, eds. *Elizabeth I: Collected Works.* Chicago: University of Chicago Press, 2000.

May, Steven W. ed. *Queen Elizabeth I: Selected Works.* New York: Washington Square Press, 2004.

McCollum, John I., ed. *The Age of Elizabeth: Selected Source Materials in Elizabethan Social and Literary History.* Boston: Houghton Mifflin, 1960.

Meads, Chris, ed. *Elizabethan Humour.* London: Robert Hale, 1995.

Nichols, John, ed. *The Progresses and Public Processions of Queen Elizabeth.* 2 vols. London: Printed by and for John Nichols and Son, 1823.

Prothero, G.W., ed. *Select Statutes and Other Constitutional Documents Illustrative of the Reigns of Elizabeth and James I.* Oxford: Clarendon Press, 1894.

Raleigh, Walter Alexander, Sidney Lee, and C.T. Onions, eds. *Shakespeare's England: An Account of the Life and Manners of His Age.* 2 vols. Oxford: Clarendon Press, 1917.

Rice, George, P., Jr., ed. *The Public Speaking of Queen Elizabeth: Selections from Her Official Addresses.* New York: Columbia University Press, 1951.

Rolfe, William J., ed. *Shakespeare's Sonnets.* New York: Harper and Brothers, Publishers, 1891.

Sidney, Sir Philip. "An Apology for Poetry." In Laurie Magnus, ed. *Documents Illustrating Elizabethan Poetry.* London: George Routledge and Sons Ltd., 1906.

———. *An Apology for Poetry.* Edited by Forrest G. Robinson. New York: Macmillan, 1970.

————. *Sir Philip Sidney: The Major Works*. Edited by Katherine Duncan-Jones. Oxford World's Classics. Oxford: Oxford University Press, 2002.

————. *Sir Philip Sidney's Apology for Poetry and Astrophil and Stella: Texts and Contexts*. Edited by Philip C. Herman. Glen Allen, VA: College Publishing, 2001.

Smith, Sir Thomas. *De Republica Anglorum: A Discourse on the Commonwealth of England*. Edited by L. Alston. Cambridge: Cambridge University Press, 1906.

Snow, Vernon F., ed. *Parliament in Elizabethan England: John Hooker's Order and Usage*. New Haven, CT: Yale University Press, 1977.

Speed, John. *The Counties of Britain: A Tudor Atlas*. Introduction by Nigel Nicolson. County Commentaries by Alasdair Hawkyard. New York: Thames and Hudson, 1989.

Spenser, Edmund. *Edmund Spencer's Poetry*. Edited by Hugh Maclean and Anne Lake Prescott. Norton Critical Editions. New York: W.W. Norton and Company, 1993.

————. *The Faerie Queene*. Edited by Thomas P. Roche and C. Patrick O'Donnell. New York: Penguin Classics, 1979.

Stow, John. *A Survey of London Written in the Year 1598*. London: J.M. Dent and Sons, 1997.

Strickland, Agnes, ed. *Letters of Mary, Queen of Scots*. Vol. II. London: Henry Colburn, 1848.

Tarbox, Increase N., ed. *Sir Walter Ralegh and His Colony in America*. Boston: Printed for the Prince Society by John Wilson and Son, 1884.

Taylor, Gary, and John Lavagnino, eds. *Thomas Middleton: The Collected Works*. Oxford: Oxford University Press, 2008.

Tyler, Thomas, ed. *Shakespeare's Sonnets*. London: David Nutt, 1890.

Vere, Edward de. *The Poems of Edward de Vere*. Chapel Hill: University of North Carolina Press, 1981.

Warren, Kate M., ed. *The Faerie Queene: By Edmund Spenser*. Book IV. Westminster: Archibald Constable and Company, 1899.

Wells, Stanley, Gary Taylor, John Jowett, and William Montgomery, eds. *William Shakespeare: The Complete Works*. Oxford: Clarendon Press, 1988.

Wilson, Thomas. "The State of England, anno dom. 1600." Edited by F.J. Fisher. *Camden Miscellany* xvi. Camden, third series. London: Royal Historical Society, 1936.

Wright, Thomas, ed. *Queen Elizabeth and Her Times: A Series of Original Letters Selected from the Unedited Private Correspondence of the Lord Treasurer Burghley, the Earl of Leicester, the Secretaries Walsingham and Smith, Sir Christopher Hatton, and Most of the Distinguished Persons of the Period*. 2 vols. London: Henry Colburn, Publisher, 1838.

Youngs, Frederic A., Jr. *The Proclamations of the Tudor Queens*. Cambridge: Cambridge University Press, 1976.

General Works and Reference Works

Auchter, Dorothy. *Dictionary of Literary and Dramatic Censorship in Tudor and Stuart England*. Westport, CT: Greenwood Press, 2001.

Black, J.B. *The Reign of Elizabeth 1558–1603*. 2nd ed. Oxford: Oxford University Press, 1994.

Boyce, Charles. *Shakespeare A to Z*. New York: Dell Publishing, 1990.

Elton, G.R. *England Under the Tudors*. 3rd ed. London: Routledge, 1991.

Fritze, Ronald H., ed. *Historical Dictionary of Tudor England, 1485–1603*. Westport, CT: Greenwood Press, 1991.

Haigh, Christopher, ed. *The Reign of Elizabeth I*. Athens: University of Georgia Press, 1987.

Hurstfield, Joel. *Elizabeth I and the Unity of England*. London: The English Universities Press, 1960.

MacCaffrey, Wallace. *Elizabeth I: War and Politics 1588–1603*. Princeton, NJ: Princeton University Press, 1992.

———. *Queen Elizabeth and the Making of Policy, 1572–1588*. Princeton, NJ: Princeton University Press, 1981.

———. *The Shaping of the Elizabethan Regime: Elizabethan Politics 1558–1572*. Princeton, NJ: Princeton University Press, 1968.

O'Day, Rosemary. *The Longman Companion to the Tudor Age*. London: Longman, 1995.

Olsen, Kirstin. *All Things Shakespeare: An Encyclopedia of Shakespeare's World*. 2 vols. Westport, CT: Greenwood Press, 2002.

Palliser, D.M. *The Age of Elizabeth: England Under the Later Tudors, 1547–1603*. 2nd ed. London: Longman, 1992.

Palmer, Alan, and Veronica Palmer. *Who's Who in Shakespeare's England*. New York: St. Martin's Press, 1981.

Rosenblum, Joseph. *The Greenwood Companion to Shakespeare: A Comprehensive Guide for Students*. 4 vols. Westport, CT: Greenwood Press, 2005.

Routh, C.R.N. *Who's Who in Tudor England*. Chicago: St. James Press, 1990.

Smith, Lacey Baldwin. *The Elizabethan World*. Boston: Houghton Mifflin, 1991.

Wagner, John A. *Bosworth Field to Bloody Mary: An Encyclopedia of the Early Tudors*. Westport, CT: Greenwood Press, 2003.

———. *Encyclopedia of the Wars of the Roses*. Santa Barbara, CA: ABC-Clio, 2001.

———. *Historical Dictionary of the Elizabethan World: Britain, Ireland, Europe, and America*. Phoenix: Oryx Press, 1999.

Williams, Penry. *The Later Tudors: England 1547–1603*. Oxford: Oxford University Press, 1995.

Youings, Joyce. *Sixteenth-Century England*. New York: Penguin Books, 1984.

Politics and the Court

Doran, Susan. *Monarchy and Matrimony: The Courtships of Elizabeth I*. London: Routledge, 1996.

Guy, John. *The Tudor Monarchy*. Oxford: Oxford University Press, 1997.

Hopkins, Lisa. *Elizabeth I and Her Court*. New York: St. Martin's Press, 1990.

Jones, Norman. *The Birth of the Elizabethan Age: England in the 1560s*. Oxford: Basil Blackwell, 1993.

Levin, Carole. *The Heart and Stomach of a King: Elizabeth I and the Politics of Sex and Power*. Philadelphia: University of Pennsylvania Press, 1994.

Levine, Mortimer. *The Early Elizabethan Succession Question 1558–1568*. Stanford, CA: Stanford University Press, 1966.

Pulman, Michael B. *The Elizabethan Privy Council in the Fifteen Seventies*. Berkeley: University of California Press, 1971.

Read, Conyers. *Lord Burghley and Queen Elizabeth*. New York: Alfred A. Knopf, 1960.

———. *Mr. Secretary Cecil and Queen Elizabeth*. London: Jonathan Cape, 1965.

Smith, A.G.R. *The Babington Plot*. London: Macmillan, 1936.

———. *The Government of Elizabethan England*. New York: W.W. Norton, 1967.

Somerset, Anne. *Ladies-in-Waiting*. New York: Alfred A. Knopf, 1984.

Williams, Neville. *All the Queen's Men: Elizabeth I and Her Courtiers*. New York: Macmillan, 1972.

Economic and Social History

Abbott, Mary. *Life Cycles in England, 1560–1720: Cradle to Grave*. London: Routledge, 1996.

Amussen, Susan D. *An Ordered Society: Gender and Class in Early Modern England, 1560–1725*. Oxford: Basil Blackwell, 1988.

Appleby, Andrew B. *Famine in Tudor and Stuart England*. Stanford, CA: Stanford University Press, 1978.

Archer, Ian W. *The Pursuit of Stability: Social Relations in Elizabethan London*. Cambridge: Cambridge University Press, 1991.

Beier, A.L. *Masterless Men: The Vagrancy Problem in England 1560–1640*. New York: Metheun, 1985.

———. *The Problem of the Poor in Tudor and Stuart England*. London: Routledge, 1983.

Beier, A.L., and Roger Finaly, eds. *London 1500–1700: The Making of the Metropolis*. London: Longman, 1986.

Bisson, Douglas R. *The Merchant Adventurers of England*. Newark: University of Delaware Press, 1993.

Bowden, Peter J., ed. *Chapters from the Agrarian History of England and Wales. Volume 1: Economic Change: Prices, Wages, Profits and Rents, 1500–1750*. Cambridge: Cambridge University Press, 1990.

———. *The Wool Trade in Tudor and Stuart England*. New York: St. Martin's Press, 1962.

Brown, Henry Phelps, and Shiela V. Hopkins. *A Perspective of Wages and Prices*. London: Methuen, 1981.

Cahn, Susan. *Industry of Devotion: The Transformation of Women's Work in England 1500–1660*. New York: Columbia University Press, 1987.

Camden, Carroll. *The Elizabethan Woman*. Rev. ed. Mamaroneck, NY: P.P. Appel, 1975.

Cantor, Leonard. *The Changing English Countryside, 1400–1700*. London: Routledge & Kegan Paul, 1987.

Charlton, Kenneth. *Education in Renaissance England*. London: Routledge & Kegan Paul, 1965.

Cioni, Maria L. *Women and Law in Elizabethan England*. New York: Garland, 1985.

Clarkson, Leslie A. *Death, Disease, and Famine in Pre-Industrial England*. New York: St. Martin's Press, 1976.

Clay, C.G.A. *Economic Expansion and Social Change: England 1500–1700. Vol. 1: People, Land and Towns*. New York: Cambridge University Press, 1984.

Coleman, D.C. *The Economy of England 1450–1750*. Oxford: Oxford University Press, 1977.

———. *Industry in Tudor and Stuart England*. London: Macmillan, 1975.

Cressy, David. *Birth, Marriage and Death*. Oxford: Oxford University Press, 1997.

———. *Bonfires and Bells: National Memory and the Protestant Calendar in Elizabethan and Stuart England*. London: Weidenfeld and Nicolson, 1989.

———. *Education in Tudor and Stuart England*. New York: St. Martin's Press, 1976.

Dietz, F.C. *English Public Finance, 1485–1641*. 2nd ed. London: F. Cass, 1964.

Dovey, Zillah. *An Elizabethan Progress*. Herndon, VA: Sutton Publishers, 1996.

Emerson, Kathy Lynn. *Wives and Daughters: The Women of Sixteenth Century England*. Troy, NY: Whitston Publishing Co., 1984.

Emmison, F.G. *Elizabethan Life: Home, Work and Land*. Chelmsford, England: Essex County Council, 1976.

———. *Elizabethan Life: Morals and the Church Courts*. Chelmsford, England: Essex County Council, 1973.

Fisher, F.J. *London and the English Economy 1500–1700*. London: Hambledon Press, 1990.

Fletcher, Anthony. *Gender, Sex, and Subordination in England 1500–1800*. New Haven, CT: Yale University Press, 1995.

Foster, Frank F. *The Politics of Stability: A Portrait of the Rulers in Elizabethan London*. London: Royal Historical Society, 1977.

Fox, Harold G. *Monopolies and Patents*. Toronto: University of Toronto Press, 1947.

Greaves, Richard L. *Society and Religion in Elizabethan England*. Minneapolis: University of Minnesota Press, 1981.

Haynes, Alan. *Sex in Elizabethan England*. Stroud, England: Sutton, 1997.

Heal, Felicity. *Hospitality in Early Modern England*. Oxford: Oxford University Press, 1990.

Heal, Felicity, and Clive Holmes. *The Gentry in England and Wales 1500–1700*. Stanford, CA: Stanford University Press, 1994.

Hogrefe, Pearl. *Tudor Women*. Ames: Iowa State University Press, 1975.

Holmes, Martin. *Elizabethan London*. New York: Frederick A. Praeger, 1969.

Hurstfield, Joel. *The Queen's Wards: Wardship and Marriage under Elizabeth I*. 2nd ed. London: Frank Cass, 1973.

Hurstfield, Joel, and A.G.R Smith. *Elizabethan People: State and Society*. New York: St. Martin's Press, 1972.

Hutton, Ronald. *The Rise and Fall of Merry England: The Ritual Year 1400–1700*. Oxford: Oxford University Press, 1994.

Jack, Sybil M. *Towns in Tudor and Stuart Britain*. London: Macmillan, 1996.

———. *Trade and Industry in Tudor and Stuart England*. London: George Allen and Unwin, 1977.

Jardine, Lisa. *Still Harping on Daughters: Women and Drama in the Age of Shakespeare*. Totowa, NJ: Barnes and Noble, 1983.

Kerridge, Eric. *Agrarian Problems in the Sixteenth Century and After*. Reprint ed. London: Routledge, 2006.

Laslett, Peter. *The World We Have Lost: England Before the Industrial Age*. 2nd ed. New York: Scribner, 1971.

———. *The World We Have Lost: Further Explored*. 3rd ed. New York: Scribner, 1984.

Macfarlane, A.D.J. *Witchcraft in Tudor and Stuart England*. New York: Harper and Row, 1970.

Macfarlane, Alan. *Marriage and Love in England 1300–1840*. Oxford: Blackwell, 1986.

McRae, Andrew. *God Speed the Plough: The Representation of Agrarian England, 1500–1660*. Cambridge: Cambridge University Press, 2002.

Mendelson, Sara, and Patricia Crawford. *Women in Early Modern England 1550–1720*. Oxford: Oxford University Press, 2000.

Osborne, Jane. *Entertaining Elizabeth: The Progresses and Great Houses of Her Time*. London: Bishopsgate Press, 1989.

Outhwaite, R.B. *Inflation in Tudor and Early Stuart England*. 2nd ed. London: Palgrave Macmillan, 1982.

Patten, John. *English Towns 1500–1700*. Hamden, CT: Archon Books, 1978.

Porter, Roy. *London: A Social History*. Cambridge, MA: Harvard University Press, 1994.

Pound, John. *Poverty and Vagrancy in Tudor England*. London: Longman, 1971.

Prior, Mary, ed. *Women in English Society, 1500–1800*. New York: Methuen, 1985.

Ramsay, G.D. *The English Wollen Industry, 1500–1750*. London: Macmillan, 1982.

Rowse, A.L. *The Elizabethan Renaissance*. New York: Scribner, 1971, 1972.

———. *Eminent Elizabethans*. Athens: University of Georgia Press, 1983.

———. *The England of Elizabeth: The Structure of Society*. Madison: University of Wisconsin Press, 1978.

St. Clare Byrne, Muriel. *Elizabethan Life in Town and Country.* 7th ed. Gloucester, England: Alan Sutton, 1987.

Salgado, Gamini. *The Elizabethan Underworld.* Stroud, England: Alan Sutton Publishing, 1992.

Sharpe, J.A. *Early Modern England: A Social History, 1550–1760.* 2nd ed. Oxford: Oxford University Press, 1997.

———. *Instruments of Darkness: Witchcraft in England 1550–1750.* New York: Penguin, 1996.

Simon, Joan. *Education and Society in Tudor Englan*d. Cambridge: Cambridge University Press, 1966.

Singman, Jeffrey L. *Daily Life in Elizabethan England.* Westport, CT: Greenwood Press, 1995.

Slack, Paul. *The English Poor Law, 1531–1782.* Cambridge: Cambridge University Press, 1995.

———. *The Impact of Plague in Tudor and Stuart England.* Oxford: Clarendon Press, 1985.

———. *Poverty and Policy in Tudor and Stuart England.* London: Longman, 1988.

Spring, Eileen. *Law, Land, and Family: Aristocratic Inheritance in England, 1300 to 1800.* Chapel Hill: University of North Carolina Press, 1997.

Stone, Lawrence. *The Crisis of the Aristocracy 1558–1641.* Abridged ed. Oxford: Oxford University Press, 1967.

———. *The Family, Sex and Marriage: In England 1500–1800.* New York: Harper & Row, 1977.

———. *Social Change and Revolution in England 1540–1640.* London: Longman, 1965.

Tawney, R.H. *The Agrarian Problem in the Sixteenth Century.* New York: Harper and Row, 1967.

Warnicke, Retha M. *Women of the English Renaissance and Reformation.* Westport, CT: Greenwood Press, 1983.

Willis, Deborah. *Malevolent Nurture: Witch-Hunting and Maternal Power in Early Modern England.* Ithaca, NY: Cornell University Press, 1995.

Intellectual and Cultural History

Adams, John Cranford. *The Globe Playhouse: Its Design and Equipment.* 2nd ed. New York: Barnes and Noble, 1961.

Astington, John H., ed. *The Development of Shakespeare's Theater.* New York: AMS Press, 1992.

Barker, Deborah E., and Ivo Kamps, eds. *Shakespeare and Gender: A History.* New York: Verso, 1995.

Bates, Catherine. *The Rhetoric of Courtship in Elizabethan Language and Literature.* Cambridge: Cambridge University Press, 1992.

Bates, Jonathon. *The Genius of Shakespeare.* London: Picador, 1997.

Beckerman, Bernard. *Shakespeare at the Globe, 1599–1609.* New York: Macmillan, 1962.

Berry, Herbert. *Shakespeare's Playhouses.* New York: AMS, 1987.

Berry, Philippa. *Of Chastity and Power: Elizabethan Literature and the Unmarried Queen.* London: Routledge, 1989.

Bevington, David, ed. *The Complete Works of Shakespeare.* 5th ed. New York: Longman, 2003.

Blagden, Cyprian. *The Stationers' Company: A History.* Cambridge, MA: Harvard University Press, 1960.

Blake, N.F. *Shakespeare's Language: An Introduction*. New York: St. Martin's Press, 1983.

Booth, Stephen, ed. *Shakespeare's Sonnets*. New Haven, CT: Yale University Press, 2000.

Carroll, William C. *The Matamorphoses of Shakespearean Comedy*. Princeton, NJ: Princeton University Press, 1985.

Chambers, E.K. *The Elizabethan Stage*. 4 vols. Oxford: Clarendon Press, 1923.

Clare, Janet. *"Art Made Tongue-Tied by Authority": Elizabethan and Jacobean Dramatic Censorship*. New York: St. Martin's Press, 1990.

Clegg, Cyndia Susan. *Press Censorship in Elizabethan England*. Cambridge: Cambridge University Press, 1997.

Dutton, Richard. *Mastering the Revels: The Regulation and Censorship of English Renaissance Drama*. Iowa City: University of Iowa Press, 1991.

Eastman, Arthur M. *A Short History of Shakespearean Criticism*. New York: Random, 1968.

Evans, G. Blakemore, ed. *The Riverside Shakespeare*. Boston: Houghton Mifflin, 1974.

Evans, Joan. *A History of the Society of Antiquaries*. Oxford: Society of Antiquaries, 1956.

Feather, John. *A History of British Publishing*. New York: Croom Helm, 1988.

Felperin, Howard. *Shakespearean Romance*. Princeton, NJ: Princeton University Press, 1972.

Fineberg, Nona. *Elizabeth, Her Poets, and the Creation of the Courtly Manner: A Study of Sir John Harington, Sir Philip Sydney, and John Lyly*. New York: Garland, 1988.

Fisher, John H. *The Emergence of Standard English*. Lexington: University of Kentucky Press, 1996.

Frye, Northrop. *Fools of Time: Studies in Shakespearean Tragedy*. Toronto: Toronto University Press, 1967.

Gassner, John, and William Green, eds. *Elizabethan Drama*. New York: Bantam Books, 1967.

Gerrard, Ernest A. *Elizabethan Drama and Dramatists: 1583–1603*. New York: Cooper Square Publishers, 1972.

Girouard, Mark. *Robert Smythson and the Architecture of the Elizabethan Era*. South Brunswick, NJ: Barnes, 1967.

———. *Robert Smythson and the Elizabethan Country House*. New Haven, CT: Yale University Press, 1983.

Goldman, Michael. *Shakespeare and the Energies of Drama*. Princeton, NJ: Princeton University Press, 1972.

Greenblatt, Stephen. *Shakespearean Negotiations*. Berkeley: University of California Press, 1988.

Gurr, Andrew. *The Shakespearean Stage 1524–1642*. 2nd ed. Cambridge: Cambridge University Press, 1980.

Harrison, G.B. *Elizabethan Plays and Players*. Ann Arbor: University of Michigan Press, 1956.

Heinemann, Margot. *Puritanism and Theatre: Thomas Middleton and Opposition Drama Under the Early Stuarts*. Cambridge: Cambridge University Press, 1982.

Helgerson, Richard. *Forms of Nationhood: The Elizabethan Writing of England*. Chicago: University of Chicago Press, 1992.

Hosley, Richard, ed. *Shakespeare's Holinshed: An Edition of Holinshed's Chronicles*. New York: Putnam, 1968.

Hotson, Leslie. *Shakespeare's Wooden O*. London: Hart-Davis, 1959.

Houston, John Porter. *Shakespearean Sentences: A Study in Style and Syntax*. Baton Rouge: Louisiana State University Press, 1988.

Inglis, Fred. *The Elizabethan Poets: The Making of English Poetry from Wyatt to Ben Jonson*. London: Evans Brothers, 1969.

Ingram, William. *The Business of Playing: The Beginnings of Adult Professional Theater in Elizabethan London*. Ithaca, NY: Cornell University Press, 1992.

Jorgens, Jack. *Shakespeare on Film*. Bloomington: Indiana University Press, 1977.

Kastan, David Scott, ed. *A Companion to Shakespeare*. Oxford: Blackwell, 1999.

Kelley, Donald R. *Renaissance Humanism*. Boston: Twayne Publishers, 1991.

Kermode, Frank. *Shakespeare's Language*. New York: Farrar Straus Giroux, 2000.

Knutson, Roslyn L. *The Repertory of Shakespeare's Company, 1594–1613*. Fayetteville: University of Arkansas Press, 1991.

Lenz, Carolyn, ed. *The Woman's Part: Feminist Criticism of Shakespeare*. Urbana: University of Illinois Press, 1980.

Lever, J.W. *The Elizabethan Love Sonnet*. London: Methuen, 1978.

Mack, Maynard. *Everybody's Shakespeare*. Lincoln: University of Nebraska Press, 1993.

McCoy, Richard C. *The Rites of Knighthood: The Literature and Politics of Elizabethan Chivalry*. Berkeley: University of California Press, 1989.

McCrum, Robert, William Cran, and Robert MacNeil. *The Story of English*. Rev. ed. Boston: Faber and Faber, 1992.

Mercer, Eric. *English Art 1553–1625*. Oxford: Clarendon Press, 1962.

Muir, Kenneth. *The Sources of Shakespeare's Plays*. London: Methuen, 1977.

Norwich, John Julius. *Shakespeare's Kings: The Great Plays and the History of England in the Middle Ages, 1337–1485*. New York: Scribner, 2001.

Orrell, John. *The Quest for Shakespeare's Globe*. New York: Cambridge University Press, 1983.

Patterson, Annabel. *Reading Holinshed's Chronicles*. Chicago: University of Chicago Press, 1994.

———. *Shakespeare and the Popular Voice*. Oxford: Blackwell, 1989.

Pomeroy, Elizabeth W. *Reading the Portraits of Queen Elizabeth I*. Hamden, CT: Archon Books, 1989.

Prior, Moody E. *The Drama of Power: Studies in Shakespeare's History Plays*. Evanston, IL: Northwestern University Press, 1973.

Rossiter, A.P. *English Drama from Early Times to the Elizabethans: Its Background, Origins, and Development*. Folcroft, PA: Folcroft Library Editions, 1977.

Rostenberg, Leona. The *Minority Press and the English Crown: A Study in Repression, 1558–1625*. Nieuwkoop, Netherlands: B. De Graaf, 1971.

Smith, Irwin. *Shakespeare's First Playhouse*. Dublin: Liffey Press, 1981.

Snyder, Susan. *The Comic Matrix of Shakespeare's Tragedies*. Princeton, NJ: Princeton University Press, 1979.

Strong, Roy. *The Cult of Elizabeth: Elizabethan Portraiture and Pageantry*. London: Thames and Hudson, 1977.

———. *Gloriana: The Portraits of Queen Elizabeth I*. London: Thames and Hudson, 1987.

Styan, J.L. *Shakespeare's Stagecraft*. Cambridge: Cambridge University Press, 1967.

Thomson, Peter. *Shakespeare's Theatre*. 2nd ed. London: Routledge, 1992.

Tillyard, E.M.W. *The Elizabethan World Picture*. New York: Vintage, 1967.

Wells, Stanley, ed. *The Cambridge Companion to Shakespeare Studies*. Cambridge: Cambridge University Press, 1986.

Wilson, Jean. *Entertainments for Elizabeth I*. Totowa, NJ: Rowman and Littlefield, 1980.

Wulstan, David. *Tudor Music*. Iowa City: University of Iowa Press, 1986.

Parliamentary, Administrative, and Legal History

Dean, D.M., and Norman L. Jones, eds. *The Parliaments of Elizabethan England*. Oxford: Basil Blackwell, 1990.

Elton, G.R. *The Parliament of England 1559–1581*. Cambridge: Cambridge University Press, 1986.

Gleason, John H. *The Justices of the Peace in England, 1558–1640*. Oxford: Clarendon Press, 1969.

Graves, Michael A.R. *Elizabethan Parliaments, 1559–1601*. 2nd ed. London: Longman, 1996.

Guy, John. *The Court of Star Chamber and Its Records to the Reign of Elizabeth I*. London: HMSO, 1985.

Hartley, T.E. *Elizabeth's Parliaments: Queen, Lords and Commons 1559–1601*. New York: St. Martin's Press, 1992.

Hurstfield, Joel. *Freedom, Corruption and Government in Elizabethan England*. London: Jonathan Cape, 1973.

Jones, W.J. *The Elizabethan Court of Chancery*. Oxford: Clarendon Press, 1967.

Neale, J.E. *Elizabeth I and Her Parliaments 1559–1581*. New York: St. Martin's Press, 1958.

———. *Elizabeth I and Her Parliaments 1584–1601*. New York: St. Martin's Press, 1958.

———. *The Elizabethan House of Commons*. Rev. ed. Harmondsworth, England: Penguin Books, 1963.

Prest, Wilfrid R. *The Inns of Court under Elizabeth I and the Early Stuarts, 1590–1640*. London: Longman, 1972.

Smith, A.G.R. *The Government of Elizabethan England*. New York: W.W. Norton, 1967.

Snow, Vernon F. *Parliament in Elizabethan England: John Hooker's Order and Usage*. New Haven, CT: Yale University Press, 1977.

Religious History

Acheson, R.J. *Radical Puritans in England, 1550–1660*. London: Longman, 1990.

Adair, John. *Puritans: Religion and Politics in Seventeenth-Century England and America*. Gloucester, England: Sutton Publishing, 1998.

Basset, Bernard. *The English Jesuits from Campion to Martindale*. New York: Burns and Oates, 1968.

Bloomfield, Edward H. *The Opposition to the English Separatists, 1570–1625*. Washington, DC: University Press of America, 1981.

Bossy, John. *The English Catholic Community 1570–1850*. New York: Oxford University Press, 1976.

Brachlow, Stephen. *The Communion of Saints*. New York: Oxford University Press, 1988.

Collinson, Patrick. *The Elizabethan Puritan Movement*. Oxford: Clarendon Press, 1990.

———. *The Religion of Protestants: The Church in English Society 1559–1625*. Oxford: Clarendon Press, 1982.

Cross, Claire. *The Elizabethan Religious Settlement*. Bangor, ME: Headstart History, 1992.

———. *The Royal Supremacy in the Elizabethan Church*. New York: Barnes and Noble, 1969.

Dickens, A.G. *The English Reformation*. 2nd ed. University Park: Pennsylvania State University Press, 1989.

Garrett, Christina. *The Marian Exiles*. Cambridge: Cambridge University Press, 1966.

Haller, William. *The Elect Nation: The Meaning and Relevance of Foxe's Book of Martyrs*. New York: Harper & Row, 1963.

———. *Elizabeth I and the Puritans*. Ithaca, NY: Cornell University Press, 1964.

———. *The Rise of Puritanism*. New York: Harper and Brothers, 1957.

Haugaard, William P. *Elizabeth and the English Reformation: The Struggle for a Stable Settlement of Religion*. Cambridge: Cambridge University Press, 1968.

Holmes, Peter. *Resistance and Compromise: The Political Thought of Elizabethan Catholics.* Cambridge: Cambridge University Press, 1982.

Houliston, Victor. *Catholic Resistance in Elizabethan England: Robert Person's Jesuit Polemic, 1580–1610.* Farnham, Surrey: Ashgate, 2007.

Hudson, Winthrop S. *The Cambridge Connection and the Elizabethan Settlement of 1559.* Durham, NC: Duke University Press, 1980.

Jones, Norman L. *Faith by Statute: Parliament and the Settlement of Religion 1559.* London: Royal Historical Society, 1982.

Knappen, M.M. *Tudor Puritanism: A Chapter in the History of Idealism.* Chicago: University of Chicago Press, 1966.

Lake, Peter. *Anglicans and Puritans.* Boston: Allen & Unwin, 1988.

———. *Moderate Puritans and the Elizabethan Church.* Cambridge: Cambridge University Press, 1982.

Lunn, David. *The Catholic Elizabethans.* Bath, England: Downside Abbey, 1998.

McGrath, Patrick. *Papists and Puritans Under Elizabeth I.* New York: Walker and Company, 1967.

McNeill, John Thomas. *The History and Character of Calvinism.* New York: Oxford University Press, 1954.

Meyer, A.O. *England and the Catholic Church under Elizabeth.* Translated by J.R. McKee. New York: Barnes and Noble, 1967.

Morey, Adrian. *The Catholic Subjects of Elizabeth I.* Totowa, NJ: Rowman and Littlefield, 1978.

Parker, T.H.L. *Calvin: An Introduction to His Thought.* London: Geoffrey Chapman, 1995.

Primus, John Henry. *The Vestments Controversy.* Kampen, Netherlands: J.H. Kok, 1960.

Pritchard, Arnold. *Catholic Loyalism in Elizabethan England.* Chapel Hill: University of North Carolina Press, 1979.

Reynolds, E.E. *Campion and Parsons: The Jesuit Mission of 1580–1.* London: Sheed and Ward, 1980.

Seaver, Paul S. *The Puritan Lectureships.* Stanford, CA: Stanford University Press, 1970.

Simpson, Alan. *Puritanism in Old and New England.* Chicago: University of Chicago Press, 1972.

Tittler, Robert. *The Reformation and the Towns in England: Politics and Political Culture, 1540–1640.* Oxford: Clarendon Press, 1998.

Trimble, W.R. *The Catholic Laity in Elizabethan England, 1558–1603.* Cambridge, MA: Harvard University Press, 1964.

Walsham, Alexandra. *Church Papists: Catholicism, Conformity and Confessional Polemic in Early Modern England.* Rochester, NY: Boydell Press, 1993.

Watt, Tessa. *Cheap Print and Popular Piety 1550–1640.* Cambridge: Cambridge University Press, 1991.

White, B.R. *The English Separatist Tradition.* London: Oxford University Press, 1971.

Military History, Foreign Policy, and Europe

Andrews, K.R. *Elizabethan Privateering: English Privateering During the Spanish War 1585–1603.* Cambridge: Cambridge University Press, 1964.

Baumgartner, Frederic J. *France in the Sixteenth Century.* New York: St. Martin's Press, 1995.

Boynton, Lindsay. *The Elizabethan Militia, 1558–1638.* London: Routledge and Kegan Paul, 1967.

Briggs, Robin. *Early Modern France, 1560–1715.* 2nd ed. Oxford: Oxford University Press, 1998.

Crowson, P.S. *Tudor Foreign Policy.* New York: St. Martin's Press, 1973.

Cruickshank, C.G. *Elizabeth's Army.* 2nd ed. Oxford: Clarendon Press, 1966.

Dulles, F.R. *Eastward Ho: The First English Adventurers to the Orient.* Freeport, NY: Books for Libraries Press, 1969.

Fernandez-Armesto, Felipe. *The Spanish Armada: The Experience of War in 1588.* Oxford: Oxford University Press, 1988.

Geyl, Pieter. *The Revolt of the Netherlands, 1555–1609.* London: Cassell, 1988.

Greengrass, Mark. *France in the Age of Henri IV.* New York: Longman, 1984.

Grierson, Edward. *The Fatal Inheritance: Philip II and the Spanish Netherlands.* Garden City, NY: Doubleday, 1969.

Hanson, Neil. *The Confident Hope of a Miracle: The True Story of the Spanish Armada.* New York: Vintage, 2006.

Howarth, David. *The Voyage of the Armada: The Spanish Story.* New York: Viking Press, 1984.

Kingdon, Robert McCune. *Myths about the St. Bartholomew's Day Massacres, 1572–1576.* Cambridge, MA: Harvard University Press, 1988.

Knecht, R.J. *The French Wars of Religion, 1559–1598.* 2nd ed. London: Longman, 1996.

Lewis, Michael A. *The Spanish Armada.* New York: Macmillan, 1960.

Loomie, Albert J. *The Spanish Elizabethans: The English Exiles at the Court of Philip II.* New York: Fordham University Press, 1963.

Lynch, John. *Spain, 1516–1598: From Nation State to World Empire.* Oxford: Blackwell, 1992.

Martin, Colin, and Geoffrey Parker. *The Spanish Armada.* Rev. ed. Manchester: Manchester University Press, 2002.

Mattingly, Garrett. *The Armada.* Boston: Mariner Books, 2005.

McDermott, James. *England and the Spanish Armada: The Necessary Quarrel.* New Haven, CT: Yale University Press, 2005.

Neale, J.E. *The Age of Catherine de Medici.* New York: Barnes and Noble, 1959.

Nogueres, Henri. *The Massacre of Saint Bartholomew.* Translated by Claire Elaine Engel. New York: Macmillan, 1962.

Oosterhoff, F.G. *Leicester and the Netherlands, 1586–1587.* Utrecht: HES, 1988.

Parker, Geoffrey. *The Dutch Revolt.* Ithaca, NY: Cornell University Press, 1977.

———. *Spain and the Netherlands, 1559–1659.* Short Hills, NJ: Enslow Publishers, 1979.

Quinn, David B., and A.N Ryan. *England's Sea Empire, 1550–1642.* Boston: G. Allen & Unwin, 1983.

Ramsay, G.D. *The Queen's Merchants and the Revolt of the Netherlands.* Manchester: Manchester University Press, 1986.

Rodger, N.A.M. *The Safeguard of the Sea: A Naval History of Britain.* New York: W.W. Norton, 1998.

Rothrock, George A. *The Huguenots: A Biography of a Minority.* Chicago: Nelson-Hall, 1979.

Rowse, A.L. *The Expansion of Elizabethan England.* New York: Scribner, 1972.

Smith, Lacey Baldwin. *The Elizabethan World.* Boston: Houghton Mifflin, 1991.

Solari, Giovanni. *The House of Farnese.* Garden City, NY: Doubleday, 1968.

Sutherland, N.M. *The Massacre of St. Bartholomew and the European Conflict, 1559–1572.* London: Macmillan, 1973.

Tracy, James D. *Holland under Habsburg Rule, 1506–1566: The Formation of a Body Politic.* Berkeley: University of California Press, 1990.

Waldman, Milton. *Biography of a Family: Catherine de Medici and Her Children.* Boston: Houghton Mifflin, 1936.

Wernham, R.B. *After the Armada: Elizabethan England and the Struggle for Western Europe, 1588–1595.* Oxford: Clarendon Press, 1984.

———. *The Expedition of Sir John Norris and Sir Francis Drake to Spain and Portugal, 1589.* Aldershot, England: Gower, 1988.

———. *The Making of Elizabethan Foreign Policy 1558–1603.* Berkeley: University of California Press, 1980.

———. *The Return of the Armadas: The Last Years of the Elizabethan War Against Spain, 1595–1603.* Oxford: Oxford University Press, 1994.

Wilson, C.H. *Queen Elizabeth and the Revolt of the Netherlands.* Berkeley: University of California Press, 1970.

Scotland, Ireland, Wales, and America

Ashley, Maurice. *The House of Stuart: Its Rise and Fall.* London: J.M. Dent, 1980.

Bingham, Caroline. *The Stewart Kingdom of Scotland 1371–1603.* New York: St. Martin's Press, 1974.

Bristol, Michael D. *Shakespeare's America, America's Shakespeare.* Oxford: Routledge, 1990.

Canny, Nicholas P. *The Elizabethan Conquest of Ireland: A Pattern Established, 1565–1576.* New York: Barnes and Noble, 1976.

Cowan, Ian B. *The Scottish Reformation: Church and Society in Sixteenth-Century Scotland.* New York: St. Martin's Press, 1982.

Davies, John. *A History of Wales.* London: Penguin Press, 1993.

Donaldson, Gordon. *All the Queen's Men: Power and Politics in Mary Stewart's Scotland.* London: Batsford Academic and Educational, 1983.

———. *The Scottish Reformation.* Cambridge: Cambridge University Press, 1960.

Durant, David N. *Raleigh's Lost Colony.* New York: Atheneum, 1981.

Edwards, R.D. *Ireland in the Age of the Tudors.* New York: Barnes and Noble, 1977.

Ellis, Steven G. *Ireland in the Age of the Tudors, 1447–1603: English Expansion and the End of Gaelic Rule.* 2nd ed. London: Longman, 1998.

Falls, Cyril. *Elizabeth's Irish Wars.* London: Metheun, 1950.

Ford, Alan. *The Protestant Reformation in Ireland, 1590–1641.* Portland: Four Courts Press, 1997.

Foss, Michael. *Undreamed Shores: England's Wasted Empire in America.* New York: Scribner's, 1974.

Jones, J. Gwynfor. *Early Modern Wales, 1525–1640.* New York: St. Martin's Press, 1994.

———. *Wales and the Tudor State: Government, Religious Change and the Social Order, 1534–1603.* Cardiff: University of Wales Press, 1989.

Kilfeather, T.P. *Ireland: Graveyard of the Spanish Armada.* Minneapolis: Irish Books and Media, 1979.

Kupperman, Karen Ordahl. *Roanoke: The Abandoned Colony.* New York: Barnes and Noble, 1993.

Lennon, Colm. *The Lords of Dublin in the Age of the Reformation.* Dublin: Irish Academic, 1989.

———. *Sixteenth-Century Ireland: The Incomplete Conquest.* Dublin: Gill & Macmillan, 1994.

Lounsburg, R.G. *The British Fishery at Newfoundland.* Hamden, CT: Archon Books, 1969.

McCarthy-Morrogh, Michael. *The Munster Plantation: English Migration to Southern Ireland, 1583–1641.* Oxford: Clarendon Press, 1986.

McGurk, John. *The Elizabethan Conquest of Ireland: The 1590s Crisis.* Manchester: Manchester University Press, 1997.

Morgan, Hiram. *Tyrone's Rebellion: The Outbreak of the Nine Years War in Tudor Ireland.* Rochester, NY: Boydell Press, 1993.

Morison, Samuel Eliot. *The European Discovery of America: The Northern Voyages A.D. 500–1600.* New York: Oxford University Press, 1971.

Morton, Grenfell. *Elizabethan Ireland.* London: Longman, 1971.

Neatby, Leslie H. *In Quest of the North West Passage.* New York: Crowell, 1958.

Quinn, David B. *The Elizabethans and the Irish.* Ithaca, NY: Cornell University Press, 1966.

———. *England and the Discovery of America, 1481–1620.* New York: Knopf, 1974.

———. *Explorers and Colonies, 1500–1625.* London: Hambledon Press, 1990.

———. *Set Fair for Roanoke: Voyages and Colonies, 1584–1606.* Chapel Hill: University of North Carolina Press, 1984.

Rowse, A.L. *The Elizabethans and America.* New York: Harper, 1959.

Sanderson, Margaret H.B. *Mary Stewart's People: Life in Mary Stewart's Scotland.* Tuscaloosa: University of Alabama Press, 1987.

Silke, John. *Kinsale: The Spanish Intervention in Ireland at the End of the Elizabethan Wars.* New York: Fordham University Press, 1970.

Thomas, W.S.K. *Tudor Wales, 1485–1603.* Llandsul, Wales: Gomer Press, 1983.

Thomson, George M. *Search for the North-West Passage.* New York: Macmillan, 1975.

Williams, Neville. *The Sea Dogs: Privateers, Plunder and Piracy in the Elizabethan Age.* New York: Macmillan, 1975.

Williamson, James A. *The Age of Drake.* New York: World Publishing, 1965.

Wilson, Derek A. *The World Encompassed: Francis Drake and His Great Voyage.* New York: Harper and Row, 1977.

Wormald, Jenny. *Court, Kirk, and Community: Scotland, 1470–1625.* Toronto: University of Toronto Press, 1981.

Biography: Elizabeth I

Bassnett, Susan. *Elizabeth I: A Feminist Perspective.* New York: St. Martin's Press, 1988.

Doran, Susan. *Queen Elizabeth I.* New York: New York University Press, 2003.

Dunn, Jane. *Elizabeth and Mary: Cousins, Rivals, Queens.* New York: Alfred A. Knopf, 2004.

Erickson, Carolly. *The First Elizabeth.* New York: Summit Books, 1983.

Frye, Susan. *Elizabeth I: The Competition for Representation.* New York: Oxford University Press, 1993.

Haigh, Christopher. *Elizabeth I.* London: Longman, 1988.

Hibbert, Christopher. *The Virgin Queen: Elizabeth I, Genius of the Golden Age.* Reading, MA: Addison-Wesley, 1991.

Gristwood, Sarah. *Elizabeth and Leicester: Power, Passion, Politics.* New York: Viking, 2007.

Jenkins, Elizabeth. *Elizabeth the Great.* New York: Coward-McCann, 1959.

Johnson, Paul. *Elizabeth I: A Biography.* New York: Holt, Rinehart and Winston, 1974.

Loades, David. *Elizabeth I.* New York: Hambledon Continuum, 2006.

MacCaffrey, Wallace. *Elizabeth I.* London: Edward Arnold, 1993.

Neale, J.E. *Queen Elizabeth I: A Biography.* Chicago: Academy Chicago Publishers, 1992 (originally published 1934).

Perry, Maria. *The Word of a Prince: A Life of Elizabeth I.* Woodbridge, England: Boydell Press, 1990.

Rex, Richard. *Elizabeth I: Fortune's Bastard*. Stroud, Glocestershire, Tempus, 2003.

Ridley, Jasper. *Elizabeth I: The Shrewdness of Virtue*. New York: Viking, 1988.

Smith, Lacey Baldwin. *Elizabeth Tudor: Portrait of a Queen*. Boston: Little, Brown and Company, 1975.

Somerset, Anne. *Elizabeth I*. New York: Alfred A. Knopf, 1991.

Starkey, David. *Elizabeth: The Struggle for the Throne*. New York: HarperCollins, 2001.

Weir, Alison. *The Life of Elizabeth I*. New York: Ballantine Books, 1998.

Williams, Neville. *Elizabeth the First: Queen of England*. New York: E.P. Dutton, 1968.

Biography: William Shakespeare

Akrigg, G.P.V. *Shakespeare and the Earl of Southampton*. Cambridge, MA: Harvard University Press, 1968.

Andrews, John F., ed. *William Shakespeare: His World, His Works, His Influence*. 3 vols. New York: Scribner, 1985.

Bentley, G.E. *Shakespeare: A Biographical Handbook*. New Haven, CY: Yale University Press, 1961.

Chambers, E.K. *Short Life of Shakespeare With the Sources*. Oxford: Oxford University Press, 1933.

Drakakis, John, ed. *Alternative Shakespeares*. 2nd ed. Oxford: Routledge, 2002.

Eagleton, Terry. *William Shakespeare*. Oxford: Blackwell, 1987.

Eccles, Mark. *Shakespeare in Warwickshire*. Madison: University of Wisconsin Press, 1961.

Fields, Bertram. *Players: The Mysterious Identity of William Shakespeare*. New York: Regan Books, 2005.

Greenblatt, Stephen. *Will in the World: How Shakespeare Became Shakespeare*. London: W.W. Norton & Company, 2004.

Holland, Norman, et al., eds. *Shakespeare's Personality*. Berkeley: University of California Press, 1989.

Holmes, Martin. *Shakespeare and Burbage*. Totowa, NJ: Rowman and Littlefield, 1978.

Honan, Park. *Shakespeare: A Life*. Oxford: Oxford University Press, 1998.

Honigmann, E.A.J. *Shakespeare: The "Lost Years."* Manchester: Manchester University Press, 1985.

Hyland, Peter. *An Introduction to Shakespeare: The Dramatist in His Context*. New York: St. Martin's Press, 1996.

Jones, Emrys. *Origins of Shakespeare*. Oxford: Clarendon Press, 1977.

Kay, Dennis. *Shakespeare: His Life, Work, and Era*. New York: William Morrow, 1992.

———. *William Shakespeare: His Life and Times*. New York: Twayne Publishers, 1995.

Lee, Sidney. *A Life of William Shakespeare*. New York: The Macmillan Company, 1909.

Levi, Peter. *The Life and Times of William Shakespeare*. New York: Henry Holt and Company, 1988.

McCrea, Scott. *The Case for Shakespeare: The End of the Authorship Question*. Westport, CT: Praeger, 2005.

O'Connor, Garry. *William Shakespeare: A Popular Life*. New York: Applause, 2000.

Ogburn, Charlton. *The Mysterious William Shakespeare*. 2nd ed. McLean, VA: EPM Publications, 1992.

Phillips, Graham, and Martin Keatman. *The Shakespeare Conspiracy*. London: Century, 1994.

Price, Diana. *Shakespeare's Unorthodox Biography: New Evidence of an Authorship Problem*. Westport, CT: Greenwood Press, 2001.

Rowse, A.L. *William Shakespeare: A Biography.* New York: Harper & Row, 1963.

Sammartino, Peter. *The Man Who Was William Shakespeare.* New York: Cornwall Books, 1990.

Schoenbaum, S. *Shakespeare's Lives.* Oxford: Clarendon Press, 1991.

———. *William Shakespeare: A Compact Documentary Life.* Oxford: Oxford University Press, 1988.

———. *William Shakespeare: Records and Images.* Oxford: Oxford University Press, 1981.

Whalen, Richard. *Shakespeare: Who Was He?* Westport, CT: Praeger, 1994.

Wilson, Ian. *Shakespeare: The Evidence.* New York: St. Martin's Press, 1994.

Other Biography

Adamson, Jack H., and H.F. Follard. *The Shepherd of the Ocean: An Account of Sir Walter Ralegh and His Times.* Boston: Gambit, 1969.

Anderson, Mark. *Shakespeare by Another Name: A Biography of Edward de Vere, Earl of Oxford, the Man Who Was Shakespeare.* New York: Gotham Books, 2005.

Archer, Stanley. *Richard Hooker.* Boston: Twayne, 1983.

Atkinson, Nigel. *Richard Hooker and the Authority of Scripture, Tradition and Reason.* Vancouver: Regent College Publishing, 2005.

Beckingsale, B.W. *Burghley: Tudor Statesman 1520–1598.* New York: St. Martin's Press, 1967.

Bowen, Marjorie. *Mary, Queen of Scots.* London: Sphere Books Limited, 1971 (originally published 1934).

Brewster, Eleanor. *Oxford: Courtier to the Queen.* New York: Pageant Press, 1964.

Caraman, Philip. *Henry Garnet, 1555–1606, and the Gunpowder Plot.* London: Longmans, Green, and Company, 1964.

Cecil, Algernon. *A Life of Robert Cecil, First Earl of Salisbury.* Westport, CT: Greenwoood Press, 1971.

Cecil, David. *The Cecils of Hatfield House: An English Ruling Family.* Boston: Houghton Mifflin, 1973.

Chrimes, S.B. *Henry VII.* Berkeley: University of California Press, 1972.

Connell, Charles. *They Gave Us Shakespeare: John Heminge and Henry Condell.* Boston: Oriel Press, 1982.

Cook, Judith. *Dr. Simon Forman: A Most Notorious Physician.* London: Chatto & Windus, 2001.

Coote, Stephen. *A Play of Passion: The Life of Sir Walter Raleigh.* London: Macmillan, 1993.

Crupi, Charles W. *Robert Greene.* Boston: Twayne, 1986.

Cummins, John. *Francis Drake.* New York: St. Martin's Press, 1995.

Devlin, Christopher. *The Life of Robert Southwell: Poet and Martyr.* New York: Greenwood Press, 1969.

Dewar, Mary. *Sir Thomas Smith.* London: University of London, Athlone Press, 1964.

Donaldson, Gordon. *Mary, Queen of Scots.* London: English Universities Press, 1974.

Duncan-Jones, Katherine. *Sir Philip Sidney: Courtier Poet.* New Haven, CT: Yale University Press, 1991.

Edwards, Francis. *The Marvellous Chance: Thomas Howard, Fourth Duke of Norfolk, and the Ridolfi Plot, 1570–1572.* London: Hart-Davis, 1968.

Erickson, Carolly. *Bloody Mary.* Garden City, NY: Doubleday, 1978.

Faulkner, Robert K. *Richard Hooker and the Politics of Christian England.* Berkeley: University of California Press, 1981.

Fraser, Antonia. *King James VI of Scotland and I of England.* London: Sphere Books Limited, 1977.

———. *Mary, Queen of Scots.* New York: Delacorte Press, 1969.

Freedman, Sylvia. *Poor Penelope: Lady Penelope Rich, an Elizabethan Woman.* Abbostbrook, England: Kensal Press, 1983.

Greenblatt, Stephen J. *Sir Walter Raleigh: The Renaissance Man and His Roles.* New Haven, CT: Yale University Press, 1973.

Greer, Germaine. *Shakespeare's Wife.* New York: HarperCollins, 2007.

Guy, John. *Queen of Scots: The True Life of Mary Stuart.* Boston: Houghton Mifflin, 2004.

Hales, John W. *A Biography of Edmund Spenser.* London: Dodo Press, 2007.

Hamilton, A.C. *Sir Philip Sidney: A Study of His Life and Works.* Cambridge: Cambridge University Press, 1977.

Haynes, Alan. *Robert Cecil, Earl of Salisbury, 1563–1612: Servant of Two Sovereigns.* London: Peter Owen, 1989.

———. *The White Bear: Robert Dudley, the Elizabethan Earl of Leicester.* London: Peter Owen, 1987.

Herendeen, Wyman H. *William Camden: A Life in Context.* Rochester, NY: Boydell Press, 2007.

Houppert, Joseph W. *John Lyly.* Boston: Twayne, 1975.

Houston, S.J. *James I.* 2nd ed. London: Longman, 1995.

Howell, Roger. *Sir Philip Sidney: The Shepherd Knight.* Boston: Little, Brown, 1968.

Hunter, G.K. *John Lyly: The Humanist as Courtier.* Cambridge, MA: Harvard University Press, 1962.

Jenkins, Elizabeth. *Elizabeth and Leicester: A Biography.* New York: Coward-McCann, 1962.

Jordan, John Clark. *Robert Greene.* New York: Octagon Books, 1965.

Kamen, Henry. *Philip of Spain.* New Haven, CT: Yale University Press, 1997.

Kassell, Lauren. *Medicine and Magic in Elizabethan London: Simon Forman, Astrologer, Alchemist, and Physician.* Oxford: Oxford University Press, 2005.

Kelsey, Harry. *Sir Francis Drake: The Queen's Pirate.* New Haven, CT: Yale University Press, 1998.

Lacey, Robert. *Robert Devereux, Earl of Essex.* New York: Atheneum, 1971.

———. *Sir Walter Ralegh.* New York: Atheneum, 1974.

Lloyd, Christopher. *Sir Francis Drake.* London: Faber and Faber, 1979.

Marshall, Rosalind K. *Queen of Scots.* Edinburgh: HMSO, 1986.

Mathew, David. *James I.* London: Eyre & Spottiswoode, 1969.

Mozley, J.F. *John Foxe and His Book.* New York: Octagon Books, 1970.

Mulryne, J.R. *Thomas Middleton.* New York: Longman Publishing Group, 1979.

Nelson, Alan H. *Monstrous Adversary: The Life of Edward de Vere, 17th Earl of Oxford.* Liverpool: Liverpool University Press, 2003.

Olsen, V.N. *John Foxe and the Elizabethan Church.* Berkeley: University of California Press, 1973.

Parker, Geoffrey. *Philip II.* 3rd ed. Chicago: Open Court, 1995.

Parry, G.J.R. *A Protestant Vision: William Harrison and the Reformation of Elizabethan England.* Cambridge: Cambridge University Press, 1987.

Pierson, Peter. *Commander of the Armada: The Seventh Duke of Medina Sidonia.* New Haven, CT: Yale University Press, 1989.

Prescott, H.F.M. *Mary Tudor.* New York: Macmillan, 1953.

Quinn, David B. *Raleigh and the British Empire.* Rev. ed. New York: Collier Books, 1962.

Rae, Wesley D. *Thomas Lodge.* New York: Twayne, 1967.

Rebholz, Ronald A. *The Life of Fulke Greville, First Lord Brooke.* Oxford: Clarendon Press, 1971.

Read, Conyers. *Lord Burghley and Queen Elizabeth.* New York: Alfred A. Knopf, 1960.

———. *Mr. Secretary Cecil and Queen Elizabeth.* London: Jonathan Cape, 1965.

———. *Mr. Secretary Walsingham and the Policy of Queen Elizabeth.* Hamden, CT: Archon Books, 1967.

Reid, Aileen, and Robert Maniura, eds. *Edward Alleyn: Elizabethan Actor, Jacobean Gentleman.* London: Dulwich Picture Gallery, 1994.

Richards, Judith M. *Mary Tudor.* London: Routledge, 2008.

Ringler, William A. *Stephen Gosson: A Biographical and Critical Study.* London: Octagon Press, 1972.

Rowse, A.L. *Sex and Society in Shakespeare's Age: Simon Forman the Astrologer.* New York: Charles Scribner's Sons, 1974.

———. *Shakespeare's Southampton: Patron of Virginia.* New York: Harper and Row, 1965.

———. *Sir Walter Ralegh: His Family and Private Life.* New York: Harper, 1962.

Ryan, Lawrence V. *Roger Ascham.* Stanford, CA: Stanford University Press, 1963.

Scarisbrick, J.J. *Henry VIII.* Berkeley: University of California Press, 1968.

Stewart, Alan. *The Cradle King: The Life of James VI and I, the First Monarch of a United Great Britain.* New York: St. Martin's Press, 2003.

———. *Philip Sidney: A Double Life.* New York: St. Martin's Press, 2000.

Strachey, Lytton. *Elizabeth and Essex.* Oxford: Oxford University Press, 1981.

Sugden, John. *Sir Francis Drake.* New York: Simon & Schuster, 1990.

Traister, Barbara Howard. *The Notorious Astrological Physician of London: Works and Days of Simon Forman.* Chicago: University of Chicago Press, 2001.

Trevelyan, Raleigh. *Sir Walter Raleigh: Being a True and Vivid Account of the Life and Times of the Explorer, Soldier, Scholar, Poet, and Courtier—The Controversial Hero of the Elizabethan Age.* New York: Henry Holt, 2004.

Wagner, J.A. *The Devon Gentleman: The Life of Sir Peter Carew.* Hull, England: University of Hull Press, 1998.

Waller, Gary F. *Edmund Spenser: A Literary Life.* London: Macmillan, 1994.

Warnicke, Retha M. *Mary Queen of Scots.* London: Routledge, 2006.

Waugh, Evelyn. *Edmund Campion.* London: Cassell, 1987.

Williams, Neville. *A Tudor Tragedy: Thomas Howard Fourth Duke of Norfolk.* London: Barrie and Jenkins, 1964.

Williams, Norman Lloyd. *Sir Walter Raleigh.* Baltimore: Penguin Books, 1965.

Williamson, Hugh Ross. *Sir Walter Raleigh.* Westport, CT: Greenwood Press, 1978.

Willson, D. Harris. *King James VI and I.* New York: Henry Holt and Company, 1956.

Wilson, Derek A. *Sweet Robin: A Biography of Robert Dudley, Earl of Leicester.* London: H. Hamilton, 1981.

Winton, John. *Sir Walter Ralegh.* New York: Coward, McCann & Geohegan, 1975.

Wooding, Lucy. *Henry VIII.* London: Routledge, 2009.

Wormald, Jenny. *Mary, Queen of Scots: Pride, Passion, and a Kingdom Lost.* Revised ed. London: Tauris Parke Paperbacks, 2001.

WEB SITES

Barlowe, Arthur. Barlowe's "First Voyage to Roanoke": http://docsouth.unc.edu/nc/barlowe/menu.html

Bond of Association: http://ccat.sas.upenn.edu/~jmcgill/bond.html

Camden, William. *Annales Rerum Gestarum Angliae et Hiberniae Regnante Elizabetha* (English and Latin): http://www.philological.bham.ac.uk/camden

Elizabeth I. Selected Poetry of Elizabeth I: http://rpo.library.utoronto.ca/poet/112.html

Elizabeth I: Tudor History: Poetry of Elizabeth I: http://www.tudorhistory.org/poetry/elizabeth.html

Elizabeth I, Writings of. Luminarium: Anthology of English Literature: http://www.luminarium.org/renlit/elizabib.htm

Elizabethan Catholics (J.P. Sommerville): http://history.wisc.edu/sommerville/361/361-18.htm.

Elizabethan Clothing: http://www.elizabethan-era.org.uk/elizabethan-clothing.htm

Elizabethan Costume: http://www.elizabethancostume.net

Elizabethan Education: http://www.elizabethan-era.org.uk/elizabethan-education.htm

Elizabethan Women. Voices of English Renaissance Women: http://www.albertrabil.com/projects2000/walters/part%206.html

Folger Shakespeare Library (Washington, DC): http://www.folger.edu/Home_02b.html

Forman, Simon. Dr. Simon Forman: http://www.mysteriousbritain.co.uk/occult/dr-simon-forman.html

Golden Speech. Modern History Sourcebook: http://www.fordham.edu/halsall/mod/elizabeth1.html#The%20Farewell%20Speech,%201601

Golden Speech. Renascence Editions: http://www.uoregon.edu/~rbear/eliz1.html

Gossen, Stephen. The Schoole of Abuse: http://www.uoregon.edu/~rbear/gosson1.html

Greene, Robert. Cony-Catching Pamphlets: http://darkwing.uoregon.edu/~rbear/greene4.html

Greene, Robert. Groats-worth of Wit: http://darkwing.uoregon.edu/~rbear/greene1.html

Hakluyt, Richard. Principal Navigations, Voyages, Traffiques and Discoveries of the English Nation: http://ebooks.adelaide.edu.au/h/hakluyt/voyages

Harrison, William. "Description of England": http://www.fordham.edu/halsall/mod/1577harrison-england.html

Hayward, John. *Annals of the First Four Years of the Reign of Queen Elizabeth*: http://books.google.com/books

Holinshed Project at Oxford: http://www.cems.ox.ac.uk/holinshed/news.shtml

Holinshed's *Chronicles*: http://www.gutenberg.org/browse/authors/h#a5166

Hooker, Richard. Works of Richard Hooker: http://anglicanhistory.org/hooker

Hooker, Richard. Works of Richard Hooker: http://www.luminarium.org/renlit/hookbib.htm

Kempe, William. Kempe Biography: http://www.globe-theatre.org.uk/william-kempe-actor.htm

Kempe, William. Kempe's Nine Daies Wonder: http://darkwing.uoregon.edu/~rbear/arte/arte.htm

Laneham, Robert. Description of Entertainments at Kenilworth Castle: http://books.google.com

Letters and Memorials of William Cardinal Allen (ed. Knox): http://books.google.com/books

Letters of Queen Elizabeth and James VI of Scotland (ed. Bruce): http://books.google.com/books

Lyly, John. Biography of Lyly and discussion of Euphuism: http://www.luminarium.org/renlit/lylybio.htm

Lyly, John. Selected Works of Lyly: http://www.luminarium.org/renlit/lylybib.htm

Mary of Scotland. Execution of Mary, Queen of Scots: http://www.eyewitnesstohistory.com/maryqueenofscots.htm

Mary of Scotland. Tudor History: Execution of Mary, Queen of Scots: http://www.tudor history.org/primary/exmary.html

Middleton, Thomas. Life of Thomas Middleton: http://www.luminarium.org/sevenlit/ middleton/thomasbio.htm

Middleton, Thomas. Plays of Thomas Middleton: http://www.tech.org/~cleary/middhome .html

Oxford Authorship Site: http://www.oxford-shakespeare.com/marprelate.html

Poor Law of 1601: http://www.victorianweb.org/history/poorlaw/elizpl.html

Raleigh, Sir Walter. Raleigh's American Colonies: http://www.britishexplorers.com/woodbury/ raleigh.html

Shakespeare Magazine: http://www.shakespearemag.com

Shakespeare Oxford Society: http://www.shakespeare-oxford.com

Shakespeare Oxford Society, *The Ever Reader* Online Magazine: http://www.everreader.com

Shakespeare, William. Complete Works of Shakespeare: http://shakespeare.mit.edu

Shakespeare, William. Educating Shakespeare: http://www.likesnail.org.uk/welcome-es .htm

Shakespeare, William. *Hamlet*: http://www.online-literature.com/shakespeare/hamlet

Shakespeare, William, Life and Times: http://web.uvic.ca/Shakespeare/Library/SLT/intro/ introsubj.html

Shakespeare, William, Links to His Life and Work: http://www.bardweb.net

Shakespeare, William. *Richard III*: http://www.uoregon.edu/~rbear/shake/riii.html

Shakespeare, William. Sonnets: http://www.shakespeares-sonnets.com/sonn01.htm

Shakespeare, William. Sources: http://www.shakespeare-online.com/sources/macbethsources .html

Sidney, Sir Philip. "An Apology for Poetry": http://books.google.com/books

Sidney, Sir Philip. Works of Sir Philip Sidney: http://www.luminarium.org/renlit/ sidbib.htm

Smith, Sir Thomas. *De Republica Anglorum*: http://www.constitution.org/eng/repang.htm

Smith, Sir Thomas. *Life of Camden* (1691): http://www.philological.bham.ac.uk/smith

Spenser, Edmund. The Faerie Queene: http://www.uoregon.edu/~rbear/fqintro.html

Spenser, Edmund. Works of Edmund Spenser: http://www.luminarium.org/renlit/spensbib .htm

Tilbury Speech. Luminarium: Anthology of English Literature: http://www.luminarium.org/ renlit/tilbury.htm

Tilbury Speech. Modern History Sourcebook: http://www.fordham.edu/halsall/mod/ 1588elizabeth.html

Wentworth, Peter Wentworth's 1576 Commons Speech: http://www.uark.edu/depts/ comminfo/cambridge/wentworth.html

Wentworth, Sir Peter Wentworth's Biography: http://www.tudorplace.com.ar/Bios/ PeterWentworth.htm

What Every Schoolboy Knows: http://www.elizabethan.org/compendium/54.html

INDEX

Boldface page references indicate that the index entry is the source or subject of a document excerpt.

ABOUT THE AUTHOR

John A. Wagner has taught British and U.S. history at Phoenix College and at Arizona State University. He holds a BA from the University of Wisconsin-Oshkosh and an MA and PhD from Arizona State University. He is the author of *The Devon Gentleman: The Life of Sir Peter Carew* (1998); the *Historical Dictionary of the Elizabethan World* (1999), a History Book Club and *Booklist* Editor's Choice Selection; the *Encyclopedia of the Wars of the Roses* (2001); *Bosworth Field to Bloody Mary: An Encyclopedia of the Early Tudors* (2003); and the *Encyclopedia of the Hundred Years War* (2006). He is also a contributor to the *Historical Dictionary of Late Medieval England, 1272–1485* (2002); *Women in the Middle Ages: An Encyclopedia* (2004); the *Encyclopedia of American Race Riots* (2006); *The Greenwood Encyclopedia of Love, Courtship, and Sexuality* (2008); and *The Greenwood Encyclopedia of Global Medieval Life and Culture* (2009).